THE BACKYARD HOMESTEAD Guide to GROWING ORGANIC FOOD

THE BACKYARD HOMESTEAD *Guide to* GROWING ORGANIC FOOD

A Crop-by-Crop Reference for 62 Vegetables, Fruits, Nuts, and Herbs

TANYA DENCKLA COBB

Storey Publishing

The mission of Storey Publishing is to serve our customers by publishing practical information that encourages personal independence in harmony with the environment.

EDITED BY Carleen Madigan, Anne Nelson Stoner, and Sarah Guare Slattery
ART DIRECTION AND BOOK DESIGN BY Bredna Lago
TEXT PRODUCTION BY Jennifer Jepson Smith
COVER ILLUSTRATION BY © Mike Austin
INTERIOR ILLUSTRATIONS BY © Elara Tanguy

Storey Publishing
210 MASS MoCA Way
North Adams, MA 01247
storey.com

Storey Publishing is an imprint of Workman Publishing, a division of Hachette Book Group, Inc., 1290 Avenue of the Americas, New York, NY 10104. The Storey Publishing name and logo are registered trademarks of Hachette Book Group, Inc.

ISBNs: 978-1-63586-790-9 (paperback); 978-1-63586-677-3 (ebook)

Printed in China by R. R. Donnelley on paper from responsible sources
10 9 8 7 6 5 4 3 2

Library of Congress Cataloging-in-Publication Data on file

For Cecil, my best friend, life partner,
and husband, who fully supported all of
my gardening efforts and experiments
and whose best Valentine's gift was his surprise
delivery of a truckload of high-grade compost

Contents

Preface

In times of change and uncertainty, one thing remains solid: The simple actions of digging into the earth, planting a seed, picking a tomato, pulling a carrot, reaching for an apple, and snipping fresh herbs are grounding and revitalizing. Through my work in sustainable food systems over the last few decades, I've learned that planting and tending a garden is often far more than a pleasant pastime. It can be a radical act that transforms lives.

Studies have shown that personal and community gardens—whether urban or rural—can relieve stress, slow anxieties, ease attention deficit disorder, support mental health, support rehab from numerous conditions including post-traumatic stress syndrome, help us stay focused, increase our patience, contribute to longevity, and advance personal growth. They can even foster leadership, organizational, and business skills. Put simply, a garden delivers far more than beauty and food. So it's no surprise that gardening remains one of the most widespread and popular endeavors throughout the world.

The other side of this story is that the relationship between garden and gardener has continued to evolve. Just as gardens can feed and transform the gardener, today's gardener understands that we can feed and transform the garden through a reciprocal and nurturing relationship. A gardener can do this by paying attention to and nurturing the health of the garden soil as well as its microecosystem. Just as we humans are healthier and more resilient if we take care of our bodies with healthy food and exercise, the garden is healthier and more resilient when we nourish soil health and take preventive action to help it weather microclimate stresses.

So often old wisdom, once scoffed at, comes around to being understood in a new light. The term *regenerative agriculture* refers to the coupling of the latest scientific knowledge with time-tested knowledge that dates back to indigenous stewardship of our lands. This knowledge has resurfaced at various times in our history in different approaches, such as biodynamic, permaculture, organic, and sustainable agriculture. Regenerative approaches foster specific outcomes such as improving soil health, sequestering carbon, and increasing biodiversity through specific processes such as using cover crops, reducing or eliminating tillage, and integrating livestock into the food production landscape system.

If any of these regenerative goals appeal to you, this book is for you. Whether gardening is a hobby or a necessity to put food on the table, whether you've got a small backyard garden or are a longtime gardener who wants to step up your game, this book is for you. I realize these may sound like overly bold claims. But many readers have thanked me over the years for the previous edition of this book, writing to say how they value having all the information they need in one place, in a format that is easy to access. What's more, this book wouldn't exist if it weren't for a request from an organic U-Pick market farm outside of Washington, D.C., whose owners took a look at my personal compendium of information and told me that I must make it available to others, as it would have saved them 10 years of heartache.

Every gardener knows that when you're ready to start your seeds, or you want to know which plants support each other as good companion plants, or you seek help controlling a specific pest, you want the information at your fingertips. All this information, and more, can be easily found in this book. We have worked hard to create a book that is maximally useful while also being a joy to use.

Life on planet Earth is a delicate balance. As a gardener you can contribute to restoring and sustaining that balance through the simple, radical act of caring for, regenerating, and sustaining your own patch of earth.

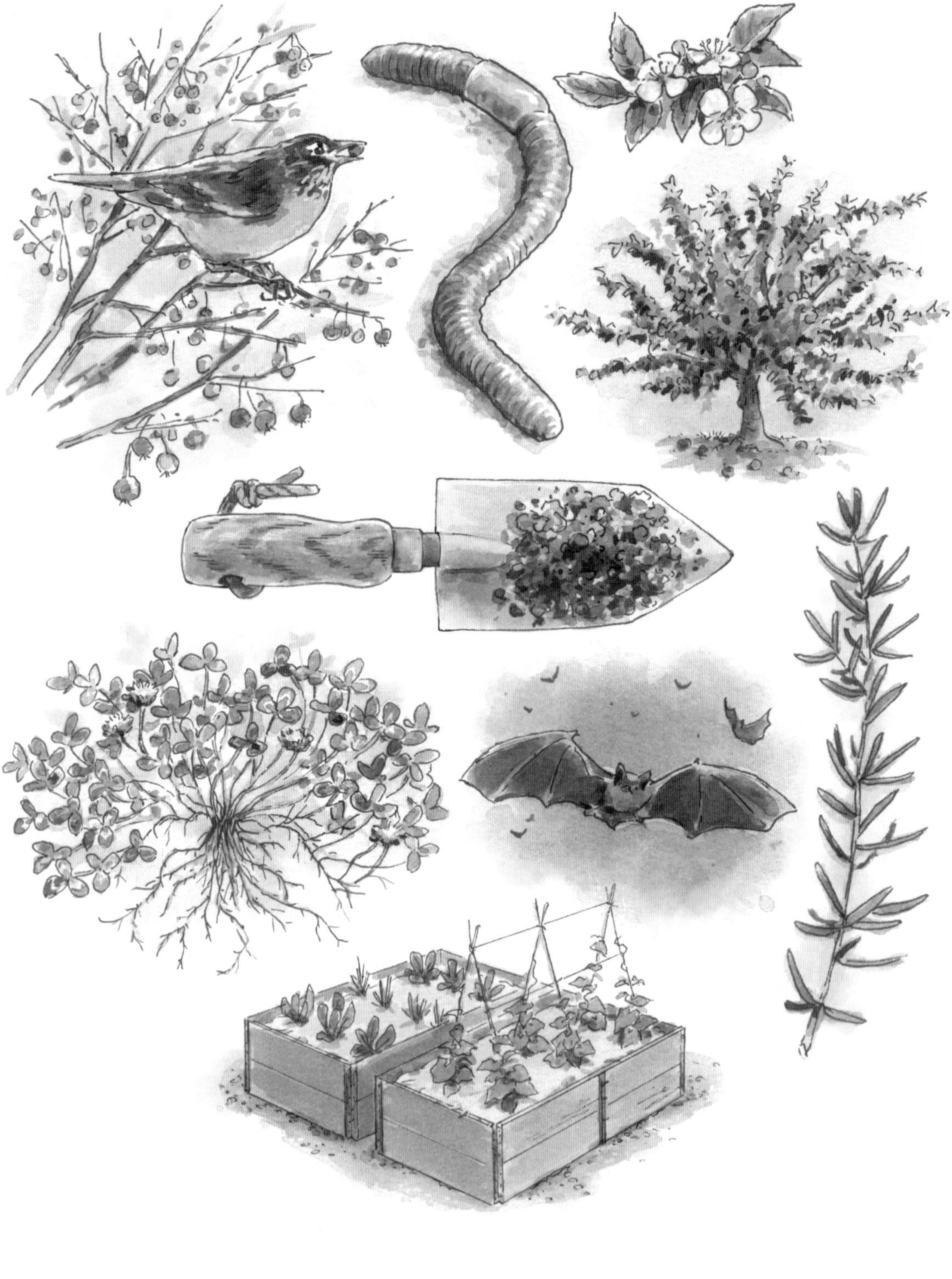

CHAPTER ONE

creating a self-sustaining garden

An organic garden is a living system that is always in flux. Soil composition, air quality, water, birds, insects, and weeds are just a few of the forces that influence the nature and health of a garden. Your role as garden steward is to work with these forces, encouraging the balance to shift in your favor, not to dominate them with the goal of achieving perfection.

The role of garden steward is not difficult to achieve, particularly if you embrace it at the outset. One of its most important precepts is feed the soil, not the plants. The role of steward is perhaps most demanding during the planning phases, when crucial decisions must be made about where to put the garden, what varieties to plant, when and where to plant them, how to feed the soil, where to put the compost pile (or whether to have one), what kind of mulch to use, and how to support pollinators.

The Self-Sustaining Garden

In addition to choosing to become a garden steward, a backyard gardener might aspire to create a self-sustaining garden. A self-sustaining garden or farm differs from a *sustainable* garden in one major respect: It supplies all of its own essential nutrients for balanced growth, from organic matter for compost to micronutrients for healthy plants, whereas the sustainable garden or farm may import many of these materials from off-site. A self-sustaining garden doesn't require importation of beneficial insects because they are already there. It doesn't require the application of imported lime to buffer the effects of acid soil, because earthworms and compost generated on-site are present to do the buffering.

Becoming a steward of a self-sustaining garden is eminently achievable. Most of us will probably need to begin with a sustainable garden—bringing in soil amendments, beneficial insects, and whatever else might be needed to improve the quality and productivity of our soils and growing environment. But our vision need not end there. Why not aim to create a healthy garden ecosystem that eventually provides for itself, does not require chronic soil amendments or importation of beneficial insects, and that becomes self-sustaining? With our increasingly demanding lifestyles, this approach may ultimately be the most time and energy efficient and rewarding.

As steward of a self-sustaining garden, your first job is to recognize that your garden will never be "perfect." There will always be some plant damage. In fact, a garden with no plant damage would suggest that something is unbalanced. Because your garden is not a machine, and because your plants do not come from a factory, you will see variations in your garden conditions and plant productivity from year to year.

Your second job is patience. It usually takes at least several years to establish an ecosystem that operates in your favor—an ecosystem with earthworms, insect-eating birds, beneficial predatory insects, soil with organic matter sufficient to drain well yet retain water to prevent runoff, and soil nutrient levels that support healthy plant growth.

The advantage of a self-sustaining garden is that it requires the least amount of money and time in the long term. You may need to invest in a first colony of earthworms, build or buy birdhouses, buy compost and organic matter before your garden produces it for you, and perhaps even buy irrigation soaker hoses and row-cover material. But in several years, these investments should reward you with a healthy garden that doesn't require lots of imported materials or time-consuming pest controls.

As steward of a sustainable garden that is evolving toward a self-sustaining garden, your strategy is simple: Focus on building healthy soil and ecosystems. Key ways of achieving this are explored in detail in Chapter Five (see pages 171–277). Above all, do not panic when you see pests or diseases in your garden. The plant world is amazingly resilient, and studies have shown that plants can lose up to 20 percent of their foliage without a significant reduction in yields.

SAFEGUARD EARTHWORMS

Originally from Europe, earthworms are now common throughout the United States and eastern Asia. Before taking any action about earthworms in your garden, it is important to first learn from local experts such as Cooperative Extension agents whether they are invasive pests or beneficial in your region. Earthworms are typically known as beneficial organisms for aerating and releasing nutrients into the soil, as well as breaking down organic matter, but they have been documented as a nuisance invasive pest in some native forests. If they are beneficial in your region, take the following steps to protect your earthworms:

- Till minimally, because tilling can disturb and kill earthworms and other soil microorganisms through mechanical abrasion, drying out, and disruption of their environment.
- When you do till, keep it shallow. An optimal tilling depth is 3 inches. To expose the eggs and cocoons of some insects to hungry birds, you may need to till up to 6 inches. Generally, unless you are creating a first-year bed and need to rototill up to 12 or even 14 inches, you should never till deeper than 6 inches.
- Avoid heavy doses of chemical fertilizers because they can harm soil microorganisms and decrease earthworm activity. Excessive nitrogen fertilizer, regardless of its source, harms the soil, and the USDA has shown that it can reduce the vitamin C content in some green vegetables. Use compost instead to provide a slow-release food to the soil and plants.
- Avoid uncomposted manure of any kind because it contains disease pathogens and seeds. If you must use manure, make sure it has been composted up to 160°F/71°C.
- Water regularly, and avoid excesses. Flooding or overwatering, and drought or drying out of the soil, can kill soil microorganisms as well as earthworms.

Partners in a Self-Sustaining Garden

A self-sustaining garden has many natural supportive partners. Chief among them, in order of importance, are earthworms, compost, mulch, and flying creatures.

EARTHWORMS

Earthworms are a gardener's best friend. Their tunneling and production of nitrogen-rich castings (excrement) accomplish many important soil-improving tasks, free of charge. Earthworms enhance the soil's environment for growing healthy, self-sustaining plants in all of the following ways.

- Aerate soil, improving the availability of oxygen to plant roots.
- Improve water retention capacity, decreasing the need to water.
- Keep the soil loose and friable, creating fertile channels for plant roots and improving plants' capacity for root growth.
- Raise important minerals from the subsoil to the topsoil where plants can use them.
- Counteract leaching out of nutrients by improvement of water retention.
- Break up hardpan soils, which are inhospitable to plant growth.
- Homogenize soil elements so they're more evenly available to plants.
- Liberate essential nutrients into a form that is soluble and available to plants.
- Neutralize soils that are too acid or too alkaline for healthy plant growth.
- Balance out organic matter in the soil, so you needn't worry about exceeding the 5 to 8 percent optimal level.

It is possible to have healthy soil without earthworms, and if you have good garden soil, earthworms will probably show up on their own. Purchasing worms to add to the soil is not necessary, nor is moving them from one location to another. While earthworms can benefit vegetable beds and compost piles, they can seriously damage natural ecosystems by consuming vast quantities of organic matter and altering nutrient and carbon cycles, especially in forested places throughout the Northeast and upper Midwest, where there are no native earthworms and the forests developed without them. They can also modify the structure of the soil, speeding up leaching of water and nutrients, while at the same time reducing the organic matter layer and replacing it with castings. For home gardens, however, earthworms should not pose these risks. In conclusion, if you have good soil in your garden, earthworms will probably show up on their own, and if they don't, your plants will likely thrive anyways.

COMPOST

Compost is another major player in the self-sustaining garden. Essentially, compost is any organic material, including manure, that has decayed into a simpler form. Humus is any partially decomposed organic material, vegetable or animal, that is mixed into the soil to improve soil quality. Mulch is any material used to cover the soil; it can be nutrient-poor, such as newspaper, nutrient-neutral, such as plastic, or nutrient-rich, such as compost.

Compost can be used wherever humus or mulch is recommended. The process of composting reduces the original bulk of the organic material by one-fourth to one-tenth. So where a thick mulch is desired, you might prefer to use uncomposted material such as straw or chopped leaves. On the other hand, if you have access to large amounts of compost, it is a highly beneficial mulch because it feeds the soil. Compost is easy to make in any home garden or farm and does the following:

- Feeds the soil and its creatures gently, unlike chemical fertilizers that can kill earthworms and other beneficial organisms.
- Lasts a long time because it releases nutrients slowly in a readily available form, unlike chemical fertilizers that provide a quick boost and then peter out.
- Improves soil drainage by adding porous organic matter (humus).
- Improves water retention, again by the addition of organic matter (humus).
- Provides food that usually has a neutral pH (unlike some chemical fertilizers) and also buffers the soil against rapid pH changes.
- Builds organic matter in the soil, which improves oxygen diffusion.
- Feeds earthworms.

Compost is a multipurpose tool. Some people apply large quantities to their garden, but a healthy minimum is to spread 1 inch of compost through your garden in spring each year before planting. It's helpful to apply another layer during the growing season. You can use compost as a fertilizer, before planting, at planting, after planting, and in fall after harvest; as a mulch, to help retain soil moisture, to keep summer soil cool, to keep winter soil warm, to smother weeds, and in some cases to discourage pests; and as a side-dressing during the growing season, as an extra food boost to the plant.

BASIC COMPOSTING PRINCIPLES

There are so many benefits to starting a compost bin or pile. By recycling your waste, you reduce your carbon footprint, minimize your contribution to landfills, and feed the soil.

Size of the pile. For rapid composting on a small scale, build a pile at least 3′ × 3′ × 3′.

Materials that go into it. Combine roughly equal parts of dry plant material and green plant material to achieve the desired carbon-to-nitrogen ratio of 30:1. Dry plant material can include autumn leaves, straw, dried and cut-up woody material, sawdust, and shredded white paper, newspaper, paper bags, and cardboard boxes and cartons. Straw consists of the hollow dried stems of grain-producing plants, whereas hay ("green" material) is the entire plant (stem and leaves) and therefore much higher in nitrogen. Some studies suggest that when added to compost, birch and blackthorn (*Prunus spinosa*) leaves can help restore exhausted soil. Green plant material can include grass clippings, old flowers, weeds, fresh fruits and vegetables, and kitchen wastes. Leafy materials that were cut green and allowed to dry are still considered green.

If possible, use a wide variety of materials in the compost, because this provides a better balance of pH, nutrients, and microbial organisms. Shred or cut material (including kitchen waste) when possible before adding it to the pile; smaller particles decompose faster, but having some larger materials helps improve aeration.

For the most rapid results, do not add material to the heap once it has started composting.

What not to add to it. Do not add carnivorous-animal manure, wood ashes, charcoal, animal meat, soils with a basic pH (such as those in California), or diseased or bug-infested plants.

Caring for the compost pile. Cover the pile with a tarp, black plastic, or a lid of some kind. Sunlight kills the bacteria that do the composting work, so a pile exposed to sunlight will not compost well in the outer layers.

Water the pile regularly to keep it evenly moist. It should have the consistency of a damp sponge: moist but not soggy, a moisture level of about 50 percent. A dry pile will not compost at all, whereas an overwatered or soggy pile will simply rot. One option is to uncover the pile during rain and re-cover it promptly to trap the moisture.

Turn the pile regularly, every 2 to 7 days, to aerate it and provide sufficient oxygen to the bacteria. Backyard piles often fail because oxygen cannot penetrate the pile. It is possible to overventilate, but this problem generally occurs only when the pile is ventilated through the sides and bottom and if it is turned on a daily basis. Some sources warn that turning piles reduces nitrogen levels in the final product, all the more reason to avoid overzealous turning.

You may want to add commercially available composting activator, a fine powder that contains helpful bacteria to speed along decomposition. The composting activator is not necessary but can be used to hasten results.

You can buy commercially produced compost, but it's also simple to make. Compost is an ideal way to recycle many different household items such as kitchen waste, newspaper, typing paper (no gloss, no colored ink), paper napkins, unwaxed cardboard, sawdust, and other carbon-rich materials.

There are many ways to compost and results can vary, from production of 50 pounds in the backyard to thousands of tons on a commercial scale. It can be made in dug holes or in windrows, in silos or in barrels, in layers on top of the ground or in huge concrete vats. Because there are so many different methods and possible ingredients, a full discussion of composting is beyond the scope of this book. (See the Basic Composting Principles box on page 5 for some general guidelines.)

Understanding that bacteria are living organisms that chemically "chew up" the organic material in a compost pile will help you identify the optimal conditions for compost. Aerobic (oxygen-requiring) bacteria work faster, are usually less smelly, and generate higher temperatures in the compost pile, which can help kill certain disease pathogens. To favor these bacteria, you must turn the pile regularly, introduce oxygen into the pile (such as with perforated pipes), or make the pile small enough for oxygen to readily diffuse into it. In contrast, anaerobic bacteria do not require oxygen to work, take longer to accomplish the job, and do not generate high temperatures. In an anaerobic compost pile, earthworms encourage some aerobic activity and thereby expedite the composting process. Their castings also make it a richer source of nutrients. Aerobic methods can produce compost in as little as 14 days, but the pile needs to be built all at once. Anaerobic methods may take up to 1 year to produce compost, but the pile can be built slowly over the summer.

Both aerobic and anaerobic composting methods require moisture, because dry bacteria are "dead" bacteria. Both also need a large excess of carbon compared to nitrogen, usually a ratio of 30:1. In the absence of a large excess of carbonaceous material, bacteria digest their meal in a malodorous way. An odoriferous compost pile is usually working anaerobically and either needs more carbon material, needs to be turned, or both.

Certain materials are to be avoided. Under most circumstances, extremely rich sources of nitrogen (for example, animal meat and carnivorous-animal manure) give the pile indigestion, produce bacterial flatulence, and attract nuisance insects, but more importantly can contain disease pathogens. Diseased plant materials should never be added to a compost pile. Destroy diseased plant material by burying it in an area away from the garden or by burning it, if permitted. Although some diseases can be destroyed by the high temperatures generated in aerobic composting, backyard gardeners cannot rely on this result. The hottest temperatures occur at the center of the compost pile, so unless the pile is turned adequately and evenly mixed, certain parts of the pile may never reach the temperatures needed to destroy the disease pathogens. (For a fuller discussion of composting, consult sources in the bibliography, such as Stu Campbell's *Let It Rot!*)

ALONG CAME A SPIDER...

Research has shown that spiders regularly migrate hundreds of miles. To attract spiders, apply a thin layer of mulch before hot summer weather sets in. In spring, spiders "balloon" or drift through the air on fine silk threads in search of hospitable summer homes. Mulch offers the cool, damp environment spiders need to remain hydrated, and garden pests provide their food.

MULCH

Any material spread to cover the soil completely is considered mulch. Examples include compost, straw, chopped leaves, wood chips, cocoa bean shells, pebbles, plastic, and landscape fabric. Mulch plays many roles in a self-sustaining garden: It suppresses weed growth, keeps moisture in the soil by reducing evaporation, insulates the ground to keep it warm in winter and cool in summer, and can help prevent the emergence of certain harmful insects. Thick mulch around potatoes, for example, can help deter the Colorado potato beetle. In moister climates, some gardeners have reported using thick mulches of 4 to 8 inches or more during the growing season and never having to water or fertilize again. In hot, dry climates, a thick layer of mulch is not advisable because it absorbs rain and irrigation water, preventing them from reaching the soil. Thick mulch can also be counterproductive in areas that experience slug problems because slugs are attracted to cooler, moister environments.

Contrary to what some believe, grass clippings can be an effective mulch as long as they have not been sprayed with herbicides or pesticides and aren't loaded with weeds that are in the process of reseeding. In fact, studies show that grass clippings promote an abundance of pest-controlling spiders, another good friend of organic gardeners. Grass clippings can sometimes retard germination and emergence, as is the case with carrots, so delay application until after shoots have emerged through the soil.

Colored mulch, such as painted plastic, can serve other purposes as well, among them raising yields and deterring specific insects. In South Carolina, red mulch increased yields of cowpeas as much as 12 percent over the yields achieved with white or black mulch. Red is also believed to increase tomato yields, particularly early in the season, but has also been found to attract some pests. Orange mulch repels sweet potato whiteflies, but may attract other pests. Studies show that of all available colors, red attracts the most whiteflies, blue attracts the most aphids and thrips, and white aluminum is the least attractive to all three pests.

FLYING CREATURES

Birds and bats that eat insects play an important role in a self-sustaining garden. They help keep the garden free of flying and crawling insects, such as ants, aphids, caterpillars, beetles and beetle larvae, crickets, flies, grasshoppers, leafhoppers, moths and moth eggs, sowbugs, wasps, and weevils.

Because of development and associated land-use changes, habitat for many bird species is shrinking. Pesticides also play a role and have been implicated in the diminishing habitat of the eastern bluebird. Providing habitat for birds significantly reduces your need for pest controls and can help restore much-needed sources of uncontaminated food for birds.

To attract more birds to your garden, incorporate in your landscape tall trees, smaller flowering trees, shrubs, berries, flowers, and native tall grasses that provide a range of seasonal nesting and feeding opportunities.

In the United States, some notable tall trees that provide habitat for a variety of birds include ash, balsam fir, birch, black gum, elm, hemlock, hornbeam, maple, mountain ash, oak, pine, spruce, and wild cherry. Smaller trees attractive to birds are those that flower and offer berries and fruits, such as crab apple, dogwood, hawthorn, holly, mesquite, mulberry, palmetto, persimmon, red cedar, serviceberry, and sumac. Shrubs and cactus attractive to birds for food and cover include algerita, all berry bushes (blackberry, blueberry, elderberry, hackberry, huckleberry, raspberry, snowberry), bitterbrush, buckthorn, filaree, grape, lote bush, juniper, madrone, manzanita, mountain laurel, multiflora rose, pinyon, prickly pear, spicebush, viburnums, Virginia creeper, and wisteria. Most wildflowers attract birds, as do bee balm, lupines, and sunflowers. A small area of tall ornamental or native grasses can provide yet another important type of bird habitat.

Bats are far from the blood-sucking horror legend would suggest. They have a voracious appetite for the insects they eat at night and are thought to be helpful in keeping down mosquito populations. To attract more bats to your property, erect bat houses; these simple wooden structures are widely available at garden and home centers, or you can build your own.

Bees, wasps, and other beneficial insects are vital garden friends. Bees are nature's best pollinators, making possible the fruits and vegetables we all enjoy. Wasps, like other beneficial insects, not only prey on various destructive insects but also parasitize eggs, larvae, and adult insects. To attract wasps and other beneficial insects, plant companion herbs (especially Apiaceae herbs), flowers, and clovers at the edge of your garden. (For more on beneficial insects, see page 178.)

Planning and Maintaining a Healthy Garden

Choosing your garden's physical location. To be self-sustaining, your garden should be able to defend itself from severe damage from most pests most of the time. Such natural defense is promoted by four major factors: sun, water, soil, and air circulation. Choose a sunny spot for your garden—preferably one with both morning and afternoon sun. In humid, moist, or rainy regions where fungus can be expected, morning sun is especially important to dry the dew as quickly as possible. Try to locate the garden where it will get good air circulation. Avoid low areas susceptible to pockets of fog and high locations exposed to harsh winds.

Testing and amending your soil. Perhaps the most critical element in a successful garden is the quality of your soil. Soil is far more than the substrate or physical structure for growing plants. It is teeming with micro and macro life—microorganisms (bacteria, fungi, algae), macroinvertebrates (insects, nematodes, slugs, earthworms), and larger macro vertebrate animals (moles, mice, gophers). It also contains a host of micro- and macronutrients that are taken up through plant roots and work to create

CONSIDER RAISED BEDS

Whatever the condition of your soil, consider building raised beds. Although they require a modest initial investment of time and money, raised beds will pay you back in many different ways over the years. They are an excellent first step toward attaining a self-sustaining garden. Consider some of the advantages of raised beds:

- They minimize soil compaction, because you never walk on the growing medium.
- They offer oxygen more readily to plant roots, because there is little soil compaction.
- They drain better, because there is little soil compaction.
- They retain water better, because there is little soil compaction.
- They are easier to plant, weed, and maintain, because there is little or no soil compaction.
- They have greater yields because of better penetration of air, water, and sunlight; they also achieve higher germination rates for early plantings.
- They allow earlier and later planting, because they warm up earlier in spring and hold heat longer in fall.
- They allow greater root development, because of low soil compaction, good drainage, and oxygen diffusion.
- They save space. Plants can be spaced closer because you need walking space only between the beds, not between each row.

There are different types of raised beds and different ways to prepare them. My preferred method is to build a contained raised bed, 12 to 16 inches high, which allows you to sit on the edge while planting or weeding. An ideal size for a raised bed is 4 by 12 feet. This size allows you to easily reach into the center of the bed without having to stretch your arms too far or step on the soil.

You can build contained raised beds with a variety of nontoxic substances (e.g., stone, brick, concrete blocks) or with untreated wood that is naturally rot-resistant (e.g., cedar, cypress, and locust). In a food garden, never use pressure-treaded lumber. Since 1984, the EPA has directed that treated wood products not be used where they might come into contact with food, animal feed, or drinking water, either directly or indirectly, because of the possibility and increasing evidence that toxic substances will leach into the soil and enter the food chain.

Studies on treated wood have found that the chemicals chromium, copper, and arsenic leach out in significant amounts into soil, food crops, and beehives and onto hands in "wipe" tests on playground equipment. If treated lumber has been used for your raised beds, create a plastic or other barrier between the lumber and soil. You may also want to test your soil to determine the amount of leachate already present.

nutrient-dense foods. These nutrients include the macro nutrients of calcium (Ca), carbon (C), hydrogen (H), magnesium (Mg), nitrogen, oxygen (O), phosphorus (P), potassium (K), and sulfur (S), and the micronutrients boron (B), chlorine (Cl), copper (Cu), iron (Fe), manganese (Mn), molybdenum (Mo), and zinc (Zn). Healthy soil is important because it enables thriving healthy plants.

In turn, according to numerous long-term studies, foods produced with organic methods (which focus on healthy soils) are consistently higher in nutritional content than food produced with nonorganic methods. More specifically, organically produced foods score higher in vitamins and phytochemicals—particularly antioxidants, carotenoids, flavonoids, and phenolic compounds, all of which are important for human health.

Finally, an important part of your soil quality is its ability to hold and transport water, along with its ability to offer sufficient air pockets that provide oxygen and pathways for growing roots. A sandy soil doesn't hold water well, and though it may have a surfeit of air pockets, without frequent irrigation plants may die of thirst. At the opposite extreme, a heavy clay soil that is overly compacted can hold too much water and have too few air pockets, causing plants to die of rot. Plants need sufficient access to water and air pockets to thrive and produce healthy foods. To understand your soil quality and what it may need to sustain a healthy organic garden, seek the assistance of your local Cooperative Extension agent in obtaining a soil test for an organic food garden, which will give you information on your garden soil's condition and needs for organic matter (ability to hold water), texture, and micro- and macro nutrients.

Preventing pests. Bed planning and maintenance are essential components of a pest-control program. See pages 171–180 for a detailed discussion of essential steps to take during the planning stage to aid in pest prevention and in finding remedies.

How to Use This Book

You can use this book in many different ways. Information is organized and cross-referenced for easy retrieval. Plants are divided into three categories: vegetables, fruits and nuts, and herbs. You will find an overview of each plant under its own entry, and an overview of insects and diseases in the charts beginning on page 181. For major topics, particularly those concerning fruit and nut trees, we cover only the basics. For more complete discussions of these topics, consult the books listed in the bibliography. Following are explanations of the categories used in the plant entries; where entries are specific to a plant type, they are so noted.

PLANT NAMES

The genus and species, family name (Latin and English), and the common name are listed for each plant. Latin names have been included to help you problem solve. Plants in the same family don't always resemble each other. When planning crop rotations and preparing for insect and disease problems, therefore, it can be useful to be aware of any family ties.

SITE (FRUITS & NUTS ONLY)

Avoid planting fruit and nut trees in low pockets or in areas where fog and frost may collect. Most fruit trees require full sun. Morning sun is especially important to dry dew as rapidly as possible, which helps prevent fungus problems. Some fruit trees that are susceptible to late-frost damage are better sited on a north-sloping hill, or 12 to 15 feet away from a north wall, in order to delay budding as long as possible. To avoid nematode and verticillium wilt problems, you might choose a site where grass or cover crops have been grown for the previous 2 years.

TEMPERATURE

For germination. The optimum soil temperature for seed germination, in degrees Fahrenheit/Celsius. Seeds can germinate at temperatures outside the noted optimum range, but generally plan on longer germination at lower temperatures and shorter germination times at higher temperatures.

For growth. The optimum air temperature for plant growth, in degrees Fahrenheit/Celsius.

SOIL & WATER NEEDS

pH. On this scale of soil alkalinity/acidity, a 7.0 is neutral. Most plants will grow well in a pH range from 6.0 to 7.0. Home test kits are widely available.

Fertilizer. Organic gardeners typically fertilize twice in one season, often just with compost: once before planting and again in the middle of the growth cycle. For fruit trees, special attention is paid to the quality and extent of new growth, because this is one of the easiest ways, all other factors (e.g., light, soil, moisture, temperature) being equal, to determine whether a tree is obtaining proper nourishment. If tree growth is not within the appropriate range, it may need more nitrogen, assuming all other conditions are favorable. If tree growth is greater than the appropriate range, it might be receiving too much nitrogen.

Side-dressing. Any addition to the soil (such as fertilizer, compost, or soil amendments) after the plant is already set in the soil is considered side-dressing. To add, create a narrow furrow 1 to 3 inches deep at the plant's drip line, or 6 inches from the plant base, whichever is greater; sprinkle the amendment into the furrow and cover with soil.

Water. The individual plant's watering needs: *heavy* = 1 gallon per square foot, or 1.4 to 1.6 inches per week; *medium* = ¾ gallon per square foot, or 1 to 1.2 inches per week; and *low* = approximately ½ gallon per square foot, or 0.8 inch per week.

MEASUREMENTS

Planting depth. Best planting depth for germination and root lodging.

Root depth. When possible, a range of average to maximum recorded root depth has been given. If a range isn't given, the average root depth has been provided. The better worked your soil is, the deeper the roots extend, but ideally you shouldn't till more than 3 to 6 inches once a bed is established.

Height. The maximum height the plant is likely to grow to under optimal growing conditions. Different varieties are likely to have different heights, hence a range is given for planning purposes. Place taller plants toward the middle of a bed and shorter plants on the outer edges.

Breadth. The maximum breadth that the plant is likely to grow under optimal growing conditions. Different varieties may have different breadths, hence a range is given for planning purposes. Plan parallel rows to allow sufficient space for the maximum breadth of both plants.

Space between plants. In beds: This is the closest spacing recommended between plants under optimal conditions in raised beds and any other garden in which plants are spaced close together. (*Note:* If your climate is damp and humid, you should probably use broader spacing to allow for more air circulation and sun penetration, which prevent fungal and other diseases.)

In rows: Spacing recommended between plants in conventional rows, as opposed to raised beds.

Space between rows. Spacing needed between conventional rows.

PROPAGATION (HERBS)

Whether perennial or annual, herbs can often be propagated at home. Some herbs, for example, go "to seed" at the end of their growing season and can be propagated by saving the dried seed for replanting next year. Other perennial herbs are propagated by dividing the roots or taking cuttings for rooting in water or a moist growing medium. Some perennials tend to peter out after several years and need to be divided and replanted to retain their vigor.

GROWING & BEARING (FRUITS & NUTS)

Bearing age. The average number of years required for a fruit or nut tree to bear fruit from the time of planning in your garden. Bearing age may vary among cultivars of the same fruit or nut; be aware of this at the time of purchase.

Chilling requirement. The number of hours a fruit or nut tree needs below a certain temperature, usually 45°F/8°C, before it will blossom. Trees with lower chilling requirements bloom earlier and, therefore, are more susceptible to late-spring frosts.

Pollination. Many fruit and nut trees require pollination, some by the same variety or cultivar of tree and some by a different cultivar in the same family. For cross-pollination to occur, the trees must be flowering at the same time, so check a catalog or nursery to be sure that you have correctly matched trees that can pollinate each other. Some fruits and nuts may be *self-fruitful* and therefore do not require pollination by another tree.

SHAPING (FRUITS & NUTS)

Training. It is possible to train certain berries and fruit trees to grow in a two-dimensional form by pruning and training the plant along a multistrand wire structure. For grapes, raspberries, and blackberries, this may be done to increase air circulation to reduce fungal diseases, improve ease of harvest, and improve ability to manage and prune the fruiting canes. For fruit trees, this is usually done for aesthetic purposes, but it can also ensure good air circulation.

Pruning. Major pruning is almost always done when a tree is dormant. Prune new transplants only after the first year of growth. Pruning at the time of transplanting to bring a tree's top growth into balance with root growth was once recommended, but research now shows that such pruning can stunt a tree's growth for years. Summer pruning is usually limited to balanced thinning to ensure high-quality fruit.

A major goal of pruning is to remove diseased, damaged, dead, and disfigured material. Judicious pruning can also increase light penetration and air circulation for better-quality fruit and better disease control. Compost pruned material, unless it is diseased, in which case it should be destroyed.

The information provided on pruning is primarily intended as a reminder for the experienced gardener. Both a science and an art, pruning is above all a visual experience and, in my opinion, cannot be taught without diagrams and hands-on experience. (For books with more extensive discussions of pruning, consult the bibliography. *Pruning Made Easy* by Lewis Hill is an excellent choice.)

FIRST SEED-STARTING DATE (VEGETABLES & HERBS)

The seed-starting dates in most catalogs and books are based on a national average. Some may even break down starting dates by USDA hardiness zone. Such dates are not necessarily the best for your backyard, however, because your microclimate may differ significantly from these average temperatures. The formulas included enable you to calculate the seed-starting dates appropriate for your particular garden, no matter your location and no matter how idiosyncratic your microclimate. They also give you the flexibility to plant varieties of the same vegetable that have different maturation times. These formulas should increase your confidence that seed started will grow safely to maturity. After you've done several trials, feel free to substitute into the equation your own numbers for each variable.

Germinate. The average number of days for a seed to germinate, which is when green shoots emerge through the soil.

Transplant. The average number of days after germination that the plant needs to grow inside until it is transplanted outside. (*Note:* This number includes the 4 to 7 days that may be needed for hardening off.)

Last frost date. Average date of last frost in spring, available from your local Extension agent. If possible, keep records to determine the average last frost date for your own area.

Days before/after last frost date. The average number of days before (or after) the last frost date that a plant can tolerate living in outdoor soil. Use this number to determine the approximate dates you should transplant seedlings outside. This number also gives you a more precise measurement of the plant's frost hardiness. Because different sources suggest different setting-out dates, I've given the broadest possible range.

Maturity. The average number of days required for a plant to reach horticultural maturity for harvest. For plants that are transplanted, the plant will need the number of days noted under "Maturity" to complete maturation for harvest. If you don't want to start your seeds inside and prefer to direct-sow outside, calculate the total days to horticultural maturity by adding together the Germinate, Transplant, and Maturity.

Short-day factor. Horticultural maturity times noted in seed catalogs assume long days and warm temperatures. For late-summer or fall plantings of many vegetable species, you need to adjust horticultural maturity times by 2 weeks to accommodate shorter and cooler days. Some species, like the radish, require short days to form and don't need such adjustments. When possible, I have noted which species require an SD factor adjustment.

Frost tender. An additional 2-week adjustment for frost-tender vegetables, which need to mature at least 2 weeks before frost in order to produce a full harvest.

First frost date. Average date of first frost in autumn, available from your local Extension agent. If possible, keep records to determine the average FFD for your own area.

IMPORTANT NOTE ON CROSS-REFERENCING

For planning purposes, all allies, companions, and incompatibles in this text are cross-referenced. If a source says that squash hinders potato growth, for example, that does not necessarily mean that potatoes hinder squash growth. Still, if one plant is alleged to harm the growth of another, they should be considered incompatible. So in this text, squash is listed as an incompatible in the potato entry and vice versa. The same cross-referencing is done for companions and allies.

INSECT AND DISEASE PESTS

No matter how many insects and diseases are listed in each plant entry, you are unlikely to encounter more than a few in your garden at one time. The diseases listed in each entry are limited to those that are transmitted by an insect vector, are highly infectious, or for which there are remedies over and above the standard preventive measures described on pages 171–180. Insect, animal, and disease pests are described in more detail in Chapter Five.

ALLIES

In the context of this book, allies are plants purported to actively repel insects or to enhance the growth or flavor of the target plant. Chapter Six offers important caveats on allies and a listing of the reputed function of each, which may be helpful in determining if it will be useful in your garden.

Some evidence. The effects of these allies have been tested in field trials. If the source and location of the field test are unknown, the claim is listed as anecdotal because its relative merits are unknown. This is an important distinction, because a plant that may function as an ally when tested in the tropics may not offer the same benefits in northern Maine. The names of research sources are listed when possible.

Anecdotal. Allies classified as anecdotal have not undergone scientific testing or field trials and often hark back to tradition, folklore, and word of mouth. Presumably, for most of these anecdotal sources, positive correlations have been made, which have prompted the perpetuation of the information. Keep in mind that observations made at an unknown place and time are far from hard evidence. Use of allies categorized as anecdotal would constitute experimentation.

COMPANIONS

Companions are alleged to share space and growing habits well but do not necessarily play an active role in each other's insect protection or growth. Use your garden as a test bed. Some companions may work well, and others not at all. One might even prove a true ally by offering insect protection.

INCOMPATIBLES

Incompatibles are alleged to play an actively negative role in each other's growth by diminishing vigor or flavor, increasing the risk of insect or disease invasion, or decreasing yields. Although these claims may not be conclusive, it may be safer to avoid planting alleged incompatibles near one another.

HARVEST

Outlines when and how to harvest and includes special tips on how to recognize that a vegetable is ready for harvest. Special preparations or directions for curing the vegetable before eating or storing are also provided.

If for health purposes you are concerned about nitrate levels in your vegetables, not to worry. Studies show that the way you harvest can help to reduce nitrate levels. The morning of harvest, use a long pitchfork or another implement to break up the soil around the vegetables, severing the roots; this stops nitrogen uptake. Then simply harvest crops late the same day, when nitrate levels are at their lowest.

STORAGE REQUIREMENTS

Here you'll find tips on the best ways to store the edible harvest.

Fresh. How long fresh harvest will keep, at optimum storage temperature and humidity.

Preserved. The number of months the harvest will keep by specific preservation methods.

Note: Portions of the storage information are reprinted from Donald N. Maynard and George J. Hochmuth, eds., *Knott's Handbook for Vegetable Growers*, Fourth Edition, and from Jeff Ball, *The Self-Sufficient Suburban Gardener*.

ROOTSTOCKS (FRUITS & NUTS ONLY)

Most fruit and some nut trees sold today are grafted onto a rootstock. Grafting seeks to combine the desired fruit variety with a rootstock that controls the ultimate size of the tree. A more rapid form of propagation than seed starting, grafting also is beneficial because it hastens the onset of bearing. Rootstocks are numerous and not easy to sort through because most nursery catalogs and books mention certain characteristics and omit others, making it difficult to get an overview. Choice of rootstock should depend on such things as desired tree size, the natural growing height of the tree variety, soil drainage, soil fertility, and the specific insect and disease problems in your area. When buying a tree, find out what rootstock it is attached to, if any, and the growing characteristics of the rootstock, as this will affect things such as tree size, how early it bears, and disease resistance. To determine which rootstock is best for your garden, consult reliable nurseries.

CHAPTER TWO

vegetables

"A seed wants to grow," a Native American farmer in northwest Arizona once told me. I was stunned. After learning so much about when and how to grow and sustain a garden, it was a revelation that a seed wants to grow. It has everything it needs within the seed coat and just needs our help with three things: water, warmth, and light. We can plan and organize all we want, but in the end the seed does the real work of transforming sun and water into food that keeps us alive.

This new clarity about a seed's programming and readiness to sprout was liberating. One year when work and weather prevented me from planting my garden at the typical time, I remembered this lesson and decided that an unprecedented 2-month delay should not deter me. And I learned four things: The seeds still wanted to grow, harvest was delayed by fewer days than the planting delay, yields seemed about the same as prior years, and a very late planting avoided squash bugs.

So be brave and bold in trying new things. A garden is very forgiving. Let the seeds and their desire to grow be a source of great joy, learning, and discovery.

Artichoke

Cynara scolymus
Asteraceae (Sunflower Family)

Artichoke is a cool-season crop, tender to frost and light freezes. Plan an average of three plants per person. In warm climates with mild winters, artichoke is grown as a perennial; in cold climates, as an annual. Choose a sunny, sheltered location. Add plenty of compost or rotted manure to the soil before planting and again when the plants are 6 to 8 inches high. In cold climates, plant artichokes in large containers to keep the roots alive through winter. In warm climates, cut the plants to the ground in fall. In cooler areas, to prepare for winter either cut the plants to the ground and bring containers indoors, or cut them to 15 to 20 inches above the ground, bend over the stalks, mulch heavily with leaves, and cover with a waterproof tarp or basket.

Some recommend removing side shoots during the growing season. This increases the size of the central head but reduces overall yield. One gardener harvested almost 30 heads from just the side shoots of one plant. If not harvested for your table, the bud will blossom into beautiful purple-blue flowers suitable for arrangements.

TEMPERATURE

For Germination: 60°F–70°F/16°C–22°C

For Growth: 60°F–65°F/16°C–19°C

SOIL & WATER NEEDS

pH: 6.5

Fertilizer: Heavy feeder, lots of well-rotted manure or compost

Side-Dressing: Every 3–4 weeks

Mulch: Apply over winter, and when plants are 6″–8″ high.

Water: Heavy

MEASUREMENTS

Planting Depth: Set buds just above the soil surface.

Root Depth: More than 4′

Height: 3′–6′

Breadth: 3′–6′

Space between Plants:

- In beds: 2′–3′
- In rows: 4′–6′

Space between Rows: 6′–8′

PROPAGATION

Seed or suckers. To propagate by sucker, use a trowel to slice off the parent plant's 10″-tall suckers, each with a section of root. In warm climates, plant the suckers in a 4″ hole. In cold climates, plant the suckers in a pot to overwinter indoors.

PESTS

Aphid, plume moth, slug

DISEASES

Curly dwarf (virus), southern blight, verticillium wilt

ALLIES

None

COMPANIONS

Brassicas

INCOMPATIBLES

None

FIRST SEED-STARTING DATE

Start 6 weeks before the last frost date in 4″-deep pots in an area where the temperature is about 65°/19°F. When germinated, put in full sun where the temperature is around 50°F/10°C for 9–10 days. Transplant when 4 true leaves have appeared.

HARVEST

When heads are still closed, about the size of an orange, and while the stem 2″ below the bud is still supple, cut off 1″–2″ of stem with the head. Heads that have already opened are tough. Always harvest the central bud first. After harvest, cut the stems to the ground, or cut to 12″ above the ground to encourage side shoots. Side shoots produce buds smaller than the first central bud.

Storage Requirements		
Store in a paper bag in the refrigerator to increase humidity and avoid drying out.		
Fresh		
Temperature	**Humidity**	**Storage Life**
32°F/0°C	95%–100%	2–3 weeks
Preserved		
Method	**Taste**	**Shelf Life**
Canned hearts	Good	12+ months
Frozen hearts	Good	4+ months
Dried	N/A	N/A

Asparagus

Asparagus officinalis
Liliaceae (Lily Family)

Asparagus is a perennial, early-spring crop. Plan an average of 10 plants per person. Best planting time is early spring. Plant in a sunny spot protected from the wind. Because asparagus roots often extend both downward and outward 5 to 6 feet, plant in deeply rototilled soil that has incorporated green manure and compost. Traditionally, roots are planted in furrows 8 to 10 inches deep and 10 inches wide. Spread the roots, cover the crowns with 2 to 3 inches of sifted compost and humus, and water well. As the plant grows through summer, add more soil, but do not cover the tip. If you prefer to plant individually, dig holes 8 to 10 inches deep and 5 inches wide, then proceed with the same method for furrow planting.

Every spring, asparagus rows should be "ridged" by drawing up several inches of topsoil or, better, newly applied compost. This counters the tendency of the crown to get too close to the surface. After harvest, sow a cover crop of cowpeas or other legume between the asparagus rows, which discourages weeds and adds to the organic matter when dug under. University of Minnesota trials have shown that fall plantings of 9- to 11-week-old seedlings equal or exceed the growth of spring transplants. Carl Cantaluppi of the University of Illinois confirmed that you can increase yields by up to 40 percent by planting crowns at a depth of 5 to 6 inches, rather than at 10 to 12 inches. He also claims that asparagus is not a heavy nitrogen feeder because the ferns return most of the nitrogen to the soil. Decide for yourself.

TEMPERATURE

For Germination: 60°F–85°F/15°C–30°C
For Growth: 60°F–70°F/16°C–22°C

SOIL & WATER NEEDS

pH: 6.0–8.0
Fertilizer: Heavy feeder, apply compost to first-year beds in autumn, and again after harvest to established beds in spring. Apply fish emulsion twice yearly. Beds may need P and K before planting, and N after planting.
Mulch: Use straw or light material during winter and remove it in spring. Use compost during the growing season.
Water: Heavy

MEASUREMENTS

Planting Depth: 8″–10″ (see above)
Root Depth: More than 4′
Height: 3′–8′ (fern growth, depending on soil and climate)
Breadth: 2′–4′ (fern growth, depending on soil and climate)

Space between Plants:

- In beds: 12″
- In rows: 15″–18″

Space between Rows: 3′–4′

AVERAGE BEARING AGE

3 years from seeds, 2 years from crowns

PESTS

Aphid, asparagus beetle (early May), cucumber beetle, garden centipede, gopher, Japanese beetle, mite, slug, snail, spotted asparagus beetle

DISEASES

Asparagus rust, fusarium wilt

ALLIES

Uncertain: Basil, goldenrod, nasturtium, parsley, pot marigold, rye, tomato

INCOMPATIBLES

Onion family, weeds (during first 6 weeks of asparagus growth)

HARVEST

When spears are ⅜″ thick and 6″–8″ high, cut spears ½″ below the soil surface to lessen the chance of disease and pest infestation. Heads should be tight and spears brittle. Stop harvesting when stalks are less than ⅜″ thick. When grown from roots, do not harvest the first year. Let the plants go to foliage, and when they brown in fall, cut them to ground level. The second year, harvest spears for about 4 weeks. In following years, the harvest will continue for 8–10 weeks.

Storage Requirements

Wrap spears in moist towels or stand upright in a glass of water, then refrigerate in plastic bags. Blanch asparagus before freezing it.

Fresh		
Temperature	**Humidity**	**Storage Life**
32°F–35°F/0°C–2°C	95%–100%	2–3 weeks
Preserved		
Method	**Taste**	**Shelf Life**
Canned	Good	12+ months
Frozen	Excellent	12 months
Dried	Fair	12+ months

Dried Beans

Phaseolus vulgaris
Fabaceae (Pea Family)

Beans are a warm-season crop, tender to light frosts and freezes. Plan an average of 10 to 20 plants per person. Cold, wet weather fosters disease. To prevent disease, do not sow or transplant too early, touch the plants when wet, or touch healthy plants after working with diseased ones. Most dried beans, whether bush or semi-vining, require long growing seasons. To direct-sow them, layer grass mulch 4 to 6 inches deep on the bed in fall. This will decompose to about 2 inches by spring, keep the soil warm 6 inches deep, and won't pull nitrogen out of the soil, slowing you to plant earlier in spring. (See Snap Beans, page 27, for comments on presoaking and inoculation.) Dried beans are very high in protein. Like other legumes, soybeans and cowpeas are excellent green manure crops that enrich soil with organic matter and nitrogen.

TEMPERATURE

For Germination: 60°F–85°F/16°C–30°C

For Growth: 60°F–75°F/16°C–24°C

SOIL & WATER NEEDS

pH: 6.2–7.5

Fertilizer: Light feeder. Because bean plants fix N when inoculated properly, they should require low N. After the plant flowers, apply fertilizer low in N, medium P and K. Avoid low K at all times.

Water: Average and constant

First Seed-Starting Date

Transplant or direct-sow when soil temperature is 60°F/16°C.

Germinate	+	Transplant	–	Days after LFD	=	Count Back from LFD
4–10 days	+	21–28 days	–	0–10 days	=	25–28 days

Last Seed-Starting Date

Germinate	+	Transplant	+	Maturity	+	SD Factor	+	Frost Tender	=	Count Back from FFD
4–10 days	+	0 (direct)	+	98–125 days	+	14 days	+	14 days	=	130–163 days

MEASUREMENTS

Planting Depth: 1″
Root Depth: 36″–48″
Height: 10″–24″
Breadth: 4″–8″
Space between Plants: 2″–6″
Space between Rows: 12″–30″; 8″ on center in raised beds

PESTS

Aphid, bean leaf beetle, beet and potato leafhopper, cabbage looper, corn earworm, cucumber beetle, cutworm, flea beetle, garden webworm, Japanese beetle, leaf-footed bug, leaf miner, Mexican bean beetle, mite, root-knot nematode, seedcorn maggot, slug, tarnished plant bug, thrips, webworm, weevil, whitefly, wireworm

DISEASES

Anthracnose, bacterial blight and wilt, bean mosaic, common mosaic, curly top, damping off, powdery mildew, rust, southern blight, white mold, yellow mosaic. (*Note:* If legal, burn diseased plants.)

ALLIES

Some Evidence: Goosegrass, red sprangletop, sorghum mulch (for cowpeas)
Uncertain: Catnip, celery, chamomile, corn, goldenrod, marigold, nasturtium, oregano, potato, rosemary, savory

COMPANIONS

Beet, cabbage, carrot, celery, corn, cucumber, eggplant, pea, potato, radish, strawberry

INCOMPATIBLES

Fennel, garlic, gladiolus, onion family

HARVEST

Wait until the plant's leaves have fallen in autumn to pick dry pods or to pull the entire plant. Harvest before the first frost. Soybeans and limas, however, should be picked when any split pods are spotted because beans often drop from the shells as they dry. Cure for several weeks in a well-ventilated area, piling them on screens or slatted shelves. Beans are dry and ready to thresh when they don't dent when bitten. Following are four methods of threshing.

- Thrash the plant back and forth inside a clean trashcan.
- Place the plant in a large burlap bag with a hole in the corner and flail.
- Put plants in a cone-shaped bag, tie the bottom, and walk or jump on the bag.
- Put the beans into a bag with a hole in the bottom and tie the bottom closed. Hang the bag from a tree and beat well, then untie the hole. With the help of a good wind, the chaff will blow away and the beans will fall into a container placed below.

STORAGE REQUIREMENTS

Remove all bad beans. Place on shallow trays and heat at 170°F–180°F/77°C–83°C for 10–15 minutes. Cool. Store in a cool, dry area in tight jars. To avoid weevil damage, see page 274.

Lima Beans

Phaseolus lunatus

Fabaceae (Pea Family)

Lima beans are a warm-season crop, very tender to frost and light freezes. Plan an average of 10 to 20 plants per person. For every 2 pounds of filled pods, you should get 1 pound of shelled beans. Limas are more sensitive to cold soil and calcium deficiency than are snap beans. Limas don't like transplanting, so it's often recommended to sow them directly in the beds; however, seeds will not germinate if the soil isn't warm enough. (See Snap Beans, page 27, for comments about presoaking, inoculation, and cold, wet weather.) For direct sowing, plant five to six seeds in a hill and thin to 3 to 4 inches.

Bush beans usually mature more quickly than pole beans and are determinate, with one clean harvest. Pole limas generally have better flavor and are indeterminate, with a continuous harvest, but they require a trellis and some extra effort. Bush limas don't do well in wet weather; they develop an unpleasant earthy taste if pods touch the ground. Corn plants can provide a substitute support for nonrampant pole beans; plant the beans between 6- to 8-inch-tall corn plants.

TEMPERATURE

For Germination: 65°F–85°F/19°C–30°C

For Growth: 60°F–70°F/16°C–22°C

SOIL & WATER NEEDS

pH: 6.0–7.0

Fertilizer: Light feeder. Beans fix N when inoculated properly, so most need low N, medium P and K.

Side-Dressing: 4 weeks after planting, apply a balanced or low N fertilizer, or compost.

Water: Average, constant

First Seed-Starting Date

Germinate	+	Transplant	–	Days after LFD	=	Count Back from LFD
7–18 days	+	21–35 days	–	14–28 days	=	14–25 days

Last Seed-Starting Date

Germinate	+	Transplant	+	Maturity	+	SD Factor	+	Frost Tender	=	Count Back from FFD
7–18 days	+	0 (direct)	+	60–80 days	+	14 days	+	14 days	=	95–126 days

MEASUREMENTS

Planting Depth: 1½″ to 2″

Root Depth: 36″–48″

Height:

- Pole: 8′–15′
- Bush: 10″–18″

Breadth:

- Pole: 6″–8″
- Bush: 4″–8″

Space between Plants:

- Pole: 6″ (in beds); 10″–18″ (in rows)
- Bush: 4″–6″ (in beds); 6″–8″ (in rows)

Space between Rows: 36″–48″

SUPPORT STRUCTURES

Use a 6′ post, A-frame, tepee (3 poles tied at the top), or trellis for pole beans.

PESTS

Aphid, bean leaf beetle, beet and potato leafhopper, cabbage looper, corn earworm, cucumber beetle, cutworm, flea beetle, garden webworm, Japanese beetle, leaf-footed bug, leaf miner, Mexican bean beetle, mite, root-knot nematodes, seedcorn maggot, slug, tarnished plant bug, thrips, webworm, weevil, whitefly, wireworm

DISEASES

Anthracnose, bacterial blight and wilt, bean mosaic, common mosaic, curly top, damping off, powdery mildew, rust, southern blight, white mold, yellow mosaic. (*Note:* If legal, burn diseased plants.)

ALLIES

Some Evidence: Goosegrass, marigold, red sprangletop

Uncertain: Catnip, celery, corn, nasturtium, oregano, potato, rosemary, savory

COMPANIONS

Carrot, corn, cucumber, eggplant, lettuce, pea, radish

Bush only: Beet, all brassicas, strawberry

INCOMPATIBLES

Fennel, garlic, onion family

Pole Only: Beet, all brassicas, kohlrabi, sunflower

HARVEST

For the best fresh flavor, pick beans when young. To encourage the plant to set more beans, pick when beans are bulging through pods. For dried beans, wait until pods turn brown or leaves drop in fall. Pick pods and cure for several weeks in a well-ventilated area, piling them on screens or slatted shelves. Beans are dry and ready to thresh when they don't dent when bitten. See Dried Beans, page 22, for threshing methods.

Storage Requirements		
Blanch before freezing. Store dried beans in jars in a cool, dry place.		
Fresh		
Temperature	**Humidity**	**Storage Life**
37°F–41°F/3°C–5°C	95%	5–7 days
Preserved		
Method	**Taste**	**Shelf Life**
Canned	Fair	12+ months
Frozen	Excellent	12 months
Dried	Excellent	12+ months

Snap Beans

Phaseolus vulgaris
Fabaceae (Pea Family)

Beans are a warm-season crop, tender to light frosts and freezes. Plan an average of 10 to 20 plants per person. Bush beans are usually determinate with one clean harvest, so plant every 10 days for continuous harvest. Pole beans are usually indeterminate with a continuous harvest for 6 to 8 weeks if kept picked, so only one planting is necessary. Bean roots don't tolerate disturbance so handle seedlings minimally. Plant outside at the same depth they grew in the pot.

Some gardeners recommend presoaking seeds before planting, but research indicates that presoaked seeds absorb water too quickly, causing the outer coats to spill out essential nutrients, which encourages damping-off seed rot. Yields can increase 50 to 100 percent by inoculating with *Rhizobium* bacteria. To inoculate, simply roll seeds in the powder. Cold, wet weather fosters disease, so do not sow or transplant too early, touch plants when wet, or touch healthy plants after working with diseased ones. Pinch off the growing tips of pole beans when plants reach the top of their support.

TEMPERATURE

For Germination: 60°F–85°F/16°C–30°C

For Growth: 60°F–70°F/16°–22°C

SOIL & WATER NEEDS

pH: 6.2–7.5

Fertilizer: Because bean plants fix N when inoculated properly, they should require low N; after they flower, apply light N, avoid low K.

Water: Low until the plant flowers, then average

First Seed-Starting Date

Germinate	+	Transplant	–	Days after LFD	=	Count Back from LFD
4–10 days	+	21–28 days	–	7–14 days	=	18–24 days

Last Seed-Starting Date

Germinate	+	Transplant	+	Maturity	+	SD Factor	+	Frost Tender	=	Count Back from FFD
4 –10 days	+	0 (direct)	+	48–95 days	+	14 days	+	14 days	=	80–133 days

MEASUREMENTS

Planting Depth:

- Spring: 1″
- Fall: 2″

Root Depth: 36″–48″

Height:

- Pole: 8″–15″
- Bush: 10″–24″

Breadth:

- Pole: 6″–8″
- Bush: 4″–8″

Space between Plants:

- Pole: 6″ (in beds); 12″ (in rows)
- Bush: 2″–4″ (in beds); 4″–6″ (in rows)

Space between Rows: 18″–36″ (pole or bush)

SUPPORT STRUCTURES

Use 6′ posts, A-frame, tepee (3 poles tied together at the top), or trellis to support pole beans.

For an alternate support, plant nonrampant pole beans between corn that isn't too densely planted, when the corn is 6″–8″ tall.

PESTS

Same as for Lima Beans (see page 24), with the addition of the European corn borer

DISEASES

Anthracnose, bacterial blight and wilt, bean and common mosaic, curly top, damping off, powdery mildew, rust, southern blight, white mold, yellow mosaic. (*Note:* If legal, burn diseased plants.)

ALLIES

Some Evidence: Goosegrass, red sprangletop

Uncertain: Catnip, celery, corn, marigold, nasturtium, oregano, potato, rosemary, savory

COMPANIONS

Pole and Bush: Carrot, chard, corn (corn rows can be windbreaks for dwarf beans), cucumber, eggplant, pea, radish, strawberry

Bush Only: Beet, all brassicas

INCOMPATIBLES

Pole and Bush: Basil, fennel, garlic, gladiolus, onion family

Pole Only: Beet, all brassicas, sunflower

HARVEST

For best flavor, pick early in the morning, after leaves are dry. Harvest before seeds bulge, when beans snap off the plant and snap in half cleanly. Continual harvest is essential for prolonged bean production.

Bush, Snap: Pick when ¼″–⅜″ diameter.

Filet: Pick daily and, for peak flavor, when no larger than ⅛″ diameter, regardless of length.

Storage Requirements		
Blanch before freezing.		
Fresh		
Temperature	**Humidity**	**Storage Life**
40°F–45°F/5°C–8°C	95%	7–10 days
Preserved		
Method	**Taste**	**Shelf Life**
Canned	Fair	12+ months
Frozen	Excellent	12 months
Dried	Excellent	24 months

Beet

Beta vulgaris
Chenopodiaceae (Goosefoot Family)

Beets are an annual cool-season crop, half-hardy to frost and light freezes. Plan an average of 10 to 20 plants per person. Most beet cultivars are open-pollinated and multigerm, where one seed yields a clump of four to five plants that need to be thinned. These multigerm seeds, also known as "seed balls," germinate better if soaked an hour before planting.

There are three main types of eating beets: long (cylindra), medium (semiglobe), and short (globe). Cylindra types mature slowly and, because they grow as long as 8 inches, require deep soil. They can also be a good organic matter crop. For all types, look for cultivars resistant to bolting and downy mildew. Yellow and white beets are sweeter than red varieties. Newer hybrids are usually sweeter than older varieties and offer more green leaves. Most beets contain 5 to 8 percent sugar, whereas newer hybrids such as Big Red run 12 to 14 percent. Hybrids tend to mature 7 to 14 days earlier, are more upright, and tend to have higher yields.

Like kale and some other vegetables, in hot weather most beets get tough, woody, and develop an "off" flavor. An exception, according to some, is Detroit Crimson Globe. If your summers are hot, generally choose a variety that matures in 45 to 60 days. In greenhouses, beets are often grown for their greens only.

TEMPERATURE

For Germination: 50°F–85°F/10°C–30°C

For Growth: 60°F–65°F/16°C–19°C

SOIL & WATER NEEDS

pH: 5.8–7.0 (5.3 to deter scab)

Fertilizer: Heavy feeder. Needs high P; avoid high N; good tops may mean the roots are poorly developed and the plant is getting too much N.

First Seed-Starting Date

Germinate	+	Transplant	+	Days before LFD	=	Count Back from LFD
5–10 days	+	0 (direct)	+	9–18 days	=	14–28 days

Last Seed-Starting Date

Germinate	+	Transplant	+	Maturity	+	SD Factor	+	Frost Tender	=	Count Back from FFD
5–10 days	+	0 (direct)	+	55–80 days	+	14 days	+	0 days	=	74–104 days

Side-Dressing: Every 2 weeks provide a light and balanced feeding; when tops are 4″–5″ use low N.
Water: Average and evenly moist

MEASUREMENTS

Planting Depth: ¼″
Root Depth: 24″–10′
Height: 12″
Breadth: 4″–8″
Space between Plants:

- In beds: 3″–4″
- In rows: 6″

Space between Rows: 18″–24″

PESTS

Mostly pest-free; occasional beet leafhopper, carrot weevil, earwig (seedlings), garden webworm, leaf miner, mite, spinach flea beetle, whitefly, wireworm

DISEASES

Mostly disease-free; occasionally cercospora, downy mildew, leaf spot, rust, scab

ALLIES

Uncertain: Broccoli, garlic, onion family

COMPANIONS

All brassicas, bush beans, head lettuce

INCOMPATIBLES

Field mustard, all pole beans

HARVEST

In late June, or before the hot season enters its prime, scrape some soil away from the beets to check their size. Pull or dig when the beets are 1″–2″ across. They can become tough and woody flavored when allowed to grow much larger, depending on the variety.

Storage Requirements

Remove all top greens, leaving about 1″ of stem with the beet. Do not wash. Pack beets in straw or moist sand. Beets can also be left in the ground and dug up from under the snow.

Fresh		
Temperature	**Humidity**	**Storage Life**
32°F/0°C	98%–100%	4–7 months topped; 10–14 days bunched
Preserved		
Method	**Taste**	**Shelf Life**
Canned	Good	12+ months
Frozen	Fair	8 months
Dried	Fair	12+ months

Broccoli

Brassica oleracea
Botrytis Group
Brassicaceae (Mustard Family)

Broccoli is an annual cool-season crop, hardy to frost and light freezes. Plan an average of 5 to 10 plants per person. Transplant seedlings when they're 6 inches high, and place in the ground 1 inch deeper than they were grown in the pots. Broccoli is usually sensitive to heat. If the weather is too hot, it will flower quickly and won't produce an edible head. Cover with fabric immediately after planting. This not only protects broccoli from pests but also helps trap heat for early plantings. To prevent spreading clubroot and other soilborne diseases, don't compost brassica roots. Some gardeners won't compost any part of a plant in the brassica family. Pull and destroy infected plants. Also, rotate the placement of brassica plants in your garden so they aren't in the same 10-foot radius for at least 3 years. Some experts recommend a rotation of 7 years.

TEMPERATURE

For Germination: 50°F–85°F/10°C–30°C
For Growth: 60°F–65°F/16°C–19°C

SOIL & WATER NEEDS

pH: 6.0–7.5 (7.2 deters clubroot)
Fertilizer: Heavy feeder. Before planting, add compost to the soil. If clubroot is a problem, raise the pH by adding lime or taking other measures (see Acid Soil on page 181).
Side-Dressing: When buds begin to form, side-dress the plant with compost.
Water: Medium and evenly moist

MEASUREMENTS

Planting Depth: ¼″
Root Depth: 18″–36″
Height: 18″–4′
Breadth: 15″–24″

First Seed-Starting Date

Germinate	+	Transplant	+	Days before LFD	=	Count Back from LFD
3–10 days	+	42 days	+	14 days	=	59–66 days

Last Seed-Starting Date

Germinate	+	Transplant	+	Maturity	+	SD Factor	+	Frost Tender	=	Count Back from FFD
3 –10 days	+	21 days	+	55–74 days	+	14 days	+	0 days	=	93–119 days

Space between Plants:

- In beds: 15″
- In rows: 18″–24″

Space between Rows: 24″–36″

PESTS

Aphid, cabbage butterfly, cabbage looper, cabbage maggot, cutworm, diamondback moth, flea beetle, harlequin bug, imported cabbageworm, mite, cabbage maggot, slug, weevil, whitefly

DISEASES

Alternaria leaf spot, black leg, black rot, clubroot, damping off, downy mildew, leaf spot, rhizoctonia, yellows

ALLIES

Some Evidence: Candytuft, celery, collard greens, mint, shepherd's purse, thyme, wormseed mustard
Uncertain: Catnip, chamomile, dill, garlic, nasturtium, onion family, radish, rosemary, sage, savory, tansy, tomato, wormwood

COMPANIONS

Artichoke, beet, bush beans, chard, cucumber, lettuce, pea, potato, spinach

INCOMPATIBLES

Pole lima and snap beans, strawberry, tomato (latter may also be an ally)

HARVEST

Harvest when the heads are dark green, or dusky violet for purple varieties. If heads turn yellow, you've waited too long. For most varieties, small compact heads offer the best flavor. The exception is Romanesco, whose head can grow up to 1′ in breadth and whose natural color is chartreuse. Harvest the central head first. Some varieties will produce side shoots that develop small head clusters; these plants will provide for 1–2 months, or until frost. Cut the stalk so that several inches remain on the plant.

Storage Requirements

Fall crops are better than summer crops for freezing.

Fresh		
Temperature	**Humidity**	**Storage Life**
32°F/0°C	95%–100%	10–14 days
32°F–40°F/0°C–5°C	80%	1 month

Preserved		
Method	**Taste**	**Shelf Life**
Canned	Fair	12+ months
Frozen	Good	12 months
Dried	Fair	12+ months

Brussels Sprouts

Brassica oleracea
Gemmifera Group
Brassicaceae (Mustard Family)

Brussels sprouts are an annual cool-season crop, hardy to frost and light freezes. Plan an average of two to eight plants per person. There are two basic types of Brussels sprouts varieties: (1) the dwarf, which matures early and is winter hardy but more difficult to harvest; and (2) the taller, which is less hardy but easier to harvest. Brussels sprouts have shallow roots, so as they become top-heavy you may need to stake them, particularly if exposed to strong winds.

As with other brassicas, Brussels sprouts are susceptible to pests and diseases that must be kept under control early in the season. Row covers are one of the easiest pest controls to use, provided no pest eggs are already present. To prevent spreading soilborne diseases, don't compost brassica roots. Rotate at least on a 3-year basis, or optimally on a 7-year basis.

This vegetable is high in calcium and iron, as well as a good source of vitamins A and C.

TEMPERATURE

For Germination: 50°F–80°F/10°C–27°C

For Growth: 60°F–65°F/16°C–19°C

SOIL & WATER NEEDS

pH: 6.0–7.5

Fertilizer: Heavy feeder, use compost, or 2–3 bushels of manure per 100 square feet.

Side-Dressing: Apply 2 weeks after transplanting, and twice more at monthly intervals.

Water: Medium and evenly moist

First Seed-Starting Date

Germinate	+	Transplant	+	Days before LFD	=	Count Back from LFD
3–10 days	+	28–49 days	+	14–21 days	=	45–80 days

Last Seed-Starting Date

Germinate	+	Transplant	+	Maturity	+	SD Factor	+	Frost Tender	=	Count Back from FFD
3–10 days	+	21 days	+	80–100 days	+	14 days	+	0 days	=	118–145 days

MEASUREMENTS

Planting Depth: ¼″
Root Depth: 18″–36″
Height: 24″–48″
Breadth: 24″
Space between Plants:

- In beds: 16″–18″
- In rows: 18″–24″

Space between Rows: 24″–40″

PESTS

Aphid, cabbage butterfly, cabbage looper, cabbage maggot, cutworm, flea beetle, harlequin bug, mite, cabbage maggot, slug, thrips, weevil, whitefly

DISEASES

Black leg, black rot, clubroot, damping off, leaf spot, rhizoctonia, yellows

ALLIES

Some Evidence: Candytuft, celery, clover (white), cover grass, French beans, mint, shepherd's purse, thyme, weedy ground cover, wormseed mustard
Uncertain: Chamomile, dill, garlic, onion family, radish, rosemary, sage, savory, tansy, tomato, wormwood

COMPANIONS

Artichoke, beet, pea, potato, spinach

INCOMPATIBLES

Kohlrabi, all pole beans, strawberry, tomato (latter may also be an ally)

HARVEST

For the best sprout growth, when a node begins to bulge, remove the leaf below it. Harvest from the bottom of the stalk up. When sprouts are firm and no more than about 1″ across, use a sharp knife to cut off the sprouts and remove lower leaves. Leave enough trunk so that new sprouts can grow. As the harvest slows, pinch the top of the plant to direct nutrients to the sprouts. For maximum vitamin C, harvest when the temperature is around freezing. Some say never to harvest unless you've had at least two frosts, because frost improves flavor. It has also been reported that sprouts can be harvested throughout summer and still be tender if continuously picked when they reach the size of marbles. If you want to harvest all at once instead of continuously, cut or pinch off the stalk top 4–8 weeks before your intended harvesttime. After harvest, remove the entire plant from the ground to minimize the chance of disease next season.

Brussels Sprouts

Storage Requirements		
Store the entire plant in a cool root cellar. Otherwise, leave the stalk in the ground and pick sprouts when ready to eat. Some report harvesting through the snow.		
Fresh		
Temperature	**Humidity**	**Storage Life**
32°F/0°C	95%–100%	3–5 weeks
Preserved		
Method	**Taste**	**Shelf Life**
Canned	Fair	12+ months
Frozen	Good	12 months
Dried	Poor	

Cabbage

Brassica oleracea
Capitata Group
Brassicaceae (Mustard Family)

Cabbage is an annual cool-season crop, hardy to frost and light freezes. Plan an average of three to five plants per person. Young plants may bolt if grown at 50°F/10°C for a long time; mature plants of late varieties improve flavor in cold weather. A smaller cabbage head has better flavor and can stay in the field longer without splitting. To keep them small, plant close together or, when the head is almost full, give the plant a sharp twist to sever feeder roots.

After harvest, continued growth causes cabbage to need additional food reserves. Rapid growers keep poorly, as they use up their food reserves faster. Early varieties are generally the smallest, juiciest, and most tender, but they store poorly and split easily. Midseason varieties keep better in the field. Late varieties, best for sauerkraut, provide the largest and longest-keeping heads. Yellow varieties tend to be hotter than white. To prevent spreading soilborne diseases, don't compost any brassica roots; pull and destroy infected plants. Also, rotate these plants on at least a 3-year basis, or optimally on a 7-year basis.

TEMPERATURE

For Germination: 45°F–95°F/8°C–35°C

For Growth: 60°F–65°F/16°C–19°C

SOIL & WATER NEEDS

pH: 6.0–7.5 (7.2 deters clubroot)

Fertilizer: Heavy feeder, high N and K, may need to add lime to raise the pH to deter clubroot

Side-Dressing: Every 2 weeks

Water: Heavy early and medium late in the season

First Seed-Starting Date

Germinate	+	Transplant	+	Days before LFD	=	Count Back from LFD
7–12 days	+	42 days	+	14–21 days	=	63–75 days

Last Seed-Starting Date

Germinate	+	Transplant	+	Maturity	+	SD Factor	+	Frost Tender	=	Count Back from FFD
4 days	+	21 days	+	65–95 days	+	14 days	+	0 days	=	104–134 days

MEASUREMENTS

Planting Depth: ¼″–½″
Root Depth: 12″–5′
Height: 12″–15″
Breadth: 24″–40″
Space between Plants:

- In beds: 15″
- In rows: 18″

Space between Rows: 24″–30″

PESTS

Aphid, cabbage butterfly, cabbage looper, cabbage maggot, cabbageworm, cutworm, diamondback moth, flea beetle, green worm, harlequin bug, leaf miner, mite, mole, cabbage maggot, seedcorn maggot, slug, stink bug, weevil

DISEASES

Black leg, black rot, clubroot, damping off, fusarium wilt, leaf spot, pink rot, rhizoctonia, yellows

ALLIES

Some Evidence: Anise, candytuft, celery, cilantro, collard greens, clover (red and white), green chop, hyssop, marigold, mint, sage, shepherd's purse, thyme, wormseed mustard, wormwood

Uncertain: Chamomile, dill, garlic, nasturtium, onion family, radish, rosemary, rye, savory, southernwood, tansy, tomato

COMPANIONS

Artichoke, beet, bush beans, cucumber, lettuce, pea, potato, spinach

INCOMPATIBLES

Basil, all pole beans, strawberry, tomato. (*Note:* Some evidence that tomato is also an ally [see page 293].)

HARVEST

For eating fresh, cut the head at ground level as soon as it feels solid. Smaller heads may grow from the remaining leaves and stems. For the best storage heads, pick when still firm and solid and before the top leaves lose green color. Pull the entire plant and roots from the ground. If left too long in the ground, the cabbage core becomes fibrous and tough, and the head may split.

Storage Requirements

Some recommend curing heads in the sun for a few days before storing for long periods. Such curing requires covering at night. Because of the strong odors emitted, store in either a well-ventilated place or a separate room reserved for brassicas. To store, trim off all loose outer leaves. Hang by its roots, or wrap individually in paper, or layer in straw in an airy bin, or place several inches apart on shelves.

Fresh		
Temperature	**Humidity**	**Storage Life**
32°F–40°F/0°C–5°C	80%–90%	About 4 months

Preserved		
Method	**Taste**	**Shelf Life**
Canned	Poor	
Frozen	Good	8 months
Dried	Fair	12+ months

Carrot

Daucus carota var. *sativus*
Apiaceae (Parsley Family)

Carrots are an annual cool-season crop, half-hardy to frost and light freezes. Plan an average of 10 to 40 plants per person. One way to break the soil crust for carrot seeds is to plant a few fast-germinating radish seeds in the carrot bed. Carrots produce best in friable soil, so dig well before planting or grow smaller carrots that don't need deep soil. Sow seeds evenly in a very shallow furrow, about ¼ inch deep, and keep seeds moist so they will germinate. When the first leaves emerge, thin to 1 inch apart; when true leaves emerge, thin to 3 inches apart. If you delay the final thinning a bit, you can use the removed roots as baby carrots. The darkest and greenest tops indicate the largest carrots. To prevent greening at the shoulders, hill dirt up around the greens.

The sweetest and best-textured carrots are the Nantes types, cylindrical and blunt-tipped. The long and tapered characteristics are typical of Imperator varieties. Nantes types absorb more water and therefore have less dry matter, making them more succulent and crisp. They are also lower than other types in terpenoids, which cause a soapy turpentine-like taste; the amount of terpenoids depends entirely on variety, not on the soil. Terpenoids break down in cooking so that carrots taste sweeter when cooked. *Nantes* now describes any carrot with the above traits, not true lineage to the French region where the type originated.

TEMPERATURE

For Germination: 45°F–85°F/8°C–30°C
For Growth: 60°F–65°F/16°C–19°C

First Seed-Starting Date						
Germinate	+	**Transplant**	+	**Days before LFD**	=	**Count Back from LFD**
6–14 days	+	0 days	+	8–14 days	=	14–28 days

Last Seed-Starting Date										
Germinate	+	**Transplant**	+	**Maturity**	+	**SD Factor**	+	**Frost Tender**	=	**Count Back from FFD**
6–14 days	+	0 days	+	65–70 days	+	14 days	+	0 days	=	85–98 days

SOIL & WATER NEEDS

pH: 5.5–6.5

Fertilizer: Light feeder; too much top growth may mean too much N.

Side-Dressing: Apply 3 weeks after germination and again when 6″–8″ high.

Water: Medium

MEASUREMENTS

Planting Depth: ¼″–½″

Root Depth: 2′–4′

Height: 12″

Breadth: 12″–24″

Space between Plants:

- In beds: 2″–3″
- In rows: 6″

Space between Rows: 16″–30″

PESTS

Carrot rust fly, carrot weevil, cutworm, flea beetle, leafhopper, nematode, parsleyworm, slug, snail, weevil, wireworm

DISEASES

Alternaria leaf spot, cercospora, damping off, leaf blight, soft rot, yellows

ALLIES

Some Evidence: Onion family

Uncertain: Black salsify, chives, coriander, flax, lettuce, pea, pennyroyal, radish, rosemary, sage, wormwood

COMPANIONS

All beans, leek, pepper, tomato

INCOMPATIBLES

Celery, dill (retards growth)

HARVEST

Gently pull the roots out by their green tops. For most newer varieties, don't let carrots grow fatter than 1½″ across or they'll become woody. Some older varieties can still be succulent and delicious when large.

Storage Requirements

Remove the green tops, but do not wash the carrot before storing. Store in sawdust or sand in containers.

Fresh		
Temperature	**Humidity**	**Storage Life**
32°F/0°C	90%–95%	4–5 months
35°F/2°C	95%–100%	7–9 months

Preserved		
Method	**Taste**	**Shelf Life**
Canned	Fair	12+ months
Frozen	Good	8 months
Dried	Fair	12+ months

Cauliflower

Brassica oleracea
Botrytis Group
Brassicaceae (Mustard Family)

Cauliflower is an annual cool-season crop, half-hardy to frost and light freezes. Plan an average of three to five plants per person. Cauliflower can be difficult to grow as a spring crop because it bolts in the heat. While it is the most sensitive of all brassicas to frost, it is generally easier to grow as a fall crop. Note on the seed-starting dates that cauliflower shouldn't be transplanted outdoors until all danger of frost is past, unless covered. It also needs to mature before hot summer weather arrives. A compromise might be to choose an intermediate starting date and cover the plants when set out to protect them from cold. Purple cauliflower is an easier crop because it's more pest resistant and hardier than white varieties. Early in the season it looks and tastes more like broccoli, but after a cold snap, its flavor is more like cauliflower. Depending on your area, cauliflower might be better grown as a fall crop to reduce the threat of insect damage and bolting.

Plant transplants 1 inch deeper than they were grown in starting pots, and cover with netting to protect from pests. Spacing between plants determines head size: The closer together, the smaller the head. When heads start forming, prevent yellowing by tying several upright leaves loosely together with string, covering the rest of the head against direct exposure to the sun. To prevent spreading clubroot and other soilborne diseases, don't compost any brassica roots. Pull and destroy all infected plants. Also, rotate brassica plants on at least a 3-year basis, or optimally on a 7-year basis. Researchers in India report best yields were attained by spraying with a 1.2% concentration of zinc sulfate in water, while highest levels of ascorbic acid (vitamin C) were attained with zinc sulfate concentrations of either 0.6% or 0.9%.

TEMPERATURE

For Germination: 45°F–85°F/8°C–30°C

For Growth:

- Day: 60°F–70°F/16°C–22°C
- Night: 50°F–60°F/10°C–16°C

SOIL & WATER NEEDS

pH: 6.0–7.5

Fertilizer: Heavy feeder; needs high N and K.

Side-Dressing: Every 3–4 weeks

Water: Medium; critical early in season and during warm weather

First Seed-Starting Date

If covered, transplants can be set out almost 4 weeks earlier (see below).

Germinate	+	Transplant	+	Days before LFD	=	Count Back from LFD
4–10 days	+	35–49 days	–	14 days (no cover)	=	25–45 days (uncovered at transplanting)
4–10 days	+	35–49 days	+	14 days (covered)	=	53–73 days (covered once transplanted)

Last Seed-Starting Date

Germinate	+	Transplant	+	Maturity	+	SD Factor	+	Frost Tender	=	Count Back from FFD
4–10 days	+	21 days	+	50–95 days	+	14 days	+	N/A	=	89–140 days

MEASUREMENTS

Planting Depth: ¼″–½″

Root Depth: 1½′–4′

Height: 18″–24″

Breadth: 2′–2½′

Space between Plants:

- In beds: 12″–15″
- In rows: 18″

Space between Rows: 24″–46″

PESTS

Aphid, cabbage butterfly, cabbage looper, cabbage maggot, cutworm, diamondback moth, harlequin bug, mite, root fly, slug, snail, striped flea beetle, weevil

DISEASES

Black leg, black rot, clubroot, damping off, downy mildew, leaf spot, rhizoctonia, seed rot, yellows (*Note:* Two British horticulturists have found hollow stems to be caused by large head size, not boron deficiency as commonly believed.)

ALLIES

Some Evidence: Candytuft, celery, collard greens, corn spurry (*Spergula arvensis*), lamb's quarters, mint, shepherd's purse, thyme, tomato, white or red clover, wormseed mustard

Uncertain: Chamomile, dill, nasturtium, onion, rosemary, sage, savory, wormwood

COMPANIONS

Aromatic plants, artichoke, beet, bush beans, garlic, lettuce, pea, potato, spinach

INCOMPATIBLES

Pole beans, strawberry, tomato (latter also might be an ally)

HARVEST

When heads are 8″–10″ in diameter, harvest by pulling the entire plant from the soil. Cauliflower heads deteriorate quickly, so check periodically and harvest when ready.

Storage Requirements		
Wrap individual plants, head and roots, in plastic. Store in a root cellar or cool place.		
Fresh		
Temperature	**Humidity**	**Storage Life**
32°F/0°C	95%–98%	3–4 weeks
Preserved		
Method	**Taste**	**Shelf Life**
Frozen	Good	12 months
Pickled	Good	12 months

Celeriac

Apium graveolens var. *rapaceum*
Apiaceae (Parsley Family)

Celeriac is a cool-season root crop, half-hardy to frost and light freezes. Plan an average of one to five plants per person. It is a pest-, disease-, and problem-free biennial vegetable that is usually grown as an annual. In Zones 5 and north, this root can be overwintered in the ground if mulched heavily with straw to prevent frost penetration. Sow seeds thickly in pots indoors. Thin seedlings to one per pot. Set out when 2 to 2½ inches tall. Remove side shoots from the base of the plant. When transplanting, keep as much as possible of the original potting soil around the roots. After setting in the roots, reach under and gently squeeze the soil around the roots to eliminate air gaps. Too much oxygen exposure during transplanting will cause them to dry out and die. Root quality drops when watered regularly, so water deeply and less frequently. To achieve the deep fertile soil needed for celeriac, try adding 1 bushel of well-rotted manure for every 20 row-feet and spading it in 8 to 10 inches deep.

Celeriac has been enjoyed in Europe for ages and only recently has begun to make a showing in the United States. It is an unsightly root that tends to develop involutions filled with dirt, which cause wastage in food preparation. With a delicious, delicate flavor similar to that of celery heart, celeriac is worth the effort of cutting off all of the skin and the involutions. It can be boiled and added to potatoes, or eaten raw as an addition to salads. We cut it into thin strips, blanch and tenderize it for 30 minutes by adding lemon juice and a little salt, then toss and serve it with a remoulade sauce.

First Seed-Starting Date

Usually 8 to 12 weeks before last frost

Germinate	+	Transplant	–	Days after LFD	=	Count Back from LFD
10–21 days	+	46–60 days	–	0–14 days	=	56–67 days

Last Seed-Starting Date

Germinate	+	Transplant	+	Maturity	+	SD Factor	+	Frost Tender	=	Count Back from FFD
10–21 days	+	50 days	+	110–120 days	+	14 days	+	N/A	=	184–205 days

TEMPERATURE

For Germination: 70°F/22°C

For Growth: 60°F–65°F/16°C–19°C

SOIL & WATER NEEDS

pH: 6.0–6.5

Fertilizer: Heavy feeder

Water: Heavy, infrequently, but keep evenly moist, especially during hot spells.

MEASUREMENTS

Planting Depth: ⅛″

Root Depth: 18″–24″

Height: 12″

Breadth: 12″

Space between Plants:

- In beds: 4″–7″
- In rows: 12″

Space between Rows: 15″–26″

PESTS

Aphid, celeryworm, slug, weevil, wireworm

DISEASES

Septoria leaf spot

ALLIES

None

COMPANIONS

Squash, tomato

INCOMPATIBLES

None

HARVEST

After the first fall frost, and when the bulbs are 2″–4″, carefully dig or pull out the roots. The larger the root (more than 4″), the more it will be contaminated by involutions of the skin.

Storage Requirements

Celeriac is best stored fresh. The results of various preservation methods are unknown. Do not wash the root before storing. Rub off side shoots. Store in boxes of moist peat. When covered with a thick mulch, the roots will keep in the ground for about 1 month beyond the first frost.

Fresh		
Temperature	**Humidity**	**Storage Life**
32°F/0°C	97%–99%	6–8 months

Celery

Apium graveolens var. *dulce*
Apiaceae (Parsley Family)

Celery is a cool-season crop, half-hardy to frost and light freezes. Plan an average of three to eight plants per person. Soak seeds overnight to help germination. The seedlings need to be transplanted at least once before setting outside. Transplant outside when seedlings are 4 to 6 inches tall and night temperatures don't fall below 40°F/5°C. Water plants before they are transplanted. There are two basic types of celery: self-blanching and blanching.

Self-blanching varieties are much easier to grow, as they can be grown in flat soil without trenches. Their harvest, however, is earlier and more limited. For celery that needs blanching, (1) plant in the center of 18-inch-wide trenches, (2) remove suckers in midseason and wrap stalk bunches with brown paper, newspaper, or cardboard to prevent soil from getting between the stalks, (3) fill the trench with soil up to the bottom of the leaves 2 months before harvest, and (4) keep mounding soil around the base of the plant every 3 weeks. Make sure the mound is sloped to help drainage.

TEMPERATURE

For Germination: 60°F–70°F/16°C–22°C

For Growth: 60°F–65°F/16°C–19°C, with nights higher than 40°F/5°C

SOIL & WATER NEEDS

pH: 6.0–7.0

Fertilizer: Heavy feeder; 2–3 weeks before planting, apply compost worked 12″ into soil.

Side-Dressing: Apply every 2 weeks, especially 3 weeks after transplanting; repeat 6 weeks later.

Water: Heavy

First Seed-Starting Date

Germinate	+	Transplant	–	Days after LFD	=	Count Back from LFD
5–7 days	+	70–84 days	–	14–21 days	=	61–70 days

Last Seed-Starting Date

Germinate	+	Transplant	+	Maturity	+	SD Factor	+	Frost Tender	=	Count Back from FFD
6 days	+	30 days	+	90–135 days	+	14 days	+	0 days	=	140–185 days

MEASUREMENTS

Planting Depth: ¼″–½″

Root Depth: Shallow, upper 6″–12″

Height: 15″–18″

Breadth: 8″–12″

Space between Plants:

- In beds: 6″–8″
- In rows: 8″–12″

Space between Rows: 18″–36″

PESTS

Aphid, cabbage looper, carrot rust fly, carrot weevil, celery leaftier, earwig, flea beetle, leafhopper, mite, nematode, parsleyworm, slug, tarnished plant bug, weevil, wireworm

DISEASES

Black heart, celery mosaic, damping off, early and late blight, numerous fusariums, pink rot, yellows

ALLIES

Uncertain: Black salsify, cabbage, chive, coriander, garlic, nasturtium, pennyroyal

COMPANIONS

All beans, all brassicas, spinach, squash, tomato

INCOMPATIBLES

Carrot, parsnip

OTHER

Cucumbers provide shade and moisture to other plants such as celery.

HARVEST

Harvest self-blanching celery before the first frost. Harvest blanched varieties after the first frost. Dig out each plant whenever needed.

Storage Requirements

Celery is best stored at cold temperatures in a perforated plastic bag. To refresh wilted stalks, simply place them in a tall glass of cold water.

Fresh		
Temperature	**Humidity**	**Storage Life**
32°F/0°C	98%–100%	2–3 months
32°F/0°C	80%–90%	4–5 weeks

Preserved		
Method	**Taste**	**Shelf Life**
Canned	Fair	12+ months
Frozen	Good	5 months
Dried	Good	12+ months

Corn

Zea mays
Gramineae or Poaceae (Grass Family)

Corn is a warm-season crop, tender to frost and light freezes. Plan an average of 12 to 40 plants per person, depending on your needs. For good pollination and full ears, plant in blocks of at least four to six rows and about 15 inches on center. If birds are a problem in your garden, stealing seeds or eating seedlings, cover your corn patch with a floating row cover immediately after planting seeds.

Corn easily cross-pollinates, so isolate popcorn and field corn from sweet corn by at least 50 to 100 feet, or plant varieties that have different pollination times, which is when tassels appear. For seed saving, isolate corns by 1000 feet for absolute purity. Once pollinated, corn matures rapidly, usually 15 to 20 days after the first silks appear. Corn has shallow roots, so mulch heavily and avoid cultivating deeper than 1½ inches. In small patches, don't remove suckers; they may bear corn if well side-dressed. White and yellow corn vary in nutrition; white corn contains twice as much potassium, and yellow corn contains about 60 percent more sodium.

TEMPERATURE

For Germination: 60°F–95°F/16°C–35°C

For Growth: 60°F–75°F/16°C–24°C

SOIL & WATER NEEDS

pH: 5.5–7.0

Fertilizer: Heavy feeder; apply manure in fall, or compost a few weeks before planting.

Side-Dressing: Apply every 2 weeks and additionally when stalks are 8″–10″ and knee high.

Water: Medium; provide more when the stalks flower.

First Seed-Starting Date

Sow every 10 to 14 days for continuous harvest.

Germinate	+	Transplant	–	Days after LFD	=	Count Back from LFD
4–21 days	+	0 (direct)	–	0–10 days	=	4–11 days

Last Seed-Starting Date

Germinate	+	Transplant	+	Maturity	+	SD Factor	+	Frost Tender	=	Count Back from FFD
4 days	+	0 days	+	65–95 days	+	14 days	+	14 days	=	97–127 days

MEASUREMENTS

Planting Depth: 1″–2″ (sh2 types, ½″)
Root Depth: 18″–6′
Height: 7′–8′ (but some flour and field corns grow much taller)
Breadth: 18″–4′
Space between Plants:

- In beds: 8″–12″
- In rows: 18″

Space between Rows: 30″–42″

PESTS

Aphid, birds, corn borer, corn earworm, corn maggot, corn rootworm, cucumber beetle, cutworm, earwig, flea beetle, garden webworm, Japanese beetle, June beetle, leafhopper, sap beetle, seedcorn maggot, thrips, webworm, white grub, wireworm

DISEASES

Bacterial wilt, mosaic viruses, rust, smut, southern corn leaf blight

ALLIES

Some Evidence: All beans, chickweed, clover, giant ragweed, peanut, pigweed, shepherd's purse, soybean, sweet potato
Uncertain: Alfalfa, goldenrod, odorless marigold, pea, potato, white geranium

COMPANIONS

Cucumber, melon, pumpkin, squash

INCOMPATIBLES

Tomato (attacked by some similar insects)

HARVEST

Sweet Corn (var. *rugosa*): About 18 days after silks appear, when they're dark and dry, make a small slit in the husk (don't pull the silks down), and pierce the kernel with a fingernail. If the liquid is (1) clear, wait a few days to pick, (2) milky, pick and eat, or (3) pasty, the ear is past its prime and is best for canning.
Popcorn (var. *praecox*): Pick when the husks are brown and partly dried. Finish drying corn on the husks. A solar drier is the most rapid method, drying the corn in about 5 days. The kernels are ready for storage if they fall off easily when rubbed by a thumb or twisted. Before using, store in bags or jars to even out the moisture content.
After Harvest: Cut stalks and till under or compost immediately.

SELECTED VARIETIES

Flour Varieties. These have soft starch, are easiest to grind, and make flour not meal.
Dent or Field Varieties. These have hard starch on the side and soft starch on the top of the kernel, are easier to grind than flint types, and are good for fresh eating, roasting, and grinding, versatile.
Flint Varieties. These have very hard starch and make cornmeal. Generally, they have good insect resistance and store well.
Sweet Varieties

- Supersweet corn has the Shrunken-2 (sh2) gene, which causes shriveled seeds with weak seed coats, resulting in poor germination. Supersweets are often twice as sweet as eh types. They develop a watery texture when frozen.
- Everlasting heritage corn has the eh gene designed for sweetness and texture.

- Sugar Enhanced corn has the se gene, which causes sugar levels that are higher than in eh types and that last up to 14 days.

Popcorn. These have the hardest starch of all corns.

Notes: Studies show hybrid varieties have greater ear and kernel growth rates, bigger kernel size, a longer period of kernel filling, as well as greater redistribution of stalk-stored food to the kernel.

Storage Requirements

Corn is best eaten immediately. Some gardeners won't even go out to pick ears until the cooking water is already boiling.

Fresh		
Temperature	**Humidity**	**Storage Life**
40°F–45°F/5°C–8°C	80%–95%	4–10 days
Preserved		
Method	**Taste**	**Shelf Life**
Canned	Excellent	12+ months
Frozen	Good	8 months
Dried	Good	12+ months

Cucumber

Cucumis sativus
Cucurbitaceae (Gourd Family)

Cucumbers are a warm-season crop, very tender to frost and light freezing. Plan an average of three to five plants per person, depending on your pickling needs. In warm climates, some recommend planting cucumbers in hills spaced 3 to 5 feet apart, with six to eight seeds per hill. In cooler climates, transplant seedlings on a cloudy day or in the afternoon to minimize transplanting shock.

Most cucumbers are *monoecious*, producing both male and female (fruit-bearing) flowers. *Gynoecious* types bear only female flowers, therefore a few male-flowering pollinators are included in the seed packets. Both require pollination by bees. *Parthenocarpic* types produce few if any seeds and require no pollination, so they can be grown to maturity under row covers. *Bitter-free* are resistant to damage from cucumber beetles. *Dwarfs* are good candidates for intercropping with tomatoes and peppers, but they must have a constant water supply. All types must be picked daily in warm weather.

TEMPERATURE

For Germination: 60°F–95°F/16°C–35°C

For Growth: 65°F–75°F/19°C–24°C

SOIL & WATER NEEDS

pH: 5.5–7.0

Fertilizer: Heavy feeder; before planting apply compost.

Side-Dressing: Every 2–3 weeks

Water: Heavy during fruiting; all other times average and evenly moist; deep watering

First Seed-Starting Date

Germinate	+	Transplant	–	Days after LFD	=	Count Back from LFD
6–10 days	+	28 days	–	14–21 days	=	17–20 days

Last Seed-Starting Date

Germinate	+	Transplant	+	Maturity	+	SD Factor	+	Frost Tender	=	Count Back from FFD
6–10 days	+	28 days	+	22–52 days	+	14 days	+	14 days	=	84–118 days

MEASUREMENTS

Planting Depth: ½″–1″

Root Depth: 12″, taproot to 2′–3′

Height: 6′

Breadth:

- **Trellis:** 12″–15″
- **On ground:** 12–20 square feet

Space between Plants:

- In beds: 12″
- In rows: 24″–48″

Space between Rows: 4′

SUPPORT STRUCTURES

Use a 6′ post, A-frame, tepee (3 poles tied together at the top), or a trellis.

PESTS

Aphid, cucumber beetle, cutworm (seedlings), flea beetle, garden centipede, mite, pickleworm, root-knot nematode, slug, snail, squash bug, squash vine borer

DISEASES

Alternaria leaf spot, anthracnose, bacterial wilt, belly rot, cottony leak, cucumber wilt, downy mildew, leaf spot, mosaic, powdery mildew, scab

ALLIES

Some Evidence: Broccoli, corn

Uncertain: Beans, catnip, goldenrod, marigold, nasturtium, onion, oregano, radish, rue, tansy

COMPANIONS

All beans, cabbage, eggplant, kale, melon, pea, sunflower, tomato

INCOMPATIBLES

Anise, basil, marjoram, potato, quack grass, rosemary, sage, strong herbs, summer savory

OTHER

Radish can be used as a trap plant; celery is a companion plant under the cucumber's A-frame.

HARVEST

Allow the main stem to grow as high as possible by pinching back some of the lateral shoots and letting others grow into branches. By picking the fruit early you won't have to support heavy fruit or risk arresting plant production.

When the fruit is slightly immature, before seed coats become hard, pick with 1″ of stem to minimize water loss. In warm weather, all cucumber plant types should be picked daily. Always pick open-pollinated varieties underripe. Harvest pickling cucumbers at 2″–6″ and slicing cucumbers at 6″–10″.

Storage Requirements		
Keep the short piece of stem on each fruit during storage.		
Fresh		
Temperature	**Humidity**	**Storage Life**
45°F–55°F/8°C–13°C	85%–95%	10–14 days
Preserved		
Method	**Taste**	**Shelf Life**
Canned	Good (as pickles)	12+ months
Frozen	Poor	
Dried	Poor	

Eggplant

Solanum melongena var. *esculentum*
Solanaceae (Nightshade Family)

Eggplant is a warm-season crop, extremely tender to frost and light freezes. Plan an average of two plants per three people. All parts of the plant except the fruit are poisonous. For indoor seed starting in flats, block out the plants once the seedlings are well established, by running a knife through the soil midway between the plants, cutting the roots, and leaving each plant with its own soil block. If you start seeds in individual pots, this procedure is unnecessary. Make sure outdoor soil temperature is at least 55°F to 60°F/13°C to 16°C before transplanting; otherwise they become stunted, turn yellow, and are slow to bear.

Difficulties growing eggplant are often related to cool conditions. Plant them in the hottest, sunniest spot available and cover with plastic jugs (bottom cut out, cap off) until leaves poke through the top. As frost approaches, pinch back new blossoms so that plant nutrients are channeled into the remaining fruits. Eggplant is a versatile fruit often used in Italian dishes such as ratatouille, caponata, and lasagna. It easily absorbs the flavors of whatever sauce it is cooked in.

TEMPERATURE

For Germination: 75°F–90°F/24°C–33°C

For Growth: 70°F–85°F/22°C–30°C

SOIL & WATER NEEDS

pH: 5.5–6.5

Fertilizer: Heavy feeder; apply manure water or tea every 2 weeks.

Side-Dressing: Apply after the first fruit appears.

Water: Heavy

First Seed-Starting Date

Germinate	+	Transplant	–	Days after LFD	=	Count Back from LFD
5–13 days	+	42–56 days	–	14–28 days	=	33–41 days

Last Seed-Starting Date

Germinate	+	Transplant	+	Maturity	+	SD Factor	+	Frost Tender	=	Count Back from FFD
5–13 days	+	42–56 days	+	50–80 days	+	14 days	+	14 days	=	125–177 days

MEASUREMENTS

Planting Depth: ¼″

Root Depth: 4′–7′

Height: 24″–30″

Breadth: 3′–4′

Space between Plants:

- In beds: 18″
- In rows: 18″–30″

Space between Rows: 24″–48″

PESTS

Aphid, Colorado potato beetle, cucumber beetle, cutworm, flea beetle, harlequin bug, lace bug, leafhopper, mite, nematode, tomato hornworm, whitefly

DISEASES

Anthracnose, bacterial wilt, botrytis fruit rot, phomopsis blight, tobacco mosaic, verticillium wilt

ALLIES

Some Evidence: Cilantro, dill, marigold

Uncertain: Coriander, goldenrod, green beans, potato

COMPANIONS

All beans, pepper

INCOMPATIBLES

None

OTHER

Potato can be used as a trap plant for eggplant pests.

HARVEST

Pick when the fruit is no more than 3″–5″ long or 4″ in diameter, and before the skin loses its luster. Cut the fruit with a small amount of stem. Fruit seeds should be light-colored. Brown seeds indicate the fruit has ripened too long. Eggplant vines are spiny, so be careful to avoid pricking yourself.

Storage Requirements

Keep a small piece of stem on the eggplant during storage, and don't pierce the skin. Eggplant is best used fresh.

	Fresh	
Temperature	**Humidity**	**Storage Life**
46°F–54°F/8°C–13°C	90%–95%	1 week
32°F–40°F/0°C–5°C	80%–90%	6 months
	Preserved	
Method	**Taste**	**Shelf Life**
Canned	Fair	12+ months
Frozen	Fair	8 months
Dried	Fair	12+ months

Kale

Brassica oleracea var. *acephela*
Brassicaceae (Mustard Family)

Kale is a cool-season crop, hardy to frost and light freezes. Plan an average of four plants per person. Kale's flavor is reputed to improve and sweeten with frost. An easy vegetable to grow, it is generally more disease and pest resistant than other brassicas, although it can occasionally experience similar problems. Kale also uses less space than other brassicas. Use it as a spinach substitute in a wide variety of dishes. Kale maintains body and crunch much better than spinach and so can be used in dishes where spinach might not be suitable; it's especially delicious in stir-fry dishes.

Author and edible landscaper Rosalind Creasy recommends cooking kale over high heat to bring out the best flavor and prevent bitterness. Creasy also noted that "many specialty growers are planting kale in wide beds only ½ to 12 inches apart and harvesting kale small as salad greens." In England, close plantings of kale have been shown to prevent aphid infestations through visual masking. Although kale is usually disease- and pest-free, some gardeners won't compost any brassica roots to prevent spreading clubroot and other soilborne diseases. Pull and destroy infected plants. Kale is not as likely as other brassicas to suffer from clubroot, but if you experience problems, be sure to rotate plantings so they're not in the same 10-foot radius for at least 3 years, optimally for 7 years.

TEMPERATURE

For Germination: 45°F–95°F/8°C–35°C

For Growth: 60°F–65°F/16°C–19°C

SOIL & WATER NEEDS

pH: 6.0–7.0

Fertilizer: Heavy feeder; use compost.

Side-Dressing: Apply when plants are about one-third grown.

Water: Heavy

First Seed-Starting Date

Germinate	+	Transplant	+	Days before LFD	=	Count Back from LFD
3–10 days	+	35–70 days	+	14–28 days	=	52–108 days

Last Seed-Starting Date

Germinate	+	Transplant	+	Maturity	+	SD Factor	+	Frost Tender	=	Count Back from FFD
3–10 days	+	21 days	+	56–63 days	+	14 days	+	N/A	=	94–108 days

MEASUREMENTS

Planting Depth: ½″

Root Depth: 6″–12″

Height: 12″–18″

Breadth: 8″–12″

Space between Plants:

- In beds: 15″–18″
- In rows: 18″–24″

Space between Rows: 24″–46″

PESTS

Aphid, cabbage looper, cabbage maggot, celery leaf-tier, diamondback moth, flea beetle, harlequin bug, imported cabbageworm, Mexican bean beetle, mites, thrips, weevil

DISEASES

Alternaria leaf spot, black leg, clubroot

ALLIES

Some evidence: Collard greens, dill

Uncertain: Chamomile, garlic, mint, nasturtium, rosemary, sage, tansy, tomato

COMPANIONS

Artichoke, beet, bush bean, celery, cucumber, lettuce, onion, pea, potato, spinach

INCOMPATIBLES

Pole beans, strawberry, tomato (latter may also be an ally; see plant ally chart on page 280.)

HARVEST

Harvest younger leaves from the middle and work your way up the stalk as it grows. Keep some of the leaves on the bottom to feed growth at the top. You can also harvest the plant all at once by cutting its stem near the bottom.

Storage Requirements

For fresh storage, don't wash the leaves. For drying, cut the leaves into strips and steam for 2–5 minutes. Spread on trays no more than ½″ thick, and dry. If using an oven, set the temperature below 145°F/65°C; check and turn every hour.

Fresh		
Temperature	**Humidity**	**Storage Life**
32°F/0°C	95%–100%	2–3 weeks
32°F–40°F/0°C–5°C	80%–90%	10 months (only fair taste)
Preserved		
Method	**Taste**	**Shelf Life**
Canned	Good	12+ months
Frozen	Good	12 months
Dried	Fair	12+ months

Lettuce

Lactuca sativa
Asteraceae (Sunflower Family)

Lettuce is a cool-season crop, half-hardy to frost and light freezes. Plan an average of 10 to 12 plants per person. Closer spacing results in smaller heads, which may be preferable for small families. Specialty growers are spacing lettuce very close for selling baby lettuces, a rapidly growing produce market.

There are two basic categories of lettuce: heading and nonheading. Head lettuces include crisphead (e.g., iceberg) and butterhead (e.g., Bibb and Boston). Nonhead lettuces include leaf and romaine (also known as *cos*). For head lettuce, one source suggests that you strip transplants of outer leaves to help the inner leaves "head up" better. This is not tested, so treat it as experimental. Head lettuces tend to be milder in flavor but are more difficult to grow. Lettuce doesn't do well in very acidic soils, and some say the pH shouldn't be lower than 6.5. During hot weather, sow lettuce in partial shade, as it doesn't do well in the heat, and use heat-resistant varieties.

TEMPERATURE

For Germination: 40°F–80°F/5°C–27°C

For Growth: 60°F–65°F/16°C–19°C

SOIL & WATER NEEDS

pH: 6.0–7.5

Fertilizer: Heavy feeder

Side-Dressing: Apply balanced fertilizer or foliar spray every 2 weeks.

Water: Low to medium; heavy in arid climates; water early in the morning to minimize diseases.

First Seed-Starting Date

Germinate	+	Transplant	+	Days before LFD	=	Count Back from LFD
4–10 days	+	14 days (leaf and head)	+	7–28 days	=	25–52 days

Last Seed-Starting Date

Germinate	+	Transplant	+	Maturity	+	SD Factor	+	Frost Tender	=	Count Back from FFD
4 days	+	14 days	+	60–95 days	+	14 days	+	0 days	=	92–127 days (head)
4 days	+	14 days	+	45–65 days	+	14 days	+	0 days	=	77–97 days (leaf)
4 Days	+	14 days	+	55–80 days	+	14 days	+	0 days	=	87–112 days (romaine)

MEASUREMENTS

Planting Depth: ¼″–½″

Root Depth: 18″–36″, taproot to 5′

Height: 6″–12″

Breadth: 6″–12″

Space between Plants:

- In beds: 10″–12″ (head); 6″–8″ (leaf); 10″ (romaine)
- In rows: 12″–14″

Space between Rows: 14″

PESTS

Aphid, beet leafhopper, cabbage looper, cutworm, earwig, flea beetle, garden centipede, leaf miner, millipede, slug, snail

DISEASES

Bacterial soft rot, botrytis rot, damping off, downy mildew, fusarium wilt, lettuce drop, mosaic, pink rot, powdery mildew, tip burn

ALLIES

Some evidence: Dill, sweet alyssum

Uncertain: Chive, garlic, radish

COMPANIONS

Beet (to head lettuce), all brassicas (except broccoli; see Incompatibles below), carrot, cucumber, onion family, pole lima bean, strawberry

INCOMPATIBLES

None; some studies have shown lettuce to be sensitive to plant residues of barley, broccoli, broad bean, vetch, wheat, and rye

HARVEST

For leaf lettuce, start picking the leaves when there are at least 5–6 mature leaves of usable size. Usable size means about 2″ long for baby lettuce and 5″–6″ long for more mature lettuce. Keep picking until a seed stalk appears or the leaves become bitter. For head lettuce, when the head feels firm and mature simply cut it off at the soil surface. Harvest all lettuce in early morning for the maximum carotene and best taste. Refrigerate immediately.

Storage Requirements

Lettuce doesn't store well for long periods and is best eaten fresh.

Fresh		
Temperature	**Humidity**	**Storage Life**
32°F–40°F/0°C–5°C	80%–90%	1 month
32°F/0°C	98%–100%	2–3 weeks

Muskmelon

Cucumus melo
Reticulatus Group
Cucurbitaceae (Gourd Family)

Melons are a warm-season crop, very tender to frost and light freezes. Plan an average of two to six plants per person. Muskmelons are often called cantaloupes, but they're not the same botanical variety. True cantaloupes are rarely grown in North America. Winter melons (Inodorus group) include honeydew and casaba. Like all cucurbits, melons need bees for pollination.

Melons can be sown directly outside, but some gardeners report better germination with presprouted seeds. If you start melons indoors, use individual cells or peat pots, not flats, as the roots are too succulent to divide. When you direct sow, plant four or five seeds in a hill and then thin to appropriate spacing, depending on whether you train them on a trellis or let them spread on the ground. For direct sowing and transplants, cover seedlings with cloches or hot caps to protect from frost, speed growth, and keep out pests. To encourage side shoots, when seedlings have three leaves pinch out the growing end. When new side shoots have three leaves, pinch out the central growing area again. When fruits begin to form, pinch back the vine to two leaves beyond the fruit.

Make sure fruits on a trellis are supported by netting or pantyhose, and fruits on ground vines are elevated by empty pots to prevent disease and encourage ripening. Troughs near the plants can be flooded for effective watering. Melon rinds are good for compost; they decompose rapidly and are high in phosphorus and potassium.

First Seed-Starting Date

Germinate	+	Transplant	–	Days after LFD	=	Count Back from LFD
4–10 days	+	21–28 days	–	14–21 days	=	11–17 days

Last Seed-Starting Date

Germinate	+	Transplant	+	Maturity	+	SD Factor	+	Frost Tender	=	Count Back from FFD
4 days	+	21 days	+	59–91 days	+	14 days	+	14 days	=	112–144 days

TEMPERATURE

For Germination: 75°F–95°F/24°C–35°C

For Growth: 65°F–75°F/19°C–24°C

SOIL & WATER NEEDS

pH: 6.0–6.5

Fertilizer: Heavy feeder; before planting, work in compost or rotted manure.

Side-Dressing: Apply balanced fertilizer or compost when vines are 12″–18″ long and again when fruits form.

Water: Medium. Apply deep watering; withhold water when fruits begin to ripen.

MEASUREMENTS

Planting Depth: ½″

Root Depth: Shallow, some to 4′

Height: 24″

Breadth:

- Bush: 36″–48″
- Vine: 30–40 square feet on ground

Space between Plants:

- In beds: 2′
- In rows: 4′–8′

Space between Rows: 5′–7′

SUPPORT STRUCTURES

Use an A-frame or trellis to grow vines vertically.

PESTS

Aphid, cucumber beetle, cutworm, flea beetle, mite, pickleworm, slug, snail, squash bug, vine borer, whitefly

DISEASES

Alternaria leaf spot, anthracnose, bacterial wilt, cucumber wilt, curly top, downy mildew, fusarium wilt, mosaic, powdery mildew, scab

ALLIES

Uncertain: Chamomile, corn, goldenrod, nasturtium, onion, savory

COMPANIONS

Pumpkin, radish, squash

INCOMPATIBLES

None

OTHER

Morning glories, radish, and zucchini are succession trap plants for cucumber beetles.

HARVEST

Melon is ready for harvest as soon as it is at "full slip": The end is soft (i.e., separates easily from the stem), a crack develops around the stem, and it smells "musky." The skin netting should be cordlike, grayish, and prominent. Winter melons don't "slip" but should be soft. Dip muskmelons in hot water (136°F–140°F/58°C–60°C) for 3 minutes to prevent surface mold and decay during storage. Store in polyethylene bags to reduce water loss and associated softening of the flesh.

Storage Requirements

Store fruits in a cool area.

Fresh		
Temperature	**Humidity**	**Storage Life**
35°F–55°F/2°C–13°C	80%–90%	About 1 month
Preserved		
Method	**Taste**	**Shelf Life**
Frozen	Good	3 months

Onion

Allium cepa
Liliaceae (Lily Family)

Onions are a cool-season crop, hardy to frost and light freezes, although certain varieties are exceptions. Plan an average of 40 plants per person. Onions are actually easy to grow, although the daylight requirements and numerous varieties for flavor and storage can be confusing. To start, the best strategy is to plant sets of a variety known to do well locally about 4 weeks before the last frost date. Onions started from seeds generally grow larger and store longer, while sets are easier and faster to grow but are more subject to bolting and rot.

Multiplier onions (*A. cepa* var. *aggregatum*), such as shallots and perennial potato onions, reproduce vegetatively and are usually started by sets. Similarly, bunching onions (*A. fistulosum*), such as scallions, Welsh, and Japanese, don't form full bulbs and are usually started by sets. Sets should be started with small bulbs no larger than ⅜ to ⅞ inches. Sweet onions are best started from seed, as is the common or regular onion. Sweet onions generally store poorly, whereas pungent varieties store well because of a high content of aromatics, which act as preservatives. For an easy perennial onion patch, grow potato onions. Almost a lost variety, with a flavor stronger than shallots, they can substitute for regular onions. Buy them once, plant in fall or spring, and enjoy harvests for decades. (For details, consult catalogs.)

TEMPERATURE

For Germination: 50°F–95°F/10°C–35°C

For Growth: 55°F–75°F/13°C–24°C

SOIL & WATER NEEDS

pH: 6.0–7.5 (multiplier types: 6.5–7.0)

Fertilizer: Light feeder; use compost.

Water: Medium; dry soil will cause the onion to form 2 bulbs instead of 1; don't water 1 week before harvest.

First Seed-Starting Date

The average time to maturity is 100 to 160 days for spring starts. (See Notes, page 66.)

Germinate	+	Transplant	+	Days before LFD	=	Count Back from LFD
4–10 days	+	28–42 days	+	14–40 days	=	46–92 days

MEASUREMENTS

Planting Depth:

- Seed: ½″
- Sets: 1″

Root Depth: 18″–3′

Height: 15″–36″

Breadth: 6″–18″

Space between Plants:

- To grow scallions: 1″
- To grow bulbs: 3″

PESTS

Japanese beetle, onion eelworm, onion maggot, slug, thrips, vole (storage), white grub, wireworm (Try radish as trap crop for onion root maggot; when infested, pull and destroy.)

DISEASES

Botrytis, damping off, downy mildew, pink root, smut, storage rot, sunscald, white rot

ALLIES

Some Evidence: Basil, caraway, carrot, marigold

Uncertain: Beet, chamomile, flax, summer savory

COMPANIONS

Lettuce, pepper, spinach, strawberry, tomato

INCOMPATIBLES

All beans, asparagus, pea, sage

HARVEST

Wait until tops fall over; pushing them can shorten storage life. When bulbs pull out very easily, rest them on the ground to dry and cure. Treat gently as they bruise easily. Turn once or twice in the next few days; cover if it rains. When completely brown, they're ready for further curing. For regular onions, clip tops 1″ from the bulb. Do not clip tops of multipliers or separate bulbs. Spread onions no more than 3″ deep on wire screens in a shady, warm, dry,

Storage Requirements

Onions sprout in the presence of ethylene gas, so never store with apples, apricots, avocadoes, bananas, figs, kiwis, melons, peaches, pears, plums, or tomatoes. Eat the largest first—they're most likely to sprout.

Fresh		
Temperature	**Humidity**	**Storage Life**
36°F–40°F/3°C–5°C	65%–70%	1–8 months (dry)
Preserved		
Method	**Taste**	**Shelf Life**
Canned	Good	12+ months
Frozen	Fair	3 months
Dried	Good	12 months

well-ventilated area. Cure for up to 2 months before storing for winter. The flavor and quality of multipliers keeps improving. After 2 months, check for spoilage and remove bad or marginal onions. Separate multiplier bulbs by cleaning and cutting off dried tops about 1″ above the bulbs. Keep the smallest bulbs for spring planting.

SELECTED VARIETIES

Long-Day Onions. These need 15+ daylight hours to properly bulb. Plant these in early spring at latitudes 37–47° (Virginia and northward) to obtain large bulbs.

Intermediate-Day Onions. These need 12–14 daylight hours and are best for intermediate latitudes between 37–47°.

Multiplier (Perennial) Onions. These include potato onions, Welsh onions, shallots, Egyptian walking onions, and bunching green onions. Multiplier onions can produce a larger yield per area than any other vegetable except staked tomatoes. They produce a cluster of bulbs at ground level from a single planted bulb. The larger bulbs are saved for eating, and the medium and small bulbs are stored and replanted. You can divide them at any time of year, but spring is best.

NOTES

Onions are usually easier to start from sets, which are planted in spring an average of about 4 weeks before the last frost date in order to receive enough daylight growing hours for bulb maturation before harvest in mid- to late summer. Seeds for summer harvest should be started inside in early spring for the same reason. For small storage onions, seed can be sown outside shortly after the last frost date. For overwintering onions, sow seed in midsummer to early fall. For more planting advice, see specific day requirements and variety requirements.

Pea

Pisum sativum

Fabaceae (Pea Family)

Peas are a cool-season crop, hardy to frost and light freezes. Plan an average of 25 to 60 plants per person, depending on how much you want to freeze, dry, or can for winter. Add organic matter to the beds in fall; in spring when the soil is thawing, gently rake the soil surface. Gardeners with mild winters can plant peas in both spring and fall. Peas have fragile roots and don't transplant well.

While some gardeners recommend presoaking seeds, research indicates that presoaked legume seeds absorb water too quickly, split their outer coatings, and spill out essential nutrients, which encourages damping-off seed rot. Yields can increase 50 to 100 percent by inoculating with *Rhizobium* bacteria. Peas can cross-pollinate, so for seed saving, space different varieties at least 150 feet apart. Dwarf varieties don't need a trellis if you plant them close together. Pole and climbing peas produce over a longer period and up to five times more than dwarf bush varieties. After the harvest, turn under the plant residues to improve the soil.

TEMPERATURE

For Germination: 40°F–70°F/5°C–22°C

For Growth: 60°F–65°F/16°C–19°C

SOIL & WATER NEEDS

pH: 6.0–7.5

Fertilizer: Light feeder. When inoculated, peas are N-fixing and need low N. Apply liquid seaweed 2–3 times per season.

Side-Dressing: When vines are about 6″ tall, apply compost or an amendment high in P and K, and light in N.

Water: Low initially; heavy after bloom; shallow watering is said to increase germination.

First Seed-Starting Date

Plant every 10 days in case of poor germination.

Germinate	+	Transplant	+	Days before LFD	=	Count Back from LFD
7–14 days	+	0 (direct)	+	28–42 days	=	35–56 days

Last Seed-Starting Date

Germinate	+	Transplant	+	Maturity	+	SD Factor	+	Frost Tender	=	Count Back from FFD
6 days	+	0 (direct)	+	50–80 days	+	14 days	+	0 days	=	70–100 days

MEASUREMENTS

Planting Depth: 1″ or ½″–¾″

Root Depth: Shallow to 3′

Height:

- Garden peas: 21″–4′
- Snap peas: 4′–6′

Breadth: 6″–10″

Space between Plants:

- In beds: 2″–4″
- In rows: 1″–3″

Space between Rows: 18″–48″

SUPPORT STRUCTURES

Use a 6′ post, A-frame, or trellis.

PESTS

Most problems affect seedlings: aphid, cabbage looper, cabbage maggot, corn earworm, corn maggot, cucumber beetle, cutworm, garden webworm, pale-striped flea beetle, seedcorn maggot, slug, snail, thrips, webworm, weevil, wireworm

DISEASES

Bacterial blight, downy mildew, enation mosaic, fusarium wilt, leaf curl, powdery mildew, root rot, seed rot

ALLIES

Some Evidence: Tomato

Uncertain: Brassicas, caraway, carrot, chive, goldenrod, mint, turnip

COMPANIONS

All beans, coriander, corn, cucumber, radish, spinach

INCOMPATIBLES

Garlic, onion, potato

HARVEST

If a plant has only a few peas on it, pinch back the growing tip to encourage further fruiting. When pea pods are plump and crisp, and before they begin to harden or fade in color, harvest them with one clean cut. Sugar snaps are best picked when plump and filled out. Harvest snow peas when the pods are young and peas undeveloped. Pick peas every day for continuous production. Harvest pea shoots for salads.

Storage Requirements

Blanch shelled regular peas and whole snap and snow peas before freezing.

Fresh		
Temperature	**Humidity**	**Storage Life**
32°F/0°C	95%–98%	1–2 weeks
Preserved		
Method	**Taste**	**Shelf Life**
Canned	Good	12+ months
Frozen	Excellent	12+ months
Dried	Good	12+ months

Peanut

Arachis hypogaea
Fabaceae (Pea Family)

Also known as goober peas and groundnuts, peanuts are a warm-season crop, very tender to frost and light freezes. Plan an average of 10 to 20 plants per person. Peanuts require full sun and can be grown wherever melon grows, as far north as Canada, although commercial production is generally limited to the South. In short-season areas, you may want to start seeds (which are the nuts) inside. For higher yields, inoculate seeds with special peanut inoculants available from nurseries.

Plant nuts that are not split and still have their papery skin. Nuts sprout more easily without their shell but filled shells can also be planted. Transplant seedlings outside into soil warmed with plastic, choosing a sheltered, south-facing site. They need loose, enriched, sandy soil. For succession planting, peanuts are good planted after early crops of lettuce or spinach. The plant produces peanuts after the stem blossoms; its lower leaves drop and in their place peduncles grow. The peduncles eventually bend over and root in the nearby soil, where clusters of peanuts then grow. When the plants reach 6 inches, begin to cultivate the rows to control weeds and keep the soil aerated. When about 1 foot high, hill the plants in the same manner as potatoes, mounding soil high around each plant. Hilling is important to help the peduncle root quickly. Mulch between rows with 8 inches of grass clippings or straw.

Research at Auburn University has shown that extra soil calcium can minimize the fungal-produced aflatoxins in peanuts; calcium applied at 10 pounds per 1000 square feet can be a justifiable "insurance" against cancer-causing aflatoxins in peanuts. Peanut hulls are good for mulching and composting as they're rich in nitrogen. For rotation planning, follow peanuts with nitrogen-loving plants.

First Seed-Starting Date

Try presprouting extralarge peanuts, which germinate poorly in wet, cool soil.

Germinate	+	Transplant	+	Days before LFD	=	Count Back from LFD
7–14 days	+	0 days	+	15–28 days	=	22–42 days

Last Seed-Starting Date

Germinate	+	Transplant	+	Maturity	+	SD Factor	+	Frost Tender	=	Count Back from FFD
7–14 days	+	0 (direct)	+	110–120 days	+	14 days	+	14 days	=	145–162 days

TEMPERATURE

For Germination: 60°F–80°F/16°C–27°C

For Growth: 70°F–85°F/22°C–30°C

SOIL & WATER NEEDS

pH: 5.0–6.0

Fertilizer: Add rotted manure in fall so its decomposition won't affect peanut seeds; at blossom time, add calcium (calcium sulfate or limestone); additional potassium may also be required.

Water: Average. When the plant begins to blossom, stop all watering.

MEASUREMENTS

Planting Depth: 1″–1½″

Root Depth: Shallow

Height: 12″–18″

Breadth: 15″–20″

Space between Plants: 3″–6″ (in 4″-high ridge), thin to 12″

Space between Rows: 30″–36″

PESTS

Weeds are the most significant, beyond that backyard gardeners may experience only occasional corn earworm, cutworm, pale-striped flea beetle, potato leafhopper, spider mite, thrips, and different caterpillars.

DISEASES

No significant diseases, except occasional leaf spot and southern blight

ALLIES

Some Evidence: Corn

INCOMPATIBLES

None

HARVEST

As the first frost approaches, when the leaves turn yellow-white, kernels drop, and pod veins darken, dig up the entire plant. In short-season areas, you may delay harvest until after the first few light frosts; although top growth may be killed, the pods continue to mature. Shake off all loose dirt. Dry roots in the sun for a few days to facilitate separation of the pods, or hang in a dry, airy place. Keep out of reach of small animals.

GREENHOUSE

The smaller dwarf bushes (Spanish) might be grown in a greenhouse.

Storage Requirements		
Preserved (Cured or Dried)		
Temperature	**Humidity**	**Storage Life**
32°F/0°C	Low	12 months

Spread peanuts on shallow trays or hang the entire plant from rafters in a garage or attic. Cure this way in a warm, dry place for a minimum of 3 weeks and no more than 3 months. Peanuts are best stored shelled, in airtight containers in the refrigerator for short periods, or in the freezer for long periods—they are very susceptible to a fungus that produces a highly toxic substance called aflatoxin. To be safe, don't eat any moldy peanuts. Roast nuts at 300°F/150°C for 20 minutes before eating.

Pepper

Capsicum annuum
Solanaceae (Nightshade Family)

Peppers are a warm-season crop, very tender to frost and light freezes. Plan an average of five to six plants per person. All parts of the plant except the fruit are poisonous. To start indoors use pots at least 1½ inches wide to minimize transplant shock, make a stockier plant, and encourage earlier production.

Growers report that the following cold treatment of seedlings significantly improves yields and early growth: (1) When the first leaves appear, lower the soil temperature to 70°F/22°C and ensure 16 hours of light with grow lamps; (2) when the first true leaf appears, thin seedlings to 2 to 3 inches apart or transplant into 4-inch pots; (3) when the third true leaf appears, move the plants to a location with night temperatures of 53°F to 55°F/12°C to 13°C and keep there for 4 weeks; (4) return the seedlings to a location with average temperature of 70°F/22°C; (5) transplant into the garden 2 to 3 weeks after all danger of frost has passed. Soil temperature should be at least 55°F to 60°F/13°C to 16°C for transplanting, or the plants turn yellow, become stunted, and are slow to bear.

Some recommend feeding seedlings weekly with half-strength liquid fertilizer until transplanted. Peppers do better planted close together. Except in the West, where peppers may be mostly pest-free, use row covers immediately because pepper pests will be out. If the temperature rises over 95°F/35°C, sprinkle plants with water in the afternoon to try to prevent blossom drop.

TEMPERATURE

For Germination: 65°F–95°F/19°C–35°C

For Growth: 70°F–85°F/22°C–30°C

SOIL & WATER NEEDS

pH: 5.5–7.0

Fertilizer: Medium-heavy feeder; high N; rotted manure or compost; some soils may need calcium.

Side-Dressing: Apply at blossom time and 3 weeks later. Apply liquid seaweed 2–3 times per season. At blossom time, try spraying leaves with a weak Epsom salts mixture (1 teaspoon per quart) to promote fruiting.

Water: Medium-heavy

MEASUREMENTS

Planting Depth: ¼″

Root Depth: 8″, some to 4′

Height: 2′–3′

Breadth: 24″

Space between Plants:

- In beds: 12″
- In rows: 12″–24″

Space between Rows: 18″–36″

PESTS

Aphid, Colorado potato beetle, corn borer, corn earworm, cutworm, flea beetle, leaf miner, mite, slug, snail, tomato hornworm, weevil

DISEASES

Anthracnose, bacterial spot, cercospora, mosaic, soft rot, southern blight, tobacco mosaic

Environmental Disorders: Blossom-end rot, sunscald

ALLIES

Uncertain: Alliums, caraway, catnip, nasturtium, tansy

COMPANIONS

Basil, carrot, eggplant, onion, parsley, tomato

INCOMPATIBLES

Fennel, kohlrabi

HARVEST

For sweet peppers, pick the first fruits as soon as they're usable in order to hasten growth of others. For storage peppers, cut the fruit with 1″ or more of stem. For maximum vitamin C content, wait until peppers have matured to red or yellow colors.

First Seed-Starting Date

Germinate	+	Transplant	–	Days after LFD	=	Count Back from LFD
10–12 days	+	32–44 days	–	14–21 days	=	28–35 days

Last Seed-Starting Date

Germinate	+	Transplant	+	Maturity	+	SD Factor	+	Frost Tender	=	Count Back from FFD
6–9 days	+	21 days	+	60–90 days	+	14 days	+	14 days	=	115–148 days

Storage Requirements

Hot varieties are best stored dried or pickled. Pull the entire plant from the ground and hang it upside down until dried. Alternately, harvest the peppers and string them on a line to dry. For sweet peppers, refrigeration is too cold and encourages decay.

Fresh

Temperature	Humidity	Storage Life
45°F–55°F/8°C–13°C	90%–95%	2–3 weeks

Preserved

Method	Taste	Shelf Life
Canned	Good	12 months
Frozen	Fair	3 months
Dried	Excellent	12 months
Pickled	Excellent	12+ months

Potato

Solanum tuberosum
Solanaceae (Nightshade Family)

Potatoes are a warm-season crop in the North, tender to frost and light freezes, and a cool-season crop in the South and West. Plan an average of 10 to 30 plants per person. All plant parts except the tubers are poisonous. Start potatoes with seed potatoes, each containing one to three "eyes," or small indentations that sprout foliage.

To prepare seed potatoes for planting: (1) Cut the potato into 2-inch pieces 2 days before planting and cure indoors at about 70°F/22°C in high humidity to help retain moisture and resist rot, or (2) plant small whole potatoes, which are less apt to rot, have more eyes, and don't need curing prior to planting. If desired, prespout seed potatoes by refrigerating at 40°F to 50°F/5°C to 10°C for 2 weeks before planting to break dormancy.

Place in trenches 6 inches deep by 6 inches wide, spaced 10 to 12 inches apart, and cover with 3 to 4 inches of soil. One week after shoots emerge, mound soil around the base, leaving a few inches exposed. This "hilling" prevents greening. Side-dress and "hill" again 2 to 3 weeks later. Cover plants if a hard frost is expected.

TEMPERATURE

For Germination: 65°F–70°F/19°C–22°C
For Growth: 60°F–65°F/16°C–19°C

SOIL & WATER NEEDS

pH: 5.0–6.0
Fertilizer: Light feeder; apply compost at planting.
Side-Dressing: 2–3 weeks after first hilling, apply fertilizer 6″ away from the plant and hill again.
Water: Medium; heavy when potatoes are forming, from blossom time to harvest

First Seed-Starting Date
2–4 or 6–8 weeks before last frost date. In the South and West, potatoes are usually started in February or March and harvested in June and July.

Last Seed-Starting Date
90–120 days (average days to maturity) before first frost date

MEASUREMENTS

Planting Depth: 3″–4″

Root Depth: 18″–24″

Height: 23″–30″

Breadth: 24″

Space between Plants:

- In beds: 9″–12″ (seed potatoes)
- In rows: 10″–12″

Space between Rows: 24″

PESTS

Aphid, cabbage looper, Colorado potato beetle, corn borer, corn earworm, cucumber beetle, cutworm, earwig, flea beetle, Japanese beetle, June beetle, lace bug, leaf-footed bug, leafhopper, leaf miner, nematode, slug, snail, tomato hornworm, white grub, wireworm

DISEASES

Black leg, early blight, fusarium wilt, late blight, mosaic, powdery mildew, psyllid yellows, rhizoctonia, ring rot, scab, soil rot or scurf, verticillium wilt

Environmental Disorders: Black heart

ALLIES

Uncertain: All beans, catnip, coriander, dead nettle, eggplant, flax, goldenrod, horseradish, nasturtium, onion, tansy

COMPANIONS

All brassicas, corn, marigold, pigweed

INCOMPATIBLES

Cucumber, pea, pumpkin, raspberry, spinach, squash, sunflower, tomato

HARVEST

For small "new" potatoes, harvest during blossoming; for varieties that don't blossom, harvest about 10 weeks after planting. Harvest regular potatoes when the vines have died back halfway, about 17 weeks after planting. Gently pull or dig out tubers with a garden fork. If not large enough, pack the soil back and try again at 2–3 week intervals. If you have many plants, remove the entire plant when harvesting to make room for another crop. For storage potatoes, dig near the first frost when plant tops have died back. To minimize tuber injury, always dig when the soil is dry.

NOTES

Potatoes are very disease prone, so use only certified disease-free potatoes as seed potatoes.

Storage Requirements

Spring- or summer-harvested potatoes aren't usually stored, but keep for 4–5 months if cured first at 60°F–70°F/16°C–22°C for at least 4 days and stored at 40°F/5°C. Dry fall-harvested potatoes for 1–2 days on the ground, then cure at 50°F–60°F/10°C–16°C and a high relative humidity for 10–14 days. Don't cure potatoes in the sun; they turn green. Once cured, store in total darkness in a single layer. Never layer or pile potatoes more than 6″–8″ deep.

Laboratory experiments conducted in Greece have shown that several aromatic herbs and their essential oils can suppress sprouting of potatoes in storage and have antimicrobial activity against potato pathogens. English lavender, pennyroyal, spearmint, rosemary, and sage suppressed growth of potato sprouts, but two oreganos did not. English lavender was the most effective sprout inhibitor.

Fresh		
Temperature	**Humidity**	**Storage Life**
55°F–60°F/13°C–16°C	90%–95%	5–10 months

Preserved		
Method	**Taste**	**Shelf Life**
Canned	Fair	12+ months
Frozen	Good	8 months
Dried	Good	12+ months

Spinach

Spinacia oleracea
Chenopodiaceae (Goosefoot Family)

Spinach is a cool-season crop, hardy to light frosts and freezes. Plan an average of 10 to 20 plants per person. Spinach can be grown as soon as the soil is workable. After thinning to 4 to 6 inches, cover the plants with row covers to keep pests away. Fall crops usually taste better and suffer no leaf miners or bolting. Also, if you plant a late fall crop and mulch it, a very early crop will come up in spring. Spinach bolts when there's 14 to 16 hours of light, regardless of the temperature, although warmer temperatures will cause it to bolt faster. The exceptions are New Zealand and Malabar "spinach," which thrive in warm weather. They aren't true spinach, but when cooked they taste like the real thing. Malabar is also a pretty ornamental vine that is easily grown on arbors, where it provides summer shade and a constant supply of summer greens.

TEMPERATURE

For Germination: 45°F–75°F/8°C–24°C
For Growth: 60°F–65°F/16°C–19°C

SOIL & WATER NEEDS

pH: 6.0–7.5
Fertilizer: Heavy feeder; before planting apply compost.
Side-Dressing: Apply 4 weeks after planting, and thereafter every 2 weeks.
Water: Light but evenly moist

First Seed-Starting Date

Sow directly every 10 days, starting 4–6 weeks before last frost.

Germinate	+	Transplant	+	Days before LFD	=	Count Back from LFD
7–14 days	+	28 days	+	21 days	=	56–63 days

Last Seed-Starting Date

Sow later crops directly, as transplanting encourages bolting.

Germinate	+	Transplant	+	Maturity	+	SD Factor	+	Frost Tender	=	Count Back from FFD
5 days	+	0 days	+	40–50 days	+	14 days	+	N/A	=	59–69 days

MEASUREMENTS

Planting Depth: ½″

Root Depth: 1′, taproot to 5′

Height: 4″–6″

Breadth: 6″–8″

Space between Plants: 2″, thin to 6″–12″ as leaves touch

Space between Rows: 12″–14″

PESTS

Aphid, beet leafhopper, cabbage looper, cabbageworm, flea beetle, leaf miner, slug, snail

DISEASES

Curly top (spread by beet leafhopper), damping off, downy mildew, fusarium wilt, leaf spot, spinach blight (caused by cucumber mosaic virus spread by aphids; see page 209)

ALLIES

Uncertain: Strawberry

COMPANIONS

All beans, all brassicas, celery, onion, pea

INCOMPATIBLES

Potato

HARVEST

Cut individual leaves when they're large enough to eat. Continual harvest prevents bolting. When the weather warms, cut the plant to ground level. Its leaves will grow back. For the best nutrition, harvest leaves in the morning.

Storage Requirements

For freezing and drying, cut the leaves into thick strips. Blanch for 5 minutes before drying, or 2 minutes before freezing. It's best to use only the smallest and most tender leaves for freezing.

Fresh		
Temperature	**Humidity**	**Storage Life**
32°F/0°C	95%–100%	10–14 days
Preserved		
Method	**Taste**	**Shelf Life**
Canned	Good	12+ months
Frozen	Good	12 months
Dried	Unknown	

Squash

Cucurbita pepo and others
Cucurbitaceae (Cucumber Family)

Squash is a warm-season crop, very tender to frost and light freezes. Plan an average of two winter plants per person and two summer plants per four to six people. Winter squash does not transplant well but can be sown inside in individual pots to minimize root disturbance. Squash is usually planted in small hills. To prepare, dig 18-inch-deep holes, fill partly with compost; complete filling with a mixture of soil and compost. Traditionally, six to eight seeds are placed 1 inch deep in each hole (others recommended only one or two seeds due to high germination rate); when seedlings reach 3 inches, thin to two seedlings. Raise fruits off the ground to prevent rot.

Fabric row covers boost and prolong yields. In cooler climates, keep row covers on all season; when the female (fruit) blossoms open, lift the cover for 2 hours in early morning twice a week to ensure bee pollination, which is essential. To keep vines short for row covers, pinch back the end, choose the best blossoms, and permit only four fruits per vine.

TEMPERATURE

For Germination: 70°F–95°F/22°C–35°C
For Growth: 65°F–75°F/19°C–24°C

SOIL & WATER NEEDS

pH: 6.0–7.5
Fertilizer: Heavy feeder; apply lots of compost; high N requirements.
Side-Dressing: Apply compost midseason; in boron-deficient soils, apply 1 teaspoon borax per plant.
Water: Heavy

First Seed-Starting Date

Germinate	+	Transplant	–	Days after LFD	=	Count Back from LFD
7–10 days	+	28–42 days	–	21–28 days	=	14–24 days

Last Seed-Starting Date

Germinate	+	Transplant	+	Maturity	+	SD Factor	+	Frost Tender	=	Count Back from FFD
3 days	+	0 (direct)	+	40–50 days	+	14 days	+	14 days	=	71–81 days (summer)
3 days	+	0 (direct)	+	80–110 days	+	14 days	+	14 days	=	111–141 days (winter)

MEASUREMENTS

Planting Depth:

- In hills: ½″–1″
- Vine: 72″–96″

Root Depth: 18″–6′

Height:

- Winter: 12″–15″
- Summer: 30″–40″

Breadth:

- Bush: Up to 4 square feet
- Vining: Up to 12–16 square feet

Space between Plants:

- In beds: 12″–18″
- In rows: 24″–28″

Space between Rows:

- Bush: 36″–60″

SUPPORT STRUCTURES

Use an A-frame or trellis to grow vines upright.

PESTS

Aphid, beet leafhopper, corn earworm, cucumber beetle, Mexican bean beetle, pickleworm, slug, snail, squash bug, squash vine borer, thrips, whitefly

DISEASES

Alternaria leaf spot, anthracnose, bacterial wilt, belly rot, cottony leak, cucumber wilt, downy mildew, mosaic, powdery mildew, scab

ALLIES

Some Evidence: Clover (medium red), mustard (yellow)

Uncertain: Borage, catnip, goldenrod, marigold, mint, nasturtium, onion, oregano, radish, tansy

COMPANIONS

Celeriac, celery, corn, melon

INCOMPATIBLES

Potato, pumpkin (cross-pollinates with other pepo plants, which is only important if you are saving seeds; keep pumpkin distant or plant 3 weeks later)

HARVEST

Cut all fruit except Hubbard types with a 1″ stem. Don't ever lift squash by the stem. Treat even those with hard skins gently to avoid bruising.

Summer: Cut before 8″ long, when the skin is still soft, and before seeds ripen.

Patty Pans: Cut when 1″–4″ in diameter and the skin is soft enough to break with a finger.

Winter: Cut when the skin is hard and not easily punctured, usually after the first frost has killed the leaves and the vine begins to die back but before the first hard frost.

SELECTED SPECIES

C. *pepo*. Almost all bush varieties are pepo, including the most commonly grown such as summer squash, acorn, spaghetti, and pumpkin.

C. *maxima*. These are excellent keepers, tolerant of borers, and include the largest fruit, such as buttercup and banana.

C. *moschata*. The sweetest squashes, such as butternut, cushaws, and cheese, are all *C. moschata*. They have high pest resistance and also have the highest vitamin content.

C. *mixta*. This is a Southern-growing group like *C. moschata*.

Storage Requirements

Cure winter squash after picking by placing in a well-ventilated, warm or sunny place for 2 weeks. If you cure fruit in the field, raise them off the ground and protect from rain. Or, dip fruit in a weak chlorine bleach solution (9 parts water: 1 part bleach), air-dry, and store. Store only the best fruit. Don't allow fruit to touch. Wipe moldy fruit with a vegetable-oiled cloth.

Fresh		
Temperature	**Humidity**	**Storage Life**
50°F–60°F/10°C–16°C	60%–70%	4–6 months
Preserved		
Method	**Taste**	**Shelf Life**
Canned	Good	12+ months
Frozen	Good	8 months
Dried	Good	12+ months

Sweet Potato

Ipomoea batatas
Convolvulaceae (Morning Glory Family)

The sweet potato is a warm-season crop, very tender to frost and light freezes. Plan an average of five plants per person. Other than extreme sensitivity to frost, sweet potatoes are easy to grow, mostly pest-free, and, once the transplants are anchored, drought hardy. Start slips with a sweet potato cut in half lengthwise. Lay the cut side down in a shallow pan of wetted peat moss or sand. Cover tightly with plastic wrap until sprouts appear, then unwrap. The slip is ready when it has four or five leaves, is 4 to 8 inches tall, and has roots.

A second method is to place a whole potato in a jar, cover the bottom inch with water, and keep warm. When leaves form above the roots, twist the sprouts off and plant in a deep flat or, if warm enough, outdoors. A third method is to take 6-inch cuttings from vine tips in fall just before frost. Place the cuttings in water and, when rooted, plant in 6-inch pots set in a south-facing window for the duration of winter. By late winter you can take more cuttings from these.

To prepare the ground in April, fill furrows with 1 to 2 inches of compost. Mound soil over the compost to form at least 10-inch-high ridges. This mini raised bed optimizes both tuber size and quality, because tuber growth is easily hindered by obstructions in the soil. After all danger of frost is past, transplant slips into these ridges. Unlike potatoes, sweets are not true tubers and keep expanding as the vine grows.

TEMPERATURE

For Germination: 60°F–85°F/16°C–30°C
For Growth: 70°F–85°F/22°C–30°C

SOIL & WATER NEEDS

pH: 5.0–6.0
Fertilizer: Light feeder. Low N. Before planting, place 1″–2″ of compost in furrows.
Side-Dressing: Once anchored, apply high P fertilizer like bonemeal, about 1 cup per 10 row-feet.
Water: Dry to medium. Water well the first few days until anchored, then ease back on water.

MEASUREMENTS

Planting Depth: 4″–6″
Root Depth: Length of the potato
Height: 12″–15″
Breadth: 4–8 square feet
Space between Plants:

- In beds: 10″–12″
- In rows: 12″–16″

Space between Rows: 36″–40″

PESTS

Flea beetle, nematode, weevil, wireworm. (Problems vary by region, so check with your Extension agent.)

DISEASES

Black rot (fungal), fusarium surface rot (storage), rhizoctonia, soil rot or scurf

ALLIES

Uncertain: Radish, summer savory, tansy

COMPANIONS

None

INCOMPATIBLES

None

HARVEST

Some harvest after the vines are killed by frost, but most warn that frost damages the root. Always harvest on a dry day. Start digging a few feet from the plant to avoid damage. Bruises or cuts as small as a broken hair root will shorten the shelf life by serving as an entry point for fusarium surface rot. Dry for 1–3 hours on the ground. Do not wash unless absolutely necessary; never scrub.

First Seed-Starting Date

Germinate	+	Transplant	–	Days after LFD	=	Count Back from LFD
8–12 days	+	42–56 days	–	7–21 days	=	43–47 days (6–7 weeks)

Last Seed-Starting Date

Germinate	+	Transplant	+	Maturity	+	SD Factor	+	Frost Tender	=	Count Back from FFD
8–12 days	+	42–56 days	+	100–125 days	+	14 days	+	14 days	=	178–221 days

Storage Requirements

Cure sweet potatoes before dry storage to seal off wounds and minimize decay. Place in a warm, dark, well-ventilated area at 85°F–90°F/30°C–33°C and high humidity for 4–10 days. Store in a cool place, making sure they don't touch. Temperatures below 55°F/13°C cause chill injury. Don't touch until ready to use.

Fresh

Temperature	Humidity	Storage Life
55°F–60°F/13°C–16°C	85%–90%	4–7 months

Preserved

Method	Taste	Shelf Life
Canned	Good	12+ months
Frozen	Excellent	6–8 months
Dried	Good	12+ months

Tomato

Lycopersicon esculentum
Solanaceae (Nightshade Family)

Tomatoes are a warm-season crop, very tender to frost and light freezes. Plan an average of two to five plants per person. All parts of the plant except the fruit are poisonous. Never plant near the walnut family trees (see Walnut on page 135).

To start in flats, sow seeds at least ½ inch apart. Seedlings will be spindly with less than 12 to 14 hours of light per day. When seedings have four leaves, transfer to a deeper pot and again when 8 to 10 inches tall. Allow up to 10 days to harden off. Soil temperature should be at least 55°F to 60°F/13°C to 16°C to transplant, otherwise plants turn yellow, become stunted, and are slow to bear. To transplant, pinch off the lower leaves again, and lay the plant on its side in a furrow about 2½ inches below the soil surface. This shallow planting speeds up growing since the plant is in warmer soil. Put in stakes on the downwind side of the plants. Some sources suggest that indeterminate and larger semideterminate varieties be pruned of all suckers (tiny leaves and stems in the crotches of larger stems) because they may steal nourishment from the fruits. However, the Erie City Extension Service has demonstrated that removing leaves decreases photosynthetic production. Hand-pollinate in greenhouses.

Unlike most crops, you may solarize soil as you grow tomatoes because they're very heat tolerant. Solarizing helps control disease, particularly verticillium wilt. Wet the soil and cover with clear plastic for the entire season for best results.

First Seed-Starting Date

Set out 2–4 weeks after the last frost. In Florida, Texas, and southern California, tomatoes can be transplanted in late winter and removed in summer when they stop bearing.

Germinate	+	Transplant	–	Days after LFD	=	Count Back from LFD
7–14 days	+	42–70 days	–	14–28 days	=	35–56 days (avg 6 weeks/42 days)

Last Seed-Starting Date

In Florida, Texas, and southern California, gardeners often plant fall crops.

Germinate	+	Transplant	+	Maturity	+	SD Factor	+	Frost Tender	=	Count Back from FFD
7–14 days	+	42–70 days	+	55–90 days	+	14 days	+	14 days	=	132–202 days

TEMPERATURE

For Germination: 60°F–85°F/16°C–30°C

For Growth: 70°F–75°F/22°C–24°C

SOIL & WATER NEEDS

pH: 5.8–7.0

Fertilizer: Heavy feeder. Fertilize 1 week before and on the day of planting. Avoid high N and K at blossom time. Too much leaf growth may indicate too much N or too much water.

Side-Dressing: Every 2–3 weeks apply light supplements of weak fish emulsion or manure tea. When blossoming, side-dress with a calcium source to prevent blossom-end rot.

Water: Medium and deep watering until harvest. Even moisture helps prevent blossom-end rot.

MEASUREMENTS

Planting Depth: ½″

Root Depth: 8″, some to 6′

Height:

- Determinate: 3′–4′
- Indeterminate: 7′–15′

Breadth: 24″–36″

Space between Plants:

- In beds: 18″
- In rows: 24″–36″

Space between Rows: 3′–6′

SUPPORT STRUCTURES

Use a wire cage, stake, or trellis; most gardeners prefer cages.

PESTS

Aphid, beet leafhopper, cabbage looper, Colorado potato beetle, corn borer, corn earworm, cucumber beetle, cutworm, flea beetle, fruit worm, garden centipede, gopher, Japanese beetle, lace bug, leaf-footed bug, mite, nematode, slug snail, stink bug, thrips, tobacco budworm, tomato hornworm, whitefly

DISEASES

Alternaria, anthracnose, bacterial canker, bacterial spot, bacterial wilt, botrytis fruit rot, curly top, damping off, early blight, fusarium wilt, late blight, nematode, psyllid yellows, septoria leaf spot, soft rot, southern blight, spotted wilt, sunscald, tobacco mosaic, verticillium wilt.

Environmental Disorders: Blossom-end rot, sunscald

ALLIES

Some Evidence: Basil

Uncertain: Asparagus, bee balm, borage, coriander, dill, goldenrod, marigold, mint, parsley, sage

COMPANIONS

Brassicas, carrot, celery, chive, cucumber, marigold, melon, nasturtium, onion, pea, pepper

INCOMPATIBLES

Corn, dill, fennel, kohlrabi, potato, walnut

HARVEST

Pick when fruit is evenly red but still firm. If warmer than 90°F/33°C, harvest fruit earlier.

Storage Requirements

Wash and dry before storing. Pack no more than two deep.

Fresh		
Temperature	**Humidity**	**Storage Life**
Ripe: 45°F–50°F/8°C–10°C	90%–95%	4–7 days
Green: 55°F–70°F/13°C–22°C	90%–95%	1–3 weeks
Preserved		
Method	**Taste**	**Shelf Life**
Canned	Excellent	12+ months
Frozen	Good	8 months
Dried	Good	12+ months

CHAPTER THREE

fruits & nuts

Always plant fruits and nuts when the tree, bush, cane, or vine is dormant and the ground is workable. In climates with milder winters, you can plant in late fall. Where winters are cold, plant in early spring. One evolving rule is that you can plant in Zones 5 and below in fall and should plant in Zones 4 and above in spring. There are many advantages to fall planting, but if you're at all uncertain about your microclimate, you might opt to wait until spring.

All fruit trees should be mulched with organic matter, ideally compost. To discourage rodents and prevent rot, keep mulch at least 3 to 12 inches away from the base of the trunk. Spread a 3- to 6-inch-deep layer of mulch out to the drip line or to 6 feet, whichever is greater. In spring, lightly hoe the mulch into the ground. In some places, urban foresters are fighting the "volcano" epidemic, in which people pile mulch high around the trunk stem so it resembles a volcano. This practice fosters ideal conditions for disease, rot, and animal invasion of the tender root collar area and can even lead to the demise of the tree. Avoid large amounts of hay, which release nitrogen late in the season when tree growth slows.

Planting a Tree

Prepare a hole that is 3 to 5 times greater in diameter than the root ball. The hole should be no deeper than the depth of the root system, or 10 percent shallower than the root ball. Studies indicate that it is more important for fruit trees to be given a wide planting hole, rather than a deep planting hole, because of their tendency to grow shallow roots. Add humus and compost to the hole to improve drainage. Install around the trunk a ¼- to ½-inch hardware cloth barrier that extends 4 inches belowground to deter gophers and other rodents, and that rises 18 to 24 inches aboveground to prevent rabbit damage (especially in winter months).

For trees on dwarf rootstock characterized by poor anchorage, nestle in a 4- to 6-foot stake before filling the hole. Form a small trench, mounding up the sides of the trench, about 18 inches away from the trunk. Fill the trench to the top with water. This drenching helps eliminate soil air pockets, which are not good for roots. Wrap the bark with a spiral white plastic tree guard to protect it from mice, rodents, and other pests. If you use a wire tree guard, whitewash the trunk first while it is still dormant with a commercial whitewash or interior white latex (never oil-based) paint.

Almond

Prunus dulcis
Rosaceae (Rose Family)

All almond trees, even those grown for nuts, are pretty ornamentals. Their culture is very similar to the peach. Almonds bloom extremely early in spring, with white or pink blossoms, and are even more susceptible than peaches to bud damage from spring frosts. As a result, cold northern areas require hardy, late-blooming varieties. Before you plant, cultivate the soil as deeply as possible to accommodate the almond's deep roots. Rain and high humidity during the bloom season can interfere with pollination, reduce yields, and promote fungal and bacterial diseases. Also, in humid summers the hulls may not split. If your area is noted for this type of spring or summer, almonds may not be for you. Almonds thrive in long, dry summers when supplemented by irrigation and can produce nuts for up to 50 days.

SITE

Full sun; south or southeast exposure; can withstand poor soil.

SOIL & WATER NEEDS

pH: 6.0–6.5
Fertilizer: Heavy feeder; low N for trees under 2 years; appropriate new growth is 6″–10″.
Side-Dressing: Apply compost in late autumn.
Water: Medium. Water deeply and let roots dry out between applications. Watering in fall and winter is very important. Mature trees are drought resistant and prefer dry summers.

MEASUREMENTS

Root Depth: Very deep
Height:

- Dwarf: 8′–10′
- Semidwarf: 10′–20′
- Standard: 20′–30′

Spacing:

- Dwarf: 8′
- Semidwarf: 8′–20′
- Standard: 24′–30′

GROWING & BEARING

Bearing Age: 3–4 years
Chilling Requirement: 300–600 hours below 45°F/8°C
Pollination: Most need cross-pollination; the pollinate cultivar can be grafted to the main cultivar.

SHAPING

Training:

- Freestanding tree: Open center, vase
- Wire-trained: N/A

Pruning: Prune young trees minimally with little or no heading back (i.e., cutting back to a promising bud or lateral branch), which stimulates extra leaf growth and delays bearing. When more mature, thin out crowded or competing branches, as well as the short, stubby spurs that bear nuts.

PESTS

Boxelder bug, brown almond mite, codling moth, filbertworm, leaf-footed bug, mite, navel orangeworm, nematode, peach twig borer

DISEASES

Bacterial canker, brown rot, crown gall, crown rot, leaf blight, leaf scab, peach leaf curl

ALLIES

Uncertain: Caraway, coriander, dill, wildflowers

INCOMPATIBLES

None

HARVEST

Unlike walnuts, as almonds mature the outer hulls split to expose the inner nuts; as the nuts dry, they fall to the ground. The nuts can also be knocked down onto canvas sheets. Don't harvest until the hulls of the nuts on the inner part of the tree have split open; these will be the last to do so. Spread nuts in a thin layer before hulling those that haven't fallen out of the hull. Unless wet, hull immediately.

ROOTSTOCKS

Almond seedlings grow more slowly than those grafted onto peach rootstock but mature to a large height and produce well. They resist drought but are susceptible to crown rot, crown gall, and nematodes. Peach rootstocks produce rapidly growing trees that have a better survival rate than almond seedlings. Some are nematode resistant. All need irrigation. Marianna 2624 is a good semidwarfing rootstock (see the Plum Rootstocks chart on pages 128–29). The almond × peach hybrid is a good rootstock for poor soils because it is vigorous and has deep roots.

Storage Requirements

Place hulled nuts in water. Remove the rotten or diseased nuts that float. Dry immediately at 110°F/44°C. They're ready for storage when the kernels rattle in the shell, or, when unshelled, the nutmeat snaps when bent. Avoid big piles of nuts, which encourage rot.

Fresh or frozen (shelled or unshelled)		
Temperature	**Humidity**	**Storage Life**
Below 40°F/5°C	Low	12+ months

Apple

Malus pumila
Rosaceae (Rose Family)

Thousands of apple varieties have been grown since ancient times. Many are lost to posterity, but more varieties of apple exist today than of any other fruit. Breeding for disease resistance has focused on the apple more than other fruits, so organic orchardists may have the greatest chance of success with this fruit.

After the June drop and when the fruit is no more than 1 inch in diameter, thin to 8 inches apart, or remove about 10 percent of the total fruit. Also thin all clusters to just one fruit; this will help produce large fruit and encourage return bloom the next year. The inclination of the apple branch is thought to determine its fruitfulness—the more horizontal, the more fruit. U.S. researchers have shown that shining red lights on apple trees for 15 minutes each night, beginning 2 weeks before harvest, delays fruit drop for 2 weeks. Other researchers are experimenting with inoculating bare roots with hairy root organisms, previously thought to be a problem disease but now shown to promote early root growth and fruiting.

To reduce the need for pest management, some growers have shown that, after early-season management of diseases and pests that attack trees, apples can be covered with small paper bags when they reach ½ to ¾ inch in diameter. Fruit can be thinned at the same time the apples are bagged. Apple bags are now available commercially.

SITE

Southeast exposure. Clay loam. To espalier, some suggest siting apples on an eastern wall or slope in very hot summer climates to avoid sunburn.

SOIL & WATER NEEDS

pH: 6.5–7.0 (6.0–6.5 for bitter pit)

Fertilizer: Low N for young trees. Appropriate new growth is 6″–14″.

Side-Dressing: Apply compost in late autumn and work into soil.

Water: Medium

MEASUREMENTS

Root Depth: 10′ or more, with a spread 50 percent beyond drip line

Height:

- Dwarf: 6′–12′
- Semidwarf: 12′–18′
- Standard: 20′–40′

Spacing:

- Dwarf: 8′–20′
- Semidwarf: 15′–18′
- Standard: 30′–40′

GROWING & BEARING

Bearing Age:

- Dwarf and semidwarf: 2–3 years
- Standard: 4–8 years

Chilling Requirement: 900–1000 hours below 45°F/8°C, though some require less.

Pollination: Most require cross-pollination.

SUPPORT STRUCTURES

Branch may need support when fruiting; branch separators can increase yields.

SHAPING

Training:

- Freestanding: Central leader
- Wire-trained: all cordons, espalier, fans, stop-overs, palmettes

Pruning: Spur types require little annual pruning because spurs bear for about 8 years, but each spring remove 1 out of 10 spurs and thin fruit by 10%. Tip-bearers fruit on 1-year-old wood. For these, prune back some of the long shoots and some of the spurs. For bitter pit, a sign of unbalanced growth, remove the most vigorous shoots at the end of summer.

PESTS

Aphid, apple maggot, cankerworm, codling moth, European apple sawfly, European red mite, flea beetle, fruit worm, leafhopper, leafroller, mice, oriental fruit moth, pear slug, plum curculio, potato leafhopper, scale, spongy moth, tent caterpillar, weevil, whitefly, white grub, woolly apple aphid

DISEASES

Apple scab, baldwin spot, canker dieback, cedar apple rust, crown gall, crown rot, cytospora canker, fire blight, powdery mildew, sunscald

ALLIES

Some Evidence: Buckwheat, *Eryngium* genus of herbs (e.g., button snakeroot and sea holly), *Phacelia* genus of herbs (e.g., California bluebells), weedy ground cover

Uncertain: Caraway, coriander, dill, garlic, nasturtium, tansy, vetch, wildflowers, wormwood

INCOMPATIBLES

Mature walnut tree, potato

HARVEST

For summer apples, pick fruit just before fully ripe, otherwise the apples become mealy. In fall, pick fruit only when fully ripe. Make sure you pick with the stems, or a break in the skin will occur that will permit bacteria to enter and foster rot. Be aware that ripening apples give off small amounts of ethylene gas that may inhibit the growth of neighboring plants and cause early maturing of neighboring flowers and fruits.

ROOTSTOCKS

Most growers now choose dwarf apples; standard trees grow very large, don't bear for years, and are difficult to harvest because of their height. To choose a rootstock you must know your soil type, drainage, and depth; then consider the specific variety's natural growing habit and size. These factors determine how much dwarfing you need in a rootstock. In rich, fertile soil all rootstocks grow more vigorously than predicted and need extra spacing. Buy smaller trees when possible because they suffer less transplanting shock and are more productive and vigorous.

Most nurseries don't offer a choice of rootstocks for a particular variety, but choice can be found between nurseries. The purpose of the charts on pages 94–95 is not to help you make an independent decision; it is to help you conduct an informed discussion with the nursery. We urge you to seek and follow the nursery growers' advice.

Note that extremely dwarfing rootstocks won't do well for most gardeners. Malling 9 is difficult because its roots are shallow and brittle, so make sure to securely stake and wrap the stems in polyethylene film to 6″ aboveground.

Storage Requirements

Wrapping in oiled paper or shredded paper helps prevent scald. Some apples stored over winter develop a rich flavor that is excellent for pies. Summer apples keep better if held at high temperatures several days before storage. Do not store apples with potatoes because apples will lose their flavor and potatoes will develop an off flavor.

Fresh		
Temperature	**Humidity**	**Storage Life**
32°F–40°F/0°C–5°C	80%–90%	4–8 months
Preserved		
Method	**Taste**	**Shelf Life**
Canned	Good	Up to 2 years
Dried	Good	6–24 months

Apple Rootstocks

Rootstock Name	Size (percent of standard)	Height/Width	Best Soil
Malling 27 EMLA 27/M27	Minidwarf 15%–30%	H: 4′–8′ / W: 2′–8′	Clay loam
Poland 22P22	Minidwarf 15%–30%	H: 5′–6′ / W: 2′–8′	———
Malling 9 EMLA 9/M9	Dwarf 20%–40%	H: 8′–10′ / W: 8′–10′	Sandy and grainy loam
Malling 26 EMLA 26/M26	Dwarf 30%–40%	H: 8′–14′ / W: 10′–14′	Sandy and grainy loam
Mark Mac-9	Dwarf 30%–45%	H: 8′–14′ / W: 8′–12′	Clay
M9/111	Dwarf 25%–50%	H: 10′–15′ / W: 10′–15′	———
M7a Malling VII EMLA 7	Dwarf 40%–60%	H: 11′–20′ / W: 12′–16′	Most soils; avoid heavy clay.
MM106 Merton-Malling 106	Dwarf 55%–85%	H: 14′–21′ / W: 14′–18′	Sandy loam; avoid poor drainage.
MM111 Merton-Malling 111	Dwarf 65%–85%	H: 15′–24′ / W: 15′–20′	All soils; can also tolerate wet soils.

P = precocious (early bearing); VP = very precocious

From Robert Kourik, *Designing and Maintaining Your Edible Landscape Naturally* (Santa Rosa, Calif.: Metamorphic Press, 1986), 166–67.

Apple Rootstock Pests and Diseases

Rootstock Name	Crown Rot	Woolly Aphid	Nematodes	Fire Blight	Powdery Mildew
Malling 27 EMLA 27/M27	HR	LR	———	S	MR
Poland 22P22	———	———	———	———	———
Malling 9 EMLA 9/M9	HR	S-LR	S	VS	MR
Malling 26 EMLA 26/M26	S-MR	S-LR	———	S-VS	MR
Mark Mac-9	R	S-LR	———	S	———
M9/111	R-VR	R-LR	———	S-VS (in early years)	MR
M7a Malling VII EMLA 7	L-MR	LR	———	R	MR
MM106 Merton-Malling 106	R	HR	———	HR	S
MM111 Merton-Malling 111	R	R	———	SS	SS

HR = highly resistant; LR = low resistance; MR = moderately resistant; R = resistant; S = susceptible; SS = somewhat susceptible; VS = very susceptible

From Robert Kourik, *Designing and Maintaining Your Edible Landscape Naturally* (Santa Rosa, Calif.: Metamorphic Press, 1986), 166–67.

Anchorage	Hardiness	Drought	Precocious	Other Factors
Poor/stake	Low hardiness	———	P	Remove fruit first 2 years; stops growing when bears fruit; good for espalier when grafted to vigorous varieties.
Poor/stake	Very hardy	———	———	Roots are brittle; union with some types is brittle when young.
Poor/stake	———	———	VP	Mice love this rootstock, so use tree guard; produces large fruit; defruit or thin fruit in first 2 years to prevent loss of leader.
Fair/might stake	Very hardy	———	VP	Can form root galls at graft union; defruit or thin first 2 years to prevent loss of leader; doesn't sucker much; produces large fruit.
Good/no stake	Very hardy	———	P	Open structure and roots well in stool beds; hardy to Zone 4 but not as hardy as M26.
Good/no stake	———	Tolerant	———	Combines benefits of 111 and 9; bury rootstock so MM111 part is underground and M9 part is exposed.
Good/no stake	Very hardy	Tolerant	P	Susceptible to burr knot; better than M26 on wet soils; remove suckers each year.
Fair to good	Low hardiness	Tolerant	P	Susceptible to burr knot; good stock for spurs; fumigate site for nematodes, which spread union necrosis and ringspot. Stake in hardpan soil.
Very good/ no stake	Very hardy	Tolerant	No	Smaller harvest than a stock like M106, but still productive; ideal for an interstem or under low vigor varieties.

Apricot

Prunus armeniaca
Rosaceae (Rose Family)

Apricots are good additions to the orchard. They're pretty (with glossy green leaves), easily managed, and one of the most drought-resistant fruit trees. They are, however, vulnerable to winter damage, and their buds are particularly susceptible to late frost damage (see Site below). Apricots grow vigorously and require annual pruning and thinning. After the natural fruit drop in late spring and when the fruit is about 1 inch in diameter, thin fruit to 3 to 4 inches apart. Summer temperatures over 95°F/35°C cause pit burn, a browning around the pit. Apricots enjoy long lives of approximately 75 years.

SITE

Not too rich or sandy. In the North, plant 12′–15′ from the northern side of a building. This delays buds and minimizes late frost injury but ensures full summer sun. Avoid windy locations. Do not plant on former apricot, cherry, or peach tree sites; when waterlogged, their roots release hydrogen cyanide that may linger in the soil and hinder growth.

SOIL & WATER NEEDS

pH: 6.0–6.5
Fertilizer: Appropriate new growth on a young tree is 13″–30″; on a bearing tree 10″–18″. Because the tree is naturally vigorous, go easy on N.
Side-Dressing: Apply compost or well-rotted manure mixed with wood ashes annually in spring, before leaves appear.
Water: Medium

MEASUREMENTS

Root Depth: 50%–100% farther than drip line
Height:

- Dwarf: 6′–7′
- Semidwarf: 12′–15′
- Standard: 20′–30′

Spacing:

- Dwarf: 8′–12′
- Semidwarf: 12′–18′
- Standard: 25′–30′

GROWING & BEARING

Bearing Age: 3–9 years
Chilling Requirement: Very low, 350–900 hours, which results in early blooming
Pollination: Most are self-pollinating, but yields are higher with more than one variety.

SHAPING

Training:

- Freestanding: Open center, dwarf pyramid. In colder areas use central leader.
- Wire-trained: Fan

Pruning: If the tree bears fruit only in alternate years, prune heavily when more than half of the flowers are blooming. Pruning encourages new spurs, each of which bears fruit for about 3 years. Prune yearly to encourage fruiting spurs. Remove wood that is 6 years old or more.

PESTS

Aphid, cankerworm, cherry fruit sawfly, codling moth, gopher, mite, peach tree borer, plum curculio, spongy moth caterpillar, whitefly

DISEASES

Bacterial canker, bacterial spot, black knot, brown rot, crown gall, cytospora canker, scab, verticillium wilt

ALLIES

Some Evidence: Alder, brambles, buckwheat, rye mulch, sorghum mulch, wheat mulch
Uncertain: Caraway, coriander, dill, garlic, nasturtium, tansy, vetch, wildflowers, wormwood

INCOMPATIBLES

Persian melon, plum. Also, don't plant where any of the following have grown in the previous 3 years: eggplant, oats (roots excrete a substance that inhibits the growth of young apricot trees), pepper, potato, raspberry, strawberry, tomato.

HARVEST

When all green color is gone and the fruit is slightly soft, twist and gently pull upward. If possible, harvest apricots when fully ripe. If plagued with animal problems, you may want to pick them slightly green and ripen them at 40°F–50°F/5°C–10°C.

ROOTSTOCKS

Generally, don't use peach rootstocks because they're susceptible to peach tree borer, root-knot and lesion nematodes, root winter injury, and uneven growth, which weakens the graft. Try not to use plum rootstocks—those dwarfed on Nanking cherry (*P. tomentosa*) or sand cherry (*P. pumila*). Although more tolerant of wet soil, these sucker continuously and cause a different fruit flavor. Apricot rootstock offers the best odds for tree survival; it is resistant to nematodes and has some resistance to peach tree borers.

Storage Requirements

For canning, use only unblemished fruits, or all fruits in the container will turn to mush. For drying, split the apricot first and remove the pit. If after drying the fruit is still softer than leather, store in the freezer.

Fresh		
Temperature	**Humidity**	**Storage Life**
60°F–65°F/16°C–19°C	90%–95%	A few days
40°F–50°F/5°C–10°C	90%–95%	3 weeks

Preserved		
Method	**Taste**	**Shelf Life**
Canned	Good	Up to 2 years
Frozen (after partially drying)	Excellent	12–24 months
Dried	Good	6–24 months
As jam	Good	Up to 18 months

Blackberry

Rubus allegheniensis, R. fruticosus, R. ursinus
Rosaceae (Rose Family)

Bramble fruits are very easy to grow. The keys to good yields are adequate spacing and light, and, because of shallow roots, good weed control and thick mulch. Rather than several short, close rows that limit berry development to only the upper cane parts, plant one long, narrow row that will produce berries to the bottom of the canes.

Blackberries are biennial. *Primocanes*, first-year green stems, bear only leaves. *Floricanes*, second-year brown stems, produce fruit. Upright or erect canes are shorter, whereas trailing varieties (also known as *dewberries* in the South) grow flexible canes as long as 10 feet. Blackberries are usually hardy to Zones 5 through 8; upright varieties are the hardiest. Blackberries have become a desirable crop for small market gardeners because of their ease of culture and the premium price they can command.

SITE

Full sun; rich loam. Due to verticillium wilt, avoid planting where nightshade family plants were grown in the last 3 years. Plant at least 300 feet away from wild brambles (which harbor pests and diseases) and from raspberries (to prevent cross-pollination).

SOIL & WATER NEEDS

pH: 5.0–6.0
Fertilizer: In spring, apply well-rotted manure or compost before canes break dormancy.
Mulch: In summer, apply 4″–8″ of organic mulch; in winter apply 4″–6″ of compost.
Water: Medium; drip irrigation is essential to avoid water on the berries, which is absorbed and dilutes flavor. Water regularly because of vulnerability to water stress.

MEASUREMENTS

Root Depth: More than 12″
Height: 4′–10′ when pruned
Spacing:

- Erect and semierect blackberry: 2′–3′ in a row (suckers and new canes fill out row)
- Trailing blackberry: 6′–12′ in a row (no suckers, but canes grow very long)

GROWING & BEARING

Bearing Age: 2 years
Chilling Requirement: Hours needed depend on the variety
Pollination: Self-pollinating

PROPAGATION

Erect Blackberry: By suckers. When dormant, dig up root suckers no closer than 6″ to mother plant.

Thornless and Trailing: By tip layering. Late in the season (August to September), bend and bury the primocane tips 4″ deep in loose soil. In spring, cut off the cane 8″ from the ground and dig up the new plants.

SHAPING

Training: A trellis is critical for disease and pest reduction, quality fruit, and easy harvest. For erect blackberries use a 4′ top wire; for trailing blackberries use a 5′ top wire. Fan out canes and tie with cloth strips.

Pruning: After harvest or in spring, cut out old canes done bearing.

- Erect blackberries: Thin to 5–6 canes per row-foot; to encourage branching, cut off the top 3″–4″ when primocanes are 33″–40″; late the following winter, cut the lateral branches back to 8″–12″ long.
- Trailing blackberries: Thin to 10–14 canes per hill; don't prune in the first year; in late winter cut canes back to 10′.

PESTS

Caneborer, mite, raspberry root borer, strawberry weevil, whitefly, white grub

DISEASES

Anthracnose, botrytis fruit rot, cane blight, crown gall, powdery mildew, rust, septoria leaf spot, verticillium wilt

ALLIES

Some Evidence: Grape

COMPANIONS

If berries are planted down the center of a 3′ bed, plant beans or peas in the first summer to keep the bed in production and to add organic matter and N to the soil.

INCOMPATIBLES

Black walnut and all members of the nightshade family transmit verticillium wilt.

HARVEST

When berries slide off easily without pressure, harvest into small containers so berries on the bottom won't be crushed. After harvest, cut back floricanes to the ground. For disease control, burn or dispose of all cut canes.

Storage Requirements

Freeze within 2 days by spreading out berries on cookie sheets and freezing. When rock hard, store in heavy freezer bags. Refrigerated, they keep 4–7 days.

Preserved

Method	Taste	Shelf Life
Canned	Excellent as jam	Up to 2 years
Frozen	Excellent	12–24 months

Blueberry

Vaccinium corymbosum, *V. angustifolium*, and *V. virgatum*
Ericaceae (Heath Family)

Lowbush varieties are grown primarily in New England, highbush throughout the United States, and rabbiteye only in the South and West.

Plant 2-year-old bushes. When your plants arrive, do not put them in water. Follow directions and "heel in" until ready to plant. Try inoculating the roots with the beneficial mycorrhizal fungi, which increases yields significantly. Regular watering and thick mulch are critical to keep down the weeds. A very acid pH is necessary for the plant to extract iron and nitrogen from the soil. Most blueberry problems are caused by stress related to pH, either too much or too little fertilizer or water.

To encourage root growth, remove all blossoms for a full 2 to 3 years. The delayed harvest will reward you with higher yields and healthier plants. Blueberries mature about 50 to 60 days from pollination. For areas prone to late-spring frosts, blueberries are a good choice, with strong frost resistance.

SITE

Full sun; choose a site where plants won't be disturbed, away from paths, roads, and driveways.

SOIL & WATER NEEDS

pH: 4.0–5.6
Fertilizer: Apply 1″ of compost under mulch. Avoid high N, aluminum sulfate, or urea. Ammonium sulfate can be used, if needed, in small quantities such as ½ ounce in year 1, and 1 ounce for every additional year thereafter. Be careful not to overuse.
Mulch: 3″–6″ acid mulches such as pine needles, peat moss, shredded oak leaves, or rotted sawdust
Water: Heavy and evenly moist

MEASUREMENTS

Root Depth: Very shallow, top 14″ of soil
Height:

- Lowbush: 2′–4′
- Highbush: 5′–6′
- Rabbiteye: 6′–30′

Spacing:

- Lowbush: 3′–4′
- Highbush: 7′–8′
- Rabbiteye: 6′–7′

Rows: 10′

GROWING & BEARING

Bearing Age: 3–8 years
Chilling Requirement:

- Lowbush and highbush: 650–800 hours below 45°F/8°C
- Rabbiteye: 200 hours

Pollination: All varieties benefit from cross-pollination, but only lowbush and rabbiteye require cross-pollination by another variety.

PROPAGATION

Layering; bend and bury the tip of a lower branch and cover with soil. Rooting hormone helps plant establish. The following spring, cut off the cane 8″ from the ground and dig up the new plant.

SHAPING

Pruning: Don't prune until the third year after planting because blueberries fruit near the tips of 2-year and older branches. To prune, cut out diseased tips and, for larger fruit, cut branches back to where buds are widely spaced. Cut out weak and diseased branches, or *canes,* as well. Every 2 or 3 years you may need to cut back to the main stem canes that are 5 years old or older. Don't leave any stubs because suckers will be weaker than new canes growing from the roots. A good rule of thumb is to allow one branch per year of age plus one or two vigorous new branches. If new branch growth on an old bush (15 years) is thinner than ¼ inch, cut out half of the new canes.

PESTS

Apple maggot, birds, cherry fruitworm, fruit fly, mite, plum curculio, weevil

DISEASES

Bacterial canker, cane gall, crown gall, mummy berry, *Phytophthera cinnamomi,* powdery mildew. Many problems are due to a lack of acidity.

ALLIES

Some evidence: White clover

COMPANIONS: None

INCOMPATIBLES: None

HARVEST

Leave berries on the bush 5–10 days after they turn blue. They're fully ripe when slightly soft, come off the bush easily, and are sweet. Pick directly into the storage bowl or containers so that as little as possible of their protective wax is removed.

Storage Requirements

Don't wash the fruit if you're going to freeze it.

Fresh		
Temperature	**Humidity**	**Storage Life**
35°F–40°F/2°C–5°C (refrigerated)	80%–90%	7 days
Preserved		
Method	**Taste**	**Shelf Life**
Canned	Fair	Up to 2 years
Frozen	Good	12–24 months
As preserves	Good	Up to 18 months

Sour Cherry

Prunus cerasus
Rosaceae (Rose Family)

Sour cherries are the easiest cherries to grow because they're more tolerant than sweet cherries of cold winters, hot and humid summers, and heavy and cool soils. They also are less vigorous and therefore require less pruning. Sour cherries reportedly have a varying productive life, ranging from 15 to 35 years and averaging 20 to 25 years. Sometimes described as tart and known for their use in pies and other desserts, most sour cherries, with the exception of the Morella variety, are sweet enough to be eaten fresh. The key and perhaps the biggest challenge for cherry growers is to keep birds away long enough for the cherries to ripen on the tree. Netting, noisemakers, scare-eye balloons, scarecrows, and "trap crops" of mulberry bushes, which are preferred by birds, are all possible defensive strategies. See Sweet Cherry (page 105) for more information.

SITE

Full sun to partial shade. A southern exposure or placement 12′ from north-facing walls to delay blooming. Well-drained soil and good air circulation. Likes 4′ of topsoil. Don't plant on former apricot, cherry, or peach sites; when waterlogged, their roots release hydrogen cyanide, which may linger in the soil and hinder growth. Also don't plant between other fruit trees, because cherries bear at a time others may need to be sprayed.

SOIL & WATER NEEDS

pH: 6.0–6.5
Fertilizer: Low N until 2 years old. Appropriate new growth is 12″–24″ when young and 6″–12″ bearing.
Water: Heavy and even supply. Cherries are especially sensitive to water stress.

MEASUREMENTS

Root Depth: 50% beyond dripline
Height:
- Dwarf: 6′–10′
- Semidwarf: 12′–18′
- Standard: 15′–20′

Spacing:
- Dwarf: 8′–10′
- Semidwarf: 18′–20′
- Standard: 20′

GROWING & BEARING

Bearing Age: 2–7 years
Chilling Requirement: 800–1200 hours at below 45°F/8°C
Pollination: All sour types are self-pollinating.

SHAPING

Training:

- Freestanding: Central leader or open center
- Wire-trained: Fan-trained against a south- or north-facing wall, using the same method as for peaches. All sizes of sour cherries are suitable for training because they're not vigorous growers.

Pruning: The lowest branch should be about 2′ off the ground and limbs about 8′ apart. Both sour and sweet cherries bear on spurs as well as on 1-year-old wood. Sour cherries, however, produce several adjacent fruit blossoms on the year-old wood, which causes future bare spaces that lack foliage. If there are too many of these lateral flower buds, trim 1″–2″ off the branch ends in June to stimulate leaf buds. Sour cherry spurs bear for 2–5 years.

PESTS

Apple maggot, birds, blackberry fruit fly, cherry fruit fly, cherry fruit sawfly, codling moth, peach leaf curl, peach tree borer, plum curculio

DISEASES

Bacterial gummosis, black knot, black rot, brown rot, cherry leaf spot, crown rot, mildew, peach leaf curl, verticillium wilt

ALLIES

Some Evidence: Alder, brambles, buckwheat rye mulch, sorghum mulch, wheat mulch

Uncertain: Caraway, coriander, dill, garlic, nasturtium, tansy, vetch, wildflowers, wormwood

COMPANIONS

Alfalfa, bromegrass, clover

INCOMPATIBLES

None

HARVEST

Wait to pick until the fruit is fully ripe, which is when the flesh slides off the stem, leaving the pit behind.

ROOTSTOCKS

Mahaleb (*Prunus mahaleb*) rootstock is good for sour cherries. It produces trees 60%–75% of standard size that are susceptible to root rot and gophers, less long-lived than Mazzard, but more resistant than Mazzard is to crown gall, drought, and cold injury. Colt rootstock produces semidwarfs, about 80% of full size, that may be more resistant to bacterial diseases and crown rot. North Star rootstock also produces semidwarfs that are hardy and resistant to wet soil. Elwood Fisher, master fruit gardener, uses North Star to dwarf other types of fruit trees as well. For other sour cherry rootstocks, see Sweet Cherry, on page 105.

Storage Requirements		
Use immediately, if possible; freeze sour cherries immediately.		
Fresh		
Temperature	**Humidity**	**Storage Life**
34°F–40°F/2°C–5°C	High	Soft flesh: 7 days; firm flesh: 2–3 weeks
Preserved		
Method	**Taste**	**Shelf Life**
Canned	Good	Up to 2 years
Frozen	Good	12–24 months
Dried	Good	6–24 months

Sweet Cherry

Prunus avium
Rosaceae (Rose Family)

Standard sweet cherries grow large and require consistent pruning to be managed properly. Sweet cherries have a varying productive life, averaging 20 to 25 years and reportedly ranging as high as 50 years. Cherries are considered a fairly easy crop for the organic grower as long as sufficient attention is given to soil fertility, which keeps the trees healthy and minimizes disease and insect problems. Fertility can be accomplished through thick applications of compost (kept 1 foot away from the base of the tree) and through foliar feeding. For organic insect control of all cherries (sweet and sour), apply dormant oil spray every spring before the leaf buds open, covering all areas of the trunk and branches. If possible, buy certified virus-free trees. See Sour Cherry (page 102) for more information.

SITE

Full sun; needs light and well-drained soil for successful survival. See Growing & Bearing.

SOIL & WATER NEEDS

pH: 6.0–6.5
Fertilizer: Low N until 2 years old. Appropriate new growth is 22″–36″ when young and 8″–12″ bearing.
Water: Heavy and even supply. Cherries are particularly susceptible to water stress.

MEASUREMENTS

Root Depth: 50% beyond dripline
Height:

- Dwarf: 6′–12′
- Semidwarf: 10′–15′
- Standard: 25′–40′

Spacing:

- Dwarf: 8′–10′
- Semidwarf: 15′–18′
- Standard: 25′–30′

GROWING & BEARING

Bearing Age: 2–7 years
Chilling Requirement: 800–1200 hours below 45°F/8°C
Pollination: All sweet cherries except Stella must be cross-pollinated, although not all are compatible because of different bloom times. Further pollination difficulties arise because early-spring flowers are receptive for only about 1 week. Also, a late frost or a wet spring can interfere with bee activity.

SHAPING

Training:

- Freestanding: Central leader
- Wire-trained: Fan-trained against a south-facing wall where the summer sun is not blistering hot, or 12′–15′ away from a north-facing wall. Only dwarf sweet cherries are suitable for training.

Pruning: The lowest branch should be about 2′ off the ground and limbs about 8′ apart. Sweet cherries bear on spurs as well as on 1-year-old wood. Sweet cherry spurs produce for 10–12 years; exercise extreme caution when harvesting or pruning to avoid damaging them.

PESTS

See Sour Cherry (page 102).

DISEASES

See Sour Cherry (page 102).

ALLIES

See Sour Cherry (page 102).

COMPANIONS

See Sour Cherry (page 102).

INCOMPATIBLES

None

HARVEST

Wait until the fruit is fully ripe. Gently pull on the stem and twist upward. Be extremely careful not to damage or rip off spurs, as these bear for 10 years or more.

ROOTSTOCKS

Mazzard (*P. avium*) rootstock is good for sweet cherries. It is a vigorous grower, produces large trees, is slow to bear, and is tolerant of wet soil. Mazzard is particularly good in the West, Northwest, and areas of the East where moisture is sufficient and winter hardiness is not a problem. GM61 is considered by some to be the best overall dwarfing stock for cherry. Its trees are 50%–60% of standard size; they can be maintained below 15′, are hardy to at least -20°F/-29°C, are spreading and precocious, do well in heavier soils, and are good for both sweet and sour. For information on other rootstocks, see Sour Cherry (page 102).

Storage Requirements

Use immediately if possible. If not possible, place in an airtight container, such as a crisper, and refrigerate. There is controversy over whether sweet cherries store best with or without their stems; experiment for yourself.

	Fresh	
Temperature	**Humidity**	**Storage Life**
34°F–40°F/2°C–5°C	High	Soft flesh: 7 days; firm flesh: 2–3 weeks
	Preserved	
Method	**Taste**	**Shelf Life**
Canned	Good	Up to 2 years
Frozen	Poor	12–24 months

Chinese Chestnut

Castanea mollissima
Fagaceae (Beech Family)

The Chinese chestnut is an attractive, globe-shaped landscape shade tree. It also offers rot-resistant timber and regular annual crops of one of the sweetest nuts. In early summer, the tree is decked with pretty (but odoriferous) yellow catkins, and its glossy, dark green serrated leaves cling late into fall.

Chestnut fungal blight swept through North America in the early 1900s, destroying nearly all American (*C. dentate*) and European (*C. sativa*) chestnuts, both of which are now planted on the West Coast, where blight is less of a problem. The Chinese chestnut, introduced in 1853, resists blight and grows well in Zones 5 through 8 in a wide variety of soil and climatic conditions, although it's grown primarily in the East and Northwest. Most seedlings do better than grafted trees in the northern Zones 5 and 6. Hardy to about −20°F/−29°C; late blooming permits it to escape spring frosts. For rot-resistant poles, chestnuts can be coppiced: Cut down the tree to stimulate sucker growth, let suckers grow to desired pole thickness, and cut again. Chestnuts can live 50 years or more.

SITE

Full sun. Preferred soil is light and sandy, but it can be rocky or silty as long as it isn't alkaline or very dry. Soil must be well drained. Avoid frost pockets, areas that are subject to soil compaction, and sites with potential disruption of the root system.

SOIL & WATER NEEDS

pH: 5.0–6.0
Fertilizer: Medium feeder. Use low N for trees under 2 years; you don't want rapid growth when the tree is young. Unlike some nuts, the chestnut likes to be fed throughout its life and produces better quality initially, as the chestnut thrives in acid soil.
Side-Dressing: Apply compost in late autumn or rotted manure and leaf mold in early spring.
Water: Medium; however, established trees are fairly drought resistant.

MEASUREMENTS

Root Depth: Deep
Height: 30′–40′
Breadth: 20′
Spacing: 8′ if thinned out in 5 years; 20′ if thinned out to 40′ in 20 years; 40′ if not thinned

GROWING & BEARING

Bearing Age: 3–4 years
Chilling Requirement: 250 hours below 45°F/8°C are required for development of nut blossoms.
Pollination: All require cross-pollination; plant two of the same or different varieties.

SHAPING

Training:

- Freestanding: Central leader
- Wire-trained: N/A

Pruning: Prune young trees minimally, just enough to train the tree to a single trunk and basic scaffold; too much pruning stimulates extra vegetative growth and delays bearing.

PESTS

Chestnut weevil, gall wasp (in Georgia), mite, nut curculio, squirrel

DISEASES

Blossom-end rot, chestnut blight, oak wilt

ALLIES

None

COMPANIONS

None

INCOMPATIBLES

None

HARVEST

Use thick gloves to protect your hands from the spines of the outer chestnut hull. To minimize daily gathering, when the burs begin to crack open in late summer, pick or knock down small bunches of them onto a harvest sheet. For final ripening, store the burs at 55°F–65°F/13°C–19°C for about 1 week or until they split open. If unable to pick them in bulk, you must gather fallen nuts each day, for chestnuts on the ground are particularly susceptible to rapid degradation by fungi and bacteria.

Storage Requirements

The chestnut can be eaten raw if cured first to maximize the nut's free sugar. To cure, dry deburred nuts in a shady, warm, dry place for 1–3 days until the nut texture is spongy. To roast, cut an X in the shell and cook at 400°F/200°C for 15 minutes. If not eaten immediately, store uncured nuts in a cold place that is either dry or has high humidity but no free moisture. A good method is to mix freshly harvested and dehulled nuts with dry peat moss, pack in plastic bags, seal, and refrigerate. You can also dry and grind nuts into a baking flour.

Fresh (uncured)		
Temperature	**Humidity**	**Storage Life**
32°F/0°C	High, but no free moisture	6–12 months

Filbert/Hazelnut

Corylus spp.
Betulaceae (Birch Family)

Filberts, also known as hazelnuts, are unusual because they can be grown as shrubs, hedgerows, or trees. An ideal size for home growers, they are generally hardy. Very early blooming renders them particularly susceptible to late frosts, however. In the Northwest, they never go fully dormant.

Filberts tend to bear in alternate years, depending on how much new wood was produced and how much was pruned out the prior year. In areas that are subject to temperatures of 5°F/−15°C or lower, they do not produce nuts consistently. In the first 2 years, protect young tree trunks from sunscald. Filberts produce numerous suckers that are easily used for propagation and good for coppice management (see Chinese Chestnut, page 107).

When buying a filbert or hazelnut, make sure it is intended to be a nut-bearing tree; many are grown only as ornamentals and may be poor nut bearers. Nuts from grafted or layered trees are generally higher quality than those from seedling trees. Delicious in baked goods, filberts are also high-vitamin and -protein snacks.

SITE

Full sun in maritime climates; partial shade in very sunny, hot climates. In the East, choose a northern, cold exposure to delay premature bloom. Can adapt to clay and sand, but prefers deep, fertile, well-drained soil. Must avoid low frost pockets and poorly drained areas.

SOIL & WATER NEEDS

pH: 6.5
Fertilizer: Heavy feeder, but do not fertilize unless foliage is pale and growth is slow. Appropriate new growth is 6″–9″.
Side-Dressing: Apply compost in late autumn and organic mulch in early spring.
Water: Medium; water well in times of severe drought. In maritime climates like the Northwest, mature trees rarely need watering. Sawdust mulch helps keep moisture in the soil.

MEASUREMENTS

Root Depth: Unlike other nut trees, the filbert has no taproot.
Height: 20′
Breadth: 15′
Spacing:

- For trees: 15′–20′
- For hedges: 3′–5′

GROWING & BEARING

Bearing Age: 2–4 years

Chilling Requirement: Medium-high hours (800–1600)

Pollination: All need cross-pollination.

SHAPING

Training:

- Freestanding: Open center
- Wire-trained: N/A

Pruning: To grow a shrub, cut excessive sucker growth yearly. For a tree, prune to establish a central leader and basic scaffold, and remove all suckers. Nuts develop on 1-year-old wood, so prune lightly every year to stimulate new growth. Make thinning-out cuts only where branches are cut back to their base, not cut in half or stubbed off.

PESTS

Blue jar, filbert bud mite, filbert weevil, filbertworm, squirrel

DISEASES

Crown gall, eastern filbert blight, filbert bacterial blight, powdery mildew (*Note:* Eastern filbert blight should not be excluded as a possible problem in West Coast growing regions. It was first found on the West Coast in the Willamette Valley of Oregon in 1986.)

ALLIES

None

COMPANIONS

None

INCOMPATIBLES

None

HARVEST

Nuts usually turn brown and ripen by late summer, but an immature husk, shaped like a barely opened daffodil blossom, prevents them from dropping for almost another month. The nut is ripe when it readily turns in the husk if pressed. When ripe, you can either hand-harvest the husks or wait until nuts drop to the ground, in which case you risk competing with squirrels and birds.

SELECTED VARIETIES

European Species (*C. avellana*). Commonly known as filberts, these are a major commercial crop in the Northwest, grow best in maritime climates, and are the kind of filbert usually found in supermarkets. They have occasionally been grown in the East but generally do poorly there due to eastern filbert blight.

American Species (*C. americana*). Most often known as hazelnuts, this species grows in native, wild hedgerows throughout the northern United States and southern Canada. American hazelnuts are usually smaller than European hazelnuts. The American species serves as a host for eastern filbert blight fungus but is very tolerant of its attack. Check with suppliers about availability.

Hazelberts. A cross between the European filbert and American hazelnut, these nuts combine the large European nut size with American hardiness and early ripening.

Storage Requirements

Place hulled nuts in water; remove the rotten and diseased nuts that float to the top. Dry and cure by spreading nuts in one layer and leaving them in a cool, dry, well-ventilated place for several weeks. They're ready for storage when the kernels rattle in the shell, or, when unshelled, the nutmeat snaps when bent. Avoid big piles of nuts, which encourage rot.

Fresh		
Temperature	**Humidity**	**Storage Life**
Shelled: 65°F–70°F/19°C–22°C	Low	Several weeks
Unshelled: 34°F–40°F/2°C–5°C	Low	Several months
Preserved		
Method	**Taste**	**Shelf Life**
Frozen (shelled)	Good	12–24 months

Grape

Vitis spp.
Vitaceae (Grape Family)

Grapevines need well-drained soil and should have at least 20 inches of topsoil. They don't need especially fertile soil because of vigorous, extensive roots; vines that grow more slowly also develop more "character." Plant vines at the same depth as grown in the nursery. Mound soil over the crown to prevent wind damage, except in the West because of possible crown rot. Cut out all but one or two stems (with two or three buds each) for the central trunk. Grape roots prefer warm soil, so mulch with stones or black plastic to raise soil temperature. If vines overbear, thin flowers before berries form.

Grape seeds secrete growth hormones within the berry, so commercial growers spray seedless grapes with growth hormones. Homegrown, unsprayed seedless grapes will be smaller.

SITE

Best on a 15-degree south-facing (southeast or southwest) slope

SOIL & WATER NEEDS

pH: 6.7–7.0
Fertilizer: Apply compost only at the beginning of the growing season or during blooming. When applied late in the season, N delays ripening, inhibits coloring, and subjects vines to winter injury if they keep growing too long into fall. American grapes and hybrids are especially sensitive to N deficiency in early spring and during blooming.
Water: Low to dry. To harden off the vines for winter, don't water much after August.

MEASUREMENTS

Root Depth: In deep soil they can easily extend 12′–40′.
Height:

- Pruned: 12′–20′
- Unpruned: 50′–100′

Spacing: 8′ is best; 7′ in shallow soil and 10′ in deep soil

GROWING & BEARING

Bearing Age: 3–4 years
Chilling Requirement: None
Pollination: All are self-fertile with the exception of a few muscadine vines.

SHAPING

Training: For vigorous vines, the less common Geneva double-curtain method provides the best aeration, most sun, and highest yields. Plant vines down the center, prune each to two trunks, and grow trunks to long, 6′–8′ cordons on upper wire. Train the first vine to the front wire, the second to the back wire, and so on. The more common four-arm Kniffen method provides an attractive privacy screen but shades the lower vine parts. For both methods, bury 9′ end posts 3′ into the ground. Use heavy galvanized #11 wire.

Pruning: To spur-prune European vines, consult other sources. Cane-prune all others as follows: (1) Cut out water sprouts, which are shoots on wood older than 2 years; (2) remove winter-damaged wood; (3) cut out last year's fruiting cane; (4) identify canes receiving the most sun by their darker wood and closely spaced nodes; select the thickest to bear this season's fruit, and cut back to only 8 to 15 nodes; (5) for each selected fruiting cane, choose a cane nearby as a renewal spur for next year's fruit; cut back to 2 buds. Each year, replace the fruiting arm with a cane from a renewal spur, and select a new renewal spur for the following year.

PESTS

Grape berry moth, Japanese beetle, leafhopper, mealybug, mite, phylloxera root aphid, plum curculio, rose chafer

DISEASES

Anthracnose, black rot, botrytis fruit rot, crown gall, downy mildew, leaf spot, Pierce's disease (spread by leafhoppers), powdery mildew

ALLIES

Some Evidence: Blackberries (*Rubus* spp.), Johnson and Sudan grass (see the caution on Johnson grass on the chart on page 287), sweet alyssum

Uncertain: Chives, hyssop

HARVEST

Cut bunches when fruits are fully colored, sweet, slide off easily, and stems and seeds are brown. Grapes don't ripen further once picked. For raisins, use a hydrometer and harvest when the grapes reach 20% soluble solids. A lower percentage significantly decreases raisin weight and quality.

SELECTED VARIETIES

American. Pure strains are rich in pectin, best for jelly, and renowned for a "foxy" flavor (cloyingly sweet, like the Concord) that, if possible, winemakers avoid. Newer hybrids are good fresh and for wine.

Muscadine (*V. rotundifolia*). Indigenous to the American Southeast, these require a warm, moist climate and are good for jelly, juice, and wine. They require cross-pollination, so plant two varieties.

Hybrids (French Hybrids, American-European Hybrids). These represent an attempt to obtain the best of both worlds: European taste and American hardiness and disease resistance.

European and California (*V. vinifera*). Low in pectin, these require a frost-free season of 170–180 days and are not hardy below 10°F/–13°C without protection. Most wines are made from vinifera or the American-European hybrids. Among the many varieties, these are hardiest.

Storage Requirements		
Cool to 50°F/10°C soon after picking and spread the fruit in single layers. Dry in the sun under clear polyethylene until stems shrivel slightly; this shortens drying time and yields raisins with higher sugar and vitamin C levels than raisins dried in an oven. Store no more than 4″ deep in trays.		
Fresh		
Temperature	**Humidity**	**Storage Life**
40°F/5°C	Slightly humid	2–3 months
Preserved		
Method	**Taste**	**Shelf Life**
Jelly	Good	Up to 18 months
Dried	Excellent	6–24 months
Juice	Good	12+ months

Kiwi

Actinidia arguta, *A. chinensis*, *A. deliciosa*, *A. kolomikta*, and *A. polygama*
Actinidiaceae (Chinese Gooseberry Family)

Kiwi is a productive and tasty candidate for the home grower—but only if proper attention is paid to site, water, support, and pruning. The buds, young shoots, and fruit of all species, regardless of hardiness, are particularly frost tender and need to be protected when temperatures fall below 30°F/−2°C for any length of time, in spring or fall. Cover at night to protect from frost damage, or use overhead sprinkling until temperatures surmount 32°F/0°C. Frost-damaged fruit emits ethylene gas in storage, thereby hastening the softening of other fruit. Kiwi vines can bear for 40 to 50 years. Light pruning and fruit thinning, rather than heavy pruning and no thinning, optimize yield and fruit size. Thin to about 60 fruits per square meter before flowers open.

One male can fertilize up to eight female vines; tag them to be sure you always know which is which. Try to buy larger plants because they have a higher survival rate. Otherwise, you may want to start small rooted cuttings in 5-gallon containers.

SITE

Full sun (minimum 6 hours), except for *A. kolomikta*, which likes partial shade in hot climates. Wind protection is important. Prefers rich, fertile soil, but will tolerate heavy soil. In any soil, good drainage is vital. Avoid soggy, low areas. Best spot is to the north of a building or tree to delay bud break. Cover vines if frost threatens in spring or fall.

SOIL & WATER NEEDS

pH: 6.0–6.5

Fertilizer: Heavy feeder. Apply slow-acting organic fertilizers, very thick compost, or well-rotted manure in late winter and spring, several inches away from the crown. Don't fertilize past mid-June. Kiwi needs high K, and also Mg to prevent K-induced deficiency. Never apply boron, as above-optimum levels can be severely toxic.

Side-Dressing: Apply twice during the growing season; use only mildly nitrogenous substances.

Water: Heavy. Drip irrigation is best. Overhead sprinkling can protect fruit and foliage from frosts.

MEASUREMENTS

Root Depth: Shallow; they're susceptible to crown and root rot in wet areas.

Height: Up to 30′ long vines

Spacing:

- Between plants: 10′–20′
- Between rows: 15′–20′

(*Note:* Male and female plants must be within at least 100′ of each other.)

GROWING & BEARING

Bearing Age: 3–5 years, except for self-pollinating types, which can bear 1 year after planting

Chilling Requirement: Vines benefit from 400–600 hours below 45°F/8°C.

Pollination: Cross-pollination between male and female vines required; 1 male can pollinate 8 female vines.

SHAPING

Training: Requires trellis, arbor, T-bar fence, pergola, wall, or chain-link fence to support fruiting vines. Supports should be 6′ tall for females and 7′ tall for males. Stake when planting.

PRUNING

Similar to grapes. Kiwis fruit on the lower 6 buds of this season's fruiting shoot, off of 1-year-old wood. On planting, prune the main stem back to 4–5 buds. The first summer allow the vine to grow freely. Cut back females to 6′ and males to 7′, and remove all but 2 or 4 of the strongest cordons for each. The second winter, head back female cordons to 8–10 buds and males to half that length (4–5 buds).

General Female Winter-Pruning Guidelines: Cut out damaged wood, curled or twining growth, and all wood that has fruited for 2 seasons. Select fruiting arms that have short internodes (less than 2″ apart), are 10″–14″ apart, and are well exposed to sunlight; cut these back to 8 buds.

General Female Summer-Pruning Guidelines: Select next season's fruiting arms, remove other shoots, cut out erect water shoots, and shorten curled or tangled growth. Make sure enough light passes through to cast patterns on the ground below.

General Male-Pruning Guidelines: After July bloom cut back flowering arms to 20″–24″; if necessary, trim again in August or September to 29″–31″. Trim vines in winter.

PESTS

No significant pests reported in North America.

DISEASES

No significant diseases reported in North America.

ALLIES

None

COMPANIONS

None

INCOMPATIBLES

None

HARVEST

Allow fruit to ripen on the vine until the first signs of softening; it should give with a little finger pressure. Clip hardy kiwi with some stem. Snap off fuzzy kiwi, leaving the stem on the vine. Even minor damage causes ethylene production, which prematurely softens other fruit. In dry climates, you can let the kiwi dry on the vine; they will become intensely sweet and keep for about 6 weeks.

Storage Requirements

On a regular basis, remove from fresh storage soft, rotten, or shriveled fruit. Freeze whole kiwis in plastic bags; or freeze ¼″ unpeeled slices and then pack in plastic bags. Cut kiwi in half, then dry at 120°F/49°C for 2 hours and repeat the next day.

Fresh (whole)		
Temperature	**Humidity**	**Storage Life**
32°F/0°C	85%–95%	2 months (hardy); 4 months (fuzzy)

SELECTED VARIETIES

Very Hardy (*A. kolomikta*). Hardy to Zone 3 (–40°F/–40°C), these are beautiful plants. The male has variegated leaves, and females display some variegation, too. Fruits are smaller than fuzzy kiwi and are smooth-skinned.

Hardy (*A. arguta*). Hardy to Zone 4 (–25°F/ -32°C) and native to northern China. The fruit is smaller than fuzzy kiwi, and its smooth, grapelike skin can be eaten.

Tender or Fuzzy Kiwi (*A. deliciosa*). Native to China and first commercially grown in New Zealand. This fuzzy fruit is hardy to Zones 8–10 (5°F–10°F°/ –15°C–-13°C) and can be grown as far north as the Pacific Northwest and British Columbia, or cultivated in greenhouses.

Peach

Prunus persica
Rosaceae (Rose Family)

Peaches are considered one of the most difficult fruits to grow, particularly for growers who don't use chemical sprays, because of multiple pests and an early bloom period that makes them extremely susceptible to frost damage. Spraying flat-white interior latex paint on the trees, buds and all, in mid-January can help delay bloom by up to 5 days; this is often enough time to make a significant difference in flower survival and fruit set.

Plant at about the same depth that it was grown in the nursery; its upper roots should be only a few inches below the soil surface. Thinning is crucial to a good harvest. After the June drop, but before the fruit is 1¼ inches in diameter, thin to one fruit per 30 to 40 leaves, *or* one fruit per 10 inches on early-ripening varieties, *or* one fruit per 6 to 8 inches on late-ripening varieties.

"Cling" varieties are firm and best for canning but are rarely available to home growers. "Freestone" varieties don't can well. Peach trees live a mere 8 years in the South and up to 18 years in the North; poor drainage renders even shorter life cycles.

SITE

Full south or southeast exposure, whether or not espaliered. Will not survive on heavy clay soils. Do not plant on former apricot, cherry, or peach tree sites; when waterlogged, their roots release hydrogen cyanide that may linger in the soil and hinder growth.

SOIL & WATER NEEDS

pH: 6.0–6.5

Fertilizer: Low N when under 3 years. Appropriate new growth is 12″–15″ when young, and 8″–18″ when bearing.

Water: Keeping the peach's shallow roots evenly moist is critical.

MEASUREMENTS

Root Depth: Shallow, over 90% in top 18″. Roots won't branch out if planted too deeply.

Height:

- Dwarf: 4′–10′
- Standard: 15′–20′

Spacing:

- Dwarf: 12′–15′
- Standard: 15′–25′

GROWING & BEARING

Bearing Age: 2–3 years

Chilling Requirement: Most need 600–900 hours below 45°F/8°C.

Pollination: Most self-pollinate, but yields will be higher with cross-pollination.

SHAPING

Training:

- Freestanding: Open center
- Wire-trained: Fan, against a south-facing wall

Pruning: Unlike apple, peach bears fruits on 1-year-old wood only and should be pruned to encourage new growth. Cut out branches that shade or cross each other, intrude on the center, or are winter-damaged. Remove at least one-third of the previous year's growth or too much fruit will be set. Every few years, cut out some older wood. Cut back upright-growing shoots to the outward-pointing buds.

PESTS

Aphid, birds, cherry fruit sawfly, codling moth, gopher, Japanese beetle, mite, oriental fruit moth, peach tree borer, plum curculio, root lesion nematode, spongy moth caterpillar, tarnished plant bug, tent caterpillar, weevil, whitefly

DISEASES

Bacterial canker, bacterial spot, brown rot, crown gall, cytospora canker, peach leaf curl, scab, verticillium wilt

ALLIES

Some Evidence: Alder, brambles, buckwheat, goldenrod, lamb's quarters, ragweed, rye mulch, smartweed, sorghum mulch, strawberry, wheat mulch

Uncertain: Caraway, coriander, dill, garlic, nasturtium, tansy, vetch, wildflowers, wormwood

Bird Control: A border of dogwood, mulberry, or other aromatic fruit, all of which birds prefer

INCOMPATIBLES

None

HARVEST

Pick when fruit is firm, almost ready to eat, and easily slides off the stem by tipping or twisting. Never pull it off directly or you'll bruise the peach and hasten spoilage. If fruit has a mild case of brown rot, harvest only those peaches that are infected and dip them in hot water for 7 minutes at 120°F/49°C (or alternatively, 3 minutes at 130°F/55°C or 2 minutes at 140°F/60°C). This kills the fungi without harming the fruit and prepares it to be stored for further ripening.

ROOTSTOCKS

See the Plum Rootstocks chart on pages 128–29, as most are the same for peaches. Peaches do best on a peach-seedling rootstock, which produces standard trees. Standard trees can be kept small by pruning. Elberta rootstocks are not hardy for the North.

Storage Requirements

To freeze the fruit, peel, pit, and cut it in halves or slices. Pack it with some honey mixed with lemon or a pectin pack. Peaches don't store well in a root cellar.

Fresh		
Temperature	**Humidity**	**Storage Life**
50°F–70°F/10°C–22°C	Low	3–14 days
Preserved		
Method	**Taste**	**Shelf Life**
Canned	Fair	Up to 2 years
Frozen	Good	12–24 months
Dried	Fair	12+ month

Pear

Pyrus communis
Rosaceae (Rose)

Pears are a good choice for backyard gardeners because they require less care than apples. Although they are more tolerant of heavy clay soils than are other fruits and prefer heavy organic mulches, they do not generally do well in light, sandy soils. They grow best in cool, moist, overcast conditions, which, unfortunately, are also perfect for fire blight, the most serious pear problem.

Pear blossoms are fairly frost resistant and can withstand temperatures as low as 28°F/−3°C. European pears don't usually need thinning because of a low "set ratio" (the number of blooms producing fruit). Asian pears should be thinned to one fruit per cluster to avoid overbearing. The higher the temperature immediately after blooming, the sooner the fruit will mature, generally in 106 to 124 days. Pears are among the longest-lived fruit trees, surviving to 200 to 300 years and producing for 100 years or more.

SITE

Full south or southeast exposure

SOIL & WATER NEEDS

pH: 6.0–6.5
Fertilizer: Avoid high N; pears need a lot of boron, so periodically check soil for deficiency.
Water: Heavy and constant supply; ground irrigation is especially important to minimize fire blight.

MEASUREMENTS

Root Depth: Deep
Height:

- Dwarf: 8′–15′
- Semidwarf: 15′–20′
- Standard: 30′–40′

Spacing:
Dwarf

- Cordon: 3′
- Espalier: 15′
- Fan: 15′
- Pyramid: 5′

Semidwarf: 20′
Standard: 30′

GROWING & BEARING

Bearing Age: 2–4 years
Chilling Requirement: Most need 600–900 hours below 45°F/8°C.
Pollination: All require cross-pollination.

SUPPORT STRUCTURES

Limb spreaders strengthen joints and encourage earlier blossoming and higher yields. More than other fruit trees, pear branches sag with fruit and may need to be tied up.

SHAPING

Training:

- Freestanding: Central leader for Comice and Anjou; open center for Bartlett, Bosc, those with flexible limbs, and those susceptible to fire blight
- Wire-trained: All cordons, espalier, stepover, palmettes

Pruning: Cut as little as possible because each cut exposes tissue to fire blight.

PESTS

Aphid, apple maggot, cherry fruit fly, codling moth, European apple sawfly, flea beetle, mite, oriental fruit moth, pear psylla, pear slug, plum curculio, gypsy moth, tarnished plant bug, tent caterpillar, thrips, weevil, whitefly

DISEASES

Bitter pit, blossom blast (boron deficiency), cedar apple rust, crown gall, crown rot, cytospora canker, fire blight, pear curl, pear decline, scab

ALLIES

Some Evidence: Alder, brambles, buckwheat, mulching with rye, sorghum, or wheat

Uncertain: Caraway, coriander, dill, garlic, nasturtium, tansy, vetch, wildflowers, wormwood

INCOMPATIBLES: None

HARVEST

Pick when pears are at least 2″ in diameter. Don't allow European varieties to ripen on the tree, as they'll become mealy and coarse. Handle carefully; although the fruit appears hard, it bruises easily. Asian pears should ripen on the tree.

ROOTSTOCKS

Quince is the most dwarfing rootstock, but it isn't as hardy as the pear, increases the tree's susceptibility to fire blight, needs staking, and doesn't do well in poorly drained soils. It has some resistance to pear decline and to pear root aphids. If fire blight is a problem for you, but you must use quince to achieve the most dwarfed tree, choose varieties that have the highest natural fire blight resistance. One superior root stock, a cross of Old Home and Farmingdale (OHxF), offers resistance to fire blight and pear decline and better tolerance to heavy, wet soils. For standard trees, the most common rootstock is the Bartlett seedling, which is hardy to winter cold but very susceptible to fire blight, nematodes, pear root aphids, and pear decline.

Storage Requirements

Some pears require lengthy storage before they begin to ripen, but if left in cold storage too long some will never ripen. After cold storage, ideal ripening temperature is 60°F–70°F/16°C–22°C; some pears won't ripen after cold storage if the home temperature is too high. If you wish to avoid the need for cold storage, place pears in a paper bag with ripe apples or pears; these emit ethylene gas, which stimulates the final stages of fruit ripening.

Pear	Minimum Storage Life at 30°F–32°F/–2°C–0°C	Maximum Storage Life at 30°F–32°F/–2°C–0°C	Maximum Storage Life at 40°F–42°F/5°C–6°C
Anjou	2 months	4–6 months	2–3 months
Bartlett	None	1½ months	2–3 weeks
Bosc	None	3–3½ months	2–2½ months
Comice	1 month	2½–3 months	1½–2 months
Seckel	None	3–3½ months	None

From Diane E. Bilderback and Dorothy Hinshaw Patent, *Backyard Fruit and Berries* (Emmaus, Penn.: Rodale, 1984), 218.

Pecan

Carya illinoinensis
Juglandaceae (Walnut Family)

The pecan is a member of the walnut family and is usually cultivated in mild regions. In order to produce filled nuts, the tree requires a long and hot growing season, averaging 75°F to 85°F/24°C to 30°C, with a minimum average of 1000 cooling-degree days and 140 to 250 frost-free days. Midwest states are more suited for nut production than northeastern states such as Connecticut because, despite being at the same latitude, they usually experience higher summer temperatures.

The four major groups of pecan cultivars are adapted to the Southwest, Southeast, and North. Pecans tend to bear in alternate years. They bloom in late spring and summer. High humidity at bloom time can hinder pollination, increase disease, and at harvesttime cause nuts to sprout while still in the husks. Look for grafted trees, which produce earlier than seedling stock. In choosing cultivars, note that vigorous growers usually bear heavily, and trees that break dormancy in late spring will suffer the least frost damage. Also, the smaller the transplant, the less injury to the taproot.

SITE

Full sun and rich, well-drained soil

SOIL & WATER NEEDS

pH: 5.8–7.5
Fertilizer: Low N when young
Side-Dressing: Apply compost in late winter to early spring.
Mulch: Avoid sawdust.
Water: Medium, but during drought periods water up to 3″–4″ per week.

MEASUREMENTS

Root Depth: Very deep
Height: 75′–100′
Spacing: 25′× 25′ to 70′ × 70′ (depending on the variety)

GROWING & BEARING

Bearing Age: 3–4 years in the South; 8–10 years in the North
Chilling Requirement: Most require some chilling but the hours depend on the variety (200–1600).
Pollination: Self-fertile but nuts will be higher quality with cross-pollination.

SHAPING

Training:

- Freestanding: Central leader
- Wire-trained: N/A

Pruning: At planting, cut back one-third to one-half of the top, to 2″–3″ above a bud facing the prevailing wind. Cut out crowded and crossed branches.

PESTS

Aphid, birds, fall webworm, hickory shuckworm, pecan casebearer, pecan weevil, scale, squirrel, walnut caterpillar

DISEASES

Canker dieback, crown gall, liver spot, pecan bunch, root rot, scab, sunscald, walnut bunch

ALLIES: None

COMPANIONS: None

INCOMPATIBLES: None

HARVEST

Gather nuts from October to January. As the pecan matures, the outer hull splits to expose the inner nut; as the hull dries, the nut falls to the ground. For most varieties, the limbs must be shaken to encourage nut drop. Spread a canvas sheet on the ground before shaking to collect the nuts. Don't begin harvesting until the hulls of the nuts on the inner part of the tree have split open; they will mature last.

Storage Requirements

Place hulled nuts in water, and remove the rotten and diseased nuts that float to the top. Dry and cure by spreading a single layer of nuts in a cool, dry, well-ventilated area. They're ready for storage when the kernels rattle in the shell or when unshelled nutmeats snap when bent. Store unshelled nuts in attics over winter or in cool underground cellars, where they'll keep for a year. Store shelled nuts in ventilated plastic bags or in tightly sealed, paper-lined tins that have a hole punctured in the side beneath the lid. Shelled nuts can also be stored in the refrigerator or freezer for up to a year.

Fresh		
Temperature	**Humidity**	**Storage Life**
34°F–40°F/2°C–5°C	Dry	12+ months

Plum

Prunus domestica and *P. salicina*
Rosaceae (Rose Family)

Plums are naturally smaller than apple, pear, and peach trees and, as a rule, grow well wherever pears do. For a stone fruit, plums offer an unusual range of flavors, sizes, and shapes. Japanese plums, now common in stores, are extremely juicy and soft and make excellent dessert fruits. European plums are much sweeter and dry well as prunes. Plum curculio greatly damages plums. Thin fruit no later than 2 months after full bloom. For both European and Japanese, allow only one fruit per spur or cluster. While usually self-thinning, European plums may need to be thinned to 2 to 3 inches apart. Japanese, a more vigorous tree, should be thinned to 4 to 5 inches. When thinning, destroy any fruit having the curculio's crescent-shaped, egg-laying scar.

SITE

See Incompatibles. Plums need well-drained soil and at least 8 hours of sun.

European and Damson: Heavy loam and south or southeast exposure.

Japanese and Beach: Sandy loam, and northern slope or 12′–15′ north of a building to minimize premature bloom and frost loss

SOIL & WATER NEEDS

pH: 6.0–8.0

Fertilizer: Low N in first 3 years. They may need K and Z supplements. Appropriate new growth for European plums is 16″–18″ when young, and 10″–14″ when bearing fruit. Appropriate growth for Japanese plums is 18″–20″ when young, and 15″–18″ when bearing.

Side-Dressing: In spring, apply a layer of compost or a mixture of well-rotted manure and wood ashes.

Water: Medium. Consistent watering is critical. Avoid watering in autumn, except in droughts.

MEASUREMENTS

Root Depth: Depends on rootstock, generally shallow.

Height:

- Dwarf: 3′–5′
- Semidwarf: 14′
- Standard: 16′–30′

Spacing:

- Dwarf: 8′–12′
- Semidwarf: 12′–20′
- Standard: 20′–25′

GROWING & BEARING

Bearing Age:

- European: 4–5 years
- Japanese: 2–3 years

Chilling Requirement: European plums need 700–1000 hours below 45°F/8°C, while Japanese need 500–900 hours.

Pollination: European are usually self-pollinating; Japanese need cross-pollination.

SUPPORT STRUCTURES

Use a forked prop to support heavy fruiting branches.

SHAPING

Training:

- Freestanding: Open center for Japanese; central leader or dwarf pyramid for European
- Wire-trained: Fan

Pruning: Never prune in winter. Trees are best pruned only after the tree starts to bear fruit. Europeans require little pruning while Japanese require harder pruning. Fruit is on spurs 2″–6″ long that live 5–8 years, so don't prune these.

PESTS

Aphid, apple maggot, birds, cankerworm, cherry fruit fly, cherry fruit sawfly, European apple sawfly, fall webworm, flathead borer, mite, oriental fruit moth, peach tree borer, peach twig borer, pear slug, plum curculio, weevil, whitefly

DISEASES

Bacterial spot, black knot, brown rot, cherry leaf spot, crown gall, cytospora canker, peach leaf curl, powdery mildew, verticillium wilt

ALLIES

Some Evidence: Alder, brambles, buckwheat, mulching with rye, sorghum, or wheat

Uncertain: Caraway, coriander, dill, garlic, nasturtium, tansy, vetch, wildflowers, wormwood

INCOMPATIBLES

Don't plant where the following have grown in the previous 3 years: cocklebur, eggplant, ground cherry, horse nettle, lamb's quarters, pepper, pigweed, potato, raspberry, strawberry, tomato, weeds in nightshade family

Storage Requirements

Ripen Japanese plums at 60°F–65°F/16°C–19°C; if not too soft, they can be stacked.

Fresh		
Temperature	**Humidity**	**Storage Life**
37°F–40°F/3°C–5°C	90%	2 weeks

Preserved		
Method	**Taste**	**Shelf Life**
Canned	Good	Up to 2 years
Frozen	Good	12–24 months
Dried	Good	6–24 months

HARVEST

Plums turn color 20–30 days before harvest. Pick when the fruit starts to soften and comes off with a slight twist. Be careful not to injure the spurs.

European Plums: For fresh eating, pick when ripe; for cooking, pick underripe.

Japanese Plums: Always pick underripe; if allowed to fully ripen on the tree, they will be overripe.

SELECTED VARIETIES

European. These are the sweetest plums; pollinate them with other Europeans, damsons, or Americans.

Damson (*P. insititia*). Very small and tart, these are best suited for preserves and cooking.

Beach (*P. maritima*). These plums are good in poor soil and are extremely hardy. Pollinate with other beach.

ROOTSTOCKS

Unlike apple trees, standard-sized plum trees are naturally smaller and can be kept small by pruning. Because of this, a particularly dwarfing rootstock is not essential for espalier work. Pay attention to variety characteristics also, as each has a different growing habit. For example, a Japanese plum, which is naturally more vigorous, might be better on a more dwarfing stock than would a European plum. Buy smaller trees when possible because they suffer less transplanting shock; in several years they're more productive and vigorous than a larger transplant.

Most nurseries don't offer an in-house choice of rootstocks. The purpose of the chart at right is not to help you make an independent decision but to help you engage the nursery grower with informed questions about what will grow best in your garden.

Plum Rootstocks

Rootstock Name	Size (percent of standard)
Citation	Dwarf 70%–85%
Marianna 2624	Semidwarf 90%
Myrobolan	Standard 100%
Myrobolan 29c	Standard 100%
P. americana (Bailey)	Standard 100%
P. americana (St. Julien)	Dwarf 70%–80%
P. pumila var. *besseyi* (Western Sand Cherry)	Dwarf 20%–35%
P. domestica (Pixie)	Dwarf 30%–40%
P. persica (Nemaguard)	Augmented 110%
P. tomentosa (Nanking Cherry)	Minidwarf 15%–25%

From Robert Kourik, *Designing and Maintaining Your Edible landscape Naturally* (Santa Rosa, Calif.: Metamorphic Press, 1986), 175–76.

Plum Rootstock Pests and Diseases

Rootstock Name	Crown Rot
Citation	Low resistance
Marianna 2624	Moderately resistant
Myrobolan	Moderately resistant
Myrobolan 29c	Moderately resistant
P. americana (Bailey)	——
P. americana (St. Julien)	Low resistance
P. pumila var. *besseyi* (Western Sand Cherry)	Highly resistant
P. domestica (Pixie)	Low resistance
P. persica (Nemaguard)	Low resistance
P. tomentosa (Nanking Cherry)	Highly resistant

From Robert Kourik, *Designing and Maintaining Your Edible landscape Naturally* (Santa Rosa, Calif.: Metamorphic Press, 1986), 175–76.

Height/Width	Best Soil	Anchorage	Hardiness	Precocious	Other Factors
H: 14′/W: 13′	Sandy loam	Good	——	——	Good disease and pest resistance
H: 16′/W: 14′	Clay loam	Good	——	——	
H: 18′/W: 16′	Clay loam	Excellent	——	——	
H: 18′/W: 16′	Clay loam	Fair	——	——	
H: 18′/W: 16′	Sandy loam	——	Hardy	——	
H: 10′–15′/W: 13′	Sandy loam	Good	Hardy	——	Good disease resistance; Citation can replace this.
H: 3′–5′/W: 3′–5′	Loam	Poor	Hardy	——	Lives less than 8 years.
H: 6′/W: 5′	Loam	Good	——	Precocious	Rootstock promotes small fruit.
H: 20′/W: 18′	Clay loam	Very good	——	——	
H: 2′–4′/W: 2′–3′	Loam	Poor	Hardy	Very precocious	Lives less than 10 years.

Oak Root Fungus	Nematode	Crown Gall	Bacterial Canker	Mice	Borer
——	Moderately resistant	Susceptible	——	——	——
Moderately resistant	Resistant	Moderately resistant	Highly susceptible	Moderately resistant	——
Moderately susceptible	Resistant	Moderately resistant	Susceptible	Susceptible	Susceptible
Moderately susceptible	Susceptible	Highly susceptible	Susceptible	Susceptible	Susceptible
——	——	——	Resistant	——	——
Susceptible	——	——	Resistant	Susceptible	——
——	——	——	Susceptible	——	——
——	Moderately resistant	——	Moderately resistant	——	——
Susceptible	Resistant	Susceptible	Susceptible	Moderately resistant	Highly susceptible
——	——	——	Susceptible	——	——

Raspberry

Rubus idaeus, *R. occidentalis*, and *R. strigosus*
Rosaceae (Rose Family)

Red raspberries are one of the most delicate and prized berry types and are considered the hardiest bramble fruit. Sufficient light and adequate spacing are two critical factors in raspberry production; without these, berries may be produced only on the upper half of the canes rather than all the way to the bottom. Yield also depends on the length of the cane after pruning, winterkill effects on blossoms, and the thickness of the canes. (See Blackberry, page 98, for yields, rows, floricanes, primocanes.) The everbearing raspberry cane bears annually: Its floricanes bear a summer crop, and its primocanes bear on their tips in fall and on their bottom the following summer. For continuous harvest, try growing biennials for a spring crop and everbearers for a bumper fall crop (see Shaping, page 131). Always select certified disease-free stock.

SITE

Full sun; rich loam; good drainage; east-facing spot sheltered from late afternoon sun. Plant at least 300 feet away from any wild brambles, which harbor insect and disease pests. Also keep at a distance from different types of berries to minimize cross-pollination.

SOIL & WATER NEEDS

pH: 5.5–7.0

Fertilizer: See Blackberry, page 98.

Mulch: See Blackberry, page 98. One gardener, who has a 60-year-old blackberry patch, layers 8″–10″ of leaf mulch in autumn, and some wood ashes in winter to counter leaf acidity. He rarely needs to water.

Water: See Blackberry, page 98.

MEASUREMENTS

Root Depth: 12″

Height: 5′–10′

Spacing:

- Red and yellow: 2′–4′ in a row (suckers and new canes will fill out row)
- Black and purple: 3′–4′ in hills (no suckers, but need room for branching canes)

GROWING & BEARING

Bearing Age: 2 years

Chilling Requirement: Most require some chilling, but the amount depends on variety.

Pollination: Self-pollinating

PROPAGATION

Red and yellow by suckers; black and purple by layering. See Blackberry, page 98.

SHAPING

Training: A trellis is important for disease and pest reduction, quality fruit, and easy harvest. Place bottom wire at 2′, middle wire at 3′, and top wire at 4′ for black and purple, or 5′ for red and yellow. Fan out canes and tie with cloth strips.

Pruning: After harvest or in spring, cut out thin, weak, spindly, or sick canes, and ones finished bearing.

- Red and yellow: thin to 8 canes per 3 row-feet, or 4″–6″ soil per cane. "Topping off" canes lowers yields, so don't do it unless the cane is taller than 6′. Cut out most sucker growth.
- Everbearers: Cut to 5–7 canes per hill. To encourage branching, when primocanes are 18″–24″ cut off the top 3″–4″ of the cane ("topping off"). In late winter, cut lateral branches back to 8″–12″ long.

PESTS

Aphid, birds, caneborer, flea beetle, fruit fly (spotted wing drosophila), fungus beetle (in ripe fruits), Japanese beetle, mite, raspberry root borer, sap beetle, strawberry weevil, tarnished plant bug, weevil, whitefly

DISEASES

Anthracnose, botrytis fruit rot, cane blight, cane gall, crown gall, leaf curl, leaf spot, mosaic, powdery mildew, rust, verticillium wilt

ALLIES

Uncertain: Garlic, rue, tansy

COMPANIONS

If berries are planted down the center of a 3′ bed, plant beans or peas in the first summer to keep the bed in production and to add organic matter and N to the soil.

INCOMPATIBLES

Because of verticillium wilt, don't plant where the nightshade family was grown in last 3 years.

OTHER

Raspberries, unlike most other plants, do tolerate the juglone in black walnut roots.

HARVEST

When berries slide off easily without pressure, harvest into very small containers so berries on the bottom won't be crushed. After harvesting, cut floricanes to the ground; on everbearers cut the tips of primocanes. Burn or destroy all canes for disease control.

Storage Requirements

To freeze, spread out berries on cookie sheets and freeze within 2 days of harvest. When rock hard, store in heavy freezer bags. Refrigerated, berries keep 4–7 days.

Preserved		
Method	**Taste**	**Shelf Life**
Canned (as jam)	Excellent	Up to 2 years
Frozen	Excellent	12–24 months
Dried	Good	6–24 months

Strawberry

Fragaria × ananassa

Rosaceae (Rose Family)

Plan about 24 plants to feed a family of four strawberry lovers. Junebearer strawberries yield a single crop in June or July and make lots of runners. Everbearing strawberries yield a first crop in June or July and a second in late summer or early fall; they require 15 hours of daylight or more during summer (unless it is a newer "day-neutral" type). If your area suffers late-spring frosts, choose varieties that flower late and tolerate high humidity. Try to buy certified virus-free plants.

When planting, cover all roots, but keep the upper two-thirds of the crown above the soil line. To promote a healthier, more productive plant, deflower all Junebearers the first year and everbearers only in their first late-spring flowering. For a bumper fall crop, you can deflower everbearers yearly in June. Most strawberry plants reproduce by runners. These can be pinched off to produce larger berries but lower yields, or trained to 7 to 10 inches for smaller berries and higher yields.

Strawberries become less productive each year, so beds are renewed by various methods. For a perennial bed, try the spaced-runner system. Space plants in rows 2 to 4 feet apart; train runners to 7 to 8 inches apart by pinning them down with clothespins or hairpins. Cut off excess runners to maintain spacing. In year 2, train runners into the central paths. Immediately after harvest in years 2 or 3, mow down the original plants, till several times, spread lots of compost, till a final time, and mulch with chopped leaves or compost every 2 weeks until fall. Every 2 or 3 years the pathways and growing beds trade places. Also, University of Wisconsin studies have shown enhanced yields when Regal perennial rye grass is grown as a living mulch and mowed to 2 to 3 inches two or three times per year.

SITE

Good drainage. North-facing, sunny slope to delay blossoms in areas susceptible to late frost. The previous fall, prepare beds with 5 pounds manure per 10 square feet; repeat whenever renewing.

SOIL & WATER NEEDS

pH: 5.5–6.8

Fertilizer: Low N; apply very lightly and often rather than in two heavy feedings.

Mulch: Apply 3″–4″ after ground is frozen hard, remove in spring, and replace in hot weather. Do not cover crowns. Row covers through winter, rather than mulch, produce higher yields. Pull off covers during April bloom (replace if frost is expected).

Water: Medium

MEASUREMENTS

Root Depth: Shallow; up to 8″

Height: 8″–12″

Breadth: 6″–12″

Spacing between Plants: 8″–15″

Space between Rows: 2′–5½′

GROWING & BEARING

Bearing Age:

- Everbearing (including newer day-neutrals): At end of first summer planted
- Junebearing: 1 year after planting; in the Deep South, fall plantings may bear in early spring.

Chilling Requirement: Most require chilling hours; amount depends on variety.

Pollination: Self-fertile, self-pollinating

SHAPING

Thinning: When runners get too prolific for a solid 7″–8″ spacing, cut off excess runners.

PESTS

Aphid, birds, crownborer, earwig, flea beetle, garden webworm, Japanese and June beetles, leafroller, mice, mite, nematode, pill bug, root weevil, sap beetle, slug, snail, strawberry beetle, tarnished plant bug, weevil, white grub, wireworm

DISEASES

Anthracnose, botrytis fruit rot, leaf blight, leaf scorch, leaf spot, powdery mildew, red stele, root rot, septoria leaf spot, verticillium wilt, walnut bunch, yellows

ALLIES

Some evidence: White clover

Uncertain: Alfalfa, borage, thyme

COMPANIONS

Bush beans, lettuce, onion family, sage, spinach

INCOMPATIBLES

All brassicas

HARVEST

A few days before harvest you may want to apply foliar calcium chloride. This can lengthen storage life by slowing ripening and delaying development of gray mold. Pick all berries as soon as ripe—whether damaged or not—to prevent disease. Handle gently to avoid bruising. Berries picked with green caps last longer in storage.

SELECTED VARIETIES

Junebearers. These are usually the highest-quality berries, yielding one crop per year in late spring or early summer.

Everbearers. These plants produce two main crops per year; for one large and late crop, just pick off all early-summer blossoms. The standard everbearer needs 15 hours or more of daylight, but a newer breed—day-neutral everbearers—are reportedly not affected by day length.

Storage Requirements		
Do not wash or remove green caps.		
Preserved		
Method	**Taste**	**Shelf Life**
Canned	Not good	Up to 2 years
Frozen	Excellent	12–24 months
Dried (as fruit leather)	Good	6–24 months
As jam	Excellent	Up to 18 months

Walnut

Juglans regia, *J. nigra*, *J. cinerea*, and *J. ailantifolia*
Juglandaceae (Walnut Family)

Black walnut and butternut roots excrete an acid (juglone) that inhibits the growth of many plants, so plant them far away from vegetables and flowers. Weed control is vital to the initial years of walnut tree growth. All walnuts benefit from mulching. Walnut trees grown for nut crops require large crowns; those grown for veneers need a straight trunk. To grow for both, favor veneer requirements and prune for straight growth.

Persian walnuts grow rapidly, about 4 to 5 feet per year. Black walnuts, the largest *Juglans,* have a strong flavor, so use sparingly in cooking. Grafted trees usually yield three to four times higher kernel filling than seedlings. Butternuts, or white walnuts, are the hardiest *Juglans,* don't require as much water, and have a rich, buttery taste. Buy the smallest tree possible to minimize injury to its straight and long taproot. True nut flavor and quality may not emerge for 2 to 3 years after bearing, so don't judge trees prematurely. Walnuts do better in mixed plantings than in a monoculture walnut grove.

SITE

Full sun; deep, well-drained loam. Don't plant anywhere near vegetable garden or orchard.

SOIL & WATER NEEDS

pH: 5.5–7.0; for Persian: 6.0–7.0
Fertilizer: Don't fertilize the first year. In following years, apply compost or well-rotted manure. When 10 years old, apply ½ pound boron (borax) in deep bar holes for steady nut production.
Water: Medium

MEASUREMENTS

Root Depth: Very deep
Height: 20′–80′
Breadth: 20′–40′
Spacing between Plants: 10′; when 10″ in diameter (about 25 years), thin to 22′–50′.

GROWING & BEARING

Bearing Age: 3–5 years for nuts; 10–20 years to produce veneer for market
Chilling Requirement: All require some chilling hours (400–1500).
Pollination: All walnuts require cross-pollination.

SHAPING

Training:

- Freestanding: Central leader
- Wire-trained: N/A

Pruning: Unlike most fruit and nut trees, prune walnuts in fall. Don't start until 4–5 years old. Cut out dead or diseased wood, and crossed or competing branches.

PESTS

Aphid, bluejay, codling moth, fall webworm, mouse, navel orangeworm, squirrel, walnut caterpillar, walnut husk fly, walnut maggot

DISEASES

Crown gall, walnut anthracnose, walnut blight, walnut bunch

ALLIES

Some Evidence: Weedy ground cover

COMPANIONS

Autumn olive, black locust, European alder, popcorn (for the first few years), raspberry, soybean.

INCOMPATIBLES

Apple, azalea, potato, tomato (which is particularly sensitive to walnut root acid)

HARVEST

Due to the indelible stains imparted by the husks, always wear gloves when harvesting walnuts. Remove the outer husks within 1 week of harvest, let dry for several days, after which the husks can be easily removed. There are three methods to dehusk a nut: (1) Use a corn sheller equipped with a flywheel and pulley, driven by ¼ hp motor; (2) spread a single layer in a wooden trough on a driveway and run a car or tractor over them, which splits the husk easily; (3) take them to a professional huller.

SELECTED SPECIES

- **Black (*J. nigra*).** The black walnut tree is native to eastern North America and can grow to towering heights of 120′ by 50′ wide. Hardy in Zones 4–10. Be aware that the tree, especially the roots, produce juglone, which can prevent growth or kill certain plants growing under or near them.
- **Persian (also Called English or Carpathian) (*J. regia*).** Because they leaf early, Persian walnuts grow best where peach trees don't suffer frost-kill. *Carpathian* refers to the mountain range in Poland, a source of many imported Persian walnuts; now it usually refers just to "hardy" cultivars.
- **Butternut (*J. cinerea*).** For location in the Ohio Valley and southward, choose varieties with "clean foliage" for anthracnose resistance. Increasingly scarce, these offer high-quality lumber. Hardy in Zones 3–7.
- **Heartnut (*J. ailantifolia*).** A Japanese ornamental walnut, these grow fast and bear nuts that hang in strings or clumps of 10–15. The heart-shaped nutmeat is the sweetest of all walnuts, with no bitterness; it is easy to extract and high in protein. The tree bears even in poor soils.

Storage Requirements

Rinse off hulled nutshells and place in water. Remove any rotten and diseased nuts that float to the top. Dry and cure by spreading in a single layer in a cool, dry, well-ventilated area. They're ready for storage when the kernels rattle in the shell—generally in 1–3 weeks—or when unshelled kernels snap when bent. Store shelled nuts in plastic bags with holes, or in tightly sealed, paper-lined tins (that have a hole punctured in the side beneath the lid), or freeze. Store unshelled nuts in an unheated shed during winter; in spring move them to a cool place.

Fresh		
Temperature	**Humidity**	**Storage Life**
32°F–36°F/0°C–3°C	60%–70%	1 year
Preserved		
Method	**Taste**	**Shelf Life**
Frozen (shelled)	Excellent	12–24 months

CHAPTER FOUR

herbs

Herbs offer a magnificent range of flavors and fragrances—including sweet, savory, mild, pungent, spicy, and earthy. They also offer a host of known health benefits such as helping to moderate blood sugar, reduce blood pressure, calm anxiety, promote regularity, and so much more. Many are also good medicine for a garden: Some are wonderful companion plants that attract beneficial insects, some repel pests, and others can be grown as "trap crops" to lure pests away from other plants.

Beyond these bountiful gifts that herbs offer to us, do you know their most amazing quality of all? They are easy! They require little fuss, most are pest-free, and most are easy to grow in small spaces or on windowsills. They're also easy to harvest, store, and use. Don't hesitate to start your gardening experience with a few of the more common herbs, and then experiment with how to use them for different purposes and in different recipes. Enjoy and feel proud, for you will be contributing to the continuation of one of our most valuable and ancient traditions.

Sweet Basil

Ocimum basilicum
Lamiaceae (Mint Family)

Basil is an annual warm-season herb that is particularly tender to frost and light freezes. It transplants easily and also can be grown easily in a greenhouse. Continuous harvest benefits this herb because pruning encourages new growth. A study by the University of California at Davis advises against storing basil in the refrigerator, for it lasts longer when kept in a glass of water at room temperature. Basil, fresh or dried, is a popular seasoning. Some culinary experts suggest that dried basil simply cannot compare with the flavor of fresh basil, but few true basil lovers will pass up either. Basil comes in a range of varieties, from purple to lime green, curly to ruffled-edged leaves, and smooth to hairy leaves. An ingredient in the liqueur Chartreuse, basil may be minty or hint of clove or cinnamon.

SITE

Full sun; protected

TEMPERATURE

For Germination: 75°F–86°F/24°C–30°C

For Growth: Hot

SOIL & WATER NEEDS

pH: 5.5–7.0

Fertilizer: Light feeder

Side-Dressing: Not necessary

Water: Low, but evenly moist

First Seed-Starting Date

Germinate	+	Transplant	–	Days after LFD	=	Count Back from LFD
3–9 days	+	7 –14 days	–	14 days	=	9 days before LFD–4 days after LFD

Last Seed-Starting Date

Germinate	+	Transplant	+	Maturity	+	SD Factor	+	Frost Tender	=	Count Back from FFD
3–9 days	+	9–14 days	+	30–50 days	+	14 days	+	14 days	=	70–101 days

MEASUREMENTS

Planting Depth: ¼″

Root Depth: 8″–12″

Height: 18″–24″

Breadth: 20″–30″

Space between Plants:

- In beds: 10″–12″
- In rows: 12″–18″

Space between Rows: 15″–25″

PROPAGATION

By seed

PESTS

Japanese beetle, slug, snail

DISEASES

Botrytis rot, damping off

COMPANIONS

Pepper, tomato

OTHER

Basil is said to repel flies and mosquitoes, and to improve growth and flavor of vegetables.

INCOMPATIBLES

Cucumber, rue, snap beans. Basil is also alleged to lower cabbage yields and cause a higher incidence of whiteflies in snap beans.

HARVEST

Pick continuously before flower buds open, up to 6″ below the flower buds or ends to encourage continuous bushy growth. Cut in the morning after the dew has dried. Do not wash the leaves or aromatic oils will be lost.

GREENHOUSE

All varieties work well.

Storage Requirements

Leaves can be used fresh, dried, or preserved in oil (must be refrigerated) or vinegar. To dry, find a warm, dry, dark place and hang bunches of snipped stems with leaves, or spread leaves on a wire mesh. When thoroughly dry, strip leaves off stems. Do not crush or grind leaves until you're ready to use them. Store in airtight containers or freezer bags in a dark place. Some people believe that basil stored in oil or vinegar is more flavorful than dried. If storing frozen pesto, don't add garlic until you are ready to serve because garlic can become bitter in the freezer.

Method	Taste
Frozen	Excellent (particularly for pesto)
Dried	Fair–good (relative to fresh basil)
Fresh	Excellent

Caraway

Carum carvi
Apiaceae (Parsley Family)

Caraway is a biennial warm-season herb, tender to frost and light freezes. It is commonly grown as an annual in most areas of the United States except for northern California, where it reportedly doesn't grow well. Sow it directly, as it doesn't transplant well, or transplant it while it's still small. It flowers in spring and produces seed in its second summer—or in its first summer if sown in fall. Caraway roots, which are long taproots, can be eaten like carrots. The leaves can be used in salads, soups, or stews. Some trace the use of caraway back to the Stone Age; it has a long history of medicinal use to aid digestion and lactation, relieve flatulence, and as an antispasmodic and antiseptic. It's a popular ingredient in German and Austrian cuisine, cheeses, and breads, and its oil is used to flavor aquavit and the liqueur kümmel.

SITE

Full sun to light shade

TEMPERATURE

For Germination: 70°F/22°C
For Growth: Warm

SOIL & WATER NEEDS

pH: 5.5–7.0
Fertilizer: Light feeder
Side-Dressing: Not necessary
Water: Low, but evenly moist

First Seed-Starting Date

Germinate	+	Transplant	+	Days before LFD	=	Count Back from LFD
17 days	+	0 (direct)	+	0–7 days	=	17–24 days

Last Seed-Starting Date

Germinate	+	Transplant	+	Maturity	+	SD Factor	+	Frost Tender	=	Count Back from FFD
17 days	+	0 (direct)	+	55 days	+	14 days	+	N/A	=	86 days

MEASUREMENTS

Planting Depth: ¼″–½″

Root Depth: Long taproot

Height: 2′–3′

Breadth: 12″–18″

Space between Plants:

- In beds: 6″
- In rows: 12″–18″

Space between Rows: 18″–24″

PROPAGATION

By seed and cuttings

PESTS

Carrot rust fly

DISEASES

None

COMPANIONS

Coriander, fruit trees, pea

INCOMPATIBLES

Fennel

OTHER

Caraway is said to be good for loosening the soil and is reputed to attract beneficial insects to fruit trees.

HARVEST

When the seeds are brown and before they begin to fall, snip the stalks. Tie in bundles and hang upside down in a warm, dry, airy place. Place paper-lined trays under the stalks to collect falling seeds, or cover them with a paper bag and let the seeds drop into the bag. Shaking the stalks can dislodge the seeds. After a few weeks, when the fallen seeds are thoroughly dry, store them in an airtight jar.

GREENHOUSE

Caraway should grow well in the greenhouse if grown in a pot deep enough to accommodate its taproot.

Storage Requirements

Store in airtight jars in a cool, dark place.

Method	Taste
Frozen	Caraway leaf doesn't freeze well.
Dried	Seed is excellent dried.

Chives

Allium schoenoprasum
Liliaceae (Lily Family)

Chives are a perennial warm-season herb, hardy to frost and light freezes, and the earliest to appear in spring. This herb likes rich and well-drained soil but can be found growing wild in dry, rocky places in northern Europe and in the northeastern United States and Canada. They also thrive in a cool greenhouse or on a kitchen windowsill. Chives are virtually foolproof because they suffer no diseases or pests. After several years, you can divide them for expansion or renewal and in autumn dig up a clump to pot indoors for continuous winter cutting. Chives blossom midsummer and are an attractive ornamental addition to the garden; if allowed to bloom, cut them back after flowering so new shoots will come up in spring. With a milder flavor than onion, chives are usually snipped raw as a finishing touch for salads, soups, sauces, and vegetable and fish dishes. Chives also work well in egg dishes such as quiche and omelettes.

SITE

Full sun to light shade

TEMPERATURE

For Germination: 60°F–70°F/16°C–22°C
For Growth: Hot

SOIL & WATER NEEDS

pH: 5.5–7.0
Fertilizer: Light feeder
Side-Dressing: None
Water: Average

First Seed-Starting Date

Chives mature in 50 days, whether or not transplanted.

Germinate	+	Transplant	+	Days before LFD	=	Count Back from LFD
10–14 days	+	21–42 days	+	0 days	=	31–56 days

MEASUREMENTS

Planting Depth: ¼″–½″

Root Depth: Bulb clumps

Height: 6″–18″

Breadth: 6″–8″

Space between Plants:

- In beds: 6″
- In rows: 5″–8″

Space between Rows: 12″

PROPAGATION

Division or seed; every 3 years, in mid-May, divide plant into clumps of 6 bulbs

PESTS

None

DISEASES

None

COMPANIONS

Carrot, celery, grape, pea, rose, tomato

INCOMPATIBLES

Beans, pea

OTHER

Chives are a putative deterrent to aphids on celery, lettuce, and peas; black spot on roses; Japanese beetles; mildew on cucurbits; and scab on apples.

HARVEST

After the plant is 6″ tall cut some of the blades down to 2″ above the ground to encourage plant production. Herbs should be cut in the morning after the dew has dried. Cut near the base of the greenery, not the chive tips, so new, gender shoots will emerge. Do not wash the cuttings or aromatic oils will be lost.

GREENHOUSE

All chives grow well in a cool greenhouse or on a windowsill.

Storage Requirements

Chives are best fresh or frozen but can also be dried. To dry, tie them in small bunches and hang them upside down in a warm, dry, dark place. Do not crush or cut until ready to use. Store the stem whole, if possible. If harvested with the flower, chives can be stored whole in white vinegar to make a pretty, light lavender, mildly flavored vinegar for gifts. Another storage method—recommended by horticulturist Frank Gouin as an excellent way of preserving chive flavor—is to alternate layers, in a glass jar, of 1″ of kosher salt with 1″ of chives. Pack down each layer with a spoon. Use these chives in any dish, just as you would fresh chives; they're said to be especially good in soups. As an added bonus, the brine also can be used to flavor soups and other dishes.

Method	Taste
Frozen	Excellent
Dried	Fair–good
Fresh	Excellent

Coriander/Cilantro

Coriandrum sativum
Apiaceae (Parsley Family)

Coriander is an annual cool-season herb, tender to frost and light freezes. In some warmer climates, coriander is self-seeding. It grows easily, although it does go to seed quickly when the weather turns hot. For a steady supply of the leaf, try sowing in succession every 1 to 2 weeks. If you're growing it for seed, stake the plant at the time of sowing or transplanting.

All parts of the coriander are edible, including the root, which is similar in taste to the leaves but has an added nutty flavor. Unlike most herbs, fresh coriander leaf is usually either loved or hated. Make sure your guests can tolerate fresh coriander before including it in a dish. The coriander plant is said to attract useful insects, and coriander honey is famous for its flavor. An ancient herb with medicinal properties for aiding digestion and relieving rheumatism, coriander is recognized as the seed used in Indian and Mediterranean cuisine, whereas cilantro is the leaf used in Central and South American cuisines. Because it is used commonly in Chinese cuisine, cilantro is sometimes referred to as "Chinese parsley."

SITE

Full sun to partial shade

TEMPERATURE

For Germination: 50°F–70°F/10°C–22°C

For Growth: Cool

SOIL & WATER NEEDS

pH: 6.0–7.0

Fertilizer: Light feeder; N reduces flavor.

Side-Dressing: Not necessary

Water: Average

First Seed-Starting Date						
Germinate	+	**Transplant**	+	**Days before LFD**	=	**Count Back from LFD**
12 days	+	30 days	+	7–21 days	=	49–63 days

Last Seed-Starting Date										
Germinate	+	**Transplant**	+	**Maturity**	+	**SD Factor**	+	**Frost Tender**	=	**Count Back from FFD**
6 days	+	21 days	+	55 days	+	14 days	+	0 days	=	96 days

MEASUREMENTS

Planting Depth: ¼″–½″

Root Depth: 8″–18″

Height: 12″–21″

Breadth: 6″–12″

Space between Plants:

- In beds: 6″–8″
- In rows: 8″–12″

Space between Rows: 12″–15″

PROPAGATION

By seed

PESTS

Carrot rust fly

DISEASES

None

COMPANIONS

Caraway, eggplant, fruit trees, potato, tomato

INCOMPATIBLES

None

OTHER

Coriander is said to enhance anise growth. It is also a putative companion to fruit trees because it attracts beneficial insects.

HARVEST

Leaves, stems, roots, and seeds are used in food preparation. Snip stalks with small, immature leaves for fresh leaves with best flavor. Cut back the top growth up to 6″ below the flower buds or ends. Do not wash or aromatic oils will be lost. For seeds, harvest when the seeds and leaves turn brown but before seeds drop; cut the whole plant.

GREENHOUSE

Coriander grows well in the greenhouse.

Storage Requirements

Coriander leaves store poorly unless preserved in something like salsa, but even then its flavor can fade in a day. Coriander seeds, on the other hand, keep well in airtight jars. To dry seeds, tie the plant upside down in a warm, dry, dark place for several weeks until the seeds turn brown. Place stalks in a paper bag and thresh until all seeds are removed from stems. Sift out seeds from chaff. Another method to finish the drying process is to remove seeds from the stems and dry them in a slow oven (100°F/38°C) until they turn a light brown. You can smell the difference between properly air-dried or roasted coriander seed and seed that is still green. For best flavor, grind the seeds just before use. Store seeds in an airtight jar in a cool, dark place.

Method	Taste
Fresh	Excellent, cuttings last well 3–7 days refrigerated in water that is refreshed daily, longer if covered with a plastic bag.
Frozen	Some report excellent for leaf, some report poor.
Dried	Excellent for seed, poor for leaf

Dill

Anethum graveolens
Apiaceae (Parsley Family)

Dill is an annual or perennial warm-season herb, very sensitive to light freezes and frost. If it's not grown in a protected spot, stake it to keep the tall stocks upright. Because of its long taproot, dill does not transplant easily, so don't attempt to transplant it once it grows beyond the seedling stage. If dill is not planted early enough, seed may not develop until the beginning of the second year. It can be grown in the greenhouse if you provide a container large enough for its roots, at least 6 to 8 inches in diameter, and pot it in rich soil. In the garden, if allowed to go to seed without complete harvest, it will reseed itself and grow as a perennial. As a seed, it's used primarily for pickling. As dill weed, it's used to flavor sauces, fish, meats, soups, breads, and salads. For best flavor, snip the weed with scissors rather than mince it with a knife.

SITE

Full sun, sheltered from wind

TEMPERATURE

For Germination: 50°F–70°F/10°C–22°C
For Growth: Hot

SOIL & WATER NEEDS

pH: 5.5–6.5
Fertilizer: Light feeder; might need one application of compost or slow-release fertilizer.
Side-Dressing: Not necessary
Water: Average

MEASUREMENTS

Planting Depth: ¼″–½″
Root Depth: Very long, hollow taproot
Height: 3′–4′
Breadth: 24″
Space between Plants:

- For leaf: 8″–10″
- For seed: 10″–12″

Space between Rows: 18″–24″

PROPAGATION

By seed

First Seed-Starting Date

Sow every 3 weeks for a continuous supply of leaves.

Germinate	+	Transplant	–	Days after LFD	=	Count Back from LFD
14 days	+	21–30 days	–	14 days	=	21–30 days

PESTS

Carrot rust fly, green fly, parsleyworm, tomato hornworm

DISEASES

None

COMPANIONS

All brassicas, fruit trees

INCOMPATIBLES

Carrot, fennel (cross-pollinates with dill), tomato

OTHER

Some gardeners report that, in orchards, dill helps attract beneficial wasps, bees, and flies that pollinate blossoms and attack codling moths and tent caterpillars. Others report that it may help cabbage by repelling aphids, spider mites, and caterpillars. There is, however, no scientific study or proof of this.

HARVEST

Cut the tender feathery leaves close to the stem. Herbs should be cut in the morning after the dew has dried. Do not wash or aromatic oils will be lost. The flavor of dill foliage is best before the flower head develops and when used the same day it's cut. If you want to harvest dill seed, let the plant flower and go to seed. Harvest when the lower seeds turn brown and before they scatter. The lower seeds on a head will brown first; the upper ones can dry indoors. Finish drying by tying stems together and hanging them upside down in a cool, dark, dry place, or place in a paper bag with holes cut in the sides. Sift to remove the seed from chaff.

GREENHOUSE

Dill grows well in the greenhouse

Storage Requirements

Fresh dill keeps for up to 3 days when stored in a jar, with stems submerged in water, covered with plastic. It will store for up to 3 months in the refrigerator when layered with pickling salt in a covered jar. To use, just brush off the salt. To freeze, store on the stem in plastic bags. Cut off what you need and return the rest to the freezer. To dry the leaves, spread them over a nonmetallic screen in a dark, warm, dry place for several days. Then store in an airtight container. Crush or grind immediately before use.

Method	Taste
Frozen	Good for foliage
Dried	Good for foliage, excellent for seeds
Fresh	Excellent

Fennel

Foeniculum vulgare
Apiaceae (Parsley Family)

Fennel self-sows easily and is a perennial warm-season herb that is half-hardy to frost and light freezes. This herb is best sown in succession plantings in spring, as it tends to bolt in hot summers. For a fall crop, sow in July. If you're growing Florence fennel—renowned for its swollen and tender anise-flavored stalks—mound the soil around the base of the plant to promote more tender, blanched stalks. Fennel stems are a more common culinary item in Europe than in the United States. They're delicious raw in salads, steamed or sautéed with a little butter and wine, or added to soups, stews, and fish dishes. Fennel is reputed to have a broad range of medicinal uses that date back to the time of Hippocrates. Fennel leaves are thought by some to improve digestion, and fennel tea is believed to have antiflatulent and calming effects. With its mild aniseed flavor, fennel seed can be used whole or ground as a spice in breads, sausages, pizza and tomato sauce, stews, and fish and chicken dishes.

SITE

Full sun and rich, well-drained soil

TEMPERATURE

For Germination: 60°F–80°F/16°C–27°C
For Growth: Cool

SOIL & WATER NEEDS

pH: 5.5–7.0
Fertilizer: Light feeder
Side-Dressing: Not necessary
Water: Low, but evenly moist watering in times of drought

First Seed-Starting Date

Germinate	+	Transplant	+	Days before LFD	=	Count Back from LFD
6–17 days	+	10–28 days	+	26 days	=	42–71 days

Last Seed-Starting Date

Germinate	+	Transplant	+	Maturity	+	SD Factor	+	Frost Tender	=	Count Back from FFD
6–17 days	+	0 (direct)	+	60–70 days	+	14 days	+	14 days	=	94–115 days

MEASUREMENTS

Planting Depth: ¼″ (just barely covered with soil)
Root Depth: Taproot
Height: Up to 4′–5′ (may need staking)
Breadth: 12″–18″
Space between Plants:

- Sweet fennel: 6″
- Florence fennel: 10″–12″

PROPAGATION

By seed; divide and replant established plants every 3 years.

PESTS

Carrot rust fly

DISEASES

None

COMPANIONS

Most vegetables

INCOMPATIBLES

All beans, caraway, coriander (prevents seeds from forming), dill (cross-pollinates with fennel), pepper, tomato

HARVEST

For leaf clippings, you can start to cut the leaves once the plant is established. For fennel stems and bulbs, wait until the plant begins to bloom, pinch off the blooms, and allow the stems and bulb to fatten several more days. Cut them off at the base and use while fresh. For seeds, allow the plant to bloom. When the seeds turn brown, cut off the entire seed head and place it in a paper bag. Fennel seeds are very delicate and fall easily from the plant, so be sure to cut seed heads before the seeds are blown away. Dry in a warm, dark place for several weeks.

SELECTED VARIETIES

Sweet Fennel (*F. vulgare*). Sweet fennel is grown primarily for leaves and seeds.
Florence or Finocchio Fennel. Florence fennel is best for swollen bulbs and stalks.

Storage Requirements

Store seeds and dried leaf clippings in separate airtight jars in a cool, dark place. Dried leaf clippings lose their flavor over time. Stems and bulbs can be stored for 1–2 weeks in the refrigerator. You might also peel and store the stems in white vinegar with black peppercorns for use in salads.

Method	Taste
Frozen	Good for leaf clippings
Dried	Excellent for seed
Fresh	Excellent for fernlike leaves

Garlic

Allium sativum
Liliaceae (Lily Family)

Garlic is an annual or perennial cool-season crop and is hardy to frost and light freezes. Plant cloves in a sunny location in rich, deep, moist, well-drained soil. You may have to add compost to the soil before planting. Although it can be started from seed, it's easiest to grow from individual cloves. Garlic bulbs mature in an average of 6 to 10 months. Cloves may be planted in either fall or spring, but fall plantings yield larger bulbs the next summer than do spring plantings harvested in fall. Remove flower buds if they develop. Early cultivars store poorly and have inferior quality. Garlic is renowned for its broad range of culinary and medicinal uses, from reportedly imparting strength to laborers who built the pyramids to more modern studies about its antibacterial and beneficial circulatory effects.

SITE

Full sun

TEMPERATURE

For Germination: 60°F–80°F/16°C–27°C

For Growth: Cool

First Seed-Starting Date

Cloves can be planted about 6 weeks before the last frost.

Germinate	+	Transplant	+	Days before LFD	=	Count Back from LFD
7–14 days	+	0 (direct)	+	14–21 days	=	21–35 days

Last Seed-Starting Date

Cloves can be planted in autumn for harvest in spring.

Germinate	+	Transplant	+	Maturity	+	SD Factor	+	Frost Tender	=	Count Back from FFD
7 days	+	0 (direct)	+	90 days	+	14 days	+	0 days	=	111 days

SOIL & WATER NEEDS

pH: 4.5–8.3

Fertilizer: Light feeder; use compost and liquid seaweed extract.

Side-Dressing: Not necessary

Water: Low, for perennial bulbs, withhold all water during summer, except in arid, dry areas.

MEASUREMENTS

Planting Depth: 1″–2″ (pointed end up)

Root Depth:

- Bulbs: 2″–2′

Height: 1′–3′

Breadth: 6″–10″

Space between Plants:

- In beds: 3″
- In rows: 4″–6″

Space between Rows: 12″–15″

PROPAGATION

Usually propagated by cloves (easiest method), though garlic can be started from seeds.

PESTS

Nematode

DISEASES

Botrytis rot, white rot

COMPANIONS

Beet, brassicas, celery, chamomile, fruit trees, lettuce, raspberry, rose, savory, tomato

INCOMPATIBLES

All beans, pea

OTHER

Garlic spray has been found to have some antifungal properties in controlling bacterial blight of beans, bean anthracnose, brown rot of stone fruit, cucumber and bean rust, downy mildew, early tomato blight, leaf spot of cucumber, and soft-bodied insects such as aphids and leafroller larvae.

HARVEST

Green garlic shoots, a gourmet treat in many locales, can be cut from the bulbs going to flower and used like scallions. Garlic bulbs are ready to harvest when the tops turn brown and die back. Do not knock the tops down to hasten harvest; some research indicates this practice shortens storage life. Withhold water and, in a few days, dig carefully to lift the plants. The tops usually are not strong enough to pull. Be careful not to bruise bulbs or they'll get moldy and attract insects when stored.

Storage Requirements

Cure bulbs in the sun for several days to 2 weeks to harden the skins and dry. To braid, keep the tops on. Otherwise, clip off dried leaves and the root bunches. Store in paper bags, net bags, or nylon stockings, tying a knot between each bulb in the stocking.

Method	Temperature	Humidity	Storage Life
Fresh	32°F/0°C	65%–70%	6–7 months

Lavender

Lavandula angustifolia
Lamiaceae (Mint Family)

Lavender is a perennial warm-season herb, hardy to frost and light freezes in Zones 5 through 8. It likes full sun and light, well-drained soil. Lavender can be easily grown in containers in the greenhouse or on windowsills and trained to different forms. In addition to serving as a pretty border plant, dried lavender flowers are touted as an effective moth repellant, and lavender oil is used as an additive to soaps and sachets. For the best oil production, lavender needs hot, dry weather from May through August.

For centuries, lavender oils have been used for a broad variety of purposes, from curing lice, repelling mosquitoes, and embalming to use in porcelain lacquers, varnishes, and paints. Lavender is also used to make a light perfume; simply add rose petals, lavender flowers, and jasmine flowers to distilled vinegar and store in airtight bottles. In the kitchen, lavender flowers and leaves can be used to flavor jellies and vinegars, herb mixes for salads, and even lavender ice cream.

SITE

Full sun protected from wind; can be stony.

TEMPERATURE

For Germination: N/A

For Growth: Hot

SOIL & WATER NEEDS

pH: 6.5–7.0

Fertilizer: Light feeder; lime may be needed to make sure soil is basic enough.

Side-Dressing: Not necessary

Water: Low

MEASUREMENTS

Planting Depth: Cover roots

Root Depth: Deep

Height: 14″–3′

Breadth: Up to 5′

Space between Plants:

- In beds: 2′
- In rows: 4′–6′

Space between Rows: 6′

PROPAGATION

By cuttings or seed. Lavender is seldom started from seed because of its long germination time. In summer, take 2″–3″-long cuttings from the side shoots; make sure there is some older wood in the cutting. Place the cuttings 3″–4″ apart in moist, sandy soil in a shaded cold frame. When they're 1 year old, plant in well-drained, dry soil that is protected from severe frost. The first year, plants should be pruned to keep them from flowering and to encourage branching.

PESTS

Caterpillars

DISEASES

Fungal diseases

COMPANIONS: None

INCOMPATIBLES: None

OTHER

Lavender leaves are reputed to repel insects.

HARVEST

Don't cut until its second year as an outdoor plant. Pick the flowers when in blossom but just before full bloom, usually in July or August. On a dry and still day, cut early in the day after the dew has dried. Cut back the top growth up to 6″ below the flower spikes. Do not wash or aromatic oils will be lost.

Storage Requirements

To dry, tie branches in small bunch and hang it upside down in a warm, dry, dark place. Then remove the flowers from the stems and keep whole in storage.

Method	Results
Dried	Excellent, remains aromatic for a long time.

Sweet Marjoram

Origanum majorana
Lamiaceae (Mint Family)

Marjoram is a perennial or annual warm-season herb, very tender to frost and light freezes. It is winter hardy only in the South, Zones 9 through 10, so most gardeners grow it outdoors as an annual or in pots that can be brought indoors through winter. Marjoram likes full sun and soil that is light, dry, well-drained, and very low acid.

This herb has played varied roles over the centuries, from medicinal and culinary purposes to aromatic uses in closets and sachets to serving as a green wool dye. Don't confuse sweet marjoram with wild marjoram or the perennial oregano (O. *vulgare*). Sweet marjoram is used for cooking, whereas wild marjoram is used for medicinal purposes. Somewhat milder and sweeter than oregano but still perky with peppery overtones, marjoram can substitute for oregano in virtually any tomato-based dish, as well as in marinades, dressings, and stews. Marjoram harmonizes well with thyme, basil, garlic, onion, and bay and is particularly complementary to eggs, fish, savory meats, and green vegetables.

SITE

Full sun

TEMPERATURE

For Germination: 65°F–75°F/19°C–24°C

For Growth: Hot

SOIL & WATER NEEDS

pH: 6.5–7.0

Fertilizer: Light feeder

Side-Dressing: Not necessary

Water: Low

MEASUREMENTS

Planting Depth: 0″; tiny seeds need light and should not be covered.

Root Depth: 6″–12″

Height: 1′–2′

Breadth: 1″–18″

Space between Plants:

- In beds: 6″–8″
- In rows: 8″–10″

Space between Rows: 15″

PROPAGATION

By seeds, cuttings, and root division. If you propagate by seed, either sow seeds directly outside after all danger of frost has passed, or start seeds indoors and then transplant in clumps of three, spaced 6″–8″ apart. Germination takes 8–14 days. Pinch back plants before they bloom. After the first year, you can divide the plant roots and pot them for your winter windowsill or greenhouse.

PESTS

Aphid, spider mite

DISEASES

Botrytis rot, damping off, rhizoctonia

COMPANIONS

Sage; marjoram is also said to generally improve the flavor of all vegetables

INCOMPATIBLES

Cucumber

HARVEST

Pick marjoram all summer and, if you want, cut it down to 1″ above the ground. In the North, don't cut it back severely in fall as it will weaken the plants. Herbs should be cut in the morning after the dew has dried. Cut back the top growth up to 6″ below the flower buds or ends. Do not wash or aromatic oils will be lost.

Storage Requirements

To dry, tie the cuttings in small bunches and hang them upside down in a warm, dry, dark place. When dried, remove the leaves from the stems and store whole. Crush or grind just before use. Store in airtight jars in a dark place.

Method	Taste
Frozen	Good
Dried	Excellent, retains much of its flavor.
Fresh	Excellent

Oregano

Origanum vulgare subsp. *hirtum, O. heracleoticum*
Lamiaceae (Mint Family)

Oregano is a perennial warm-season herb, hardy to frost and light freezes through Zone 5. It likes full sun and well-drained, average soil. Flowering doubles the concentration of oil in oregano leaves, so for the strongest flavor don't harvest until the plants start flowering. Nonflowering varieties should be harvested in late spring, as the oil concentrations rise steadily in spring and then decline. But the late-spring peak flavor of nonflowering varieties simply cannot compare with the flavor of autumn-flowering varieties. For the strongest-flavored oregano, choose a variety that is autumn flowering. It's difficult to get a good-flavored oregano, so one strategy is to start from a cutting or plant that you have tasted or one that has an established track record. The best is *O. heracleoticum*. Oregano is a stronger, more peppery version of marjoram and is a staple in Mediterranean and Latino cuisine. It is used to enhance egg dishes, tomato-based dishes, savory meats, and vegetables.

SITE

Full sun

TEMPERATURE

For Germination: 65°F–75°F/19°C–24°C
For Growth: Hot

SOIL & WATER NEEDS

pH: 6.5–7.5
Fertilizer: Light feeder
Side-Dressing: Not necessary
Water: Low

MEASUREMENTS

Planting Depth: 0″; tiny seeds should not be covered.
Root Depth: Shallow
Height: 12″–24″
Breadth: 12″
Space between Plants:

- In beds: 18″

Space between Rows: 18″–20″

PROPAGATION

By root division in spring, or by cuttings and seeds. The easiest method is to take cuttings in summer and root them in sandy compost. Seeds germinate in about 4 days.

PESTS

Aphid, leaf miner, spider mite

DISEASES

Botrytis rot, fungal disease, rhizoctonia

COMPANIONS

All beans, cucumber, squash

INCOMPATIBLES: None

HARVEST

One gardener claims that a first harvest when the plant is a mere 6″ tall fosters bushy growth. When the plant is budding prolifically in June, she cuts the plant severely so that only the lower set of leaves remains. The plant reportedly leafs out again in a few weeks. She then cuts back the plant severely again in August. Generally, herbs should be cut in the morning after the dew has dried. Cut back the top growth to as much as 6″ below the flower buds or ends. Do not wash the leaves or aromatic oils will be lost.

Storage Requirements

To dry, tie the cuttings in small bunches and hang them upside down in a warm, dry, dark place. When dried, remove the leaves from the stems, and keep leaves whole for storage. Store in airtight jars in a dark place. Crush or grind just before use. Fresh oregano has a milder flavor than does dried oregano.

Method	Taste
Frozen	Good
Dried	Good
Fresh	Excellent

Parsley

Petroselinum crispum
Umbelliferae (Parsley Family)

Parsley is a cool-season biennial herb, hardy to frost and light freezes. It is notorious for its long germination time. Several methods can help speed things along: Soak the seeds overnight or for 48 hours; refrigerate the seeds; freeze the seeds; or pour boiling water over the soil plug before covering it. If you soak the seeds longer than overnight, change the water twice. Be sure to discard the water, as it will contain some of the germination inhibitor, furanocoumarin. If you let some of the plants go to seed late in the season, they may produce seedlings that can be dug and grown on the windowsill for next year's crop. Parsley is hardy but will usually go to seed in its second year, so it's most often grown as an annual. While some say it's difficult to transplant, you can direct-sow or transplant parsley from pots. An excellent source of vitamin C, iron, and minerals, parsley is more than a pretty garnish. Its refreshing flavor is a great addition to soups, salads, sauces, and many other dishes.

SITE

Full sun to partial shade

TEMPERATURE

For Germination: 50°F–85°F/10°C–30°C

For Growth: 60°F–65°F/16°C–19°C

SOIL & WATER NEEDS

pH: 6.0–7.0

Fertilizer: Heavy feeder

Side-Dressing: 2–3 times during the season, apply compost or spray with liquid seaweed.

Water: Low

First Seed-Starting Date

Germinate	+	Transplant	+	Days before LFD	=	Count Back from LFD
11–42 days	+	7–14 days	+	10 days	=	28–66 days

Last Seed-Starting Date

Germinate	+	Transplant	+	Maturity	+	SD Factor	+	Frost Tender	=	Count Back from FFD
11–42 days	+	7–14 days	+	63–76 days	+	14 days	+	14 days	=	109–160 days

MEASUREMENTS

Planting Depth: ¼″

Root Depth: Shallow to 4′

Height: 12″–18″

Breadth: 6″–9″

Space between Plants:

- In beds: 4″
- In rows: 6″–12″

Space between Rows: 12″–36″

PROPAGATION

By seed

PESTS

Cabbage looper, carrot rust fly, carrot weevil, nematode, parsleyworm, spider mite

DISEASES

Crown rot, septoria leaf spot

ALLIES

Uncertain: Black salsify, coriander, pennyroyal

COMPANIONS

Asparagus, corn, pepper, tomato

INCOMPATIBLES

None

HARVEST

Cut as needed. To keep it productive, frequently cut back the full length of the outside stems and remove all flower stalks. Herbs should be cut in the morning after the dew has dried. Cut back the top growth to as much as 6″ below the flower buds or ends. Do not wash the leaves or aromatic oils will be lost.

Storage Requirements

To dry, tie the cuttings in small bunches and hang them upside down in a warm, dry, dark place. When dried, remove the leaves from the stems and keep whole for storage. (If you prefer, the drying job can be hastened in an oven or microwave.) Store in airtight jars in a dark place. Crush or grind just before use.

Method	Taste
Frozen	Good for curly parsley
Dried	Good for broadleaf Italian
Fresh	Excellent (stored in jar in refrigerator, with stem submerged in water, covered with plastic bag)

Rosemary

Rosmarinus officinalis
Lamiaceae (Mint Family)

Rosemary is a perennial warm-season herb, very tender to light frost and freezes. It can tolerate a wide variety of soil conditions, ranging from 4.5 to 8.7 pH, and anywhere from 12 to 107 inches of water per year. Rosemary favors a sunny location and does not transplant well. If grown from seed, do not harvest for 3 years. It benefits from frequent pruning at any time of year; don't hesitate to cut it back severely.

"Dr. Rosemary," nurseryman Thomas DeBaggio in northern Virginia, recommended that north of Zone 8 rosemary be grown in pots year-round and brought indoors for the winter, as most varieties are hardy to only 15°F to 20°F/−10°C to −7°C. Arp is the only variety that is hardy to −10°F/−24°C and can be grown outdoors north of Zone 8. If you grow Arp outside, support its limbs and shield it with burlap in winter—not polyethylene, which can capture heat underneath—leaving the top open to minimize fungal disease. Overwatering causes tips to turn brown, followed by all leaves browning and dropping off.

SITE

Full sun; good drainage essential

TEMPERATURE

For Germination: 65°F–75°F/19°C–24°C
For Growth: Hot

SOIL & WATER NEEDS

pH: 6.0–7.0
Fertilizer: Light feeder
Side-Dressing: 2–3 applications per season of liquid seaweed
Water: Low

MEASUREMENTS

Planting Depth: ¼″
Root Depth: 12″–24″
Height: 2′–6′
Breadth: 12″–24″
Space between Plants: 12″–24″

PROPAGATION

Stem-tip cuttings taken in spring or fall root easily in sandy compost. Propagating from seed is not recommended because the seeds are unreliable and rapidly lose viability. If you do start from seeds, however, use seeds that are less than 2 years old. Rosemary seeds take a long time to germinate—up to 3 weeks—so be patient. Make sure the seed pots have excellent drainage and keep soil moist.

PESTS

Greenhouse: Spider mite and whitefly

Outdoors: Mealybugs and scale

DISEASES

In humid climates, fungal botrytis rot, rhizoctonia

COMPANIONS

All brassicas, beans, carrot, sage

INCOMPATIBLES

Cucumber

OTHER

Rosemary is said to deter bean beetles, cabbage moth, and carrot rust fly.

HARVEST

When the plant matures you can harvest it year-round. Cut 4″ branch tips, but do not remove more than 20% of the plant's growth. Herbs should be cut in the morning after the dew has dried. Do not wash or aromatic oils will be lost.

Storage Requirements

To dry, tie cuttings in small bunches and hang them upside down in a warm, dry, dark place. When dried, remove the leaves from the stems and keep whole for storage. Store in airtight jars in a dark place. Crush or grind just before use.

Method	Taste
Frozen	Unknown
Dried	Good
Fresh	Excellent

Sage

Salvia officinalis
Lamiaceae (Mint Family)

Sage is a perennial shrub and is hardy to −30°F/−35°C, if covered. In the North, cover with a loose mulch or hay or evergreen boughs. A June bloomer, sage likes well-drained and moderately rich soil, though it will tolerate poor soil and drought. Sage seeds store and germinate poorly. When started from seed, sage takes about 2 years to grow to a mature size. Most gardeners start sage from cuttings or division, using the outer, newer growth. Some gardeners recommend replacing sage plants every several years when they become woody and less productive.

Sage has putative antibacterial activity and has been used as a natural preservative for meats, poultry, and fish. Distilled sage extracts have been made into antioxidants that are used to increase the shelf life of foods. Some research also indicates that sage lowers blood sugar in diabetics and may have estrogenic properties, which might account for the popular folk belief that sage dries up milk. Fresh sage has a lemony and slightly bitter flavor, while dried sage has a mustier flavor. It adds depth to egg dishes, breads, and a variety of meats.

SITE

Full sun; good drainage essential

TEMPERATURE

For Germination: 60°F–70°F/16°C–22°C
For Growth: Warm

SOIL & WATER NEEDS

pH: 6.0–7.0
Fertilizer: Light feeder
Side-Dressing: An occasional spray of liquid seaweed will benefit the plant.
Water: Average

MEASUREMENTS

Planting Depth: ¼″
Root Depth: Shallow
Height: 12″–40″
Breadth: 15″–24″
Space between Plants:

- In beds: 18″–20″

Space between Rows: 3′

PROPAGATION

By layering, stem cuttings, or seed. Crowns of old sage plants can rarely be divided successfully, but dividing may work on younger plants. Start seeds indoors 1–2 months before the last frost or sow directly outdoors 1–2 weeks before the last frost; they germinate in about 21 days. Transplant outdoors about 1 week before the last frost. In fall, take a 4″ cutting and root it for planting the following spring.

PESTS

Slug, spider mite, spittlebug

DISEASES

Powdery mildew, rhizoctonia, verticillium wilt

COMPANIONS

All brassicas, carrot, marjoram, rosemary, strawberry, tomato

INCOMPATIBLES

Cucumber, onion family

OTHER

Sage can be used to deter cabbage moths and carrot flies.

HARVEST

If you want to keep these plants through winter, harvest lightly in the first year and no later than September. Herbs should be cut in the morning after the dew has dried. Cut back the top growth to as much as 6″ below the flower buds or ends. Don't wash or aromatic oils will be lost.

Storage Requirements

To dry, tie cuttings in small bunches and hang them upside down in a warm, dry, dark place. When dried, remove the leaves from the stems, and keep whole for storage.

Method	Taste
Frozen	Good
Dried	Fair
Fresh	Excellent

Tarragon

Artemisia dracunculus
Asteraceae (Sunflower Family)

Tarragon is an aromatic, perennial herb, hardy to frost and light freezes through Zone 4. It likes full sun to partial shade and rich, sandy, well-drained loam. The plants should be divided every 2 or 3 years for flavor and vigor. All flower stems should be removed to keep the plant productive. Tarragon most often fails due to soil that is too wet or too acidic. It can be grown in containers with good drainage in the greenhouse or on a windowsill.

The only tarragon worth growing for culinary use is French tarragon, but it is somewhat harder to find than Russian tarragon. Tarragon is an excellent flavor enhancer in vinegars, salad dressings, and chicken, cheese, and egg dishes. It is important in French cuisine, particularly in béarnaise, hollandaise, tartar sauces, and herb mixtures such as herbes de Provence. Tarragon reportedly aids digestion and when made as an infusion is said to soothe rheumatism, arthritis, and toothaches.

SITE

Full sun to partial shade

TEMPERATURE

For Germination: 75°F/24°C
For Growth: Warm

SOIL & WATER NEEDS

pH: 6.0–7.0
Fertilizer: Light feeder
Side-Dressing: Not necessary
Water: Average

MEASUREMENTS

Planting Depth: Cover roots.
Root Depth: 6″–12″
Height: 12″–36″
Breadth: 24″
Space between Plants:

- In beds: 18″
- In rows: 2′

Space between Rows: 30″

PROPAGATION

By cuttings, divisions, or seed. French tarragon cannot be grown from seed, so if you grow tarragon seeds it is the less aromatic, more common Russian tarragon. To propagate French tarragon, take cuttings or divisions in early spring and transplant 2′ apart.

PESTS: None

DISEASES

Downy mildew, powdery mildew, rhizoctonia

COMPANIONS

Tarragon is alleged to enhance the growth of most vegetables

INCOMPATIBLES: None

HARVEST

Begin harvest 6–8 weeks after transplanting outside. The leaves bruise easily, so handle gently. Herbs should be cut in the morning after the dew has dried. Cut back the top growth to as much as 6″ below the flower buds or ends. Don't wash or the aromatic oils will be lost.

Storage Requirements

To dry, tie cuttings in small bunches and hang them upside down in a warm, dry, dark place. When dried, remove the leaves from the stems and keep whole for storage. The leaves will brown slightly during the drying process. Crush or grind just before use. Store in airtight jars in a dark place. Fresh tarragon can also be preserved in white vinegar (which preserves flavor better than drying) and by freezing the leaves in airtight plastic bags.

Method	Taste
Frozen	Good (better than dried)
Dried	Fair
Fresh	Excellent

Thyme

Thymus vulgaris
Lamiaceae (Mint Family)

Thyme is a perennial herb and is hardy to frost and light freezes in Zones 5 through 9. It likes full sun and does well in light, dry to stony, poor soils. Good drainage is essential or the plant will be susceptible to fungal diseases. Keep it sheltered from cold winds. It may not survive severe winters unless covered or heavily mulched.

The plant may become woody and straggly in 2 to 3 years. Either replace it or try cutting back three-fourths of the new growth during the growing season to rejuvenate it and keep it bushy. French thyme is difficult to propagate with cuttings but the following method is suggested: Prune the plant severely in mid-June, and take small ½- to 1-inch softwood cuttings in mid-July; root the cuttings in a sand bed, and cover the bed with a milky white plastic "tent" 6 to 8 inches above the top of the cuttings; mist the cuttings once a day at midday. Important in French and Greek cuisine, thyme is wonderfully versatile, enhancing everything from breads, vinegars, and butters to egg, fish, poultry, meats, and vegetables.

SITE

Full sun to partial shade

TEMPERATURE

For Germination: 60°F–70°F/16°C–22°C

For Growth: Warm

SOIL & WATER NEEDS

pH: 5.5–7.0

Fertilizer: Light feeder

Side-Dressing: Not necessary

Water: Average

MEASUREMENTS

Planting Depth: 0″–¼″

Root Depth: 6″–10″

Height: 3″–12″

Breadth: 18″–3′

Space between Plants: 8″–12″

PROPAGATION

By cuttings, divisions, layering, or seed. Start seeds indoors 2–3 weeks before the last frost, keeping seeds dry and uncovered. For layering, divisions, and cuttings, snip 3″ from fresh new green growth, place in wet sand, keep moist for 2 weeks, and transplant when rooted. The best time for divisions or cuttings is spring; also early summer.

PESTS

Aphid, spider mite

DISEASES

Botrytis rot, fungal diseases, rhizoctonia

COMPANIONS

All brassicas, eggplant, potato, strawberry, tomato

INCOMPATIBLES

Cucumber

OTHER

May repel cabbageworm and whitefly

HARVEST

Cut as needed before the plant blossoms in midsummer. Alternatively, harvest the entire plant by cutting it down to 2″ above the ground; the plant will grow back before the season ends, but this method renders the plant less hardy for winter. Herbs should be cut in the morning after the dew has dried. Cut back the top growth to as much as 6″ below the flower buds or ends. Do not wash the leaves or aromatic oils will be lost.

GREENHOUSE

Any variety does well, but keep foliage dry to prevent rot.

Storage Requirements

To dry, tie cuttings in small bunches and hang them upside down in a warm, dry, dark place. When dried, remove the leaves from the stems and keep whole for storage. Crush or grind leaves just before use. Store in airtight jars in a dark place or freeze in airtight containers.

Method	Taste
Frozen	Fair
Dried	Excellent
Fresh	Excellent

YOGURT
ORGANIC

CHAPTER FIVE

organic remedies

Prevention and a self-sustaining, balanced ecosystem are the organic gardener's most important tools for minimizing diseases. Without preventive measures, the advantages of organic gardening quickly diminish. Preventive medicine in plants means adopting a holistic approach from the beginning. Some diseases and insects can be minimized by breaking the pest cycle through proper garden siting, crop rotation, intercropping, and soil maintenance. Other pests can be minimized by ensuring good plant nutrition, because healthy plants are always less susceptible to attack.

Realistic expectations are essential to a holistic approach. Overly optimistic expectations can lead to "ghost" gardens gone to seed or to habitual quick fixes with chemicals. Abandon at the outset thoughts of 100 percent picture-perfect produce. Even a healthy garden with an advantageous balance between predators and prey suffers some damage during the growing season.

Discerning Impacts and Balancing Needs

Most plants can lose up to 20 percent of their foliage and still match yields of those with no foliage loss. As garden steward, your role is to determine the severity of the damage and the factors promoting the damage, and to decide what action, if any, is appropriate. Damage does not necessarily mean lower yields.

If you can identify an imbalance, you might be able to undertake long-term remedies. Events seemingly out of your control, such as unusually prolonged wet periods that promote fungus, might be addressed over the long term by improving soil drainage and ventilation. In the short term, however, often the best single remedy is to prevent further garden contamination: Remove and destroy the infected plants.

An organic garden is an object of sentiment, not sentimentality. It may be difficult to dispose of a plant you've lovingly nurtured and nourished, but the needs of the whole garden frequently outweigh those of a single plant. When it comes to sustaining plants that are weak, diseased, or unsuitable for your microenvironment, often the ends do not justify the means. Remedies may be deleterious to you and your garden and offer negligible benefits. Outdoors, where nature's balancing act prevails, a philosophical embrace of imperfection and a "tough love" policy toward diseased plants are critical.

A garden is a complex living organism that takes time to understand. Several years may be needed to build a productive soil and resident population of beneficial organisms. It also takes time to learn which plant varieties are suited to a particular microenvironment. A neighbor may have perfect conditions for your favorite tomato, but you may not be able to grow it well because of variations in the microenvironment.

If you can learn to accept some imperfections, some diseases, some insects, and some failures, your garden can be a continual source of nourishing food, relaxation, and pleasure.

First Line of Defense: Plan Ahead

Prevention of a host of potential garden problems begins well before a single seed is planted, even before the first garden bed is created. Resist the temptation just to start digging. Instead, if possible, observe your property through the seasons: What parts receive sun and for how long? Where does fog rise, dew linger, or frost bite latest in spring or earliest in fall? Where does water accumulate or drain? Where does wildlife move, and which can be helpful or harmful to your garden? With this knowledge, you will maximize the likelihood of your garden's success and are ready to begin planning.

GARDEN LOCATION

For any garden, selecting the right location may be the key to preventing plant disease.

Choose a location that receives bright sunlight most of the day. In humid areas, morning sun is particularly important because it helps to dry dew rapidly. This in turn helps minimize the growth and spread of fungal and bacterial pathogens.

Good drainage is also important. If your "ideal" site doesn't drain well, mix materials such as humus into the soil to improve drainage. Good drainage keeps plant roots from becoming waterlogged and, therefore, oxygen starved and severely stressed. Poor drainage increases the likelihood of root rot and various soilborne diseases.

SOIL CONDITION

Soil is "alive," teeming with organisms, large and small. Your role as steward is to encourage a healthy diversity of organisms and nutrients. Do so by feeding the soil, not the plants. The soil that results will help you grow vibrant, healthy plants.

Avoid dumping large quantities of chemical fertilizers on the soil. They may boost plant growth temporarily, but they can also kill beneficial soil organisms, such as earthworms, and can deplete the soil in the long run. Enrich the soil in your garden by taking the following steps.

Encourage earthworms. Earthworms are an excellent way to feed the soil and promote healthy plant growth. If you have good garden soil, earthworms will probably show up on their own. Purchasing worms to add to the soil is not necessary, and can end up damaging natural ecosystems. (See page 3 for more on earthworms.)

Use peat humus, compost, and composted manure. These are available from garden-supply stores.

Minimize tilling depth. After the initial tilling, double-digging, or other preparation of the garden bed, don't till more than a few inches deep (unless absolutely necessary); going deeper may kill or disturb earthworms and other soil organisms. There are a few exceptions to this rule; see "Undertake fall cultivation" on page 176, and as noted in the animal pest chart on pages 219–77.

Avoid soil compaction. If possible, don't walk on the soil. Some gardeners lay 6 to 12 inches of straw to prevent compaction where heavy machinery is used.

Sow cover crops after a harvest to replenish the soil. Use a legume or grass, such as cowpeas or winter rye. Cover crops help retain soil moisture, improve soil texture, and increase organic matter; legumes also return nitrogen to the soil.

Use raised beds where possible. They help you achieve multiple goals including good drainage, minimal soil compaction, and aeration. Contained raised beds also help to minimize the spread of disease organisms by localizing them to the infected bed. (See page 9 for more on raised beds.)

Solarize garden soil if the garden develops a soilborne disease problem. Solarization is accomplished by creating a kind of mini hothouse that raises soil temperature to 130°F to 140°F/55°C to 60°C for several days. Temperatures higher than this kill beneficial organisms. There are different methods, depending on how large and deep an area you want to solarize. An easy approach is to loosen the soil in midsummer, thoroughly drench it with water, and let it sit overnight. The next day, cover the soil with 4-millimeter-thick clear plastic, stretch the plastic tight, and seal the edges with rocks or soil. Allow the soil to heat up for 4 to 6 weeks, then remove the plastic and plant as usual. For other methods, consult the bibliography.

Pasteurize potting soil from extensive greenhouse operations and to start seeds in flats, pots, or other containers. Otherwise, use unpasteurized soil mix. Pasteurization may not be necessary if you use potting soil taken from uncultivated areas or fields growing grains or forage. An easy way to pasteurize is to place a 1- to 1½-inch layer of soil in shallow pans and bake for 1 hour at 220°F/105°C. Or, cover the soil with foil, insert a meat thermometer so it doesn't touch the bottom or sides of the pan, and bake at 350°F/180°C until the soil temperature reaches 180°F/83°C. Turn off the heat and let the soil remain in the oven for another 30 minutes. When cool, store the soil in tightly sealed plastic bags.

PLANT LOCATION AND SELECTION

Consider the garden plot to be a place in which to encourage a diversity of life. The soil is alive with microbial organisms, many of them disease pathogens. One of the best ways to minimize these pathogens is to interrupt or discourage their life cycles. The following practices will help you achieve this goal.

Rotate your crops. Plant the same vegetable in the same soil site no more frequently than once every other year (a 2-year rotation). If possible, routinely rotate on a 3- to 8-year basis. *Same soil site* is defined as a radius of 10 feet from where the vegetable has been planted. So rotation can occur within the same growing bed as long as the vegetable is planted at least 10 feet away from where it was the previous year.

Intercrop. Try to avoid *monocrops,* single crops of, say, just corn or beans. Space and time permitting, if you want to grow a large amount of one vegetable, try planting it in several different places or breaking up a large patch with plantings of another vegetable. Intercropping discourages some pests from feasting conveniently on their favorite food. In fact, studies have shown that random mixing of plant cultivars in a stand greatly reduces disease severity. Also, certain vegetables may grow better in one spot than in another, so experimentation with placement may prove helpful.

Test different varieties of the same crop. Each variety of a particular vegetable has slightly different growing habits and different disease and insect resistance. One variety may thrive where another dies. The more varieties you try, the higher intrinsic resistance your garden has to widespread disease and insect damage. Over time, you will identify the varieties that fare best in your particular microclimate.

Encourage good air circulation. Give each plant adequate space to grow to maturity. Prune trees and canes annually to prevent overcrowding of limbs and branches. In some cases, if the area becomes too crowded, you may need to remove entire trees.

Select varieties that are resistant to or tolerant of the problems specific to your climate. Your Extension agent or local organic association should be able to tell you what the predominant pest problems, whether fungal, bacterial, viral, or insect, are in your area. For some diseases, selecting resistant varieties is the only prevention and remedy.

Buy certified disease-free seed or plants whenever possible. For certain diseases predominant in the eastern United States, buying seed grown west of the Rockies is an important preventive measure.

Second Line of Defense: Prevention

Most of the defensive actions discussed in this section also happen to be organic remedies for a host of diseases and animal pests. If you adopt these practices at the outset, you will need to consult the specific remedies offered in the rest of the chapter much less frequently.

Some steps may be free, some inexpensive, others more expensive. Do what you can, when you can, choosing options that are consistent with your goals. A purple martin house, for example, may seem like a pricey investment initially, but it will last 20 years, and purple martins will greatly reduce the need for insecticidal spray, chemical or organic. Bluebird and bat houses, by contrast, can be built easily from scrap lumber or bought at modest cost. In sufficient numbers, bluebirds and bats can accomplish the same goal.

PLANT MAINTENANCE

These steps are critical for prevention. As a group, they are also the most common and important remedies for disease and insect damage. If you experience disease or insect problems, review this list. If there is a step that you haven't already taken, implement it as a remedy.

Avoid deep planting where fungal root rot (rhizoctonia) is a problem. Shallow planting encourages the early emergence of seedlings and gives them a better chance of survival.

Water from below using some form of irrigation. A cheap method is to use gallon-size plastic jugs whose bottoms have been cut out. Simply insert the necks of the jugs into the soil at intervals appropriate to the plants' needs, and fill the jugs with water. More expensive methods include soaker hoses and emitter tubes. Watering from below helps to prevent and remedy fungal disease by discouraging its growth and minimizing its spread through water droplets. It is also more efficient than regular watering and reduces evaporative loss.

Water before noon. This allows the plants to dry off in the middle of the day, before nightfall, which also discourages fungal growth.

Don't work around or touch wet plants. Diseases are frequently transmitted by human hands and infected tools, so this preventive measure is standard practice.

Don't touch healthy plants after working with diseased plants. Again, human hands and infected tools are common methods of disease transmission, so this should be avoided.

Avoid high-nitrogen fertilizers. Fertilizers can harm soil organisms and also can stimulate the plant to put its energy into leafy growth rather than fruits.

Feed the soil with compost. For some diseases, a major remedy is to spread 1 inch or more of compost through the garden. (See pages 4–6 for more information.)

Mulch in spring and fall. Mulch is another occasional remedy for fungal, bacterial, and certain insect pest problems. Apply several inches of mulch in spring and 4 to 6 inches in fall, after harvest. (See "Undertake fall cultivation," page 176; see also page 7 for more information on mulch.)

Control weeds in and around the garden. Weeds can harbor insect and disease pests. If you weed regularly in the early summer months, you should not experience a severe weed problem during the rest of the season. Removing perennial weeds and thistles within 100 yards of the garden is considered a remedy for several diseases.

Remove rotting or dead leaves, stalks, weeds, and plants. These can be a breeding ground for pests. Rid the garden of fall leaves, too, even if you aren't growing any fall crops.

Move piles of wood and garden debris to a spot away from the garden. These can be a breeding ground for pests.

Don't allow large, stagnant pools of water. Small birdbaths and running water are not a problem.

Mow grass in orchards. Orchard grass is another potential breeding ground for pests. One "natural" orchard plan involves planting companion grasses or plants that attract beneficial insects and allowing them to naturalize. Most orchards, however, are surrounded by orchard grass, which should be kept mowed to discourage pests.

Disinfect tools periodically. Even if there's no sign of disease, make an effort to disinfect tools regularly. And when working with diseased plants, always disinfect tools between pruning cuts.

Shade plants in extremely hot weather if they wilt continuously. Use a shading material such as cheesecloth. If plants wilt one day, they won't necessarily die the next, but don't be afraid to shade your plants. Studies by NASA have indicated that plants integrate light over time, and that long, sunny summer days provide more light than plants require. If plants are wilting from heat stress, make sure they are receiving adequate water.

Protect plants from freezes. Whenever a freeze is anticipated, protect plants with a light material. Even newspaper works.

Promptly harvest fruits and vegetables when ripe. Allowing fruits and vegetables to stay on the stem too long promotes certain diseases.

Remove plants immediately after harvest. Don't allow harvested plants to just sit in the garden. If they're not diseased, remove them and add them to the compost pile, or, where appropriate, work them back into the soil.

Always remove and destroy infected or diseased leaves, canes, or the entire plant when necessary. For some diseases and insect pests, removing the infected leaves may be sufficient. For other pests, which may be systemic, removing the affected leaves may not be sufficient. If all other measures discussed in this section fail to control the problem, you may need to resort to various sprays—whether simple home remedies or insecticidal soaps, or harsher remedies such as the copper-based fungicides and botanical sprays.

Undertake fall cultivation. After plants have been harvested and the garden cleaned of plant debris, leave the soil bare for a few days. For normal purposes, cultivate the soil no more than 3 inches. For certain insect pest problems, cultivate the soil to a depth of 6 to 8 inches to expose eggs and larvae to birds and other predators. Two weeks later, lightly cultivate the soil a second time with a rake, now to a depth of just 2 inches. Leave soil bare for a few more days, then plant a cover crop or apply a layer of winter mulch 4 to 6 inches deep.

HELPFUL SUPPORTS AND DEVICES

These devices may seem unnecessary, but they can make the difference between the presence or absence of a problem. In some cases, they are recommended as remedies to specific disease or animal pests.

Borders. Borders of certain plants around vegetable beds have been found by some research to be helpful in maintaining garden health. Plant in small ratios relative to the size of the garden bed. Try planting borders of dead nettle, valerian, hyssop, lemon balm, and yarrow.

Trellises, stakes, A-frames, tepees. These and other forms of plant support accomplish multiple goals. Not only do they make the most efficient use of growing space, but they promote better light penetration and air circulation, both of which help minimize disease. Supports also make it much easier to prune and harvest. Use supports for vegetables such as tomatoes, pole beans, peas, cucumbers, melons, and squash. Melons and large squash can be supported on trellises by tying them with pantyhose or similar materials. If grown on the ground, melons should be raised off the soil with steel cans or plastic containers to minimize rot. Cane fruit, such as blackberries, raspberries, and grapes, also grow effectively when trellised.

Row covers. These are helpful throughout the growing season. In spring and fall, they keep your crops warm and protected from frost, thereby prolonging the season. In spring and summer, they are an easy and effective protection against insect attack. Before applying row covers, however, make sure that harmful insects are not trapped underneath.

Row covers are usually made of a lightweight woven material, such as polyester or polyvinyl alcohol, that allows in air, light, and water and requires no supports. To enhance warmth under row covers, fill gallon jugs with water and place them every few feet along the rows. The water in the jugs absorbs heat during the day and radiates the stored warmth through the night.

Wire cages, stakes, and water-based white paint. These are critical aids to saplings. Wire cages provide an effective barrier against animals. When planting a sapling, install a ½- to ¼-inch hardware cloth around the trunk, so that it extends 4 inches below the ground to prevent rodents from burrowing under and 18 to 24 inches above the ground to prevent rabbit damage, particularly in winter months. Make sure the wire is spaced a couple of inches away from the trunk to allow for growth.

For trees on dwarf rootstock characterized by poor anchorage, place a 4- to 6-foot stake close to the trunk before filling the planting hole with soil, and secure it with special ties that permit growth and flexing. Tree trunks can be painted any time, but if done while young, it will help prevent sunscald or winter injury, a condition promoted by sunny winter days and resulting in cracks or cankers.

Electrical fences or other barriers. In rural areas, barriers against large animals such as deer are almost essential. Many a gardener has gone to bed, content with a prospering garden, only to awaken to find devastation. Some gardeners initially feel the problem doesn't warrant the expense, but their minds are changed pretty quickly when their entire garden, flowers and vegetables, are destroyed in short order. (For suggestions on different types of barriers, see the remedies for deer in the animal pest chart on page 234.)

ATTRACT BENEFICIAL ANIMALS AND INSECTS

Birds, bats, bees, predatory and parasitic wasps, ladybugs—these are just a few of the beneficial animals and insects that are critical to a self-sustaining garden. Beneficials are one of the easiest ways to prevent disease and to deter animal pests that spread disease. They save you both money and time—and time is money, after all.

In the beginning, your garden's ecosystem may not contain all of the beneficials that you want or need. You may choose to import beneficial insects to fight a specific problem, for example. Such a practice is part of integrated pest management (IPM), a common approach in commercial crop management. IPM relies extensively, but not exclusively, on precisely timed releases of beneficial insects to fight pest problems. Backyard gardeners who don't have the opportunity or inclination to investigate the proper timing or method of releasing purchased beneficial insects probably shouldn't use this remedy. If you can follow through on the timed releases, however, importation of beneficials can be an effective remedy. Beneficial insects are listed, where applicable, in the animal pest chart on pages 219–77. Always follow the supplier's instructions for quantity and timing to ensure success.

Some purists believe that the importation of beneficial insects disrupts the development of

Selected Beneficial Insects

Insect	Benefits
Assassin bugs	Eat immature insects.
Bumblebees	Pollinate blossoms from which fruits and vegetables develop. One of nature's best helpers for our food supply.
Ground beetles	Eat caterpillars, cutworms, some species of slugs and snails, and soft-bodied larvae.
Lacewing wasps	Eat aphids, corn earworms, mealybugs, mites, leafhopper nymphs, thrips, caterpillar eggs, scales, and whiteflies.
Ladybugs	Eat aphids, mealybugs, and small insects. Different species of ladybugs prefer different insects.
Praying mantises	Eat aphids and small insects.
Spiders	Eat insects and other pests.
Syrphid flies (hover flies and flower flies)	Eat aphids, leafhoppers, mealybugs, mites, scales, and small insects.
Wasps parasitoid (nonstinging)	In general, parasitize the eggs, larvae, and sometimes pupae of many insects, including aphids, caterpillars (larvae of butterflies and moths [*Lepidoptera*]), sawflies, beetles, leafhoppers, true bugs, thrips, psyllids, and flies.
Braconids	Parasitize aphids, larvae of moths, butterflies, and many beetles.
Chalcids	Parasitize aphids, mealybugs, scales, and larvae of beetles, moths, and butterflies.
Ichneumonids	Parasitize moth and butterfly larvae.
Pediobius foveolatus	Parasitizes Mexican bean beetle larvae.
Trichogrammas	Parasitize and eat eggs of the corn borer, cabbage looper, codling moth, and many caterpillars.

Note: Additional beneficial insects are mentioned in the charts that follow.

a balanced local ecosystem. This argument has some merit. But be aware that some beneficials are self-limiting: When their food source dies, they die.

Ideally, a self-sustaining garden should not need imported help, but you may decide to resort to imported beneficials when faced with acute infestations. The decision depends on your individual goals. If you've implemented the first and second lines of defense, the probability of extensive damage to any single crop or crop variety is low. To attract beneficial insects, plant herbs, flowers, and clovers around the borders of your garden. (For more information on beneficials, see pages 3–8 and also page 190.)

Third Line of Defense: Identify the Problem

Identification may seem an improbable defensive action, but it is absolutely essential in the garden. If you saw water spots on your ceiling, you wouldn't run right out to replace the roof; first you seek the cause. The spots might simply result from condensation due to inadequate ventilation of the roof rafters. Likewise, when plants get sick, make every effort to diagnose the problem accurately before attempting remedial action. What appears to be a fungus at first glance may simply be a lack of phosphorus.

The most common garden problems are frequently the simplest ones to fix: overwatering or underwatering, inadequate nutrients, poor drainage, or lack of ventilation. Take your time, and examine any problems closely before deciding which remedy or combination of remedies is appropriate.

The balance of this chapter is intended to help you pinpoint the possible causes of your plant problems and to help you conduct informed discussions with professionals. If you want to experiment with your garden—and you are not committed to saving every plant, maximizing yields, or obtaining picture-perfect produce—the guidelines and remedies that follow can be for you a source of fun, discovery, and learning. If you are a market gardener with an investment in yields, both quality and quantity, obtain an accurate diagnosis from a professional before implementing a remedy. Don't forget: Advice and soil tests from Extension agents are free.

REGULAR MONITORING

Monitor the garden daily, if you have time, or at least weekly. Act quickly to prevent a pest or disease from becoming a problem, starting with the most benign methods of control, which are also usually the easiest and least expensive. The simplest methods include handpicking and trapping, or spraying plants with strong jets of water to clear off bugs. Work your way up from these to stronger methods, such as biological predators. If the problem becomes particularly serious, you might try even stronger controls like botanical insecticides, but use them sparingly and only as a last resort. (See the warning under "Botanical controls" on page 198.) The key is to find the control for your garden that is both the most effective and the most benign.

SYSTEMATIC EXAMINATION OF THE ENVIRONMENT

Before attempting diagnosis, you must first learn how to observe. Begin by taking a general accounting of the plant and determining the parts that are affected. Following is a partial list of things you might look for.

- **Leaves:** Inspect edges (margins), veins, top side, and bottom side. Notice wilting, general coloration and distortion (curling, crinkling), holes, spots, eggs, and insects.
- **Blossoms and fruits:** Check petals, blossom end of the fruit, and skin. Look for spots, discolorations, decay, cuts, holes, premature drop, lack of fruit setting, eggs, and insects.
- **Stems or bark:** Examine from the soil level, or even slightly below the soil level, to the top. Notice cuts, cracks, or splits in the tissue, blisters, growth (cankers or galls), discoloration, wilting, stunting, twisting, spindly growth, sticky coating, gummy exudates, spots, eggs, and insects.
- **Roots and surrounding soil:** If the plant is sufficiently diseased, you may want to dig it up. Check the length and breadth of main roots and root hairs. Notice nodules, knots, decay, underdevelopment, twisting or distortions, eggs, cocoons, and insects.

START WITH THE BASICS

After examining the plant and its environment, consider the basics, not the unusual. Start with the most common garden problems—water, nutrients, drainage, air circulation—even if insects or disease are clearly present. Many pests don't attack a plant unless it is already weakened and stressed. Before reaching for the fungicide, check to see whether the roots are too wet and compacted to get oxygen. Global garden destruction can be due to animals, such as deer and rodents. And global garden sickness can be caused by acid rain, pollution, or smog, modern afflictions we often forget to consider during diagnosis.

A GUIDE TO IDENTIFYING AND TREATING COMMON PROBLEMS

For more detailed information on remedies, see the Glossary of Organic Remedies on pages 190–202.

Acid Soil

Nitrogen, phosphorus, and other nutrient deficiencies appear because an acid medium makes them less biologically available. The plant performs poorly and exhibits multiple symptoms.

Symptoms: pH below 6.0; excess aluminum and manganese, because an acid medium makes these more biologically available.

Where It Occurs: Common in areas with acid rain, especially in the Northeast.

Diagnostic Tools: Soil and pH tests

Organic Remedies

- Earthworms
- Compost
- Ground dolomitic limestone (slow release, contains magnesium and calcium)
- Ground calcitic limestone (slow release, no magnesium and calcium)
- Wood ashes (fast release, caustic)
- Organic material, because lime speeds decomposition of organic matter

Alkaline Soil

Symptoms: pH above 7.0; micronutrient deficiencies; poor plant performance

Diagnostic Tools: Soil and pH tests

Organic Remedies

- Earthworms
- Compost and other organic materials
- Gypsum (calcium sulfate)
- Aluminum sulfate or powdered sulfur

Water

Too Little: Plants wilt due to loss of tissue turgor, which is maintained by water pressure. Leaves may eventually brown and die. With prolonged water shortage, growth is stunted.

Too Much: The soil around the stem is soaked. Mold, moss, or fungus may be growing on top of the soil. Other symptoms include wilting, yellowing, and dead leaf margins.

Diagnostic Tools: Why guess? Buy a simple moisture meter to find out whether the root medium is too wet or dry. Buy a rain gauge and mount it where it can be easily checked.

Organic Remedies

- Earthworms
- Compost
- *Do what's logical:* If it's too wet, let the root medium dry out; if too dry, provide more water.

Nitrogen (N)

Nitrogen is essential for all phases of growth. Because it can be rapidly depleted, garden soil needs a slow, constant supply such as compost provides.

Too Little: Slow growth. Lighter green leaf color is followed by yellowing tips, usually starting at the bottom of the plant. Leaf undersides may become blue-purple. Plant eventually becomes spindly, and older leaves drop. Fruits are small and pale before ripening and overly colored when ripe.

Too Much: Lush, green foliage. Little or no fruit, because the plant is putting all of its energy into growth.

Where It Occurs: Usually where there is an excess of fast-acting fertilizer.

Diagnostic Tool: Soil test kit

Organic Remedies

- Earthworms
- Compost (slow release)

- Foliar spray of diluted fish emulsion or other liquid fertilizer
- Fish meal (slow release)
- Composted manure (slow release)
- Hoof and horn meal (slow release)
- Cottonseed meal (medium release)
- Blood meal (fast release)

Avoid: Urea, the various nitrates, ammonium phosphate

Phosphorus (P)

Phosphorus is essential for proper fruiting, flowering, seed formation, and root branching. It also increases the rate of crop maturation, builds plant resistance to disease, and strengthens stems.

Too Little: Leaf undersides have blue-red spots that expand to entire leaf. Darkened leaves develop a blue-green tinge. Green crops have reddish purple color in stems and leaf veins. Fruiting crops are leafy, with fruits setting and maturing late, if at all.

Where It Occurs: Widespread, except in the Northwest. Most severe in the Southeast from the Gulf of Mexico to North Carolina.

Diagnostic Tool: Soil test kit

Organic Remedies

- Earthworms
- Compost
- Bonemeal (slow release)
- Soft phosphate (even slower release)
- Phosphate rock (very slow release)

Avoid: Phosphoric acid, superphosphates, highly soluble compounds

Potassium (K)

Potassium is essential for regulating water movement in plants and helps with production of sugars, starches, proteins, and certain enzyme reactions. It also increases cold-hardiness, especially in root crops.

Too Little: Leaves at the plant base turn grayish green. Leaf edges yellow, brown, or blacken, and curl downward. Black spots appear along leaf veins. New leaves curl and crinkle. Flowers and fruit are small and inferior. Stems are hard and woody. Plant and roots are stunted. Leaves may turn bronze, yellow-brown, or mildly bluish.

Where It Occurs: Most common east of the Mississippi and in coastal fog areas; most severe in parts of Texas through Florida, and north to Virginia

Diagnostic Tool: Soil test kit

Organic Remedies

- Earthworms
- Compost
- Greensand (very slow release)
- Crushed granite (very slow release)
- Rock potash (slow release)
- Kelp meal (medium release)
- Wood ash (fast release, caustic)
- Feldspar dust

Avoid: Potassium chloride

Magnesium (Mg)

Magnesium is important for chlorophyll production and respiration.

Too Little: Lower, older leaves yellow between the leaf veins and eventually turn dark brown. Leaves get brittle and curl upward. Fruit matures late. Symptoms usually appear in late season.

Where It Occurs: Acidic soils, leached, sandy soils, or soils high in potassium and calcium

Diagnostic Tools: Soil and pH tests

Organic Remedies

- Earthworms
- Compost
- Seaweed meal
- Liquid seaweed (foliar spray)

Calcium (Ca)

Calcium is necessary for water uptake and proper cell development and division.

Too Little: Newer, upper leaves turn dark green, sometimes curl upward, and leaf edges yellow. Weak stems, poor growth, early fruit drop, fruit cracking. Fruits develop water-soaked decaying spots at the blossom end. Examples are blossom-end rot in tomato, tip burn in lettuce, black heart in celery, and Baldwin spot in apple and pear flesh (brown spots under the skin and bitter flesh).

Where It Occurs: Acidic, leached, very dry soils, or soils high in potassium

Diagnostic Tools: Soil and pH tests

Organic Remedies

- Earthworms
- Compost
- Ground limestone (slow release), applied once in fall
- Ground oyster shells (slow release)
- Crumbled eggshells (slow release)
- Avoid fertilizers high in nitrogen and potassium
- Wood ashes, applied once in spring

  Avoid: Quicklime, slaked lime, hydrated lime

Boron (B)

Boron is important for cell wall formation and carbohydrate transport.

Too Little: Bushy growth from lower stems. Newer shoots curl inward, turn dark, and die. Young leaves turn purple-black. Leaf ribs get brittle. Fruit develops cracks or dry spots.

Where It Occurs: Eastern United States, especially in alkaline soils

Diagnostic Tools: Soil and pH tests

Organic Remedies

- Granite dust (slow release)
- Rock phosphate (slow release)
- Liquid kelp foliar spray (fast acting)
- Boric acid spray on newly opened fruit blossoms (0.02 pound to 1 gallon water)

Iron (Fe)

Iron is important for chlorophyll formation.

Too Little: Similar to nitrogen deficiency, but leaf yellowing is between the veins and starts first on upper, not lower, leaves.

Where It Occurs: Often in soils with pH above 6.8

Diagnostic Tools: Soil and pH tests

Organic Remedies

- Compost
- Lower soil pH to 6.8 or less
- Add peat moss manure (lowers pH)
- Glauconite (source of iron)
- Greensand (source of iron)

Drainage

Too Much: Sandy soils do not sufficiently retain water.

Too Little: Long-standing puddles. Slowly melting snow.

Diagnostic Tools: Dig a gallon-size hole and fill it with water. Let it drain, fill it again with water, and time how long it takes the hole to drain; more than 8 hours indicates poor drainage.

Organic Remedies (*for both conditions*)

- Earthworms
- Compost or other organic matter (helps soil both retain and drain water)

Poor Ventilation

Plants wilt due to heat stress. Dew dries very slowly. Mold, moss, mildew, and other symptoms of too much moisture are present.

Organic Remedies

- Stake plants, or use some support structure to keep plants erect.
- Prune trees and plants; remove suckers between stem crotches.
- If the garden is too crowded, remove weakest, smallest, or least-desired plants.

Ozone (O_3)

This is a major photochemical irritant in smog. Plants become more brittle and generally attract more insects. Studies suggest that ozone can alter the olfactory cues, thereby altering the activity of insects, making the plant more attractive to pests.

Organic Remedies: There is no known remedy for smog pollution. If gardening in a smog-polluted area, do everything possible to maintain soil and plant health, and don't assume the plant is diseased.

Walnut Wilt

Roots of black walnut and butternut trees secrete an acid (juglone) that is toxic to tomato, potato, pea, cabbage, pear, apple, sour cherry, and others. Plants can suddenly wilt and die. Their vascular systems brown, which may cause a false diagnosis of fusarium or verticillium wilts.

Diagnostic Tools: If affected plants are growing near a black walnut or butternut tree, the acid from the tree roots is most likely the problem.

Organic Remedies: Remove the tree, or plant the garden a distance from the tree that exceeds the height of the tree.

Micropests and Macropests

Microdestructive agents receive the designation *micro* because they cannot be seen by the naked eye. They include fungi, bacteria, and viruses. By contrast, macrodestructive agents, ranging from whiteflies to deer, are those that you can see and identify.

Identification of macropests is fairly simple and normally possible without the aid of a professional. Micropests are another matter, however. A definitive diagnosis of most microscopic organisms cannot be made without specialized training, and sometimes without laboratory tests. The difficulty is compounded by the fact that microscopic organisms share numerous symptoms. Several broad differences do exist. A fungus infection frequently results in mold growth, whereas bacteria may cause bad-smelling plant parts. Mottled coloring in the leaves is often a symptom of a virus. These differences are not reliable for diagnosis, however, because they don't consistently accompany the disease. When a definitive diagnosis is necessary, consult a trained professional.

The blue-cheese syndrome. A garden is much like blue cheese, which contains about 13 critical microorganisms that produce its distinctive taste and texture. In blue cheese, about half of these microorganisms are fungal and half bacterial. Similarly, every garden contains a broad variety of microorganisms and macroorganisms, all acting and interacting to produce health or disease. In the advanced stages of disease, therefore, there is probably no such thing as a "pure" infection by a single organism or even by a single family of organisms. Disease is usually promoted by a host of factors, from nutrients to microbial activity. Once a plant is weakened, it can be attacked by several different organisms simultaneously.

The good news is that some organic remedies are broad spectrum; they help attenuate a broad range of diseases. Many of these remedies are the same preventive practices mentioned previously, such as ensuring good soil drainage or watering from below to prevent further contamination through water droplets. One of the most basic broad-spectrum remedies is to remove and destroy diseased leaves, fruit, branches, or plants. When the basics have been ruled out—and disease has been ruled in—a thorough and accurate diagnosis of the major pathogens responsible for the disease may not be necessary if the broad-spectrum remedies work.

Differential diagnosis is important, however, when insect vectors play a role, for the insects then can be controlled. A differential diagnosis also is especially critical any time the gardener wants to use remedies specific to a particular disease, such as a botanical, mineral, or other chemical spray.

OVERVIEW OF SYMPTOMS AND REMEDIES

What follows is an outline of microagents and macroagents, symptoms, and promoting factors and remedies. The list is neither definitive nor a substitute for professional advice or textbooks. A single plant may exhibit only one or multiple symptoms. And, occasionally, there are exceptions to the promoting factors and remedies listed. Remember, many of the remedies are also good preventive garden practices.

Fungal Diseases

SYMPTOMS

Fungal-Specific Symptoms: Mold on any plant part; may be fuzzy, flat, or colored. This group of diseases also includes the blights, which are characterized by rapid withering or tissue decay with no apparent rotting. The blights are perhaps the most difficult to identify because they can mimic each other and often deviate from specific symptoms.

Spots (on Leaves, Stems, or Bark, or Fruit and Flowers): Watery, soft, sunken, dry, shriveled, colored

Leaves: Yellowed, wilted, fallen, curled, wrinkled

Fruit: Shriveled, misshapen

Flowers: Spots, discolored petals

Stems: Rot (decay), sunken areas, girdling, watery blisters, and other types of cankers, cracks, and dark swellings

Roots: Rot (decay), discoloration, knots, cankers

PROMOTING FACTORS

Usually fostered and spread by prolonged periods of rain, moisture, dew, humidity. Spread by tools, gardeners, wind, seeds (sometimes), and insects. Can be soilborne and harbored in plant debris. Some fungal pathogens can live up to 15 years in the soil.

Immediate Remedies

- Remove and destroy diseased plants or parts of plants.
- Water from below.
- Don't touch plants when wet, to avoid spreading disease.
- Disinfect hands after working with diseased plants.
- Disinfect tools between cuts.
- Improve ventilation.
- Keep orchard grass mowed.
- Find out which spray is appropriate for the disease.
- Spray fruit trees with liquid seaweed every 2–3 weeks to prevent spread of fungus; this coats fruits with a protective filament.
- For some fungal problems, you can spray with copper-based fungicides, Bordeaux mixture, sulfur, or lime-sulfur. Never use sulfur on apricots or high doses on cucurbits, which are sensitive to sulfur and will be injured. Copper can kill earthworms.
- There are an increasing number of antifungal commercial sprays and wettable powders available for the organic grower. Check in catalogs and websites for sprays that might apply to your specific fungal problem.
- For certain fruit tree fungi, follow a spray program starting in spring when the tree is dormant.

Long-Range Remedies

- Encourage earthworms.
- Compost.
- Use long crop rotations of 3–5 years for all fungal wilts.
- Plant in a well-drained area.
- Select resistant varieties.
- Solarize garden soil (this is especially effective for controlling verticillium wilt).
- Where recommended, use hot-water seed treatment as follows:

- » *For brassicas:* Place seeds in 122°F/50°C water for 25 minutes.
- » *For celery:* Place seeds in 118°F/48°C water for 30 minutes.
- » *For Solanaceae:* Place seeds in 122°F/50°C water for 30 minutes.

- For fruit trees, paint trunk and lower limbs to reduce cold injury, because disease spreads through injury.
- Don't prune trees until buds swell, because disease may spread through dead buds and bark cuts.
- Prune limbs or canes 4″ below the infection (cankers, galls), and disinfect tools between cuts.
- Research plots in California's San Joaquin Valley showed that composted yard trimmings rid peaches of brown rot.
- Increase organic matter in the soil to discourage wilts.
- Store harvested produce in well-ventilated, cool, dry areas.
- Applying soil taken from underneath birch trees or surrounding birch roots to soil where diseased plants have been removed is thought to have beneficial effects.
- A biologically beneficial strain of the fungus *Gliocladium virens* is commercially available (SoilGard) and reportedly provides long protection against pathogenic fungi that live in the soil.

Bacterial Diseases

SYMPTOMS

Bacteria-Specific Symptoms: Bad smells associated with fruit, roots, stems, or leaves.

Circular and Angular Spots (on Leaves, Stems, and Bark): Sunken, raised, and water-soaked tissue may drop out of spots, leaving holes.

Leaves: Yellowed, curled, wilted, stunted

Fruit: Slimy, spots

Blossoms: Withered, dead

Stems: Lesions, wilted, blackened, dead, wartlike growth, oozing

Roots: Soft, slimy

PROMOTING FACTORS

Usually spread by rain and some beetles (e.g., cucumber beetles, flea beetles).

Immediate Remedies

- Apply insecticidal soap spray at the specific site of infection.
- Remove and destroy infected plants.
- Disinfect tools.
- Don't touch plants when wet.
- Practice clean cultivation.
- For trees, prune out infected parts, disinfect tools between cuts, and destroy removed parts.
- Where severe, remove and destroy the tree. If feasible, solarize the soil.
- Where recommended (usually for fruit trees), spray with a copper-sulfur blend. (This can kill earthworms.)
- Where recommended (usually for vegetables), apply micronized sulfur.

Long-Range Remedies

- Encourage earthworms.
- Compost.
- Plant resistant varieties.
- Practice crop rotation.
- Many peppers, tomatoes, and brassica crops have bacterial diseases inside the seed. Experimental results suggest that seeds be given hot-water treatments at 122°F/50°C for 20–25 minutes, followed by cool water. Seeds should be wrapped loosely in cloth and weighted to submerge them in the

hot-water bath. Carrots require 122°F/50°C for 10 minutes. Solanaceae plants require 122°F/50°C for 25 minutes.
- In the eastern United States, use seeds grown west of the Rockies that are free of bacterial blight.
- Improve soil drainage.

Viral Diseases

SYMPTOMS

Virus-Specific Symptoms: Mottled coloring in leaves
Leaves: Mottled coloring; misshapen growth; yellowing; curling downward; crinkling; unusual narrow, pointed, or fernlike leaves; veins may disappear.
Fruits: Misshapen, premature ripening
Blossoms or Flowers: Misshapen, underdeveloped, few
Stems: Stunted, twisted, misshapen

PROMOTING FACTORS

Usually spread by insect or human vectors (e.g., aphids, cucumber beetles, grasshoppers, leafhoppers, thrips, smokers [tobacco mosaic], human hands, and tools).

Immediate Remedies

- Control insect vector.
- Disinfect tools and hands before working with plants.
- Remove and destroy infected plants, or parts of plants.
- Practice clean cultivation.

Long-Range Remedies

- Encourage earthworms.
- Compost.
- Plant resistant varieties.
- Remove weeds that harbor insect vectors.
- Plant in areas protected from wind to minimize aphid contamination.
- Use closer spacing where leafhoppers are a problem.

Insect Pests

SYMPTOMS

Visible presence of insect (but those that suck plant juices are more difficult to spot)
Leaves: Chewed or ragged holes, defoliation, tunnels, blotches, skeletonization, wilting, webbing, leaf drop, eggs on upper or lower leaf sides
Fruit: Small, round or other-shaped holes; premature drop
Flowers: Malformed
Stems and Bark: Holes or sunken area; severed, weak, stunted or distorted, wilted
Roots: Malformed, poorly developed, eaten; decay in storage.

Immediate Remedies

- Handpick bugs off plants.
- Remove and destroy eggs.
- Use traps; most are insect specific.
- Mulch, where appropriate.
- Remove and destroy heavily infected plants.
- Practice clean cultivation.
- Where appropriate, apply sprays of insecticidal soaps, oils, etc.
- Spray fruit trees with liquid seaweed every 2–3 weeks, which masks fruit scent and protects the trees against insect damage.

Long-Range Remedies

- Encourage earthworms.
- Compost.
- Plant resistant varieties.
- Use row covers before pest emerges.

- Practice fall cultivation.
- Encourage insect-eating birds and other beneficial animals.
- Solarize soil, if feasible.

Mycoplasmas

SYMPTOMS

Because mycoplasmas are life-forms intermediate between viruses and bacteria, plant symptoms may resemble those of viruses and bacteria. Mycoplasmas are the smallest organisms lacking cell walls capable of self-replication and are known to cause diseases in humans, animals, and plants.

PROMOTING FACTORS

Usually spread by insect vectors such as leafhoppers.

Remedies

See remedies for fungal, bacterial, and viral diseases.

Glossary of Organic Remedies

Following is a detailed description of the common remedies for micropests and macropests that are given in the charts in abbreviated form.

When selecting a remedy, the rule of thumb for the noncommercial gardener is to start with the least invasive and least toxic remedies. If these are ineffective, then consider removing the pest-damaged plants. Use stronger remedies (botanical sprays) only if your need to save the pest-damaged plants outweighs the harmful effects the sprays may have on the garden ecosystem. Apply all remedies in the smallest effective quantities and in the most limited areas necessary for control.

Beneficial insects and plants. (See also "Integrated pest management" on page 195.) Beneficial insects are attracted to flowering Apiaceae, such as dill and carrots in their second year, yarrow, sweet cicely, and fennel. (For more information on beneficials, see pages 3–8 and 178.) The Henry Doubleday Research Association in Coventry, England, has shown that the following beneficial insects are attracted to the noted plants.

- **Hover fly:** Pot marigolds, baby blue eyes, bush morning glory, poached egg plant (*Limnanthes douglasii*), sweet alyssum, dill, cosmos, lemon balm, yarrow
- **Parasitic wasps and flies:** Yarrow, flowering fennel and carrots, angelica, dill, mallow, cosmos, lobelia, sweet alyssum, cinquefoil, marigold
- **Lacewings and parasitic wasps:** Mustard, yarrow, dill, angelica, coriander, cosmos, fennel, dandelion

Beneficial nematodes. Unlike the various nematodes that cause damage, beneficial nematodes such as *Steinernema carpocapsae* are a fast and totally safe control for various pests. A number of species and varieties of beneficial nematodes exist. As juvenile-stage microscopic organisms, these parasites inject the insect with bacteria that kill the host within 24 hours. They don't harm humans, plants, pets, birds, earthworms, honeybees, or beneficial insects. A self-limiting control, beneficial nematodes seek out soil grubs (young phase of certain insects), feed, reproduce, and, when their food supply is exhausted, die. Only effective in the juvenile stage, these nematodes can be stored in the refrigerator for up to 2 months.

Beneficial nematodes must be applied at sufficient rates to be effective, about 50,000 per foot of standard row, or per square foot in raised beds. Numerous destructive pests are susceptible to these nematodes, including borers, weevils, cutworms, cucumber beetles, and even spongy moths. One quart is sufficient for about 50 square feet—just sprinkle the mixture where the pests are a problem. One source suggests using nematodes in compost heaps to eradicate harmful larvae.

WHAT GOES UP MUST COME DOWN

Substances that may damage insects above the soil also have the potential to damage beneficial organisms in the soil. Such remedies may treat the plant at the expense of the ecosystem. When possible, the potential effects these remedies may have on beneficial organisms above and in the soil have been noted.

Some perspective may be helpful here. Most garden vegetable plants last for a year, whereas the soil takes years to build into a healthy medium. If one year you drive out beneficial organisms in order to get rid of a pest problem and harm the soil in the process, the following year there is a distinct possibility that your garden will have even more problems and require even more remedial measures.

Although there may be times you want to use these remedies to save some plants, do so with consideration for the soil. Apply the remedy in the smallest effective quantities and in the smallest area necessary for control. Massive preventive spraying is usually neither necessary nor recommended for the backyard gardener. Commercial growers and orchardists may have little choice at the moment, but the backyard gardener does.

Bug juice. Considered an old home remedy, bug juice may or may not be effective. It is thought that, on death, some insects release a pheromone to warn their kind to stay away. But applying bug juice might also help spread disease to other plants. If you want to try it experimentally, capture ½ cup of the pest, crush it, and liquefy it with 2 cups water. Do *not* use a household blender to accomplish this; instead, use an old blender jar or a mortar and pestle specifically intended for garden use. Strain to remove particles before spraying. Spray both sides of the leaves and stems.

Clean cultivation. (See Plant Maintenance on page 175.) Generally, *clean cultivation* means you should remove and destroy all infected plants or parts of plants, and clean out weeds, dead and rotting vegetation, piles of junk, and plants that are finished bearing. Destroy diseased plants by burning (where permitted), burial, or some other appropriate means. Remove stagnant pools of water and piles of brush, lumber, or stones near the garden. Don't work around or touch wet plants, particularly when they're diseased. Don't add diseased plant material to compost piles.

Colored mulch. Yellow mulch may serve as an attractant to plant pests and can serve as a way of "trapping" plant pests in a concentrated zone. If you are going to spray, vacuum, or do something else, applying yellow mulch may make it easier for you to accomplish your goal while having less impact on the larger garden area.

Cooking oil spray mix. The following home oil spray can be used for controlling aphids, whiteflies, and spider mites: (1) Mix 1 tablespoon plain dishwashing liquid with 1 cup cooking oil; (2) add 1 to 2½ teaspoons of the oil/detergent solution to 1 cup water; (3) spray directly on plants every 10 days.

This spray works well on carrots, celery, cucumber, eggplant, lettuce, pepper, and watermelon but be cautious that it may burn squash, cauliflower, and red cabbage.

Crop rotation. At a minimum, plant the same vegetable in the same soil site only once every other year, rotating on a 2-year basis. Some diseases require a longer minimum rotation. *Same soil site* is defined as being within a 10-foot radius of where the vegetable was planted previously. So rotation can occur within the same growing bed as long as the new site is at least 10 feet away from where the crop was grown the previous year or from where there is refuse from the planting. If possible, routinely rotate on a 3- to 5-year basis.

Diatomaceous earth (DE). This is an insect remedy with very low toxicity. Diatomaceous earth is a hydrophilic (water-loving) form of silicon dioxide (sand) that rapidly takes up water. Harvested from riverbeds, it is made from petrified skeletons of water-dwelling microorganisms known as *diatoms.* It works by desiccating insects.

Apply a dusting of diatomaceous earth after a light rain, dew, or after lightly spraying plants with water. Dust all plant surfaces, starting from the base and moving upward. You can also spray diatomaceous earth in a weak insecticidal soap solution (¼ pound diatomaceous earth to 5 gallons water to 1 teaspoon insecticidal soap), which helps the spray adhere to plant surfaces. Fruit trees can be painted with the same solution. Whether dusted or sprayed, reapply after rainfall. Diatomaceous earth is effective against most soft-bodied insects (aphids, mites, slugs, etc.) but also may work against some beetles and weevils.

Fall cultivation. Leave the soil completely bare for a few days. Cultivate the soil to a depth of 6 to 8 inches to expose eggs and larvae to birds and other predators. Two weeks later, lightly cultivate the soil a second time with a rake, this time to a depth of only 2 inches. Leave the soil bare for a few more days, then plant a cover crop or apply a layer of winter mulch 4 to 6 inches deep.

Garlic spray. This falls into the category of old home remedies, which means it may or may not work for you. Garlic has been found to have some antifungal properties (see page 153), but the methods of extraction and the quantities necessary haven't been widely tested. This spray should be considered experimental. (See "Hot pepper spray" on page 193 for ideas on how to prepare garlic spray.)

Warning: Earthworms will not eat plants in the onion family, so garlic spray could drive them away from the area sprayed.

Handpick. Handpicking is often the most effective control against insect pests. Wear gloves at all times to prevent allergic reactions. To kill bugs, drop them into soapy water, boiling water, or water that has some insecticidal soap in it. Small amounts of kerosene or oil also work but are more difficult to dispose of in an ecologically safe way.

BAD TIMES FOR APPLYING PESTICIDES

Pesticides such as botanicals and homemade sprays, soaps, and oils should not be applied under any of the following conditions.

- In the rain
- In windy conditions
- In intense sunlight
- In the middle of hot, dry days (pesticide may volatilize before reaching insect or leaf)
- When mixed with noncompatible materials
- On open blossoms, when bees are present
- When plant is moisture stressed (too much or too little)
- When leaf is wet with dew (unless such moisture is specifically recommended to assist adherence)

Horticultural oil. Horticultural grades of oil work by suffocating mature insects, larvae, and eggs. Complete coverage of the insect population is required for the treatment to be effective. Historically, horticultural oils were called "dormant" oils because they were sprayed only when plants, particularly fruit and shade trees, were in a dormant stage of growth before buds opened in spring. As refining processes improved, "superior" oils were developed. These are lighter weight than previous dormant oils, evaporate more quickly, and contain no sulfur. They are less likely to burn plants, meaning they can be applied, with some precautions, during the growing season when plants are in full leaf. The term *dormant* no longer refers to the type of oil, but instead now refers to the seasonal timing of the application, as all horticultural oils now sold are superior oils. All-season oils can be sprayed any time of the year except during freezing temperatures, temperatures above 90°F/33°C, and windy or rainy weather. Fall treatments can cause winter injury. Oils should only be applied when the plant surfaces are dry and the plant is well irrigated. If overapplied, they can clog leaf pores, thereby preventing respiration and severely injuring or killing the plant. To determine whether a plant will tolerate the oil, spray it on a few leaves. Leaf tips and margins will yellow after several days if the plant is damaged by the oil. Horticultural oils are considered relatively safe for humans, other warm-blooded animals, and beneficial insects, though can be toxic to fish and bees unless sprayed in the early morning or evening.

Hot pepper spray. Red peppers have been shown to contain an active ingredient called *capsaicin*, which is an irritant to mammals and insects. Capsaicin kills nerve fibers in mammals, so it may act against insect pests by affecting their nervous systems. Reports on the efficacy of hot peppers are mixed, though some have found that capsaicin powder repels onion fly maggots when as little as 1 milligram is sprinkled around the plant base. It is believed to be effective against other insects as well. It apparently does not work well in monocultures, but it does work well in gardens having a variety of plants and offering insects multiple feeding sites. Capsaicin can be purchased commercially, or you can make your own. University of Massachusetts Amherst Extension points out that hot pepper wax is no longer allowable for Certified Organic growers. The National Organic Program allows capsaicin, the active ingredient in hot pepper wax, but not the wax itself.

Warning: Capsaicin is toxic to bees and other beneficial insects, and an irritant for earthworms.

To make your own hot pepper spray, try one of these recipes.

Recipe 1: Chop, grind, or blend hot peppers. Mix ½ cup ground hot peppers with 2 cups water. Strain to remove particles.

Recipe 2: Mix together 2 tablespoons garlic powder, 1 to 2 tablespoons Tabasco sauce or Louisiana Hot sauce, a dash of dishwashing liquid, and 2 cups water. The soap helps the spray adhere better to leaves and bugs. The spray works well against many soft-bodied insects, such as aphids, whiteflies, mealybugs, and most larvae (except that of spongy moth). *Recipe courtesy horticulturist Carl Totemeier, Ph.D.*

Apply hot pepper spray twice, allowing a 2- to 3-day interval between each spraying. Hot pepper spray should be applied in the evening so it has all night to dry before the sun's rays hit the plant in the morning. The spray must make physical contact with the pest to be effective. Generally, pepper spray usually repels, but does not kill, the bugs.

Hot-water seed treatment. Place seeds in a cheesecloth bag; place the bag in water at the designated temperature and for the specified number of minutes. Stir continuously, adding hot water periodically to keep the water temperature consistent. Don't pour hot water directly on the seeds. When finished, remove the seeds and immerse them in cold water. Drain and dry.

Insecticidal soap spray. This is not the same thing as homemade soap, and it is not effective for household cleaning. Insecticidal soap is derived from fatty acid salts that are able to penetrate the cell membranes of insects. They work best on soft-bodied insects such as aphids, mealybugs, mites, and whiteflies. Insecticidal soap spray biodegrades in 2 to 14 days, and the residue on the plant, once dry, is considered ineffective.

Insecticidal soaps are specifically formulated to attack only harmful pests and, unless specified, are not harmful to humans, pets, and most beneficial insects. They have been used successfully in conjunction with beneficials such as *Encarsia formosa* and ladybug larvae. Insecticidal soaps are generally better for plants than are household soap sprays because they don't usually burn plant leaves, they lack the added ingredients of household soap, and they contain known quantities of active ingredients (fatty acid salts). Any phytotoxic symptoms appear within the first 48 hours of spraying, so if you're unsure whether the soap will burn or injure a plant, test it on just a few leaves and wait for 2 days to see if wilting, yellowing, or other symptoms of burn appear.

Insecticidal soap works on contact only, so spray it directly on the pest. And spray only those areas affected by the pest, not the entire patch of plants and not necessarily the entire plant. Coat both sides of any infested surface. This is called *spot spraying.*

Generally, insecticidal soap is not very effective against hard-bodied insects, but adding isopropyl alcohol increases its effectiveness. The alcohol carries the soap through the pest's protective coating. Simply add ½ cup isopropyl alcohol to every 4 cups insecticidal soap. Some commercial insecticidal soaps are premixed with alcohol, though they may not advertise this fact.

It's best to spray in early morning. Don't spray insecticidal soap at temperatures above 90°F/33°C or in full sun. And don't spray newly rooted cuttings, new transplants, or blooming fruit and nut trees. If a plant begins to wilt in the first few hours after spraying, rinse all soap residues from the plant.

Integrated pest management (IPM). In the latter twentieth century, significant advances were made in understanding how pests can be controlled through the carefully timed and controlled release of beneficial insects that eat pests and/or their larvae, interrupt the pest cycle, or otherwise reduce or prevent crop damage by pests. Once considered by many to be too experimental or too difficult, IPM has become a mainstream practice for both large- and small-scale growers due to increased education and improved technologies. IPM is one of the many effective tools that can be used by the organic gardener.

Kaolin clay. Kaolin clay is a naturally occurring mineral that is often used as a spray or dust on the foliage of plants. It acts as a physical barrier that repels insects and is an obstacle to feeding and egg-laying. In some instances, it has been shown to help reduce sunburn on crops in areas of intense sun (particularly in the Southwest). The physical barrier it creates may also offer some protection against fungal diseases by preventing spore attachment and germination.

Kaolin clay is highly recommended for use on some fruit trees (apple, citrus, and pear), wine grapes, walnut trees, brussels sprouts, cucumbers, eggplant, tomatoes, squash, and zucchini plants. It can help protect from aphids, apple maggots, Colorado potato beetles, cucumber beetles, flea beetles, thrips, Japanese beetles, leafhoppers, squash bugs, spotted asparagus beetle, pear psyllid, and certain moths and caterpillars. In particular, studies by the USDA have shown that kaolin clay is very effective in preventing thrips on small fruit trees. Specifically, an application of the powder applied at 50 pecent bloom deters thrips and provides several other horticultural benefits. The application of the clay encourages good growth and does not interfere with the activities of beneficial pollinators.

Surround WP is the most common brand of kaolin clay. To use, mix 3 cups of clay with 1 gallon of water. It is most advisable to spray on days without direct sunlight to prevent sunburning, and not too close to rainfall, which will wash the clay off. Apply the kaolin clay spray using a handheld sprayer, ensuring complete coverage of the plant foliage, including both upper and lower leaf surfaces. The goal is to create a thin, even layer of the clay on the plants. Depending on rainfall and plant growth, you may need to reapply the spray every 7 to 14 days to maintain its effectiveness.

Neem. Neem is a botanical insecticide derived from the neem tree of arid, tropical zones in Asia and Africa. The active ingredient, azadirachtin, is unlike most other botanical poisons, which typically act on the stomach or nerves. Neem acts as a feeding deterrent and interrupts normal hormonal activity so that insects cannot molt properly; they die in their own skin. It has been shown to be effective against numerous pests, including the more difficult ones: Colorado potato beetle, gypsy moth, grasshopper, Japanese beetle, and Mexican bean beetle. While neem does not persist in the soil, there have been growing concerns around its impact on nontarget insects and its potential harm to pollinators, such as bees, when not used properly.

Row covers. Row covers are an extremely effective barrier against egg-laying insects. They are made of lightweight material that lets in air, light, and water. Cover transplants immediately or as specified for pest emergence times. Seal the edges to the ground, and leave the row covers on all season, unless otherwise noted. Allow extra material to accommodate the growth of the tallest plant. For plants that need pollination, such as most cucumbers, lift the edges of the row covers during bloom time in the early morning for 2 hours, twice a week. This is all the time bees and other pollinators need to do their good work. When the blooming time is past, secure the row cover edges again until harvesttime.

Do *not* use row covers if the pest was seen in that same spot the previous season or if it overwinters or lays eggs in the soil.

Row covers usually raise the temperature underneath, which is helpful for extending the growing season in spring and fall. If you plan to keep the covers on through the warm season, however, especially if you live in one of the southern growing zones, the temperature rise may not be beneficial to plants that don't tolerate heat well.

There are many effective row covers on the market. Choose the one that suits your needs best, depending on the climate and the level of breathability and permeability your plants need.

Soap spray (homemade). Homemade soap spray is not the same as insecticidal soap spray. Tests of various types of household soap sprays show that they differ considerably in their effectiveness against bugs and in the degree to which they burn plant leaves. Begin by using 2 to 3 tablespoons of soap per gallon of water; never use more than 4 tablespoons of soap, for it will burn the plant leaves. Test different soaps to determine the brand and concentration that works best without burning the leaves. You might also choose to rinse the plant well 1 to 2 hours after spraying it, which prevents harm to the plant. Avoid using soaps that are dyed or perfumed. Soap flakes, although more difficult to prepare, seem to be the least damaging to plants. Some dishwashing liquids are mild enough to be left on the plant without rinsing. Soap spray is a contact insecticide (see "Insecticidal soap spray" on page 194).

Warning: Unless you are absolutely certain that the soap you use is biodegradable, you may do more harm than good if you spray it widely. Spot spraying, however, should not be a problem. Commercial manufacturers may label a kitchen soap "biodegradable," but that begs the questions: Under what conditions and in how many years? The label may be appropriate for a septic tank, but always check with the manufacturer to be sure the soap will biodegrade rapidly. If in doubt, use an insecticidal soap that is designed to biodegrade rapidly and to target specific pests.

Soap and lime spray. Mix agricultural lime at the rate of ¼ to ½ cup per gallon of water. Add 2 to 3 tablespoons insecticidal soap per gallon. The soap helps the lime adhere to insect bodies. The lime can dry out small insects, kill some small insects and mites, and irritate adult insects. Test the spray first on a small area of the plant, because some plants may react adversely to these materials. Wait several days before judging the results and deciding whether to spray the remainder of the plant. As with other soap sprays, spot spray to avoid harming beneficial insects.

Stem collar. Stem collars provide physical barriers against crawling pests. To make stem collars, use waxed paper cups, which hold up well in the rain, or some other weather-resistant material, such as cardboard or tar paper. Cut a hole in the bottom of each cup to accommodate the stem, then cut slits radiating out from the hole to allow for stem growth. Place the inverted cup around the base of the stem, sinking the edges into the soil at least 1 inch. If using something other than a cup, simply cut a 3- to 4-inch collar out of the material, place it around the stem, push it 1 inch into the soil, and fasten the sides together securely. Cardboard toilet paper tubes work well and eventually disintegrate.

Sticky balls. These traps may function best as early-warning devices to detect the presence of pests in sufficient numbers to require further action. Usually red, the balls are hung in trees as both warning and control devices. As a monitoring device, count the pests trapped every 2 to 3 days and recoat the ball every 2 weeks. As a pest control, use one to four balls per tree, depending on tree size. Clean and recoat the balls as needed, and remove all balls after 4 weeks to avoid catching too many beneficial insects.

Sticky bands. Sticky bands are wrapped around tree trunks to trap larvae, egg-laying females, or other pests. Use cotton batting, burlap, or heavy paper that's at least 6 inches wide. Place bands around the tree trunk at about chest height. Cover the batting with a 6- to 12-inch piece of tar paper coated with Tanglefoot or with a mixture of either pine tar and molasses or resin and oil. Wrap tightly around the trunk and secure with wire or a tie. Renew the sticky substance periodically. If you're trapping larvae, remove the bands and destroy the larvae once weekly in warm weather or biweekly in cool weather. If you're trapping a crawling insect that is not bearing or laying eggs (e.g., aphids), clean as necessary and renew the sticky substance.

Sticky traps. These traps may function best as early-warning devices to detect the presence of pests in sufficient numbers to require further action. For monitoring, count the pests trapped every 2 to 3 days; recoat the traps every 2 weeks. These traps are usually yellow or white boards, about 8 × 10 inches, coated with a sticky substance such as Tanglefoot Tangle-Trap or petroleum jelly. Do not use motor oil (recommended by some), because it will change the board's color. Place the traps adjacent to susceptible plants; do not place them above the plants. Clean and recoat traps as needed. Try not to use these traps for more than 3 to 4 weeks at a time to avoid capturing too many beneficial insects. In a greenhouse, place the traps at the height of the plants' canopy.

Traps. Traps are an easy, nontoxic way to monitor and control many different insects. They usually use pheromones and colors to attract the targeted bug. Monitoring traps is useful to determine when the insect emerges, where it comes from, and how many insects are present, before resorting to chemical remedies. Generally, traps are a safe and cost-effective tool for a self-sustaining garden. Traps are available for such insects as the slug, Japanese beetle, codling moth, spongy moth, oriental fruit moth, corn earworm, cherry fruit fly and husk fly, apple maggot (see "Sticky balls," above), and some scales, among others.

SOME CAVEATS ON TRAPS

Traps that are not pheromone-specific may capture beneficial insects as well as harmful ones; consequently, traps shouldn't be left out longer than recommended. Pheromone traps that work over long distances may actually attract more of the undesirable targeted insect to your garden. Some pheromone traps are best suited to large commercial operations. Before investing in traps, consult the supplier about your particular situation and determine whether traps are best placed in the garden or away from it.

Organic Remedies to Use with Caution

The following remedies are approved for use in organic gardening but should be used with caution due to concerns about their impact on pollinators and beneficial insects.

Bacillus thuringiensis (Bt). Bt is a naturally occurring bacterium that was discovered in 1901. It comes in a powder form and contains proteins that are toxic to insect larvae when eaten. There are many types of Bt. Each type or strain affects different insect groups, such as the M-One that attacks Colorado potato beetle larvae. This control method won't kill eggs or adults, so it is important to apply it at the right time, when the insect pests or other larvae are actively feeding. While Bt is considered safe for humans, if you are concerned about its effects, avoid the sprayed area for 30 to 90 minutes to allow the droplets to settle.

Warning: Legitimate concern exists about the possibility that exclusive or immoderate use of Bt will foster Bt-resistant pests. In 2013, reduced efficacy of Bt crops caused by field-evolved resistance was reported in between 5–13 major pest species, compared with resistant populations of only one pest species in 2005. Many specialists believe that as such problems arise, new strains of Bt can be developed to conquer the newly resistant pests. This argument is identical to one used by pharmaceutical companies to justify new strains of penicillin to combat penicillin-resistant bacteria. Although new forms of penicillin have been developed successfully, the toxicity to humans of the newer penicillins exceeds the original by 10 to 12 times. Severe allergic response to the original penicillin was less than 1 percent; severe allergic response to "improved penicillins" are as high as 10 to 20 percent. Therefore, noncommercial growers may decide, as I did, not to use Bt or, if necessary, to use it only as a last resort.

Botanical controls. Derived from naturally occurring sources, these insecticides are considered "organic" by many people because of their alleged lack of persistence in the environment. Botanicals are generally thought to be relatively safe for birds, pets, humans, and other wildlife. Some synthesized chemicals, however, which are not considered organic, seem to be gentler on beneficial insects in and above the soil than some of the older "organic" sprays. Strictly speaking, minerals, such as copper and sulfur, are not botanicals, but they are included under this rubric for easy reference.

Warning: Insecticides and botanicals should not be used unless crops have suffered significant damage. No matter how safe an insecticide is reputed to be, the introduction of botanical poisons, minerals, and other substances alters a garden's natural system of checks and balances. Pyrethrin can kill beneficial organisms in and above the soil just as easily as the pests you're trying to eradicate. It can cause allergic skin reactions in some people and pose significant health risks to mammals and other nontarget organisms, such as birds, bees, and fish.

The definition of significant damage is a matter of personal interpretation, but bear in mind that most plants can lose up to 20 percent of their foliage and still produce yields equal to those of plants with no foliage loss. Even when significant damage occurs, you might consider the size of the area you will need to spray and the value of your crop, compared to the potential damage to the ecology of the rest of your garden. Insecticides and fungicides should only be used as an absolute last resort, after all other methods have failed. Apply the botanical control just to the leaves, plants, or areas that are affected and at the minimal concentrations necessary to do the job. (For more information, see the information that follows about copper, pyrethrin, and sulfur.)

Copper. Copper is usually considered a fungicide and can be dusted, sprayed, or combined with other substances. While it is an effective control of fungal and bacterial diseases, such as anthracnose, all blights, brown rot, downy and powdery mildews, leaf spot, rust, and scab, a number of studies show that copper is highly toxic to honeybees, can cause liver disease and anemia in humans, and can be toxic to beneficial soil bacteria, fungi, and earthworms. (For a more detailed discussion of the effects of copper and other substances on earthworms, see Jerry Minnich, *The Earthworm Book*.) While the National Organic Standards Board allows garden use of copper (fixed copper in oxides, and copper sulfate), additional restrictions have been added to ensure that copper-based materials are not used as herbicides and are used in a way that minimizes accumulation in the soil.

Pyrethrin. This botanical poison is derived from the pyrethrum flower, a member of the chrysanthemum family. Pyrethrin is considered a "knockout" contact insecticide and stomach poison; it works by paralyzing the insect. If the insect receives less than a lethal dose, it may revive. Pyrethrin is still approved for use in organic gardening and is considered relatively safe for warm-blooded animals and relatively safe for honeybees and ladybug larvae, but only because it degrades within 6 hours in temperatures above 55°F/13°C. There has been growing concern in recent years about their harm to nontarget insects and aquatic life. Additionally, some insects have developed resistance to pyrethrin. Use with extra caution. Spray at dusk when honeybees are less active, and don't spray at all if a heavy dew is expected. The foliar spray is considered to be less harmful to bees than is the dust application. It is effective against most greenhouse pests, especially flying insects such as whitefly.

Spinosad. Spinosad is a natural substance, made by a soil bacterium, that acts as a broad-spectrum microbial insecticide, attacking the pest's nervous system once eaten. It is a mixture of two chemicals, called spinosyn A and spinosyn D, and is used to control a wide variety of pests, including the Colorado potato beetle, diamondback moths, cabbage looper, imported cabbageworms, European corn borer, fall armyworm, corn earworms, hornworms, thrips and leafminers. Generally, Spinosad is most effective against larvae, so look carefully for eggs and feeding insects before you spray. Like Bt, Spinosad breaks down in sunlight, so late-day applications will better expose insects to the toxins. Spinosad has a longer period of residual effectiveness compared with Bt, often providing protection from pests for 5–7 days.

Warning: The wet spray of Spinosad is toxic to bees and other beneficial insects such as ladybugs and parasitoid wasps. They are minimally affected once Spinosad residue is dry, so try to apply when pollinators are less active and avoid applying it to plants known to host butterflies and other beneficials, like milkweed. Like Bt, there are concerns around excessive use leading to the development of resistance in target pests. To manage resistance, rotate Spinosad with other organic pest control methods, use only when necessary, and read application instructions carefully.

Sulfur. Sulfur is a naturally occurring element used in organic gardening as a fungicide and pesticide, and can be dusted, sprayed, or combined with other substances. It is thought to work as a fungicide by entering fungi cells and affecting cell respiration. As a pesticide, it interferes with the insect's normal metabolic function, altering their ability to produce energy. It is effective against diseases such as powdery mildew, rust, and certain fruit tree diseases, and insects such as mites and psyllids. While sulfur it not thought to be toxic to humans, birds, bees and fish, there is concern that it can kill a variety of other beneficial insects, fungi, and other microbes and should therefore be used sparingly and with caution. Always follow label instructions and take steps to avoid exposure.

Synthetic pesticides. Designed for quick results and long-lasting activity, synthetics are totally man-made poisons, often acting on the nervous systems and digestive tracts of insects. Some synthetics are considered milder and less toxic than the more "natural" botanical poisons. They are considered less safe for organic growing, however, because their breakdown products often persist in the soil longer and are more toxic than their original formulations. Some synthetic pesticides persist so long, in fact, that they can be found in soils more than 20 years after their application. Botanicals are favored in organic growing because they don't persist in the environment and their breakdown products are safer.

Warning: Studies have shown that the residues of some pesticides, when used in greenhouses, may linger longer than specified. Therefore, safe reentry time may be longer than expected. If you are a greenhouse grower, contact the manufacturer to determine whether the pesticide has been tested under conditions similar to those in your greenhouse.

Identifying and Remedying Specific Micropests and Macropests

The two sections that follow outline in detail how to identify and remedy a range of diseases and how to control the insect and animal pests that may affect your plants. Keep in mind that the charts are meant to assist, not to discourage. If you rotate crops, destroy diseased material from garden areas, use resistant varieties, and start with pathogen-free transplants, most diseases shouldn't be a problem. As for insects, most gardens experience very few, usually no more than three to five major pests. Proper controls adopted in a timely fashion should minimize any major threats to your crops. And remember that plants can lose up to 20 percent of their foliage and still produce yields equal to those of plants with no foliage loss.

Only when you have made a positive identification of the microscopic destructive agent should you apply remedies specific to that disease. Specific-disease remedies, such as botanical sprays, are generally more injurious to an ecosystem than are the broad-spectrum, preventive remedies discussed on pages 171–180. An application of a special remedy that doesn't target the appropriate disease is not only a waste of money and time, but it also can be potentially harmful to the plant and ecosystem. An antibacterial spray used inappropriately, for example, could destroy beneficial bacteria both above and in the soil. The ecological balances above and in the soil take time to build and should not be sacrificed lightly. If you are ready to spray or use some other pest-specific remedy, take time to consult a textbook, an Extension agent, or another professional to ensure that you have correctly identified the pest.

Prevention is by far the best approach to disease and insect control, but it is most critical with diseases. Postinfection remedies for specific macropests are often more varied and usually include some easy, nontoxic methods that don't harm beneficials above or in the soil.

In the sections that follow, I have tried to avoid, or at least minimize recommendations of, controls that might be difficult to administer, could potentially harm earthworms and soil microorganisms, or could cause ecological imbalances in future years. Not everyone agrees as to the appropriate use of certain substances. When in doubt, every effort has been made to err on the side of safety.

A word about weeds. It is often said that a weed is any plant that grows where it is not desired. Some people keep meticulous gardens, weeding every last whisper of grass or dandelion green throughout the season. Research in north-central California has shown that such meticulous care may not be necessary and may even be harmful. Hoeing and other forms of weeding were shown to reduce yields in some cases. The research concluded that cucumbers, lettuce, and cauliflower require only 2 weeks of weeding to be well established. A balanced approach might be to weed meticulously during the first few weeks of plant establishment and then to follow your own aesthetic. Here are some suggestions for dealing with weeds.

- **Solarize the soil,** which kills some weed seeds.
- **Add radish juice** to the growing medium to completely inhibit germination of some important weed species. Research studies have found radish juice to be an effective herbicide.
- **Consider lamb's quarters.** Both water extracts and pulverized residues of the common weed lamb's quarters (*Chenopodium album*) have been found to strongly inhibit germination and growth of some plants, according to researchers in Oklahoma. Pulverized lamb's quarters gradually loses its herbicidal properties over time.
- **Use hot water.** Hot water melts the waxy coating on weed leaves or breaks down the plant's cellular structures. Treated plants are unable to retain moisture and dehydrate within hours or a few days. Hot water kills new as well as mature plants.

- **Consider corn-gluten meal.** Corn-gluten meal is believed by some to be an effective preemergent herbicide; it is available commercially.
- **Consider a handheld commercial propane device.** These are said to "kill weeds safely by heating—not burning." They are lightweight and portable.
- **Till in the dark.** Tilling in the dark may cut some weed problems in half, according to research from the USDA in Rosemount, Minnesota. Seeds of certain weed species need a flash of light to break dormancy, and tilling in the dark prevents this. This approach is recommended only for those with good night vision.
- **Spray white vinegar.** Studies have shown that vinegar (5 percent acetic acid) can be effective against grass and some weeds if sprayed at least three times.

A GUIDE TO CONTROLLING DISEASES

Selection criteria: Diseases are included in this chart *only* if they meet the following criteria: (1) The remedies for the disease go beyond the remedies mentioned in the earlier parts of this chapter (to avoid unnecessary repetition); (2) insects are known to spread the disease organisms (the disease may be attenuated by insect control); and (3) the disease organism is especially virulent and the affected plants need to be removed immediately.

If you do not find a disease or insect pest listed in the charts that follow, refer to pages 190–200 for generic remedies that may apply.

Pathogens: Diseases in different plants may share a common name (e.g., bacterial wilt) but are often caused by different pathogens. Consequently, the "same" disease may have distinct symptoms in different plants. To make matters more difficult, the same pathogen occasionally causes different symptoms in different species. To simplify matters in the chart, diseases have been grouped by their common names and, when possible, the different symptoms are described.

Remedies: In addition to implementing the specific remedies listed in this chart, remember *never* to work with wet plants and to practice clean cultivation as described on page 191.

Warning: Diseases are more difficult than insect pests to diagnose accurately. The information presented here is intended to help you conduct a more informed discussion with professionals; it is not meant to be a definitive diagnostic tool.

Before using sprays or instituting large-scale or costly remedies, make every effort to obtain an accurate diagnosis. Carefully read each description of possible diseases for the particular plant; don't stop at the first one, even if it seems to match the symptoms of your plant. Because this section is not exhaustive, consult other texts as well. If in doubt, take a plant sample to a local professional to obtain a diagnosis.

Anthracnose

Type: Fungus

Plants Affected: Numerous plants

Where It Occurs: Widespread. Overwinters in seed and residues of infected plants. It can be spread by wind, rain, animals, clothing, and tools. It is most common in cool wet conditions.

Symptoms

- Numerous strains of this fungus affect different crops and ornamental plants.
- Characterized by spots that become brown, grayish, or black; the spots are often sunken and may ooze.
- May cause lesions on stems and vines, and may infect the roots.
- Fruits can develop circular cankers of varying size and color, depending on the crop; in moist conditions these spots can contain salmon gelatinous spores.

Organic Remedies

- See Overview of Symptoms and Remedies for fungal diseases on page 186.
- Remove diseased refuse, use a 3-year rotation, and ensure well-drained soil and good air circulation.
- Select varieties that are resistant to this mildew.
- Commercial fungicides containing baking soda can be used on various ornamentals and fruit trees and are said to be effective against black spot, powdery mildew, leaf spots, anthracnose, phoma, phytophthora, scab, and botrytis.

Armillaria Root Rot

also known as Honey Mushroom, Mushroom Root Rot, Oak Root Fungus, Shoestring Fungus

Type: Fungus

Plants Affected: Fruit trees, nut trees, ornamentals

Where It Occurs: Western states, Atlantic Coast, Florida, and Gulf Coast. Worst in heavy, poorly drained soils.

How It Is Spread: Fungus spreads underground 1 foot at a time.

Symptoms

- White, fan-shaped fungus appears between the bark and wood.
- Lower trunk decays.
- Crown is girdled by fungus.
- Mushrooms appear in autumn around the plant base.
- Roots rot and die slowly. If stressed by other factors, the tree will die suddenly.

Organic Remedies

- ***In mild cases:*** Remove the soil around rotted trunk areas; cut out dead tissue; let the trunk dry out during summer and replace soil when a freeze approaches.
- ***In severe cases:*** Remove the plant, stump, and, if possible, the roots.

Asparagus Rust

Type: Fungus

Plant Affected: Asparagus

Where It Occurs: Widespread. Worst in moist seasons.

How It Is Spread: Wind and spores

Symptoms

- Leaves and stems develop orange-red spots or blisters that, in time, burst open with orange-red spores.
- Tops yellow and die prematurely.

Organic Remedies

- Cut, remove, and destroy affected tops.
- Do not start new plantings next to old plantings.
- Destroy wild asparagus.

- If necessary, apply a sulfur spray every 7–10 days until 1 month before harvest.
- Use heavy mulch and drip (not overhead) irrigation to minimize spreading disease through splashing.
- Select resistant varieties.

Aster Yellows

see Yellows

Bacterial Canker

also known as Bacterial Blast, Bacterial Gummosis

Type: Bacteria

Plants Affected: Almond, apricot, blueberry, cherry, peach, tomato

Where It Occurs: Widespread, especially in cool, windy, moist weather

How It Is Spread: Transmitted by wind, rain, infected seeds, and debris. It enters through skin wounds.

Symptoms

- ***In almond, apricot, peach:*** Small purple spots develop on leaves, black spots on fruits, and cankers on twigs.
- ***In blueberry:*** Stems develop reddish brown to black cankers and nearby buds die. Plants eventually die.
- ***In cherry:*** Leaves wilt and die. Cracks and stems may ooze in spring and fall. Limbs may die.
- ***In tomato:*** Oldest leaves turn downward first; leaflets curl and shrivel. Only one side may be affected. A stem cut lengthwise may reveal creamy white to reddish brown discoloration. Young infected fruits are stunted and distorted. Fruits may develop small, white round spots.

Organic Remedies

- ***For tomato:*** Hot-water seed treatment at 122°F/50°C for 25 minutes. Plant resistant varieties or certified seed. Rotate crops.
- ***For trees:*** Prune immediately. Between cuts, disinfect tools and hands. If uncontrollable by pruning, destroy tree.

Bacterial Wilt

also known as Stewart's Disease *in corn*

Type: Bacteria

Plants Affected: Beans, corn, cucurbits, eggplant, tomato

Where It Occurs

- ***Corn:*** North Central, South, and East
- ***Cucurbits:*** Northeast and North Central states. Some wilts are fostered by moist soil and soil temperatures above 75°F/24°C.
- ***Solanaceae:*** South

How It Is Spread: Transmitted in beans by seeds; in cucurbits by both types of cucumber beetle; in corn by the corn flea beetle. The pathogen affecting beans and tomatoes overwinters in debris.

Symptoms

- ***In beans:*** Seedlings usually die before reaching 3 inches tall. Mature vines wilt, especially midday, and die.
- ***In cucurbits:*** Plants wilt rapidly and, even while green, can die. Cut stems produce oozy strings. This bacteria blocks the plant's vascular system.
- ***In corn:*** Plants may wilt and leaves can develop long water-soaked or pale yellow streaks. A cut in the lower stem oozes yellowish droplets that can be drawn out into fine, small threads.
- ***In tomato:*** Plants wilt and die rapidly, starting with young leaves first. Lower foliage may yellow slightly. A lengthwise stem cut reveals an oozy gray-brown core.

Organic Remedies

- Immediately remove and destroy infected plants.
- Plant resistant varieties.
- ***For corn and cucurbits:*** Control the insect vector (see Symptoms).

- ***For beans and tomato:*** Plant only certified wilt-free seeds. Rotate crops on a 4–5 year basis. Fumigate soil.

Bean Rust

Type: Fungus

Plant Affected: Bean

Where It Occurs: Occurs along the Eastern Seaboard and in irrigated areas in the West. Fostered by relative high humidity for 8–10 days.

How It Is Spread: Spores are spread by wind and water.

Symptoms

- Leaf undersides develop small, red-orange to brown blisters full of spores.
- Leaves yellow, dry, and drop prematurely.

Organic Remedies

- Don't reuse vine stakes.
- Use long crop rotations.
- If necessary, apply a sulfur spray every 7–10 days until 1 month before harvest.
- Use heavy mulch and drip (not overhead) irrigation to minimize spreading disease through splashing.
- Select resistant varieties.

Black Heart

Type: Environmental

Plants Affected: Celery, potato

Where It Occurs: Widespread, but rare in the Northwest and North Central states

Symptoms

- ***In celery:*** A low calcium-potassium ratio causes spreading brown, water-soaked areas on leaves.
- ***In potato:*** Low oxygen levels at the tuber center cause purple, black, or gray areas.

Organic Remedies

- ***For celery:*** Make sure the soil contains adequate calcium.
- ***For potato:*** Improve soil drainage to reduce chances of it recurring. Don't leave potatoes in or on very hot soil (over 90°F/33°C).

Black Knot

Type: Fungus

Plants Affected: Apricot, cherry, plum

Where It Occurs: East of the Mississippi

How It Is Spread: Spread by wind and rain. Harbored in the tree knots.

Symptoms

- Coal-black, hard swellings appear on twigs and limbs.
- Olive green growths develop in late summer, then blacken. They can be 2–4 times the thickness of the branch.
- Limbs weaken. Trees die slowly.
- The disease is detected the year after infection.

Organic Remedies

- Cut off all twigs and branches at least 4″ below swellings. Destroy cuttings. Cover wounds with paint or wax.
- Remove all infected wild cherry and plum.
- Where significant damage is expected, spray with a lime-sulfur or Bordeaux mix at the first bud stage.
- Plant resistant varieties.

Blotch Disease

also known as Sooty Blotch

Type: Fungus

Plants Affected: Apple, citrus, pear

Where It Occurs: In the eastern, central, and southern states to the Gulf of Mexico

Symptoms

- Only skins are affected. Fruits are still edible.
- Mottled, irregularly shaped spots (up to ¼″) appear.
- "Cloudy fruit" has spots that run together.

Organic Remedies

- Scrub citrus fruit skins.
- Peel skins off fruits other than citrus before eating.
- Prune and space trees for better air circulation.
- Prune and destroy infected twigs.

Botrytis

also known as Gray Mold

Type: Fungus

Plants Affected: Numerous plants

Where It Occurs: Widespread. This fungus can overwinter in infected plant debris and can be carried into storage. It favors cold, wet weather.

Symptoms

- Several different strains of this fungus affect different crops and ornamental plants.
- On leaves, light tan or gray or whitish spots develop; leaves are then covered by a darker-colored fungus. The leaf withers and the fungus progresses into the stem. In crops like lettuce, the leaves become a slimy mass.
- Infected fruits are water-soaked and soft.
- Infected roots may have light brown and water-soaked lesions anywhere, but they occur most commonly on the crown.
- Grayish-brown mold develops on surfaces and, in storage, can spread into "nests" of mold.

Organic Remedies

- See Overview of Symptoms and Remedies for fungal diseases, page 186.
- Commercial fungicides containing baking soda can be used on various ornamentals and fruit trees and are said to be effective against black spot and powdery mildew, as well as leaf spots, anthracnose, phoma, phytophthora, scab, and botrytis.
- The broad-spectrum biological fungicide Serenade can safely treat fungal diseases such as botrytis. Serenade is nontoxic to honey bees and other beneficial insects.
- Research in Israel suggests that biological control methods might be enhanced if more than one biocontrol agent is used simultaneously; significant increases in efficacy were achieved by combining a beneficial yeast and a beneficial bacterium to suppress gray mold (*Botrytis cinerea*) on strawberry foliage.
- USDA scientists at the Appalachian Fruit Research Station in West Virginia evaluated the juices and essential oils from various plants to determine their antifungal activity, particularly their activity against gray mold due to *Botrytis cinerea.*

  Juices completely inhibiting germination for 48 hours: Garlic creeper (*Mansoa alliacea*); elephant garlic (*Allium ampeloprasum*); fragrant-flower garlic (*Allium ramosum*); serpent garlic (*Allium sativum*); society garlic (*Tulbaghia violacea*); several sweet and hot pepper cultivars, including habanero and tabasco.
- Israeli researchers have found that foliar fertilizer therapy can induce disease resistance. Leaves are sprayed with solutions that contain minor trace plant nutrients at very low concentrations, which apparently induce systemic resistance to powdery mildew in cucumbers and common rust in corn.
- Mycostop, a biological control, is the living formulation of the *Streptomyces* bacterium found in sphagnum peat. The wettable powder can be applied as a drench or soil spray or as a seed treatment to control fusarium, alternaria, phomopsis, pythium, phytophthora root rots, and botrytis gray molds, with negligible toxicity to humans and animals.

Canker Dieback

Type: Fungus

Plants Affected: Apple, pecan

Where It Occurs: Widespread. For apples, especially a problem in moist springs and early falls. For pecans, may be caused by inadequate water in winter or heavy soils with poor drainage.

Symptoms

- ***In apple:*** Watery blisters on bark. Oval dead patches (1″–1′) may become sunken. Branches wilt and die from the tip down. Eventually leaves yellow.
- ***In pecan:*** Branches wilt and die from the tip down.

Organic Remedies

- Avoid wounding tree trunks and stems.
- Cut off infected branches well below infection.
- For small cankers, gouge out with sharp knife and treat with tree paint or Bordeaux paste. Disinfect tools between cuts.
- Destroy all pruned matter.
- ***For pecan:*** Ensure adequate drainage in hardpan soils and deep watering in sandy soils.

Cedar Apple Rust

Type: Fungus

Plants Affected: Apple, pear

Where It Occurs: In the eastern and central states and in Arkansas

How It Is Spread: Transmitted in wind and rain by spores from red cedars and junipers. Has a 2-year life cycle.

Symptoms

- Light yellow spots on leaves become bright orange spots.
- Fruits may develop spots.

Organic Remedies

- Remove all red cedars, junipers, wild apple, and ornamental apples within 30 yards of infected trees. Alternatively, plant a windbreak between the disease hosts and apple trees.
- If necessary, apply a sulfur spray every 7–10 days until 1 month before harvest.
- Use heavy mulch and drip (not overhead) irrigation to minimize spreading disease through splashing.
- Select resistant varieties.
- Copper may be used, but can harm earthworms.

Celery Mosaic

Type: Virus

Plant Affected: Celery

Where It Occurs: Widespread

How It Is Spread: Spread by aphids. Continuous celery cultivation and certain weeds (wild celery, poison hemlock, wild parsnip, and mock bishop's weed) can cause virus to persist.

Symptoms

- Leaves turn yellow and mottled green.
- Stalks are stunted, twisted, and narrow.

Organic Remedies

- Control aphids.
- Destroy infected plants.

Cherry Leaf Spot & Plum Leaf Spot

also known as Yellow Leaf *in cherry*

Type: Fungus

Plants Affected: Cherry, plum

Where It Occurs: East of Rockies; particularly bad in warm, wet conditions

How It Is Spread: Harbored in debris and spread by wind.

Symptoms

- Purple spots on leaves, followed by bright yellow foliage.
- Spots often drop out of leaves, followed by defoliation.
- Heavy fruit drop in plums
- Very damaging

Organic Remedies

- Destroy fallen leaves and fruit; pick off infected leaves.
- A spray of wettable sulfur from petal fall to harvest is virtually the only control.
- Fall cultivation of soil—no more than 2″—reduces spore spread.

Common Mosaic

Type: Virus

Plant Affected: Beans

Where It Occurs: Widespread

How It Is Spread: Spread by aphids and gardeners. Overwinters in perennial weeds like Canadian thistle.

Symptoms

- Severely stunted plants with few pods
- Mottled green elongated leaves crinkle and curl downward at the edges.
- Infection occurs near bloom time.
- Plants eventually die.

Organic Remedies

- Control aphids.
- Destroy infected plants, no matter how mildly affected.
- Remove all perennial weeds within 150′ of the garden.
- Plant resistant varieties.

Cottony Rot

also known as Pink Rot *and* Watery Soft Rot *in cabbage;* White Mold *in beans*

Type: Fungus

Plants Affected: Beans, cabbage, celery, lettuce

Where It Occurs: Widespread. Most common in cool, moist conditions.

How It Is Spread: Spread by small black bodies, which can survive in soil for up to 10 years.

Symptoms

- White mold develops and small, hard black bodies form on or within the mold.
- ***In beans:*** Stems develop water-soaked spots, branches and leaves follow. White mold develops in these spots.
- ***In cabbage and lettuce:*** Stem and leaves near the ground become water-soaked, leaves wilt, and the plant collapses. White mold grows on the head.
- ***In celery:*** White, cottony growth appears at the stalk base. Stalks rot and taste bitter.

Organic Remedies

- Remove and destroy infected plants, if possible before black bodies form.
- Plant in well-drained soil; raised beds help greatly.
- Rotate with immune or resistant crops such as beets, onion, spinach, peanuts, corn, cereals, and grasses. Avoid successive plantings of beans, celery, lettuce, or cabbage.
- ***For beans and celery:*** Where flood irrigation is feasible, usually in muck or sandy soil, flood the growing area for 4–8 weeks, or alternate flooding and drying, which kills the black bodies.

Crown Gall

Type: Bacteria

Plants Affected: Almond, apple, apricot, blackberry, blueberry, cherry, filbert, grape, peach, pear, pecan, plum, raspberry, walnut

Where It Occurs: Widespread

How It Is Spread: Transmitted through wounds in the roots, crowns, and stems by tools and soil water.

Symptoms

- Fruit trees and brambles weaken and produce small, poor fruit.
- *Galls* are swellings that circle roots and crowns; they are sometimes several inches in diameter and can be spongy or hard.

- Plants can survive for many years but are very susceptible to other stresses.

Organic Remedies

- ***For brambles:*** Destroy canes and plants with symptoms.
- ***For trees:*** Prune galls and treat with tree surgeon's paint or a bactericidal paint. Cover with soil after painting. Destroy infected portions. Disinfect hands and tools between cuts.
- Remove badly infected trees, trunks, and roots and destroy. Don't plant another susceptible tree in the infected location for 3–5 years.
- Propagate fruit trees only by budding.
- Select resistant rootstocks.
- Use Galltrol (competitive bacteria) at planting.
- Ensure good soil drainage.

Crown Rot

see Southern Blight

Crown Rot

Type: Fungus

Plants Affected: Almond, apple, cherry, pear

Where It Occurs: Widespread where trunks are wet at the soil line

How It Is Spread: Like collar rots and damping off, this fungus attacks at or below the soil surface.

Symptoms

- Late in the season, one or more branches turn reddish.
- Leaves turn yellow or brown and wilt.
- Dead bark tissue appears at the soil line, with sunken and sometimes girdling cankers.

Organic Remedies

- Rake soil away from the tree crown and, if necessary, expose upper roots. This improves air circulation and may correct the problem.
- Avoid deep planting of new young trees.
- Avoid standing water or continuously wet conditions around the trunk.
- Allow soil to dry out thoroughly between watering.

Cucumber Mosaic

also known as CMV, Mosaic; Yellows *in spinach*

Type: Virus

Plants Affected: Cucurbits, lettuce, pepper, potato, raspberry, spinach, tomato

Where It Occurs: Widespread

How It Is Spread: Spread by aphids (in cucurbits, lettuce, pepper, tomato), striped or spotted cucumber beetles (in cucurbits), and gardeners. It overwinters in many perennial weeds.

Symptoms

- ***General:*** Yellow-green mottling and curled foliage. Plants are weak, stunted, may have few blossoms, poor fruit, and may die. Fruits are misshapen and mottled. Distorted leaves are common.
- ***In cucurbits:*** Leaf margins can curl downward, and cucumbers and summer squash fruits become mottled, yellow-green.
- ***In pepper and tomato:*** Older leaves look like oak leaves and develop large yellowish ring spots. Affected leaves can drop prematurely. Fruits develop concentric rings and solid circular spots, first yellow then brown. Fruits flatten and roots are stunted.
- ***In potato:*** Tubers may develop brown spots, and the plant yellows and dies.
- ***In raspberry:*** Dry, seedless, crumbly fruit. Canes may droop, blacken, and die.

Organic Remedies

- Control appropriate insect vector—aphids or cucumber beetles (see Symptoms). Apply row covers until blossom time to prevent aphids and cucumber beetles.
- Remove and destroy infected plants and, if severe, surrounding plants.

- Remove all perennial weeds within 15′ of the garden.
- Plant resistant varieties.

Curly Dwarf

Type: Virus

Plant Affected: Artichoke

Where It Occurs: Pacific Coast and southern coast of Texas

Symptoms

- Stunted plants
- Aphids and leafhoppers

Organic Remedies

- Control aphids and leafhoppers.
- Remove and destroy all infected plants.
- Remove all milk thistle and other nearby weeds.

Curly Top

Also known as CTV; Western Yellow Blight *in tomato*

Type: Virus

Plants Affected: Beans, beet, cucurbits, pepper, spinach, tomato

Where It Occurs: Widespread

How It Is Spread: Beet leafhoppers

Symptoms

- ***General:*** Stunted plants have numerous small leaves that pucker, crinkle, curl, and yellow. Fruits are few, dwarfed, or may ripen prematurely.
- ***In beans:*** Leaves are darker green. Young plants may die, but older plants usually survive. Plant produces few or dwarfed pods and looks bushy.
- ***In cucurbits:*** Leaves may be mottled.
- ***In tomato:*** Branches are very erect, leaflet veins turn purple; plant turns a dull yellow.

Organic Remedies

- Control beet leafhoppers.
- Apply row covers until blossom time to reduce leafhoppers.
- Prune and destroy infected parts of plants immediately. If serious, remove and destroy all infected plants and all nearby plants.
- Grow tomatoes away from beets, spinach, melons, or other leafhopper hosts. Also, space them closely to discourage leafhoppers.
- Select resistant varieties.

Downy Mildew

Type: Fungus

Plants Affected: Numerous plants

Where It Occurs: Widespread. Fungal spores are spread by the wind and can be carried by rain, wet clothing, and tools. Unlike some other mildews, this fungus may overwinter in some areas in seed, in diseased roots, and as tiny oospores (sexual fruiting bodies).

Symptoms

- Numerous strains of this fungus attack different crops and ornamental plants. Many may be confused with mosaic.
- ***In corn:*** Leaves develop a characteristic chlorosis (yellowing) at the base of the oldest leaf, with a distinct margin between this and the green upper portion of the leaf.
- ***In cucurbits:*** Leaves develop pale green areas that change to yellow angular spots along leaf veins. If moisture is present, the leaf underside may develop a faintly purplish hue or a range of colors from white to black. Older leaves tend to be affected first, then it moves to younger leaves. Fruit may be dwarfed and have poor flavor. In moist conditions, plants may be overcome by the fungus in days.

Organic Remedies

- See Overview of Symptoms and Remedies for fungal diseases on page 186.
- Select resistant varieties.

Enation Mosaic

also known as Pea Virus I, Leaf Enation

Type: Virus

Plant Affected: Pea

Where It Occurs: Widespread, but particularly a problem in the Northwest

How It Is Spread: Spread primarily by aphids, overwinters in various clovers, vetch, and alfalfa.

Symptoms

- Young leaves become mottled.
- Leaf undersides develop small outgrowths known as enations.
- Vine tips become misshapen and internodal distance shortens.
- Stunted plants have few, if any, pods. Pods may have yellow seeds.
- Extremely damaging

Organic Remedies

- Control aphids.
- Plant early to avoid high aphid populations.
- Select resistant varieties.

Fire Blight

Type: Bacteria

Plants Affected: Apple, pear

Where It Occurs: Widespread, particularly in areas of high humidity, dew, and rain. Bacteria remain dormant through winter inside cankers.

How It Is Spread: Aphids, psylla, bees, and rain. Enters through blossoms or new growth.

Symptoms

- Infected shoots turn brown and black, as though scorched by fire.
- Lesions may ooze orange-brown liquid.
- Blossoms wither and die. Reddish, water-soaked lesions develop on the bark.

Organic Remedies

- Control aphids and psylla.
- Remove and destroy all suckers and infected branches. Control is most effective when infected areas are removed as soon as seen, no matter the season. Cut at least 12″ below point of visible wilt. After each cut, disinfect tools in bleach solution (1:4 dilution). In winter, repeat and treat cuts with asphalt-based dressing.
- Spray the tree regularly while in bloom with a solution of 4% Clorox (4 ounces Clorox in 3 gallons water). This sterilizes the blossoms so bees do not spread the blight.
- Avoid heavy pruning or high-nitrogen fertilizer. Both stimulate rapid twig growth.
- Check soil acidity. The more acid the soil, the more prone to fire blight.
- If significant damage occurs, spray with a copper-sulfur blend labeled for fire blight.
- Plant resistant varieties.

Fusarium Wilt

also known as Fusarium Yellows *or* Yellows

Type: Fungus

Plants Affected: Asparagus, brassicas, celery, lettuce, melon, pea, potato, spinach, sweet potato, tomato, turnip, watermelon

Where It Occurs: Widespread, but occurs mainly east of the Rockies. Worst in the South; in light, sandy soil; and in dry weather with temperatures of 60°F–90°F/16°C–33°C. Temperatures above 90°F/33°C retard the disease.

How It Is Spread: Water, tools, and seeds. The disease can live in soil for 20 years. Thrives in warm, dry weather.

Symptoms

- ***General:*** Yellowing, stunting, and wilting (often rapid). Lower leaves may wilt first. Plants usually die, but seedlings can die quickly. In some plants, a sliced lower stem may reveal discoloration originating from the roots.

- ***In celery:*** Ribs also redden.
- ***In muskmelon:*** One side of the vine develops a water-soaked yellow streak near the soil line that darkens to brown.
- ***In potato:*** In storage, blue or white swellings may develop on brown decayed areas.

Organic Remedies

- Remove and destroy infected plants.
- Ensure good soil drainage.
- Don't plant susceptible crops for 8 years in places where fusarium was last seen; rotate crops on a regular basis as a preventive measure.
- Solarize garden soil where possible; sterilize potting soil.
- Select resistant varieties, one of the best controls.
- ***For asparagus:*** Use seed labeled "treated with a Clorox solution," or treat the seeds yourself with Clorox.
- Mycostop, a biological control, is the living formulation of the *Streptomyces* bacterium found in sphagnum peat. The wettable powder can be applied as a drench or soil spray or as a seed treatment to control fusarium, alternaria, phomopsis, pythium, phytophthora root rots, and botrytis gray molds with negligible toxicity to humans and animals.

Gray Mold

see Botrytis

Leaf Blight

also known as Bacterial Blight

Type: Bacteria

Plant Affected: Carrot

Where It Occurs: Arizona, Indiana, Iowa, Michigan, New York, Oregon, and Wisconsin

Symptoms: Sports on seedling leaves start out yellow-white. In time they turn brown and look water-soaked.

Organic Remedies

- Hot-water seed treatment: 126°F/53°C for 25 minutes.
- Plant disease-free seed.
- At harvest, remove and destroy carrot tops.
- Rotate on a 2- to 3-year basis.

Oak Wilt

Type: Fungus

Plants Affected: Chestnut, oak

Where It Occurs: Occurs in states bordering the Mississippi; west to Oklahoma, Kansas, Nebraska; east to Pennsylvania; and south to all states in the Appalachian Mountains.

How It Is Spread: White oak is a major reservoir for the fungus.

Symptoms

- A very serious disease in Chinese chestnut; better tolerated by white oak.
- Water-soaked spots form on leaves, usually along the tip and margin. Leaves turn brown and fall off.
- Symptoms start at the top of the tree, then move to the trunk, which develops short, bulging, vertical splits in the bark.

Organic Remedies

- Once this disease is identified, immediately cut and destroy the tree. Remove the stump and major roots.
- The fungus is thought to enter through wounds that penetrate the tree bark, so you might try dressing wounds with a fungicide or tree paint as soon as they are spotted.

Orange Rust

Type: Fungus

Plants Affected: Blackberry, raspberry

Where It Occurs: Widespread

How It Is Spread: Wind. Overwinters in plant stems and roots.

Symptoms

- Yellow spots appear on both sides of leaves in early spring.
- Several weeks later, the leaf underside ruptures with masses of orange-red powdery spores.

Organic Remedies

- Remove/destroy infected canes, roots, suckers, and wild berries within 500 yards.
- Mulch heavily with straw and leaf mold.
- Apply lots of compost in autumn with extra P and K. (Low P and K encourages rust.)
- Select resistant varieties.

Pear Decline

Type: Mycoplasma

Plant Affected: Pear

Where It Occurs: Habitat areas of the pear psylla, which are principally east of the Mississippi and northwestern states

How It Is Spread: Transmitted by the pear psylla. Especially affects those on Asian rootstocks.

Symptoms: Tree weakens and slowly dies.

Organic Remedies

- Control pear psylla.
- Use only *Prunus communis* rootstock.

Pecan Bunch

Type: Mycoplasma

Plant Affected: Pecan

Where It Occurs: Arkansas, Georgia, Kansas, Louisiana, Mississippi, Missouri, New Mexico, Oklahoma, and Texas

Symptoms: Similar to Walnut Bunch

Organic Remedies: See Walnut Bunch.

Phytophthora cinnamomi

Type: Fungus

Plant Affected: Blueberry (highbush)

Where It Occurs: Emerges in hot, moist conditions, especially in Florida, Georgia, Arkansas.

How It Is Spread: Lives indefinitely in all soil types, except perhaps sand. Most prevalent in wet soils with poor drainage.

Symptoms

- Leaves yellow; leaf margins turn brown, wilt, and fall off.
- Displays stunted growth.
- A "flag" branch (dead branch with dried leaves still attached) may be seen on an otherwise healthy-looking bush.

Organic Remedies

- Best prevention is to grow plants in raised beds to ensure good drainage.
- Avoid stressing the plant with under- or overfertilization or overwatering.
- Cut down to the ground the infected part of the bush; remove and destroy.
- Commercial fungicides containing baking soda can be used on various ornamentals and fruit trees and is said to be effective against black spot and powdery mildew, as well as leaf spots, anthracnose, phoma, phytophthora, scab, and botrytis.

Powdery Mildew

Type: Fungus

Plants Affected: Numerous plants

Where It Occurs: Widespread. Fungal spores survive in frost-free areas and are blown long distances. Insects also help spread the fungus locally. High humidity and moisture on leaves are not necessary for this fungus to take hold. Leaves are most susceptible within 2–3½ weeks of unfolding.

Symptoms

- White powdery growth like talcum powder, frequently starting on the leaf underside for cucurbits and on the upper leaf surface for lettuce.
- Growth can spread to cover most of the leaf.

- Numerous strains of powdery mildew affect different crops and ornamental plants.
- ***In crucifers:*** Talcumlike growth appears in spots or in larger areas on upper side of leaf and stems. Leaves may pale, then turn yellow or tan.
- ***In cucurbits:*** Leaves wither and die, and dry and become brittle. Vines may also wither and become whitish. Fruit can sunburn more easily, ripen prematurely, and have poor taste and quality.
- ***In lettuce:*** Lettuce leaves tend to curl before turning yellow, then brown.

Organic Remedies

- See Overview of Symptoms and Remedies for fungal diseases, page 186.
- Select varieties that are resistant to this mildew.
- Several minimally toxic fungicides including horticultural oils, neem oil, jojoba oil, sulfur, and the biological fungicide Serenade are available.
- Avoid overhead watering, as an overly damp environment increases powdery mildew spore germination.
- Kaolin clay can offer some protection against powdery mildew, as the physical barrier it creates can prevent spore attachment and germination.
- Research shows that spraying affected plants with a 5% emulsion of garlic extract can result in substantial protection against powdery mildew infection (*Erysiphe cichoracearum*).
- Researchers in Germany treated Bacchus grape plants with sodium bicarbonate (baking soda) and found that 1.0% solutions worked best against powdery mildew (*Uncinula necator*).
- Fungicides containing baking soda can be used on various ornamentals and fruit trees, and are said to be effective against black spot and powdery mildew, as well as leaf spots, anthracnose, phoma, phytophthora, scab, and botrytis.
- Plant pathologists in India report reductions in symptoms of powdery mildew after applying copper, molybdenum, or 50 ppm of gibberellic acid.
- For cucurbits, Israeli researchers report that foliar sprays containing potassium nitrate (readily available at garden centers as a fertilizer) can protect against powdery mildew. Spraying every 7 or 14 days with a 25 millimolar solution of potassium nitrate (plus surfactant) did not harm cucumber plants and did a good job of preventing infestations of powdery mildew due to *Sphaerotheca fuliginea*.

Psyllid Yellows

Type: Phytotoxemia, caused by a toxic substance thought to be a virus

Plants Affected: Potato, tomato

Where It Occurs: Habitat of psyllids, also known as "jumping plant lice," which resemble tiny cicadas. Pysllids overwinter in Texas and Mexico, and are abundant after cool, mild winters. They occur in February and March in southern Texas, then migrate to areas north, including California and Colorado.

How It Is Spread: Spread by a toxic substance released by the tomato psyllid.

Symptoms

- ***In potato:*** Young leaves yellow or redden, brown, and die. Sprouts emerge on young tubers and form new tubers, creating eventually a chain of deformed tubers.
- ***In tomato:*** Older leaves get thick and curl upward. Young leaves turn yellow with purple veins. Plant is dwarfed and spindly. Developed fruit is soft. If the plant is attacked while young, no fruit will appear.

Organic Remedies

- Clear away Chinese lantern and ground cherries, both of which are hosts.
- Control the tomato psyllid; garlic spray may work.

- 70% neem oil is approved for organic use and can be sprayed on vegetables, fruit trees and flowers to kill eggs, larvae, and adult insects. Mix 1 ounce in a gallon of water and spray all leaf surfaces (including the undersides of leaves) until completely wet.
- Spray horticultural oil in early spring to destroy overwintering adults and eggs.
- Diatomaceous earth contains no toxins and works quickly on contact. Dust lightly and evenly over vegetable crops wherever adults are found.
- Safer Insect Killing Soap will work fast on heavy infestations. A short-lived natural pesticide, it works by damaging the outer layer of soft-bodied insect pests, causing dehydration and death within hours. Apply a mixture of 2½ ounces per gallon of water when insects are present, repeat every 7–10 days as needed.
- BotaniGard ES is a highly effective biological insecticide containing *Beauveria bassiana*, an entomopathogenic fungus that attacks a long list of troublesome crop pests—even resistant strains! Weekly applications can prevent insect population explosions and provide protection equal to or better than conventional chemical pesticides.
- Kaolin clay (Surround WP) forms a protective barrier film, which acts as a broad-spectrum crop protectant for preventing damage from insect pests.

Scab

Type: Fungus (many different strains)
Plants Affected: Almond, apple, apricot, beet, cucumber, melon, peach, pecan, potato, pumpkin, squash, watermelon
Where It Occurs: Widespread, particularly in the humid Southeast. Fostered by humidity.
How It Is Spread: Spread among fruit and nut trees primarily by wind. Overwinters in fallen leaves and dead twigs. Dry soil favors this fungus, so keep soil moist.

Symptoms

- Symptoms vary in different plants.
- The disease develops rapidly at 70°F/22°C.
- ***In beet and potato:*** Ugly corky, wartlike lesions on the outside of roots. Tubers are still edible if damaged areas are removed.
- ***In cucurbits:*** Leaves develop water-soaked spots and can wilt. Stems can develop small cankers. Immature fruit develops gray concave spots that darken, become deeper, and develop a velvety green mold.
- ***In fruit trees:*** When fruit is half grown, small, greenish, dark spots eventually turn brown. Branches and twigs may develop yellow-brown spots. Fruit can crack.
- ***In pecan:*** In spring when leaves unfold, irregular, olive-brown to black spots appear, usually on leaf undersides. Concave spots appear on nuts. Nuts and leaves drop prematurely.

Organic Remedies

- Remove and destroy all diseased leaves, plants, and fruit. Mow under trees. Research shows that chopping or burning apple leaves soon after they have dropped in fall can significantly lower scab spore survival.
- ***For beet and potato:*** Lower soil pH to below 5.5.
- ***For fruit trees:*** Spray or dust with sulfur 3 weeks after petal drop and repeat 2 weeks later. The University of Tennessee has shown that dormant soybean oil, degummed ("slightly refined"), is highly effective against scale when sprayed on apple and peach trees (5% emulsion in water on a volume basis) in early February. Also, this might be a good miticide/insecticide during the growing season at a lower concentration (1%–2%).
- Commercial fungicides containing baking soda can be used on various ornamentals and fruit trees, and are said to be effective against black spot and powdery mildew, as well as leaf spots, anthracnose, phoma, phytophthora, scab, and botrytis.

- ***For pecans:*** Remove all leaves, shucks, and dead leaves. Burn, if legal. Hot composting methods will destroy the organism.
- Ensure good drainage.
- ***For all vegetable crops:*** Rotate on a 3-year basis at minimum.
- ***For melons:*** Ensure full sun by planting in a sunny location.
- Plant soybeans in infested soil and turn under.
- Select resistant varieties.
- Grow chives near the affected plant roots.
- Apply composted pigeon droppings to plant soil.
- Spray trees in spring and early summer with *Equisetum* (horsetail) tea.

Smut

Type: Fungus (different strains)

Plants Affected: Corn, onion

Where It Occurs

- Most likely to occur in climates with a hot, dry season and dry spring followed by a wet spell. Spores survive for years.
- ***Onion:*** Prevalent in northern states.

Symptoms

- ***In corn:*** Stunted or misshapen stalks. Smut develops anywhere on the leaves, stalks, ears, or tassels. Ugly white or gray galls are covered with a shiny milky membrane that ruptures and releases more black spores.
- ***In onions:*** Black spots on leaves or bulbs. Cracks containing black powder appear on the sides of spots. Onion seedlings may die in a month. If not infected by the time its first true leaves appear, the seedling will usually escape this disease.

Organic Remedies

- ***For corn:*** Remove and destroy smut balls before they break. If severe, remove and destroy infected plants. Remove all stalks in fall. To reduce injury, control corn borers when tassels first appear.
- Avoid manure fertilizer, which may contain spores.
- Rotate crops on a 3+-year basis.
- Select disease-resistant corn and disease-free onion sets.
- If you can produce it reliably, you might sell young corn smut, a new gourmet item, to specialty restaurants.

Southern Blight (*Sclerotium rolfsii*)

also known as Crown Rot, *Sclerotium* Root Rot, Southern Wilt

Type: Fungus

Plants Affected: Artichoke, bean, okra, peanut, pepper, soybean, tomato, watermelon

Where It Occurs: Prevalent in southern states below 38° latitude, coast to coast. This fungus prefers warm soil (80°F/27°C or higher), moisture, and sandy soils low in nitrogen.

How It Is Spread: This fungus can spread over the soil to other plants. It overwinters 2″–3″ below the soil line in the mustard seed–like bodies. It is known to infect 200 plant species.

Symptoms

- Leaves yellow, wilt, and drop, starting at the bottom, followed by vine wilt and death.
- White mold grows on the stem at or near the soil line. The white mold may harden and crust over.
- Round, yellow, tan, or dark brown bodies the size of mustard seeds appear on lower stems and on the soil, and may develop white mold growth.
- Some fruits and roots develop round lesions.
- Storage rot may occur in cabbage, squash, potato, and sweet potato.

Organic Remedies

- In warm climates, immediately dig up infected plants and destroy. In cool climates (above 38° latitude), some suggest this disease may not need controls.

- Black plastic mulch is reported to help control this disease and is an easier control than soil solarization.
- After harvest, plow in the plant stubbles deeply.
- Rotate crops and don't plant susceptible vegetables near each other.
- Solarize soil.
- Use wide spacing.
- Plant early where there is a history of southern blight.

Southern Wilt

see Southern Blight

Spotted Wilt

Type: Virus

Plant Affected: Tomato

Where It Occurs: Widespread

How It Is Spread: Transmitted almost entirely by thrips.

Symptoms

- Leaves develop small orange spots.
- Older leaves brown and die.
- Plant is stunted.
- Green fruits can develop yellow spots that develop concentric zones of brown, green, pink, or red shading.

Organic Remedies

- Control thrips. Use a reflective mulch such as aluminum foil or black plastic sprayed with aluminum.
- Grow 2 plants per pot and set out together. Only a maximum number of plants per given area get infected, so yields can be kept high.

Stewart's Disease

see Bacterial Wilt

Sunscald

also known as Winter Injury

Type: Environmental

Plants Affected: Apple, cherry, onion, pecan, pepper, tomato

Where It Occurs: Widespread. Dark tree bark is the most susceptible. Worst in drought years with cold, sunny winter days.

How It Is Caused: The southwestern side of the plant warms during the day, then cells rupture during cold nights.

Symptoms

- Vegetables develop white or yellow wrinkled areas.
- Onions get bleached and slippery tissue during curing.
- Fruit tree bark darkens and splits open in long cracks or cankers.

Organic Remedies

- ***For fruit trees:*** Shade bark by covering with burlap or apply a white interior latex paint.
- ***For vegetables:*** Keep as much foliage as possible to shade fruit; don't prune suckers at the plant base. If necessary, prune above the first group of leaves above fruit.
- ***Onions:*** Don't cure in direct sun.

Tobacco Mosaic (TMV)

Type: Virus

Plants Affected: Eggplant, pepper, tomato

Where It Occurs: Widespread

How It Is Spread: Spread by tools and hands (especially those of smokers). Virus is known to live in cured tobacco for up to 25 years.

Symptoms

- Misshapen leaves in young plants.
- Dark green mottled leaves tend to be pointed or fernlike; leaves may curl and wrinkle and have a grayish coloring.

- In the final disease stage, leaves drop, branches die, and fruits yellow and wrinkle.
- Very difficult to control.

Organic Remedies

- Never smoke near plants; have smokers scrub their hands before touching plants.
- Destroy infected and nearby plants. Clear nearby perennial weeds.
- Disinfect all tools.
- Spray infected seedlings with milk or reconstituted powdered-milk solution. Spray until the seedlings are dripping.
- Select resistant varieties.

Walnut Bunch

also known as Witches'-Broom, Brooming Disease

Type: Uncertain; some suspect mycoplasma or virus.

Plants Affected: Strawberry, hickory, pecan; particularly serious in butternut, walnut

Where It Occurs: Northeast and Midwest

How It Is Spread: Uncertain; insect vectors are suspected.

Symptoms

- ***In strawberry:*** Symptoms are on shoots only. On swollen stems, deformed shoots are bushlike and broomlike. Occurs on woodland borders and where balsam fir is present.
- ***In walnut:*** Lateral buds don't remain dormant but produce bushy, densely packed shoots and undersize leaves, often 2 weeks earlier than healthy branches. Few nuts are produced. Nuts are shriveled, soft-shelled, poorly developed, and have dark kernels. Diseased shoots enter dormancy in fall, very late.

Organic Remedies

- ***For strawberry:*** Remove all infected berries and plants. Eliminate nearby balsam firs.
- ***For walnut:*** Removing all diseased branches can be an effective control. Make cuts well back from the infected area. Disinfect tools. Propagate only from disease-free trees.

Western Yellow Blight

see Curly Top

Winter Injury

see Sunscald

Yellows

Type: Fungus; *see* Fusarium Wilt

Yellows

Type: Virus

Plants Affected: Beet, celery, spinach

Where It Occurs: California, Oregon, Washington, Utah, Colorado, Michigan, Nebraska, Ohio, Maryland, and Virginia

How It Is Spread: Spread by aphids.

Symptoms

- Leaves yellow, starting at tips and margins.
- Outer and middle leaves can get thick and brittle.
- Stunted plants and roots

Organic Remedies

- Control aphids, using a reflective mulch such as black plastic sprayed with aluminum.
- Don't plant winter spinach near beets.
- Plant vegetables in protected areas to minimize aphids spreading by wind.

Yellows

also known as Aster Yellows

Type: Mycoplasma

Plants Affected: Broccoli, carrot, celery, lettuce, onion, strawberry, tomato

Where It Occurs: Widespread, but particularly destructive in the West, where it affects more than 200 plant species

How It Is Spread: Leafhoppers, particularly the six-spotted leafhopper

Symptoms

- Young leaves yellow.
- Top growth is yellow and bushy like witches'-broom.
- Older leaves may become distorted.
- Carrot tops turn reddish brown in mid- to late season.
- Flowers may be absent, green, underdeveloped, misshapen, or fail to produce seed or fruit.
- Immature leaves are narrow and dwarfed.
- Stunted plants
- Sterile seeds
- Vegetables ripen prematurely.
- Yields and quality are severely affected.

Organic Remedies

- Control leafhoppers; eradicate weeds to destroy leafhopper eggs, especially early in the season.
- Immediately remove and destroy infected plants and plant residues.
- Plant tolerant varieties.

A GUIDE TO CONTROLLING INSECTS AND ANIMALS

About the information that follows:

Clean cultivation. Clean cultivation and sanitation practices are assumed (see pages 175 and 191). Both are important to the prevention and control of many diseases and insects.

Damage not requiring control. When assaulted by chewing pests, plants can tolerate up to 20 percent defoliation without significant loss in yield or quality. The exception is plants whose leaves are the product, such as spinach or cabbage.

Remedies. The use of aluminum foil mulch for prolonged periods may result in aluminum leaching into the soil. If you're planning to leave the mulch on for long periods, consider a substitute, such as silver mulch, a polyethylene sheeting coat with a thin layer of aluminum.

Experimental remedies. These remedies may or may not work; efficacy may depend on the severity of the pest problem as well as method of application. Many of these are homemade; for recipes, see the Glossary of Organic Remedies on pages 190–202.

Allies. Ally listings in this chart should be checked against the chart on allies and companions (pages 280–94), because an alleged ally may help only one of the crops listed. Also, remember that while an ally may effectively deter one insect pest it may, at the same time, attract others.

Aphid

many species

Description

- Tiny (1⁄16″–1⁄8″) soft-bodied insects are pear-shaped and can be brown, black, pink, white, or green. They have long antennae, two tubelike projections from the rear, and may have wings.
- Aphids transmit many viral diseases.
- The phylloxera aphid attacks grapes and nearly wiped out the French wine industry in the 1800s.

Plants Affected: Many herbs, most fruits, most vegetables

Where It Occurs: Widespread; produces 20+ generations per year. The phylloxera aphid is primarily a problem in the West (e.g., California and Arizona) where European vines are grown.

Signs

- Foliage curls, puckers, or yellows.
- Plants can be stunted or distorted.
- Cottony masses may appear on twigs of trees and shrubs.
- Presence of sticky "honeydew," which attracts ants and supports black sooty mold.
- Aphids of different species suck leaves, fruit, stems, bark, and roots.

Organic Remedies

- Symptoms may result from too much nitrogen or pruning. Check for the presence of aphids.
- Use row covers.
- Control aphids and ants, which carry aphid eggs, with sticky bands, sticky yellow traps, or yellow pans filled with soapy water.
- Keep grass mowed around the garden.
- A reflective mulch like aluminum foil or silver mulch repels them.
- Application of fermented extract of stinging nettle is thought to repel black aphids—use experimentally; see page 219.
- Homemade sprays—use experimentally; see page 219.
  - » Forceful water jets 2–3 times per day
  - » Bug juice (see page 191)
  - » Garlic, onion, or pepper (see pages 192–93).
  - » Oxalic acid from the leaves of rhubarb or spinach (boil 1 pound leaves for 30 minutes in 1 quart water; strain, cool, and add a touch of soap, not detergent)
  - » Tomato or potato leaf juice
- Other sprays:
  - » Light horticultural oil (3% solution), applied in the plant's dormant or active phase
  - » Insecticidal soap
  - » Strong lime solution spray
  - » Cooking oil spray mix, as recommended by USDA (see page 191)
  - » Kaolin clay spray
  - » Make sure all sprays contact the aphids.
- Dust with diatomaceous earth to dry up aphids—or with calcium to control ants.
- Practice fall cultivation.
- Rotate crops (more effective with root-feeding species).
- **Biological controls:** Larvae and adults of the green lacewing and ladybug. Syrphid fly larvae, minute pirate bug, damsel bugs, big-eyed bugs. In the greenhouse, PFR (*Paecilomyces fumosoroseus*) is a beneficial microorganism available in granule form that attacks whiteflies, mites, aphids, thrips, mealybugs, and certain other greenhouse pests and is claimed to be safe for humans.
- Cinnamon oil sprays may be highly effective for controlling mites, aphids, and even fungi that attack greenhouse-grown plants with minimal concerns about health and safety.
- **Botanical Controls:** Pyrethrin, neem
- **Allies:** Anise, broccoli, chives, clover, coriander, cover crops of rye and vetch, fennel, French beans, garlic, lamb's quarters, nasturtium, onion family, tansy (See chart on pages 280–94.)

Apple Maggot

Description

- Small (¼″) white-yellowish worms hatch in mid- to late summer. They create winding brown tunnels as they feed inside fruit. Once the fruit falls, larvae emerge to pupate in the soil.

- The adult is a small black fly with yellow legs, a striped abdomen, and zigzag black markings on its wings. Females lay eggs in puncture wounds in fruit.

Plants Affected: Apple,* blueberry, cherry, pear, plum

**Plant most frequently attacked by the insect*

Where It Occurs: Northeast, west to the Dakotas, and south to Arkansas and Georgia. Produces 1–2 generations per year.

To Monitor: Prepare traps by mixing 2 teaspoons ammonia, ¼ teaspoon soap flakes, and 1 quart water. Hang traps in jars on the sunny side of trees, shoulder high. Ten jars per orchard should give a good picture of the maggots' presence. Count the flies every 2–3 days.

Signs

- Slight cavities and holes indicate eggs are present.
- Brown streaks on fruit skins
- Premature fruit drop
- After fruit falls or is picked, flesh becomes brown pulpy mess.
- Very damaging

Organic Remedies

- Red sticky balls. Hang these on perimeter trees at shoulder height, using about 4 balls per tree.
- Make a control trap of 1 part molasses to 9 parts water; add yeast; and pour into widemouthed jars. When fermentation bubbling subsides, hang the jars in trees. Use experimentally; see page 280.
- Remove and destroy badly infested fruit or feed it to animals. Drop mildly damaged fruit into water to kill maggots; these are okay for cider.
- Practice fall cultivation.
- Apply kaolin clay spray in a visible layer to all surfaces of the tree, leaves, and fruit. This acts as a visual and physical repellent to insects.
- **Biological controls:** Beneficial nematodes, applied in late summer to early fall

Asparagus Beetle

Description

- The small (¼″) metallic blue-black beetle, with three yellow-orange squares on each side of its back, lays dark shiny eggs the size of pinheads on leaves and spears.
- Eggs develop into orange larvae with black heads and legs, then green-gray grubs with dark heads.
- Beetles overwinter in garden trash.

Plant Affected: Asparagus

Where It Occurs: Widespread, but rare in the Pacific coastal areas, the Southwest, Florida, and Texas. Produces 2 generations per year in cold areas, 3–5 in warm areas.

Signs

- Defoliation
- Misshapen spears
- Adult beetles eat leaves, fruit, and spears.

Organic Remedies

- Use row covers.
- Harvest regularly in spring.
- Vacuum adults off ferns. Immediately empty the bag and destroy the bugs or they can crawl back out.
- Practice fall cultivation to destroy overwintering pests; also in fall, let chickens in the garden to eat beetles.
- **Biological controls:** Encourage birds, and import ladybugs, chalcid and trichogramma wasps, and *Encarsia formosa*.
- **Botanical controls:** Ryania, rotenone (1% solution)
- **Allies:** Basil, marigold, nasturtium, parsley, tomato. Also, beetle allegedly dislikes bonemeal. (See chart on pages 280–94.)

Bean Jassid

see Potato Leafhopper

Bean Leaf Beetle

Description: The adult is a small, ¼″ reddish tan beetle with 3–4 black spots on each side of its back. It lays eggs in the soil at the base of seedlings. Larvae, slender and white, feed on roots. Produces 1–2 generations per year.

Plants Affected: Bean,* pea

**Plant most frequently attacked by the insect*

Where It Occurs: Primarily in the Southeast

Signs

- Holes in leaves, particularly young seedlings
- Adult beetles feed on leaf undersides and on seedling stems.
- Larvae attack roots but usually don't affect the plant.
- Not a frequent pest

Organic Remedies

- Use same controls as for Mexican bean beetle; see page 248.
- ***Biological controls:*** Ladybugs and lacewings eat the eggs. Beneficial nematodes, mixed into seed furrow and in mulch, may kill larvae and emerging adults.
- Apply kaolin clay spray in a visible layer to all surfaces. This acts as a visual and physical repellent to insects.

Beet Leafhopper

also known as Whitefly *in the West*

Description: See Leafhopper. Produces up to 3 generations per year.

Plants Affected: Beet,* bean,* cucumber, flowers, spinach, squash, tomato

**Plants most frequently attacked by the insect*

Where It Occurs: West of Missouri and Illinois, except in coastal fog areas

Signs: The beet leafhopper spreads curly top virus, which is characterized by raised leaf veins; stunted plants; small, wartlike bumps on the leaf undersides; and curled, brittle leaves.

Organic Remedies: See Leafhopper controls on page 246.

Birds

Description: Can be major pests of all fruits and berries, and corn and peas.

Plants Affected: Fruits, nuts, many vegetables

Where It Occurs: Widespread

Organic Remedies

- ***For trees:*** Netting must be held out away from the tree by supports. Otherwise birds peck through the netting. Secure the netting tightly around the bottom. For more complete protection you can use cheesecloth, which is harder to peck through.
- ***For growing beds:*** Use row covers over corn and peas.
- ***For corn seed:*** Spread lime down seed rows—use experimentally; see page 219. Plant corn seeds deeper than usual, or mulch heavily. Erect several taut strands of black thread or fishing line over each seed row. Or start seeds inside and transplant once established.
- ***For mature corn:*** When silks brown, tie small rubber bands over each ear.
- Construct growing boxes that are screened on all sides.
- ***For berries and other large plants,*** erect around the plant a tepee structure out of lumber or poles, and drape netting over it.
- ***For strawberries:*** Paint large nuts red and place in the strawberry patch before fruit has ripened. Some gardeners report that birds tire of pecking at these fake berries before the real ones ripen. Use experimentally; see page 219.
- Scare-eye balloons have been reported to be effective—use experimentally; see page 219.

- Mulberry and elderberry trees offer berries in fall that birds eat first—use experimentally; see page 219. Mulberry grows rapidly to a breadth of 50′–60′.
- Use noise-making devices to scare birds away. One gardener reported that talk shows with human voices worked best. Use experimentally; see page 219.
- BirdXPeller Pro produces specific predator sounds, which are said to alarm and deter pigeons, sparrows, starlings, gulls, woodpeckers, crows, blackbirds, grackles, and geese. It can be programmed with different predator sounds.

Blackberry Sawfly

Description

- Adults are small wasplike flies with two pairs of transparent wings hooked to each other. They lay white eggs on leaf undersides in May.
- Blue-green larvae (¾″) roll leaves closed with webs and feed inside the webs through July. They then drop to the ground to pupate in the soil.

Plant Affected: Blackberry

Where It Occurs: Unable to determine; likely widespread

Signs: Rolled and webbed leaves

Organic Remedies

- Use sticky traps to catch adults.
- Handpick eggs and larvae in spring.
- **Botanical controls:** Pyrethrin

Blister Beetle

see Striped Blister Beetle

Boxelder Bug

Description: Medium-size (½″) bugs suck plant juices. They look like squash bugs but are brown with red markings. Nymphs are bright red.

Plants Affected: Almond, ash, boxelder,* maple*

**Plants most frequently attacked by the insect*

Where It Occurs: Present wherever boxelders grow.

Signs: Damaged foliage and twigs

Organic Remedies

- Remove any nearby female boxelder trees.
- Insecticidal soap spray, though this isn't a very effective control of hard-bodied insects.

Brown Almond Mite

see Mite

Cabbage Butterfly

see Imported Cabbageworm

Cabbage Looper

Description

- This large (1½″) pale green worm with light stripes down its back doubles up, or "loops," as it crawls. It hides under leaves in hot, dry weather. The worm overwinters as a green or brown pupa in a thin cocoon attached to a plant leaf.
- The adult moth (1½″wingspan) is night-flying, brownish, and has a silver spot in the middle of each forewing. It lays greenish white round eggs, singly, on leaves.
- Eggs hatch in 2 weeks and the looper feeds for 3–4 weeks.
- Produces 4 generations or more per year.

Plants Affected: Bean, brassicas, celery, lettuce, parsley, pea, potato, radish, spinach, tomato

Where It Occurs: Widespread

To Monitor: Use pheromone traps to monitor population levels of adult moths, starting soon after planting.

Signs

- Ragged holes in leaves
- Seedlings can be destroyed.
- Worms bore into the heads of all cabbage family plants.

Organic Remedies

- Use row covers all season.
- Handpick loopers.
- Plant spring crops to avoid the cabbage looper peak.
- Stagger planting dates to avoid entire crop susceptibility.
- Hot pepper spray—use experimentally; see page 219.
- Spray with soap and lime, or dust the wet plant with lime.
- In the Deep South, practice a thorough fall cultivation and also rotate crops on a 3–5-year basis. This insect doesn't overwinter in the North, so these steps aren't necessary there.
- Make viral insecticide from loopers infected with nuclear polyhedrosis virus (NPV). Loopers are chalky white, sluggish or half-dead, may be on the top of leaves or hanging from their undersides. They turn black and liquefy within days. Capture 3 and make bug juice. Spray from 3 bugs covers ¾ acre. Loopers take 3–6 days to die, but one spraying can last the entire season. ***Note:*** Spray only when it is cool and damp, and when you see that loopers are not hiding under leaves.
- Encourage predators such as toads, bluebirds, chickadees, robins, and sparrows.
- **Biological controls:** Spinosad, applied when larvae are young; Bt, applied every 2 weeks until heads form (for broccoli and cabbage); lacewings and trichogramma wasp.
- **Botanical controls:** Pyrethrin, neem
- **Allies:** Dill, garlic, hyssop, mint, nasturtium, onion family, sage, thyme (See chart on pages 280–94.)

Cabbage Maggot

Description

- The adult resembles a housefly but is half the size and has bristly hairs. It emerges from an underground cocoon in spring at cherry blossom time, in early summer, or in autumn. It lays eggs on plant stems near the soil line or in cracks in the soil.
- The small (⅓″), white, legless worm with a blunt end attacks stems below the soil line.
- To overwinter, maggots pupate 1″–5″ deep in the soil and emerge on the first warm spring day.
- The maggot transmits both bacterial soft spot and black leg.
- In season, each life cycle takes 6–7 weeks.
- Produces numerous generations per year.

Plants Affected: Brassicas, pea, radish (late spring), turnip

Where It Occurs: Widespread, particularly in western and northern United States. It thrives in cool, moist weather.

To Monitor: Yellow sticky traps are a good early-warning device for adults. Another method is to take a scoop of soil from the plant base, place it in water, and count the eggs that float to the top to determine the extent of the problem.

Signs

- Seedlings wilt and die.
- Stems are riddled with brown, slimy tunnels.
- Stunted, off-color plants.

Organic Remedies

- Use row covers in early season.
- Maggots don't like alkaline environment. Circle plants with a mixture of lime and wood ashes (moistened to prevent blowing) or diatomaceous earth—use experimentally; see page 219. Replenish after rain. Mix wood ashes into the surrounding soil. Do not replenish more than 2 times; continued use of wood ashes raises the pH excessively by its addition of potassium.

- Use a 12″ square of tar or black paper to prevent larvae from entering the soil.
- Plant in very early spring or in fall to avoid maggot peak in May and early June.
- **Biological controls:** Beneficial nematodes are effective when applied before planting.
- **Allies:** Clover, garlic, onion family, radish, sage, wormwood (See chart on pages 280–94.)

Cabbage Moth

see Imported Cabbageworm

Cabbageworm

also known as Cross-Striped Cabbageworm

Description: New worms are gray with large round heads. Mature worms (⅔″) are green to blue-gray with long dark hairs and at least 3 distinct black bands across each segment. The adult moth is small, pale yellow with mottled brown on its forewings.

Plant Affected: Cabbage

Where It Occurs: Widespread

Signs: See Imported Cabbageworm.

Organic Remedies: See Imported Cabbageworm.

Caneborer

also known as Rednecked Cane Borer

Description

- Blue-black beetles (⅓″) with coppery red thorax appear in May and lay eggs in June in cane bark near a ragged or eaten leaf.
- Flat-headed larvae bore into canes and cause swellings or galls in late July and August. Cut open galls to find creamy white grubs.

Plants Affected: Blackberry, raspberry

Where It Occurs: Present in the Northeast; other types are prevalent in other parts of the United States.

Signs

- Large cigar-shaped swellings on canes.
- Where cane joints swell, the cane may break off and die.

Organic Remedies: Cut out all canes with swellings and burn or destroy.

Cankerworm, Fall and Spring

also known as Inchworm, Measuring Worm

Description

- Small worms (1″) are green, brown, or black, have a yellow-brown stripe down their back, and drop from trees on silky threads when ready to pupate. They pupate 1″–4″ deep in the ground in cocoons near the trees.
- Male adults are grayish moths. Females are wingless. In spring they lay brownish gray eggs in masses on tree trunks or branches; in fall they lay brown-purple egg masses beneath the bark. Eggs hatch in 4–6 months.

Plants Affected: Apple,* apricot, cherry, elm, maple, oak, plum

**Plant most frequently attacked by the insect*

Where It Occurs: Widespread. The fall variety is worst in early spring in California, Colorado, Utah, and northern United States. The spring variety is worst in the East, Colorado, and California.

Signs

- Skeletonized leaves
- Few mature fruit
- Trees may look scorched when damaged by the spring variety.
- Defoliation may occur 2–3 years in a row.

Organic Remedies

- Use sticky bands from October to December, and again in February, to catch wingless females crawling up trees to lay eggs. Renew sticky substance periodically.

- Encourage predators such as bluebirds, chickadees, and nuthatches.
- Spray horticultural oil before leaves bud in spring.
- **Biological controls:** Trichogramma wasps work on spring species. Chalcid wasps. Bt and/or spinosad, applied every 2 weeks from the end of blossom time to 1 month later.

Carrot Rust Fly

Description: Small (⅓″), yellow-white larvae burrow into roots and make rusty colored tunnels. The adult fly is slender, shiny green, and lays eggs at the plant crown in late spring. Produces several generations per year.

Plants Affected: Caraway, carrot, celery, coriander, dill, fennel, parsley, parsnip

Where It Occurs: Widespread, but mostly a problem in northern and Pacific Northwest states

Signs

- Stunted plants
- Leaves wilt and turn yellow.
- Soft rot bacteria in the carrot

Organic Remedies

- Use row covers all season.
- Fall cultivation and early-spring cultivation disrupt overwintering maggots.
- Rotate crops.
- Avoid early planting. Plant all target crops after maggot peak.
- Yellow sticky traps. British horticulturists have shown these traps are most effective for this pest when placed at a 45-degree angle.
- Sow seeds with used tea leaves—use experimentally; see page 219.
- Spread wood ashes (moistened to prevent blowing), pulverized wormwood, or rock phosphate around the plant crown to repel egg laying—use experimentally; see page 219.
- **Allies:** Black salsify, coriander, lettuce, onion family, pennyroyal, rosemary, sage (See chart on pages 280–94.)

Carrot Weevil

Description: Small (⅓″), pale, legless, brown-headed worms tunnel into roots and celery hearts. The tiny (⅕″), dark brown, hard-shelled adult is snout-nosed and overwinters in garden litter and hedgerows. Produces 2–3 generations per year.

Plants Affected: Beet, carrot,* celery, parsley, parsnip

**Plant most frequently attacked by the insect*

Where It Occurs: East of the Rockies

Signs

- Zigzag tunnels in the tops and roots of plants
- Defoliation

Organic Remedies

- Use row covers all season.
- Practice fall cultivation.
- Rotate crops.
- Encourage chickadees, bluebirds, juncos, and warblers.
- **Biological controls:** Beneficial nematodes when plants are very small

Carrotworm

see Parsleyworm

Celery Leaftier

also known as Greenhouse Leaftier

Description

- Medium (¾″), pale green-yellow worms, with white stripe down the length of their backs, eat a host of vegetables. They web foliage together as they feed, and eventually pupate in silky cocoons inside webs.
- The adult is a small (¾″), brown nocturnal moth. It lays eggs that look like fish scales on leaf

undersides. They can do great damage but don't usually appear in large numbers.

- Produces 5–6 generations per year in warm areas; 7–8 generations per year in greenhouses.

Plants Affected: Celery,* kale, many other plants

**Plant most frequently attacked by the insect*

Where It Occurs: Widespread, but worst in the Northeast and southern California. Most destructive in greenhouses.

Signs

- Holes in leaves and stalks
- Leaves folded, and tied with webs

Organic Remedies

- Handpick and destroy pests.
- Handpick damaged or rolled leaves in which the leaftier may be hiding.

Celeryworm

see Parsleyworm

Cherry Fruit Fly

Description

- These black fruit flies resemble small houseflies, with yellow margins on the thorax and two white crossbands on the abdomen.
- They emerge in early June and feed for 7–10 days by sucking sap. They then lay eggs through small slits in developing fruits.
- The maggots are small yellow or white worms with 2 dark hooks on their mouths. They feed inside fruit, then drop to the ground and pupate for 6 months 2″–3″ deep in the soil.
- Pupae overwinter in the soil.

Plants Affected: Cherry, pear, plum

Where It Occurs: Widespread, except in the Southwest and Florida

To Monitor: Use sticky red balls or pheromone traps to monitor population levels.

Signs

- Small, disfigured fruit
- Premature fruit drop
- Rotten flesh with maggots feeding inside

Organic Remedies

- Fall cultivation after the first several frosts will expose pupae to predators.
- Red sticky balls. Hang these on perimeter trees at shoulder height, using about 4 balls per tree.
- Make a control trap of 1 part molasses to 9 parts water; add yeast; and pour into widemouthed jars. When fermentation bubbling subsides, hang the jars in trees. Use experimentally; see page 219.
- Remove and destroy badly infested fruit or feed it to animals. Drop mildly damaged fruit into water to kill maggots; these are okay for cider.
- **Biological controls:** Braconid wasps
- **Botanical control:** Neem

Cherry Fruit Sawfly

Description

- Small (⅛″) adult wasplike flies have two pairs of transparent wings hooked together and yellow appendages.
- Small (¼″) larvae are white with brown heads. They bore into young fruit and feed on seeds. They exit fallen fruit to pupate and overwinter in silken cocoons in the ground.

Plants Affected: Apricot, cherry, peach, plum

Where It Occurs: Pacific Coast

Signs: Fruits shrivel and drop.

Organic Remedies

- Shallow 2″ cultivation around trees to expose pupae
- Use sticky traps to catch adults.
- Handpick eggs and larvae in spring.
- **Botanical controls:** Pyrethrin

Cherry Fruitworm

Description

- The small, gray adult moth lays single eggs on cherries in May and June.
- Small (3⁄8″) pinkish larvae hatch in 10 days and bore into fruit where they feed. They overwinter in the stubs of pruned branches or in bark crevices.
- Distinguished from the cherry fruit fly maggot by black head and caterpillar-like body.
- Produces 1 generation per year.

Plant Affected: Cherry

Where It Occurs: Prevalent in Colorado, and north and west of Colorado

Signs

- Rotten flesh with larvae feeding inside
- Can be very damaging.

Organic Remedies

- **Biological control:** Bt, sprayed in the first week of June

Cherry Slug

see Pearslug

Chestnut Weevil

also known as Snout Weevil

Description

- The adult (5⁄16″–½″) has a very long proboscis (snout), as long or longer than its body. It emerges from April to August, and in August deposits eggs into the bur through a tiny hole.
- Larvae are legless, white, plump, and curved like a crescent moon.
- Mature larvae overwinter 3″–6″ belowground.
- Completes a life cycle in 1–2 years.

Plant Affected: Chestnut

Where It Occurs: Wherever Asian chestnuts are grown

Signs: Larvae feed on kernel tissue for 3–5 weeks, sometimes hollowing out the interior, then leave the nut.

Organic Remedies

- Collect fallen nuts every day and immerse in hot water (122°F/50°C) for 45 minutes to kill all larvae. This prevents larvae from entering the soil and continuing the cycle.
- Plant away from woods or forest from which squirrels and other rodents can bring in infested nuts.
- Fall cultivation. Also, chickens can help clean up larvae.

Click Beetle

see Wireworm

Codling Moth

Description

- Large (1″) larva is white tinged with pink, has a brown head and a voracious appetite.
- Adult moths (¾″ wingspan) are gray-brown with dark brown markings on lacy forewings, fringed back wings, and dark brown edging on all wings. They lay flat white eggs, singly, on twigs or upper leaf surfaces.
- Eggs hatch in 6–20 days, and larvae tunnel into and out of fruit. Pupae overwinter in tough cocoons built in cracks of loose bark, fences, buildings, or garden debris.
- Produces 2 generations per year; the first generation attacks immature fruit; the second attacks mature fruit.

Plants Affected: Almond, apple,* apricot, cherry, peach, pear, walnut (English)

**Plant most frequently attacked by the insect*

Where It Occurs: Widespread

To Monitor: Use pheromone traps to determine population levels. More than 5 moths per trap per week indicates that controls may be needed.

Signs

- Holes and tunnels in fruit, with brown fecal material at the core and a brown mound at the hole opening
- Sometimes forms cocoons in bark crevices.

Organic Remedies

- Apply kaolin clay spray. It is suggested to begin spraying at the first petal fall and reapply once a week for 6 to 8 weeks throughout the season. Repeat applications after any major rain event.
- In spring, band tree trunks with several thicknesses of 6″-wide corrugated cardboard. Exposed ridges must be at least 3⁄16″ wide and must face the tree. This gives larvae a place to spin cocoons when they leave the fruit. Remove and kill larvae once a week in warm weather, once every 2 weeks in cool weather. Continue through harvest. Burn the cardboard.
- Use sticky bands to catch larvae.
- Make a trap for larvae of 2 parts vinegar to 1 part molasses in a widemouthed jar—use experimentally; see page 219. Hang 3–4 traps per tree, 8″ below the limb. Clean and replenish daily.
- In spring, scrape off all loose rough bark from the trunk and limbs. Catch the scrapings and destroy. Seal pruning wounds.
- Apply soap and lime spray, or fish oil spray, to the entire tree before leaves appear in late winter, and, later, weekly to tree trunk and base.
- Apply horticultural oil spray before buds open. Be sure to cover all surfaces of the tree.
- Encourage woodpeckers in winter with 1 suet ball per tree.
- **Biological controls:** 2–3 sprays of Bt, applied 3–4 days apart at peak egg-laying time, is very effective. Three timed releases of trichogramma wasps—the first at petal fall, the second 3–8 weeks later, and a final release 5–8 weeks later in early fall—are also helpful. Beneficial nematodes help most when sprayed on wet tree trunks and nearby soil in late winter.
- Pheromone-based mating disruption devices are commercially available but may not be effective in small orchards.
- **Botanical controls:** Pyrethrin
- **Allies:** Cover crops of the buckwheat, cloves, daisy families; dill; garlic; wormwood (See chart on pages 280–94.)

Colorado Potato Beetle

Description

- Small (1⁄3″), yellow, hard-shelled beetles have orange heads with black dots and black stripes down their backs. They lay bright yellow eggs on leaf undersides.
- Eggs hatch in 4–9 days and become plump red larvae with black spots and black heads.
- Produces 1–3 generations per year.

Plants Affected: Eggplant,* pepper, potato,* tomato*

**Plants most frequently attacked by the insect*

Where It Occurs: Widespread, but mostly a problem in the eastern United States. Rarely a problem in southern California through Texas, Louisiana, and Georgia.

Signs

- Skeletonized leaves and complete defoliation
- Adults and larvae chew foliage.

Organic Remedies

- Apply kaolin clay spray every 7 to 14 days, depending on rainfall and infestation severity.
- Use row covers in early season.
- Handpick immediately, when sighted, and crush adults and egg masses—a very effective control.
- Apply thick organic mulch to impede the movement of overwintered adults to plants. Beetles walk more than fly during the early season. Potatoes can be started in thick mulch aboveground.
- Practice fall cultivation.

- Where various potato and tomato varieties are grown, resistant varieties will be less susceptible. If only 1 resistant variety is grown, however, even this will be consumed. All eggplants are susceptible.
- Time plantings to avoid beetles. Plant potatoes as early as possible to allow sufficient plant growth to withstand attack of overwintered adults.
- Research in Ontario shows that potatoes can serve as an effective trap crop for tomatoes, and that crop rotation of potato and tomato crops can help reduce more overwintering Colorado potato beetles.
- University of Maine studies have shown that fish emulsion foliar spray repels these bugs.
- Research shows that ground tansy—diluted 1:100 (leaf to water weight ratio) and used as a foliar spray—dramatically reduces bug feeding.
- Garlic, onion, and hot pepper sprays, applied directly on beetles, are irritants—use experimentally; see pages 192–93.
- Foliar sprays of hydrogen peroxide (1 tablespoon to 1 gallon water) applied directly on active adults provide fair control. Do not apply in direct sunlight in the heat of the day.
- A dusting of diatomaceous earth dries out beetles. Soap and lime spray is also believed to dry out beetles, but generally soap is not effective against hard-bodied insects.
- Sprinkle fine-milled wheat bran on leaves at the first sign of beetles—use experimentally; see page 219. Found effective by an Ohio gardener.
- In fall, let chickens into the garden to eat beetles and larvae.
- Encourage predators like songbirds, toads, and ground beetles.
- *Beauveria bassiana* (Bb) is a naturally occurring soil fungus that can be applied to Colorado potato beetle larvae with a standard sprayer. It can cause defoliation damage but can help prevent egg laying and future generations. This product works well when used with Bt, spinosad, or neem earlier in larval development.
- Spinosad has been the go-to treatment for many organic growers. It's a naturally occurring substance made by soil bacterium (*Saccharopolyspora spinosa*) that can be toxic to a wide variety of insects.
- **Biological controls:** Ladybugs, lacewings, and *Edovum puttleri* eat the eggs. Beneficial nematodes. Two-spotted stink bug (*Perillus bioculatus*). Spinosad and some Bt strains (M-One, Trident, Foil) are very effective if applied in the larval stage. Once the larvae are too big, it doesn't help much.
- **Botanical controls:** Neem
- **Allies:** Bean, catnip, coriander, dead nettle, eggplant, flax, horseradish, nasturtium, onion family, tansy. Because beans are allegedly noxious to this bug, and potatoes repel the Mexican bean beetle, they might be companions. (See chart on pages 280–94.)

Corn Borer

see European Corn Borer

Corn Earworm

also known as Vetchworm, Cotton Bollworm, Tomato Fruitworm, Tobacco Budworm

Description

- Large (1½″–2″), light yellow, green, red, or brown caterpillars; striped, with "spines" at bands; feed first on leaves and corn silk. They feed on kernels and exit through the husk to pupate. Feeding lasts about 1 month, then they drop to the ground and pupate 3″–5″ deep in the soil.
- The adult (1½″ wingspan) grayish brown moth feeds on flower nectar. It lays 500–3000 tiny, single, ribbed, dirty white eggs on host plants.

- This pest is most numerous 2–3 weeks after a full moon. Some say corn should ideally silk during the full moon. Pest numbers are reduced by cold winters and wet summers.
- Extremely destructive.
- Produces 2–3 generations per year.

Plants Affected: Bean, corn (sweet),* pea, peanut, pepper, potato, squash, tomato

**Plant most frequently attacked by the insect*

Where It Occurs: Widespread, but primarily a problem in southern and central states

Signs

- Ragged holes in tender leaves
- Eaten tassels and damaged pods on developing fruits
- Chewed silk and damp castings near the silk
- Damaged kernels, often at the ear tip

Organic Remedies

- Mineral oil, applied just inside the tip of each ear, suffocates the worms. Apply only after silk has wilted and started to brown at the tip or pollination will be incomplete. Use ½ of a medicine dropper per small ear, ¾ of a dropper per large ear. You might add red pepper to the oil to see if it increases the effectiveness. Apply 2 or more applications of oil, spaced at 2-week intervals.
- Fall cultivation. In spring, cultivate the top 2″ of soil.
- Handpick worms after silks brown.
- Time plantings to avoid worms. In northern states, early plantings that silk before mid-July often avoid attack.
- Plant resistant varieties with tight husks. Or clip husks tightly with clothespins. You can also try covering ears with pantyhose.
- Some research shows that petunias, cosmos, geraniums, marigold, and thyme contain natural repellants.
- Spray light horticultural oil (2%–3% solution). Bt added to the oil spray can increase its effectiveness.
- Research suggests that spinosad, available in an organic formulation (Entrust SC), can suppress corn earworm if used on a 3–4-day spray schedule. Spinosad works well as an insecticide in the direct silk method.
- **Biological controls:** Minute pirate bugs. Lacewings. Trichogramma wasps and tachinid flies lay eggs in the moth eggs and prevent hatching. Inject beneficial nematodes into infested ears; they seek out and kill worms in 24 hours. Bt and/or spinosad can be applied to borers before they move into the stalks. Then wettable Bt, applied every 10–14 days, is effective.
- **Botanical controls:** Pyrethrin. Use pheromone traps to identify moth flight paths before spraying. Spray moths before they lay eggs.
- **Allies:** Corn, marigold, soybean (See chart on pages 280–94.)

Corn Maggot

also known as Seedcorn Maggot

Description: Small (¼″), yellow-white larvae, with long heads tapering to point, tunnel into larger vegetable seeds. The adult is a small gray-brown fly that lays eggs in April through May in the soil and on seeds and seedlings. Produces 3–5 generations per year.

Plants Affected: Bean, corn (sweet),* pea

**Plant most frequently attacked by the insect*

Where It Occurs: Widespread. Worst injury occurs early in cold, wet soil that is high in organic matter.

Signs

- Damaged seeds that fail to sprout
- Poor, stunted plants

Organic Remedies

- Plant seeds in shallow furrows to speed emergence.

- Delay planting until soil is warm; avoid planting early in soils high in organic matter and manure.
- If damage is heavy, replant immediately. Seeds will germinate before the next generation of adults emerges.
- **Ally:** Rye (See chart on pages 280–94.)

Corn Rootworm (Northern and Western)

Description

- Adult yellow-green beetles are small (¼″) and emerge in late July and August. They feed on corn silks and other plants. They lay eggs in the ground near corn roots in late summer.
- Eggs hatch in late spring. Small (½″), narrow, wrinkled white worms with brown heads feed only on corn and burrow through corn roots.
- Produces 1 generation per year.

Plant Affected: Corn (sweet)

Where It Occurs: The western variety is active in the upper Midwest, and east to Pennsylvania and Maryland. The northern variety is active in New York to Kansas and South Dakota.

Signs: Weak plants with damaged silks and brown tunnels in the roots

Organic Remedies: Crop rotation; if beetles are found feeding on silks, then plant sweet corn in a different location next year.

Cucumber Beetles (Striped/Spotted)

Spotted *also known as* Southern Corn Rootworm

Description

- Small (⅓″), thin white larvae with brown heads and brown ends feed for 2–6 weeks on roots and underground stems. Heavy larvae populations can reduce plant vigor and damage melon rind surfaces next to the ground.
- Adults of both types are small (¼″) with black heads and yellow or yellow-green backs.
- Striped beetles have 3 black stripes down the back. Spotted beetles have 11 to 12 black spots scattered across the back.
- Both types lay yellow-orange eggs in the soil near host plants. Beetles tend to congregate on one leaf or plant, so it may be possible to remove a selected plant and destroy large quantities.
- Midsummer adults feed on upper plant parts, while autumn adults feed on fruits, then weeds and trees.
- Produces 1 generation per year in cold areas; 2 generations in warm climates.

Plants Affected: Asparagus, beans (early),* corn (sweet),* cucumber,* eggplant, muskmelon,* pea, potato, pumpkin,* squash,* tomato, watermelon,* some fruit trees

**Plants most frequently attacked by the insect*

Where It Occurs: Widespread east of the Rockies, but most serious in the South and where soils are heavy

Signs

- Striped adults are the most destructive and eat mostly cucurbits.
- Both types eat stems and leaves of cucurbits before the first true leaves emerge. Spotted beetles also eat flowers and fruit. Adults transmit bacterial wilt of cucurbits, brown rot in stone fruit, cucumber mosaic, and wilt. Larvae feed on the root system.
- Break a cucumber plant stem, put it back together, pull it back apart, and see if strings (looking like pizza cheese) form. If so, it has bacterial wilt. This test is not so easy with other cucurbits.

Organic Remedies

- Apply kaolin clay spray every 7 to 14 days, depending on rainfall and infestation severity.
- Use row covers from the time of sowing or transplanting to bloom time. Lift edges during bloom time for 2 hours in early morning—just twice per week—to allow pollination; secure edges again until harvest.

- Vacuum adults with a handheld vacuum at dusk. Empty into a plastic bag immediately, or they'll crawl out.
- Select resistant varieties.
- Transplant strong seedlings.
- Practice fall cultivation.
- Circle plants with a trench 3″–4″ wide and 3″ deep. Fill with wood ashes, moistened to prevent blowing. Use experimentally; see page 219. Don't get ashes on plants.
- Handpick beetles.
- Apply thick mulch.
- Lime is thought to dry out these beetles. Apply one of the following directly on beetles: soap and lime spray, lime dust (hydrated or plasterer's lime), or a spray containing equal amounts of wood ashes and hydrated lime mixed in water. Soap alone isn't very effective against hard-bodied insects.
- Hot pepper and garlic spray—use experimentally; see pages 192–93.
- Sprinkle onion skins over plants—use experimentally; see page 219.
- Time plantings to avoid bugs.
- Plant zucchini or yellow squash to trap early infestations—use experimentally; see page 219.
- Encourage songbirds.
- **Biological controls:** Lacewings and ladybugs eat eggs. To kill adults, apply beneficial nematodes in the seed furrows, around roots, and in mulch.
- **Botanical controls:** Pyrethrin
- **Allies:** Broccoli, catnip, corn, goldenrod, marigold, nasturtium, onion skins, radish, rue, tansy (See chart on pages 280–94.)

Cutworm

Description

- Large (½″) soft-bodied larvae are gray or brownish with bristles. They curl into a circle when disturbed. They feed at night for several weeks and burrow into the soil during the day. The last generation overwinters as naked brown pupae in the soil.
- Adults are night-flying moths with ragged blotches like paint drips on their wings. They lay egg masses on leaves, tree trunks, fences, and buildings. Eggs hatch in 2–10 days.

Plants Affected: Beans, brassicas, corn (sweet), cucumber, eggplant, lettuce, melon (seedlings), pea, peanut, pepper, potato, radish, tomato, all seedlings

Where It Occurs: Widespread

Signs

- Severed stems, straight across, at or below soil surface
- Plants wilt and collapse.
- Buds, leaves, and fruit may also be eaten by the variegated cutworm.

Organic Remedies

- Install stem collars.
- Plant transplants inside ½-gallon milk cartons, with bottoms cut out and rims emerging about 1″ out of the soil.
- Diatomaceous earth, sprinkled around the base of each plant and worked slightly into the soil, is very effective.
- Sprinkle cornmeal or bran, ½ teaspoon per plant, around the plant base in a circle leading away from the stem—use experimentally; see page 219. Worms eat this and die.
- Make a trap of equal parts of sawdust (pine is best) and bran, add molasses and a little water. At dusk sprinkle several spoonfuls near plants. The sticky goo clings to cutworm bodies and dries, making them food for prey. Use experimentally; see page 219.

- Create barriers by making a trench 3″–4″ wide, 2″–3″ deep; fill with wood ashes (moistened to prevent blowing), crushed eggshells, oak leaves, or cornmeal or bran (½ teaspoon per plant).
- Fall cultivation. Following fall cultivation, allow chickens into the garden to clean out exposed pests.
- Handpick at night with a light.
- Encourage birds and toads.
- University of British Columbia student Greg Salloum claims cutworms will starve before eating plants treated with extracts of pineapple weed or sagebrush.
- **Biological controls:** Apply beneficial nematodes at a rate of 50,000 per plant. Apply Bt and/or spinosad. Lacewing, braconid, and trichogramma wasps. Tachinid flies.
- **Allies:** Shepherd's purse, tansy (See chart on pages 280–94.)

Deer

Description: Large quadruped mammal

Plants Affected: Azalea, fruit trees, holly, juniper, rose, saplings, vegetables

Where It Occurs: Widespread

Signs: Deer have 2 large and 2 small toes on each foot, a distinct print.

Organic Remedies

- Fences: Serious deer fences need to be electrified with 7 strands, at 8″, 16″, 24″, 40″, 50″, and 60″.
  - An alternative is to use a one-wire electric fence, but only if you bait the fence. All electrified fences work best if baited. Bait with attached pieces of aluminum foil smeared with peanut butter; this attracts deer, shocks them, and trains them to stay away.
  - An effective nonelectric fence is two 4′-high fences spaced 5′ apart, with bare ground between. Deer aren't broad jumpers and realize that, once they get into the middle section, there isn't enough room to clear the second fence.
  - An alternate, nonelectric is a horizontal fence. Research at the Institute of Ecosystem Studies, New York Botanical Garden, in Millbrook, New York, shows that deer won't jump a horizontal fence.
  - An Extension horticulturist from the University of Georgia Cooperative Extension Service said that a fence of fishing line with flagging tape at every 2′–3′ interval will startle and deter deer.
- Tie bags containing 1 ounce human or dog hair, dried blood meal, or fish heads to orchard trees and along perimeters of melon and sweet potato patches—use experimentally; see page 219. This allegedly provides protection for 10 months.
- Make a spray of 2 egg yolks in 1 quart water; spray fruit tree foliage. Use experimentally; see page 219. One farmer claims trees weren't bothered the entire season.
- Lay chicken wire squares wherever you find deer droppings; deer will avoid the area—use experimentally; see page 219.
- Hanging soap in outer tree limbs is reported by some to work—use experimentally; see page 219. Be aware, however, that groundhogs love soap.
- Hinder, a deer repellent, reputedly works when sprayed on leaves and branches.
- Maintain dogs to keep deer away.
- Use automated blinking lights at night to keep deer away—use experimentally; see page 219.
- Old, smelly shoes are reputed to be effective deterrents when placed around the garden perimeter—use experimentally; see page 219.
- Plant a border of plants that deer won't eat, such as *Fritillaria*.
- For trees, translucent tubes apparently accelerate growth of the tree seedlings while protecting them from rabbits and deer, although some trees are sensitive to leaf scorch and overheating.

- Spray-on liquid containing Bitrex, a bitter-tasting substance, such as Plantskydd and Tree Guard, is claimed to repel domestic pets and wild mammals, including deer.

Diamondback Moth

Description: Small (⅓″), green-yellow larva with black hairs chews leaves. When disturbed, it wriggles and drops to the ground. Gray-brown adult moth (¾″ wingspan) has fringed back wings, with a diamond that shows when the wings are at rest. Usually a minor pest.

Plants Affected: Brassicas

Where It Occurs: Widespread

Signs: Small holes in outer leaves

Organic Remedies

- Apply soap and lime spray directly on worms; before harvest, spray 3 days in a row to kill new worms.
- Southernwood is an herbal repellant—use experimentally; see page 219.
- A field trial conducted on Oahu in 2020 showed that intermittent sprinkler irrigation for 5 minutes twice during dusk (at 6:00 and 8:00 p.m.) reduced diamondback moth damage on head cabbage by 19%, though there was no significant decrease in larvae on the plants.
- **Biological controls:** Lacewings and trichogramma wasps. Spinosad can offer an effective treatment of eggs and larvae if infestation is severe.
- **Botanical controls:** Pyrethrin
- **Allies:** Cabbage, tomato (See chart on pages 280–94.)

Earwig

Description

- Nocturnal, slender, brown, beetlelike insect (¾″) with sharp pincers at its tail. It usually crawls but can fly if it takes off from a high place. Hides under and in things during the day.
- As a beneficial, it can scavenge larvae, slow-moving bugs, and aphids.
- As a pest, it feeds on soft plant tissue such as foliage, flowers, and corn silks.
- It can be particularly damaging to seedlings.

Plants Affected: Bean (seedling), beet (seedling), cabbage (Chinese), celery,* corn (sweet),* flowers, lettuce, potato,* strawberry*

**Plants most frequently attacked by the insect*

Where It Occurs: Widespread, but primarily a pest in the West, particularly the San Francisco Bay Area and northern California.

Signs: Round holes in the middle of leaves

Organic Remedies

- Probably best left alone in the areas where they're not a serious problem.
- In areas where they're a serious problem, trap and kill. Good trap locations are moist, tight areas where they spend the day. Try rolled-up moistened newspapers, rolls of moistened cardboard, or bamboo. Collect and dispose of pests in the morning.
- If very bad, use commercial earwig bait.

Eelworm

see Nematode

European Apple Sawfly

Description

- Small wasplike adult flies are brown and yellow with 2 pairs of transparent wings hooked together. They emerge at blossom time.
- Larvae are white worms, with 7 forelegs that bore into fruit and leave chocolate-colored sawdust on the fruit surface. Worms then drop to the ground, in which they pupate through the winter.
- Produces 1 generation per year.

Plants Affected: Apple, pear, plum

Where It Occurs: Present in Connecticut, Massachusetts, New Jersey, New York, Rhode Island

Signs

- Premature fruit drop
- Brown scars on fruit skin

Organic Remedies

- Clean up fallen fruit and destroy larvae by placing them in a sealed black bag in a sunny location.

European Corn Borer

also known as Corn Borer

Description

- The gray-pink caterpillar (1″) has brown spots on each segment and a dark brown head.
- The adult, night-flying, yellowish moth (½″) has dark wavy bands across its wings and lays clumps of white eggs on leaf undersides. Eggs hatch in up to 1 week.
- Larvae overwinter in corn stubble.
- Pupae are reddish brown grubs.
- Bores into ears and feeds on kernels at both tip and butt ends.
- Bores into the stem and fruit parts of pepper, potato, and green beans.
- Can attack the stems, foliage, and fruits of more than 260 different plants.
- Produces 1–3 generations per year, depending on the climate.

Plants Affected: Bean (green), chard, corn (sweet),* pepper, potato, tomato

**Plant most frequently attacked by the insect*

Where It Occurs: Widespread, except in the Southwest and far West

Signs

- Broken tassels and bent stalks
- Sawdust castings outside small holes

To Monitor

- Use black-light traps to monitor populations before spraying moths.
- Catches of more than 5 moths per night warrant sprays applied every 4–5 days, starting at full tassel.

Organic Remedies

- Remove and destroy all plant debris.
- Fall cultivation destroys larvae. Plants must be destroyed and turned under at least 1″ beneath the soil line.
- Avoid early plantings, which are more susceptible to larvae attack.
- Handpick by slitting damaged tassels and removing the borer.
- Plant resistant varieties. Small-stemmed, early-season types are less tolerant of borer injury.
- Cover ears with pantyhose.
- Encourage predators such as toads, downy woodpeckers, phoebes, swallows.
- **Biological controls:** Trichogramma wasps parasitize eggs. Braconid wasps. Tachinid flies. Ladybugs and lacewings eat the eggs. Release trichogramma when adults are first caught in a monitoring trap. Bt and spinosad are also effective.
- **Botanical controls:** Pyrethrin
- Apply Bt and botanical controls at tassel emergence if moth activity is high. Repeat sprays every 4–5 days until silks turn brown.
- **Allies:** Clover, peanuts (See chart on pages 280–94.)

European Red Mite

see Mite

Fall and Spring Armyworm

Description

- The spring species is a large (1½″) tan, brown, or green caterpillar found early in the season in the whorl leaves of corn.

- The fall armyworms have 3 light yellow hairline stripes from head to tail, and on each side a dark stripe below which is a wavy yellow stripe marked with red. Heads have a prominent V or Y.
- Both species usually feed on cloudy days and at night, but the fall species also feeds during the day.
- The adult gray moth of the spring species has 1 yellow or white spot on each forewing. Each lays up to 2000 eggs on corn and grasses. Eggs hatch in 7 days, and the cycle continues. Further generations feed through late summer.
- Produces 3–6 generations per year.

Plants Affected: Bean, cabbage, corn (sweet)*

**Plant most frequently attacked by the insect*

Where It Occurs: The spring species is widespread, but most serious in warm climates, where there is more generation turnover. The fall species overwinters in the South and migrates to northern states every year in June and July.

Signs: Chewed leaves, stems, and buds. The fall species also bores into ears and feeds on kernels; it can be very destructive to late plantings.

Organic Remedies

- Encourage natural predators such as birds, toads, and ground beetles. Skunks also prey on these, but you may not want to attract them.
- In case of a serious problem, dig a steep trench around the garden—use experimentally; see page 219. Armyworms will be trapped inside and can be destroyed by putting them in boiling water or in water laced with insecticidal soap (don't use kerosene—it is toxic to the soil and difficult to dispose of safely).
- Alternate rows of corn with sunflowers to discourage population movement—use experimentally; see page 219.
- **Biological controls:** Lacewings, ladybugs, and other insect predators eat eggs and young larvae. The Hh strain of beneficial nematodes (*Steinernema carpocapsae*) is effective against the larval stage. Ichneumon and braconid wasps. Tachinid flies. Bt and spinosad are effective against the larvae.

Fall Webworm

Description

- This yellowish caterpillar (1¼″) has long, light brown or whitish hairs, a dark stripe down its back, and is dotted with small black spots. It builds gray cocoons in secluded sites, fences, bark, or garden debris. White or green eggs are layered in clusters of 200–500 on leaf undersides.
- Adult white moths, with black- or brown-spotted wings, emerge in spring and late summer.
- Produces 2 generations per year.

Plants Affected: Fruit trees, pecan

Where It Occurs: Widespread

Signs

- Large silken tents or nests on ends of branches
- Tents include foliage, unlike tentworms.
- Very damaging
- Trees can be stripped and die.

Organic Remedies

- Cut off and destroy nests. Burn where permitted. Otherwise destroy nests by putting them in boiling water or water laced with insecticidal soap (don't use kerosene—it is toxic to the soil and difficult to dispose of safely).
- Pick off leaves with eggs and destroy.
- **Biological controls:** Trichogramma wasps eat eggs. Bt and spinosad are also effective.
- **Botanical control:** Neem

Filbert Mud Mite

Description

- Tiny white arachnids (0.3 mm), difficult to see without a magnifying lens.

- Adults invade new buds of current year's shoots, which become deformed as early as September.
- Adults breed in fall and winter, and in spring females leave deformed buds to invade young leaves and lay eggs.

Plant Affected: Filbert

Where It Occurs: Widespread

Signs

- Buds swell through summer and fall to 2–3 times their normal size. Mites will be easily recognized by December, with thousands of them feeding per bud.
- Swollen buds open, dry, and drop prematurely in spring.
- Yields are seriously diminished.
- Tiny mites migrate to newly developing buds before old buds fall in spring.

Organic Remedies

- Plant resistant cultivars. This is the best control.
- Early-spring aphid foliar sprays may help.
- You might try pruning out infested buds in early winter.

Filbert Weevil

also known as Hazelnut Weevil

Description

- Small (¼″–⅜″) adult beetle is light brownish yellow with a long snout about half the length of its body. It emerges May to June and lays eggs in late June or early July in the green shell.
- White larvae feed first on the green shell, then on the kernel. They exit through small holes and drop to the ground, where they overwinter 2″–8″ below the soil surface.

Plants Affected: Filbert, western oak

Where It Occurs: Throughout the United States

Signs

- Deformed green shells
- Hollowed-out kernels and shells

Organic Remedies: Similar to Chestnut Weevil and Plum Curculio (see pages 228 and 258, respectively)

- **Botanical control:** Neem

Filbertworm

Description

- Small (½″-long) adult moth varies in appearance. Its forewings are reddish brown, with a broad coppery band down the center.
- Larvae (½″) are white with yellowish heads. They feed on nut kernels. Larvae overwinter in cocoons on the ground and pupate in spring.

Plants Affected: Almond, chestnut, filbert, oak, Persian walnut

Where It Occurs: Throughout the United States

Signs: Small holes in the nut

Organic Remedies

- Early harvest of nuts and immediate destruction of infested nuts.
- See your Extension agent for further help.

Flathead Borer

also known as Flathead Appletree Borer

Description

- Adults (½″) are dark bronze beetles with a metallic sheen and are usually found on the warm side of trees, where they lay yellow, wrinkled eggs in cracks in the bark of unhealthy or injured trees. May and June are the worst times.
- Eggs develop into long (1½″) yellow-white, U-shaped larvae that have swollen areas just in back of their heads. They bore tunnels into the tree.
- Produces 1 generation per year.

Plants Affected: Many trees: apple, ash, beech, boxelder, dogwood, hickory, maple, oak, pecan, fruit trees

Where It Occurs: Widespread, but particularly in the South and Midwest. Oak is a prime target in the West; maple and fruit trees are prime targets in the East.

Signs

- Sunken areas in the bark, which indicate feeding tunnels, are filled with a dry powdery substance known as frass, a mixture of droppings and sawdust.
- Minor foliage damage
- The bark turns dark and may exude sap.
- Sunny sides of the tree are attacked most.

Organic Remedies

- Shade the trunks of young trees with some kind of shield.
- Protect newly transplanted trees by wrapping trunks with burlap or cardboard from the soil level up to the lower branches. Or cover with a thick coat of white interior latex paint.
- Keep young trees pruned to a low profile.
- Seal wounds with tree paint.
- Encourage predators such as crows, wasps, woodpeckers, predatory beetles, and vireos.

Flea Beetle

many species, also known as Corn Flea Beetle, Potato Flea Beetle

Description

- These tiny (1⁄6″) dark brown or black beetles jump when disturbed. They can have white or yellow markings.
- Adults lay eggs in the soil and favor the sun. The larvae feed on plant roots and can also damage tubers.
- Adults transmit bacterial wilt to sweet corn and early blight to potatoes.
- Flea beetles stop feeding and hide in wet weather.
- Usually produce 2 generations per year.

Plants Affected: Bean, brassicas, corn, eggplant, lettuce, muskmelon, pepper, potato, radish, spinach, sweet potato, tomato, watermelon

Where It Occurs: Widespread

To Monitor: Use white sticky traps for an early warning device.

Signs

- Numerous small holes in leaves in early summer
- Worst after mild winters and cool, wet springs

Organic Remedies

- Apply kaolin clay spray every 7 to 14 days, depending on rainfall and severity of infestation.
- Use row covers. (Pantyhose can be used over small cabbages.)
- Plant as late as possible.
- Seed thickly until the danger of infestation is past.
- Attach sticky bands around the base of wintering plants.
- Use yellow sticky traps for control.
- Frequent fall and spring cultivation will expose eggs to predators
- Sprinkle wood ashes (moistened to prevent blowing) around the plant base; or, mix equal parts of wood ashes and lime in small containers and place around the plants. Use experimentally; see page 219.
- A dusting of diatomaceous earth dries up beetles.
- Vacuum with a handheld vacuum. Empty immediately into plastic bag.
- Plant after a trap crop of radish or pak choi—use experimentally; see page 219.
- Sprinkle crushed elderberry or tomato leaves on vulnerable plants—use experimentally; see page 219.
- Mulch with chopped clover—use experimentally; see page 219.
- Companion plant with cover crops of clover or annual ryegrass to reduce populations—use experimentally; see page 219.
- Interplant with shading crops—use experimentally; see page 219.
- Hot pepper or garlic spray—use experimentally; see pages 192–93.

- **Biological controls:** Apply beneficial nematodes in mulch or seed furrows.
- **Botanical controls:** Pyrethrin
- **Allies:** Candytuft, catnip, mint, shepherd's purse, tansy, tomato (See chart on pages 280–94.)

Fruit Tree Leaf Roller

see Leaf Roller

Gall Wasp

Description

- The small (⅛″) adult wasp emerges in late May and early June and lays eggs inside buds.
- Eggs hatch in late July and larvae begin to grow.
- Larvae overwinter inside the bud.
- Produces 1 generation per year.

Plant Affected: Chestnut

Where It Occurs: Prevalent in the Southeast, particularly Georgia

Signs

- Vegetative buds and shoot growth are hindered by galls.
- Buds are turned into ⅓″–½″ rose-colored balls that often hang on to the branch for several years.
- Buds may have some parts of leaf or stem growth.
- Trees lose vigor and may die.

Organic Remedies: Prune and destroy infested shoots.

Garden Symphylan or Centipede

Description

- Small (½″) white wormlike creature with 12 pairs of legs thrives in damp soil, leaf mold, and manure piles. It feeds on root hairs.
- After harvest, it burrows down 12″ into the soil, where it lays clusters of white spherical eggs.
- This pest is not a true centipede, which is beneficial and grows to 3″ long.

Plants Affected: Asparagus, cucumber, lettuce, radish, tomato

Where It Occurs: Warm climates and greenhouses. Particularly damaging to asparagus in California.

Signs

- Stunted plants that slowly die
- Destroyed root hairs

Organic Remedies

- Inspect soil. Two or more of these pests per shovelful means you can expect damage. Avoid planting where you find damaging populations.
- Pasteurize potting soil.
- Solarize outdoor growing beds, where possible.
- In California, flood asparagus field for 3 weeks in late December to early January, to a depth of 1–3 feet.

Garden Webworm

Description

- Tan-brown moths (1″) with gray markings appear in spring and lay clusters of eggs on the leaves of host plants.
- Caterpillars (1″) are greenish with small dark spots and hairy. They hatch, feed, and spin webs for shelter. When disturbed, they drop to the ground or hide inside silken tubular shelters on the ground. They feed for about 1 month before pupating. The last generation overwinters in the soil in the pupal phase.

Plants Affected: Bean,* beet, corn (sweet),* pea, strawberry

**Plants most frequently attacked by the insect*

Where It Occurs: Widespread, but only serious in parts of the South and Midwest

Signs

- Holes in leaves and stems
- Folded leaves held together with fine webs
- Defoliation
- Produces several generations per year.

Organic Remedies

- Cut off and destroy webbed branches.

- Handpick caterpillars.
- Remove infested leaves and stems.
- Crush worms inside silken tubes on the ground.
- **Botanical controls:** Neem

Gopher and Groundhog

Description: Gophers eat the roots of vegetables, fruit trees, and grasses. They also dine on bulbs and tubers. Unlike groundhogs, gophers can't climb fences and, unlike the solitary mole, they invade in numbers.

Plants Affected: Flowers, fruit trees, vegetables

Where It Occurs: Widespread

Signs

- Burrows and chewed vegetation
- Fan- or crescent-shaped mounds of dirt next to holes

Organic Remedies

- Trapping or shooting are the only sure controls. Determine all openings to the tunnel system, then fumigate.
- For gophers, install ¼″ hardware cloth so that it extends 2′ down into the soil and 1′ above the ground.
- Gophers don't like *Scilla* bulbs (also known as squills)—use experimentally; see page 219. These spring-flowering bulbs require minimal care and are best for borders or rock gardens.
- Plant the animal's favorite foods (e.g., alfalfa and clover) at a distance—use experimentally; see page 219.
- Dog manure placed in animals' holes is reported to drive them away—use experimentally; see page 219.
- I Must Garden groundhog spray is a product reputed to repel groundhogs. Spray on foliage, borders, and animal paths.
- Sprinkle human hair throughout the garden (you can get a plentiful supply from your local hairdresser)—use experimentally; see page 219. This is unsightly but found to be effective by some.

Grape Berry Moth

Description

- Adult moths emerge in late spring and lay flat, round eggs on stems, flowers, and grapes.
- Larvae pupate in cocoons attached to bark, in debris, or in fallen leaves.
- Produces 2 generations per year.

Plant Affected: Grape

Where It Occurs: Prevalent in northeastern states, west to Wisconsin and Nebraska, south to Louisiana and Alabama

Signs: Young grapes are webbed together, fail to mature, brown, and fall to the ground.

Organic Remedies

- 1 month before harvest (late summer), hoe around grapevines. Create a wide raised row to seed with a winter cover crop.
- Turn under any cocoons on the soil surface. Water well to compact the soil and seal in the cocoons, after which they'll be smothered.

Grasshopper

also known as Locust

Description: The large (1″–2″), brown, gray, yellow, or green heavy-shelled adult has large hind legs, big jaws, and antennae. It lays eggs in weeds or soil. Grasshoppers can pollute well water and reservoirs. Larvae overwinter in the soil.

Plants Affected: All plants

Where It Occurs: Primarily in grassland areas, particularly in dry seasons

Signs

- Chewed leaves and stems
- Defoliation

Organic Remedies

- Repeated fall cultivation
- Use row covers.
- Encourage natural predators like birds, cats, chickens, field mice, skunks, snakes, spiders, squirrels, and toads. Also, blister beetle larvae prey on grasshopper eggs, so unless they're a pest themselves, leave these alone. If numerous, the larvae can eat up to 40%–60% of the area's grasshopper eggs.
- Fill a jar with a mixture of molasses and water. Bury it up to its mouth in the soil; clean and refresh as needed. Use experimentally; see page 219.
- Spray insecticidal soap, mixed with beneficial nematodes, directly on the grasshopper. Apply in evening hours. Soap alone is not very effective against hard-bodied insects—you can also try mixing in hot peppers.
- **Biological controls:** Praying mantis. *Nosema locustae,* a beneficial protozoan often sold as NOLO Bait or Semaspore Bait, controls most grasshopper species. It must be applied in early spring—before grasshoppers grow to more than ¾″—or they won't eat enough for it to be effective. It lasts several years, and its effects are greatest the summer following its application.
- **Botanical control:** Neem

Greenhouse Leaftier

see Celery Leaftier

Harlequin Bug

also known as Cabbage Bug, Calicoback, Terrapin Fire Bug

Description

- This small (¼″), flat, and shield-shaped bug has a shiny black and red-orange back. It sucks leaf juices and smells bad.
- The adult female lays 2 neat rows of black-ringed white eggs on leaf undersides. Eggs hatch in 4–7 days.
- Nymphs suck leaf juices, causing leaf blotches.
- The adult overwinters in cabbage stalks.
- Very destructive
- Produces several generations per year.

Plants Affected: Brassicas,* eggplant, radish

**Plant most frequently attacked by the insect*

Where It Occurs: Appears in southern half of the United States, from coast to coast.

Signs

- Wilting plants, especially seedlings
- Yellowish or black spots on leaves
- White blotches

Organic Remedies

- Handpick adults and eggs and destroy.
- Insecticidal soap. Lace the spray with isopropyl alcohol, which helps it penetrate the shells of hard-bodied insects. Soap alone is not very effective against hard-bodied insects.
- Practice fall cultivation.
- Mustard greens or turnips can be used as trap crops—use experimentally; see page 219.
- In spring, place old cabbage leaves in the garden to attract the bugs; destroy them when collected. Use experimentally; see page 219.
- **Biological control:** Praying mantis might help.
- **Botanical controls:** Pyrethrin

Hickory Shuckworm

Description

- Large (⅔″) caterpillars are cream-colored with brownish heads. They overwinter in shucks on the ground or in the tree.
- Small (½″) dark brown to black adult moths emerge when nuts begin to develop and continue emerging throughout summer. They lay eggs on foliage and nuts.

- Very damaging
- Produces 1–4 generations per year.

Plants Affected: Hickory, pecan

Where It Occurs: Prevalent in eastern Canada and United States, south to Florida, west to Missouri, Oklahoma, and Texas

Signs: Premature nut drop, poor-quality kernels, dark-stained spots on shells

Organic Remedies

- Black-light traps can reduce populations (1 per 3 trees)
- Collect all prematurely dropped nuts; at harvest, collect all shucks. If legal, burn. Otherwise, destroy larvae by dropping shucks and nuts in water laced with insecticidal soap or boiling water. (Don't use kerosene—it is toxic to the soil and difficult to dispose of.)
- **Biological controls:** Trichogramma wasp—release 2–3 times per season (mid-April; 2 weeks later; and again 2 weeks following).

Imported Cabbageworm, Moth, and Butterfly

Description

- This large (1¼″), velvety smooth worm, light to bright green, has 1 yellow stripe down its back. It feeds on foliage and pupates by suspending itself by silken threads from plants or objects.
- The adult (2″ wingspan) is a day-flying, white to pale yellow butterfly, with grayish tips and 3–4 black spots on each wing. Butterflies drop hundreds of single, light yellow-green eggs on leaf undersides, which hatch in 4–8 days.
- Produces 3–6 generations per year.

Plants Affected: Brassicas,* radish

**Plant most frequently attacked by the insect*

Where It Occurs: Widespread

Signs

- Huge ragged holes in leaves with bits of green excrement
- Tunnels inside broccoli, cabbage, and cauliflower heads

Organic Remedies

- Use row covers all season. Also try nylon stockings over cabbage heads. Nylon mesh stretches, allowing sun, air, and water through but keeping the butterfly out.
- Sprinkle damp leaves with rye flour; worms eat it, bloat, and die. Use experimentally; see page 219.
- Handpick worms in early morning. Handpick eggs off the undersides of leaves every few days.
- Practice fall cultivation; repeated again in spring.
- Any green mulch deters this moth.
- Make a viral insecticide (see directions under Organic Remedies for Cabbage Looper on page 224).
- Use butterfly nets to catch moths; each one caught means 200–300 worms destroyed.
- Encourage bluebirds, chickadees, English sparrows.
- **Biological controls:** Spinosad and/or Bt, applied every 10–14 days until heads form, is effective. Lacewings. Trichogramma and braconid wasps.
- **Allies:** Celery, dill, garlic, hyssop, mint, onion, rosemary, sage, tansy, thyme, tomato; many others (See chart on pages 280–94.)

Inchworm

see Cankerworm

Japanese Beetle

Description

- This medium-large (½″) beetle is shiny metallic green with copper-brown wing covers. The adult lays eggs in the soil and eats and flies only during the day, often up to 5 miles.

- The grub, similar to our native white grub, is gray-white with a dark brown head and 2 rows of spines. It's smaller, about 1″, and lies curled in the soil. It overwinters deep in the soil.
- Produces 1 generation per year.

Plants Affected: Asparagus, basil, bean,* corn (sweet),* grape,* grasses, okra, onion, peach, potato, raspberry, rhubarb, rose,* tomato; most fruit trees*

**Plants most frequently attacked by the insect*

Where It Occurs: Mostly in the eastern United States, but this beetle is also found in the West.

Signs

- Lacy, skeletonized leaves
- Beetles also feed on fruit and corn silk.
- Grubs feed on grass roots.

Organic Remedies

- Apply kaolin clay spray every 7 to 14 days, depending on rainfall and severity of infestation.
- Handpick in early morning by shaking tree limbs or branches. Catch them on a sheet spread on ground. Drop bugs into water laced with insecticidal soap. (Don't use kerosene—it is toxic to the soil and difficult to dispose of.)
- High soil pH discourages grubs.
- Make a bait of water, sugar, mashed fruit, and yeast. Place it at least 1′ off the ground in sunny spots on the periphery of the garden, not in the middle. Strain out beetles every evening—use experimentally; see page 219.
- Use commercially available yellow pheromone traps. Place these so the beetles already present will be lured away from the crop and new beetles from other areas won't be drawn in.
- Encourage starlings, the only bird that eats adult beetles. Other birds eat the grubs.
- Time plantings to avoid beetle peak.
- Four-o'clocks (*Mirabilis*), larkspur, and geraniums all poison the beetle. These are good interplantings.
- Try trap crops of African marigold, borage, evening primrose, four-o'clocks, soybeans, white roses, white and pastel zinnias—use experimentally; see page 219.
- **Biological controls:** Apply beneficial nematodes at a rate of 50,000 per square foot of lawn to prevent chewing damage. *Paenibacillus popilliae,* or milky spore disease, can be applied to lawns and orchard grasses. It attacks grubs and is effective for 15–20 years after just one application.
- **Botanical controls:** Pyrethrin, neem
- **Allies:** Catnip, chives, garlic, rue, tansy (See chart on pages 280–94.)

June Beetle

also known as May Beetle

Description: Night-flying adults are large brown beetles. They emerge in May or June. They lay eggs in midsummer (see White Grub, page 276). White grubs, slightly larger than the Japanese beetle grub, feed for 2 years before pupating. Has 1 emergence per year.

Plants Affected: Corn (sweet), potato, strawberry

Where It Occurs: Causes serious damage in the midwestern and southern United States.

Signs

- Damaged leaves of berry plants (adult feeding)
- Sudden wilting, especially in May or June, and roots and underground stems are chewed or severed (grub feeding).

Organic Remedies

- Fall and spring cultivation
- Don't plant susceptible crops on areas just converted from untilled sod, as grubs will come up through the grass.
- Allow chickens to pick over garden following fall and spring cultivations.
- Encourage birds.

- **Biological controls:** Beneficial nematodes in spring or early summer, as mulch or dressing. Milky spore disease, which takes a few years to spread enough to be effective.
- Handpick beetles and drop into water laced with insecticidal soap. (Don't use kerosene—it is toxic to the soil and difficult to dispose.)
- Shake beetles from the tree or shrub early in the morning while they're sluggish, letting them fall onto a sheet beneath; collect and destroy the beetles.

Lace Bug

many species; also known as Eggplant Lace Bug

Description

- Nymphs and adults suck plant juices from leaves and stems. They feed in groups on leaf undersides.
- Small adults lay black eggs on leaf undersides in either fall or spring. Eggs hatch in spring. Brown-black nymphs start feeding immediately.
- Adults overwinter in garden trash.

Plants Affected: Eggplant, potato, tomato

Where It Occurs: Prevalent in the southern half of the United States, from coast to coast

Signs

- Pale, discolored (bronzed), and curled leaves
- Plants may die.
- Leaves may be dotted with dark, shiny droppings.

Organic Remedies

- Check for eggs every 7–10 days and destroy all egg clusters.
- Insecticidal soap spray

Leaf Beetle

see Bean Leaf Beetle

Leaf-Footed Bug

Description

- This large (¾″) bug resembles the squash bug, but its hind legs are broadened and look like leaves. It is dark brown with a yellow band across its body. When handled it emits a distinctive odor.
- Adults lay barrel-shaped eggs on leaves of host plants. Nymphs look like adults.
- Adults hibernate in winter, especially in thistle, and emerge in early summer.
- Produces 1 generation per year.

Plants Affected: Almond, bean,* nuts, potato,* tomato*

**Plants most frequently attacked by the insect*

Where It Occurs: Widespread, but primarily a problem in the South and west to Arizona

Signs

- Chewed leaves in vegetables
- In almond, there may be poorly developed misshapen nuts or premature nut drop.

Organic Remedies

- Handpick and destroy bugs.
- Handpick and destroy eggs.

Leafhopper

many species, Beet Leafhopper *is also known as* Whitefly *in the West*

Description

- Small (¼″–⅓″) green, brown, or yellow slender bugs suck juices from leaves, stems, and buds. Nymphs move sideways.
- The beet leafhopper (⅓″) is yellow-green, jumps quickly into the air, and looks like a whitefly.
- The potato leafhopper (⅓″) is green with white spots.
- The six-spotted leafhopper (⅛″) is yellowish with 6 black spots.

- Adults lay eggs in early spring on leaf undersides. The second generation of eggs, 2 weeks later, may be laid in plant stems. Adults overwinter in garden trash and weeds.
- Produces 1–5 generations per year.

Plants Affected: Aster, bean, beet, carrot, celery, chard, citrus, corn, eggplant, fruit trees, grape, lettuce, potato, raspberry, rhubarb, rose, spinach, squash, tomato

Where It Occurs: Widespread. For specific regions, see Beet Leafhopper (page 222) and Potato Leafhopper (page 259).

Signs

- White or yellow mottled, curled leaves die and drop.
- Excreted honeydew attracts ants and supports black sooty mold.
- Leafhoppers transmit curly top, in which mature leaves roll upward, turn yellow with purple veins, and become stiff and brittle.
- Especially damaging in potatoes due to decreased yields
- Nymphs suck plant juices.

Organic Remedies

- Apply kaolin clay spray every 7 to 14 days, depending on rainfall and severity of infestation.
- Use row covers in early spring.
- Avoid planting, if possible, in wide open space.
- Insecticidal soap spray. If the infestation is bad, add isopropyl alcohol to the spray.
- Sprinkle diatomaceous earth or wood ashes, moistened to prevent blowing, around the plant base. Both will dry out leafhoppers.
- Remove weeds and afflicted plants.
- Practice fall cultivation.
- A reflective mulch such as aluminum foil will repel leafhoppers.
- Keep beets and spinach far from tomatoes. Also avoid planting carrots, asters, and lettuce together if your garden has a problem with the six-spotted leafhopper.
- Plant resistant varieties.
- Black lights trap adults—use experimentally; see page 219.
- Boil 1 pound tobacco in 1 gallon water; strain; and use as a spray—use experimentally; see page 219.
- Encourage songbirds.
- **Biological control:** Lacewings eat the eggs.
- **Botanical controls:** Pyrethrin, neem
- **Allies:** Bean, blackberry, clover, goosegrass, red sprangletop, rye, vetch. Geraniums and petunias allegedly repel leafhoppers. (See chart on pages 280–94.)

Leaf Miner

many species; symptoms of the spinach species are given here

Description

- Larvae (⅓″) are pale green or whitish. They tunnel through the tissue between the upper and lower surfaces of leaves, causing a scorched, blotched, and blistered appearance.
- Adults are tiny (⅙″–¼″) black or gray flies that lay eggs on leaf undersides. Eggs are tiny, white, and lined up in groups of 4–5. If hatched, the leaf will have a grayish blister.
- Produces several generations per year.

Plants Affected: Bean, beet greens, blackberry, cabbage, chard, chestnut, lamb's quarters, lettuce, oregano, pepper, radish, spinach, Swiss chard, turnip

Where It Occurs: Widespread

Signs

- White-brown tunnels or blotches on leaves
- Yellowed, blistered, or curled leaves
- Stem damage below the soil surface
- Leaf miners are disease vectors for black leg and soft rot.

Organic Remedies

- Use row covers.
- Cut out the infested parts of leaves with grayish blisters.
- Remove all lamb's quarters unless used as trap crop.
- Handpick and destroy eggs.
- Plant fall crops to avoid the insect.
- Rotate crops.
- Apply horticultural oil.
- Encourage chickadees, purple finches, robins.
- Controls are usually not warranted on the chestnut.
- **Biological controls:** Beneficial nematodes give some control. Ladybugs and lacewings may eat leaf miner eggs. Spinosad may be effective against larvae.
- **Botanical control:** Neem

Leaf Roller

also known as Fruit Tree Leaf Roller

Description

- Small (¾″) green caterpillars usually have dark heads. They feed for about 4 weeks, then spin webs around leaves and sometimes around the fruit. They pupate in these rolled leaves.
- The adult is a light brown moth that lays eggs with a camouflage coating in clusters of 30–100 in mid-summer on twigs and bark. Eggs overwinter and hatch into caterpillars in spring.
- Produces 1 generation per year.

Plants Affected: Apple; other fruit trees

Where It Occurs: Widespread, but most damage occurs in northern United States and southern Canada.

To Monitor: Use pheromone traps to monitor moth populations and to know when to spray to prevent egg laying.

Signs

- Rolled leaves with fine webbing that holds the leaves shut
- Chewed fruit, leaves, and buds

Organic Remedies

- Handpick eggs in winter.
- Spray light horticultural oil in early spring before buds appear.
- Garlic Barrier, a product containing only garlic oil and water, is supposed to repel leaf rollers.
- **Predator:** Trichogramma wasps will eat the caterpillars.
- **Biological control:** Spinosad and/or DiPel Bt is an effective control; be sure to spray inside the rolled leaf.

Locust

see Grasshopper

Mealybug

Description

- These minuscule bugs suck plant sap.
- They lay tiny, yellow, smooth eggs where leaves join the stem.
- Produces numerous generations (each cycle takes 1 month).

Plants Affected: Fruit trees, greenhouses, house-plants, rosemary, vegetables

Where It Occurs: Widespread, but particularly a problem in warm climates

Signs

- Cotton tufts on the leaf underside
- Honeydew excretions attract ants and support black sooty mold.
- Dwarfed plants
- Wilt
- Premature fruit drop

Organic Remedies

- Direct strong water jets at the undersides of leaves.
- Destroy mealybugs with cotton swabs dipped in alcohol.

- Spray light horticultural oil before buds appear, to smother eggs.
- Use insecticidal soap spray, especially in the early-spring dormant stage.
- Use sticky bands to trap ants.
- **Biological controls:** Green lacewings. *Cryptolaemus* ladybug (Australian and uncommon) is a predator and also works in the greenhouse. *Pauridia* parasites prey on bugs. In the greenhouse, PFR (*Paecilomyces fumosoroseus*) is a beneficial microorganism available in granule form that attacks whiteflies, mites, aphids, thrips, mealybugs and certain other greenhouse pests, and is claimed to be safe for humans.
- **Botanical control:** Neem

Measuring Worm

see Cankerworm

Mexican Bean Beetle

Description

- The small (¼″), copper, round-backed adult beetle, with 16 black spots in 3 horizontal rows on its back, looks like an orange ladybug.
- The female adult lays orange-yellow eggs in groups of 40–60 on leaves. Eggs hatch in 5–14 days.
- Most beans can tolerate 10%–20% defoliation (more prior to bloom) without loss in yields.
- Produces 2 generations per year in cold climates, and 3–5 in warmer regions.

Plants Affected: Bean,* kale, squash

**Plant most frequently attacked by the insect*

Where It Occurs: Widespread, but particularly a problem in the East and Southwest

Signs

- Lacy, skeletonized leaves. Pods and stems are eaten in bad infestations.
- Orange-yellow fuzzy larvae (⅓″) are longer than the adult and attach themselves to leaves, usually on the underside, or inside a curled leaf.

Organic Remedies

- Apply kaolin clay spray every 7 to 14 days, depending on rainfall and severity of infestation.
- Handpick and destroy beetles, larvae, and egg clusters.
- Use row covers.
- A reflective mulch like aluminum foil will repel them.
- A spray of crushed turnips with corn oil—use experimentally; see page 219.
- Spray cedar sawdust or chips boiled in water—use experimentally; see page 219.
- Fall: Pull up infested plants as soon as the main harvest is over but while pests are still present. Stuff vines in a plastic bag, tie, and leave in the sun for 10–14 days to kill the bugs.
- Practice fall cultivation.
- Early planting.
- Encourage insect-eating birds.
- **Biological controls:** Spined soldier bug is excellent control. Predatory mites. *Pediobius foveolatus* wasps parasitize larvae; they are excellent controls, but expensive.
- **Botanical controls:** Pyrethrin, neem
- **Allies:** Garlic, marigold, nasturtium, petunia, potatoes, rosemary, savory (See chart on pages 280–94.)

Millipede

Description

- This caterpillar-like worm (½″–1″) has a hard-shelled body divided into multiple segments and 30–400 pairs of legs.
- It moves slowly by contracting and stretching, feeds at night on decaying vegetation, and sometimes transmits diseases.

- It lays sticky sacs of hundreds of eggs on or in the soil in summer.
- Adults live 1–7 years.
- Produces 1 generation per year.

Plants Affected: Lettuce, root vegetables, rose, seeds

Where It Occurs: Widespread, but most damaging in the South and West

Signs

- Ragged holes in stems and roots, especially seedlings
- Fungal disease may be present.

Organic Remedies

- Peat compost is more hostile to millipedes than other types such as leaf or manure compost.
- Place window-screen wire under plants.

Mite

many species

Description

- Mites are very tiny red, green, yellow, black, or brown arachnids that are difficult to see without a magnifying lens. Some are beneficial. Females lay numerous eggs on webbing under leaves. Mites overwinter in the soil.
- Mites suck chlorophyll out of plants and inject toxins. They can lower chlorophyll by as much as 35%. They are worst in hot, dry conditions.
- Produces up to 17 generations per year; each life cycle takes 7–14 days.

Plants Affected: Apple, apricot, asparagus, bean, blackberry, blueberry, brassicas, celery, chestnut, cucumber, eggplant, grape, herbs, muskmelon, peach, peanut, pepper, raspberry, strawberry

Where It Occurs: Widespread. Many types exist only in specific locales, but general characteristics remain the same.

To Monitor: To detect, hold a white paper underneath and tap the leaves to see if mites, the size of salt grains, are dislodged.

Signs

- Yellowed, dry leaves, with yellow or red spots or blotches and small white dots
- Veins yellow or turn reddish brown first.
- Fine webbing between leaves and across undersides
- Poorly developed fruit that drops early

Organic Remedies

- Spray forceful jets of water in early morning, 3 days in a row, or every other day (3 times).
- Spray insecticidal soap at least 3 times, every 5–7 days.
- Mix ¼ pound glue in a gallon of water; let stand overnight. Spray on twigs and leaves. Use experimentally; see page 219. When dried it will flake off, taking trapped mites with it. Spray 3 times, every 7–10 days.
- Vacuum plants with a handheld vacuum. Empty immediately into a plastic bag or mites will crawl back out.
- ***Fruit trees:*** High-nitrogen fertilizers can increase mite populations, so avoid them.
- Spray fruit trees with horticultural oil late in the dormant period, right at bud break, when mite eggs are most vulnerable.
- Cooking oil spray mix, as recommended by USDA (see page 191).
- Garlic Barrier, a product containing only garlic oil and water, is supposed to repel spider mites.
- Ensure adequate water.
- Cinnamon oil sprays may be highly effective for controlling mites, aphids, and even fungi that attack greenhouse-grown plants with minimal concerns about health and safety.
- **Biological controls:** Predatory mites are good outdoors and in greenhouses. Green lacewings and

ladybugs feed on the mites. In the greenhouse, PFR (*Paecilomyces fumosoroseus*) is a beneficial microorganism available in granule form that attacks whiteflies, mites, aphids, thrips, mealybugs, and certain other greenhouse pests, and is claimed to be safe for humans and beneficials.

- **Botanical controls:** Pyrethrin (apply twice, 3–4 days apart)
- **Allies:** Alder, bramble berries, coriander, dill, rye mulch, sorghum mulch, wheat mulch (See chart on pages 280–94.)

Mole

Description

- Moles are solitary, unlike gophers.
- They tunnel extensively, often using each tunnel only once.
- They eat grubs and beetles, which isn't bad, but also feed on earthworms, their favorite food.
- Their tunnels can harm the root systems of young plants.

Plants Affected: Many vegetables

Where It Occurs: Appears throughout the United States but is a major problem in the West.

Signs

- Extensive tunnels
- Main runways are usually 6″–10″ belowground with frequent mounds of soil heaped aboveground.

Organic Remedies

- The best control is traps. Set out traps at the first sign of tunnels. Tunneling can occur anytime in most western states. In cooler climates, tunneling occurs in spring. Determine which runs are active before setting traps, then set the traps, mark the spots, and check again in 2 days. If spots are raised, the tunnel is active. Spear or harpoon-type traps are considered the easiest to use.
- Plant 4–5 poisonous castor bean plants (*Euphorbia lathyris*), also known as mole plants, nearby—use experimentally; see page 219. (*Note*: This plant can become a pest itself in areas of the West and South. It is also poisonous to humans.) Commercial and homemade sprays with castor oil can also be effective.
- Scatter red pepper or tobacco dust to repel moles—use experimentally; see page 219.
- Wearing gloves to prevent human scent, place Juicy Fruit gum in tunnels. Moles are alleged to love it, eat it, and die from it—use experimentally; see page 219.
- Control grubs, food for moles.
- Plant favorite foods (e.g., alfalfa and clover) at a distance.
- A New York gardener reports that soiled kitty litter placed in main tunnel openings and along the borders of areas is an effective way to get rid of moles—use experimentally; see page 219.

Mouse

many species, including Voles

Description

- The house mouse is uniformly gray.
- The vole, or field mouse, is silver-bellied with gray-brown fur on top.
- The deer mouse, or white-footed mouse, resembles the vole but has white feet.
- Mice will move into mole tunnels and feed on crop roots.

Plants Affected: Apple, fruit trees, greenhouses, onion (storage), strawberry

Where It Occurs: Widespread

Signs

- Chewed tree trunks at ground level
- Gnawed roots (by pine mice)
- In strawberry beds, you may find nests in mulch and destroyed roots.

Organic Remedies

- At planting, install hardware-cloth girdles 6″ in diameter and 18″ high around tree trunks. Set them at least 6″ into the soil, preferably in coarse gravel.
- Remove protective cover for mice by removing all vegetation within a 3′ radius of trunks. In winter, pull mulch at least 6″ away from tree trunks. Keep grass mowed.
- For strawberries, wait to mulch until mice have made winter homes elsewhere, when the ground has developed a frosty crust.
- Make gravel barriers around garden plots, at least 6″–8″ deep and 12″ or more wide. This prevents rodents from tunneling and, if kept free of weeds, from crossing the area.
- Apply a lightweight, porous, sharp-edged gravel underneath and around the bulbs to protect bulbs and roots from voles.
- Encourage owls and snakes.
- Don't mulch perennials until a few frosts have occurred.
- Sprinkle mint leaves in the garden—use experimentally; see page 219.
- **Ally:** Wormwood (See chart on pages 280–94.)

Navel Orangeworm

Description: Worms are yellow or dark gray with dark heads. They pupate in cocoons within the fruit. The gray adult moth has crescent-shaped dots along its outer margins.

Plants Affected: Almond, citrus,* walnut

**Plant most frequently attacked by the insect*

Signs: Worms burrow into fruit and nuts on the tree and in storage.

Organic Remedies

- Maintain good orchard sanitation.
- Harvest early.
- Nuts can be fumigated before storage with methyl bromide.
- Remove and destroy nuts left on the tree in winter.
- **Biological controls:** *Goniozus legneri* and *Pentalitomastix plethoricus* both parasitize the pupae. Release them in early spring or after harvest.

Nematode

many species; also known as Roundworm, Eelworm

Description: Nematodes are blind and usually microscopic. Not all are harmful; some are beneficial (see page 190).

Plants Affected: Apple, bean, carrot, celery, cucumber, dill, eggplant (in South), garlic, mustard, okra, onion, parsley, pea, potato, raspberry, strawberry, sweet potato, tomato; many others

Where It Occurs: Widespread, especially in warm areas and areas with sandy or loamy soils. Not very common in clay soils. The eggs of some nematode species remain viable in soil for years.

Signs

- Malformed flowers, leaves, stems, and roots
- Stunted, yellowing leaves
- Leaves may wilt during the day.
- Dwarfed plants, with poorly developed roots, leaves, and flowers
- Dieback
- Root-knot nematodes cause galls, knots, or branched root crops.
- Lesion nematodes cause root fungal infections and lesions on roots.

Organic Remedies

- Plant resistant varieties.
- Solarize soil.
- Increase soil organic matter. Heavy mulch or compost is one of the best deterrents. Compost is host to saprophytic nematodes and predacious fungi that destroy harmful nematodes. Compost also

releases fatty acids toxic to nematodes. Leaf mold compost is especially effective, particularly pine needles, rye, and timothy grasses.

- Disinfect tools used in infected soil.
- Long crop rotation
- Monterey Nematode Control by Arbico Organics is a concentrate to be mixed with water and applied as a soil drench. The active ingredient is saponins of *Quillaja saponaria*, which controls plant-parasitic nematodes by limiting their development past the egg stage.
- A combination of fish emulsion and a by-product of the yucca cactus is thought to be effective at knocking out nematodes. In tests with citrus trees, a mixture of 70% fish emulsion and 30% yucca extract reduced root-knot and pin nematode populations by up to 90%.
- Kelp meal and crab shell meal (chitin, sold as a *chitosan*) stimulate beneficial fungi that prey on nematodes. Dig these into the soil 1 month before planting to reduce populations.
- Sprinkle an emulsion of 1 part corn oil to 10 parts water—use experimentally; see page 219.
- Research in Egypt indicates that boric acid was effective as a nematicide in reducing nematodes on Thompson seedless grapevines. Boric acid combined with calcium nitrate or chitosan as well the bioagent *Bacillus megaterium* also decreased nematode population and enhanced grape yield and quality.
- A solution of water hyacinth leaves or flowers macerated in water (1:3 on a weight basis) has been shown to kill nematodes. Also, tomato and eggplant roots soaked in this solution for 80 minutes prior to planting grew 3 times faster than unsoaked controls.
- Various studies have recommended hot-water treatments for *Aphelenchoides ritzemabosi* in different plants, which include immersing chrysanthemums at 110°F/44°C for 20 minutes. Hot-water treatments have also been used to manage other plant parasitic nematodes by treating bulbs, bare-root plants, dormant crowns, suckers, and runners of many crops.
- **Botanical controls:** Laboratory trials have revealed root-knot nematode is highly sensitive to the essential oils derived from several plants in concentrations of 1000 micrograms per liter of water (plus a small amount of ethanol). The following oils caused immobilization of juvenile root-knot nematodes within 2 days of exposure (oils marked with asterisks also reduced hatching of nematode eggs to under 5%): wormwood (*Artemisia judaica*),* caraway,* wild thyme, lemongrass, fennel,* apple mint,* spearmint,* white-leaved savory (*Clinopodium serpyllifolium* subsp. *fruticosum*),* Syrian oregano,* and oregano.

Allies: Asparagus, barley, corn, garlic, hairy indigo, marigold, mustard (white or black). See chart on pages 280–94. (*Note*: Research shows that marigolds suppress root lesion nematodes for 3 years when planted in the entire infested area for a full season. Spot plantings are not as effective and may reduce yields of nearby crops.)

- Also, Commodore radishes grown as a green manure have been shown to greatly reduce root-knot nematode populations in potato plots. The radishes can be sown in spring, before potatoes are planted, or in fall, following potato harvest, and tilled into the soil after a couple of months.
- Cover crops of barley, castor bean, corn, cotton, joint vetch, millet, rye, sesame, or wheat reduce populations. All plants must be turned under to be effective. Winter rye, when tilled under in spring, produces an organic acid toxic to nematodes. (*Note:* The only rye that can control nematodes is cereal rye [*Secale cereale*].)

- **Companion planting:** Planting cucumbers (for which nematode-resistant cultivars are still being explored) with nematode-resistant tomatoes such as Celebrity had significantly higher yields than the same cucumber grown with nematode-susceptible tomatoes.
- Research has shown that root-knot nematode populations can be reduced in soils that have been previously planted with French marigolds or African marigolds.
- White and black mustard exude an oil hostile to nematodes.
- Plant tomatoes near asparagus; asparagus roots are toxic to tomato nematodes.

Nut Curculio

Description

- The small (3⁄16″) adult is black with reddish brown blotches and the long, curved snout of curculios.
- It emerges in May and June, occasionally feeds on foliage, and deposits eggs when the bur cracks to expose the nut.
- Larvae feed on nut kernels for about 3 weeks, then emerge through small (3⁄16″) holes.
- Produces 1 generation per year.

Plants Affected: Chestnut, oak

Where It Occurs: Southeast

Signs

- Premature nut drop
- Circular cavities in nuts and shells

Organic Remedies

- Hang white sticky traps (8″ × 10″) in trees at chest height for both monitoring and control. Use several per tree. Remove after 3–4 weeks.
- Starting at blossom time, every day in the early morning spread a sheet or tarp under the tree and knock branches with a padded board or pole. Shake collected beetles into a bucket of water laced with insecticidal soap. (Don't use kerosene—it is toxic to the soil and difficult to dispose.)
- Remove all diseased and fallen fruit immediately. Destroy larvae by burning fruit or burying it in the middle of a hot compost pile.
- Keep trees pruned; curculios dislike direct sun.
- Encourage chickadees, bluebirds, and purple martins. Domestic fowl will also eat these insects.
- Drop infected nuts into water to kill larvae.

Onion Eelworm

see Nematode

Onion Fly Maggot

also known as Onion Maggot

Description

- Small (1⁄3″), legless, white worm that tapers to a point at the head. It feeds on stems and bulbs.
- The adult fly resembles a hairy housefly. It lays eggs at the base of plants, near the bulb or neck, or in the bulb.
- Produces 3 generations per year; the last generation attacks harvest and storage onions.

Plants Affected: Onion,* radish

**Plant most frequently attacked by the insect*

Where It Occurs: Particularly prevalent in northern and coastal regions, where cool, wet weather abounds

Signs

- Rotting bulbs in storage
- Destroyed seedlings
- Faded and wilted leaves
- Lower stems of onion near the bulb are damaged or destroyed.
- Worse damage than that caused by the cabbage maggot

Organic Remedies

- Avoid close spacing and planting in rows. This discourages maggot movement between plants.
- Red onions are the least vulnerable, followed by yellow, and then white varieties.

- Sprinkle diatomaceous earth around the plant base and work it slightly into the soil. If this isn't available, then sprinkle wood ashes (moistened to prevent blowing) near the base of the plants.
- Don't store damaged bulbs.
- Encourage robins and starlings.
- **Biological controls:** Beneficial nematodes

Oriental Fruit Moth

Description

- These small larvae (½″) are yellow-pink with brown heads and are very active.
- When small, they tunnel into tender shoots and later enter fruit through the stem end. They don't tunnel to the core of apples, but in peaches they feed close to the pit. On the outside, fruit may not look damaged.
- Larvae emerge from fruit and pupate in silken cocoons attached to tree trunks, weeds, or garden debris.
- The adult moth (½″ wingspan) is gray, and lays white eggs on leaves and twigs.
- Several generations per year.

Plants Affected: Apple,* peach,* pear, plum, quince

**Plants most frequently attacked by the insect*

Where It Occurs: Prevalent east of the Mississippi and in the upper Northwest

To Monitor: Pheromone traps are available for early detection. Captures exceeding 5–10 moths per trap per week warrant control action.

Signs

- Wormy fruit
- Terminals of rapidly growing shoots wilt, turn brown in a few days, and die.
- Gummy exudates; holes in fruit and in fruit stems

Organic Remedies

- If this is a consistent pest, plant early-ripening cultivars to starve the last generation of the season.
- Prune trees annually to avoid dense growth.
- Plant early-maturing varieties of peach and apricot.
- Inspect tree trunks and destroy all cocoons.
- Pheromone-based mating disruption lures are commercially available but may not be effective in small orchards.
- **Biological control:** Import the braconid wasp *Macrocentrus ancylivorus* and release according to instructions from the supplier.
- **Botanical controls:** Pyrethrin
- **Allies:** Goldenrod, lamb's quarters, strawberries (See chart on pages 280–94.)

Parsleyworm

also known as Carrotworm, Celeryworm, Black Swallowtail

Description

- This long (2″), stunning green worm has a yellow-dotted black band across each segment. It emits a sweet odor and projects 2 orange horns when disturbed.
- The adult is the familiar black swallowtail butterfly. Its large black forewings (3″–4″ across) have 2 rows of parallel yellow spots. Its rear wings have a blue row of spots with one orange spot.
- Adults lay white eggs on leaves; they hatch in 10 days.
- Produces several generations per year.

Plants Affected: Carrot,* celeriac, celery, dill, parsley,* parsnip

**Plants most frequently attacked by the insect*

Where It Occurs: East of the Rockies, with a similar species west of the Rockies

Signs

- Chewed leaves, often down to bare stems
- Damage is usually minor because of low populations.

Organic Remedies

- Handpick in early morning.
- Encourage songbirds.

- **Biological controls:** Lacewing larvae, parasitic wasps

Peach Tree Borer (Greater)

Description

- Large (1¼″), yellow-white larvae have dark brown heads. They feed under the bark at or below the soil surface all winter. The highest they'll usually go is about 12″ above the soil.
- Adult female moths (1″ wingspan) are blue, with a wide orange stripe around the abdomen, and look like wasps; the male is gray with yellow markings and clear wings. They emerge in the North in July and August, and in the South in August and September. They lay brown-gray eggs at the trunk base in late summer to fall.
- Produces 1 generation per year.

Plants Affected: Apricot, cherry, nectarine, peach,* plum

**Plant most frequently attacked by the insect*

Where It Occurs: Appears where vulnerable plants are grown, particularly in eastern states and the lower half of the United States from coast to coast.

Signs

- Brown gummy sawdust (frass) on the bark, usually near the ground
- Very damaging
- Trees can die.

Organic Remedies

- Insert stiff wires into holes to kill larvae. Do *not* remove gummy exudates, which helps to seal wounds.
- Use sticky bands, from 2″ below the soil line to 6″ above. Destroy and replace the bands each week (see page 197).
- Encourage birds.
- **Tobacco dust ring:** Encircle the trunk with a piece of tin, 2″ away from the bark. In mid-May fill with tobacco dust. Repeat every year.
- Tie soft soap around the trunk from the soil line up to the crotch; soap drips repel moths and larvae. Use experimentally; see page 219.
- Pheromone dispensers can confuse males and stop mating but may not be effective in small orchards.
- **Biological controls:** Spray or inject beneficial nematodes into the holes. Spinosad and/or Bt can be sprayed every 10 days or syringe it into the holes.
- **Ally:** Garlic (See chart on pages 280–94.)

Peach Tree Borer (Lesser)

Description

- Larvae look the same as greater peach tree borer.
- Adult female and male moths are blue with clear wings and yellow markings.
- Life cycle is same as greater borer, except the lesser borer lays eggs higher in the limbs of the tree in rough bark or cracks.
- Completes about 1½ life cycles per year, slightly more than the greater borer.
- Produces 2–3 generations per year.

Plants Affected: Apricot, cherry, nectarine, peach,* plum

**Plant most frequently attacked by the insect.*

Where It Occurs: Appear where vulnerable plants are grown, particularly in eastern states and the lower half of the United States from coast to coast.

Signs

- Brown gummy sawdust (frass) on the bark, usually in upper limbs
- Invades through wounds created by such things as winter injury, pruning, and cankers.

Organic Remedies

- Insert stiff wires into holes to kill larvae. Do *not* remove gummy exudates, which helps to seal wounds.
- Use sticky bands on affected limbs. Destroy and replace the bands each week.

- Take measures to minimize winter injury (see Sunscald on page 217), pruning wounds, or other entry sites.
- **Tobacco dust ring:** Encircle the trunk with a piece of tin, 2″ away from the bark. In mid-May fill with tobacco dust. Repeat every year.
- Encourage birds.
- **Biological controls:** Spray or inject beneficial nematodes into the holes. Spinosad and/or Bt can be sprayed every 10 days or syringe it into the holes.
- **Ally:** Garlic (See chart on pages 280–94.)

Peach Twig Borer

Description: Small (less than ½″) red-brown larvae construct cocoons under curled edges of bark. The adult is a small (½″ wingspan), steel gray moth. Produces 3 or 4 generations per year.

Plants Affected: Almond, apricot, peach,* plum

**Plant most frequently attacked by the insect*

Where It Occurs: Widespread, but very damaging on the West Coast

Signs

- Red-brown masses of chewed bark in twig crotches
- Infested fruit late in the season

Organic Remedies

- Increase organic matter in soil.
- Take measures to minimize winter injury (see Sunscald on page 217), pruning wounds, or other entry sites.
- Insert stiff wires into holes to kill larvae. Do *not* remove gummy exudates, which helps to seal wounds.
- Tie soft soap around the trunk from the soil line up to the crotch; soap drips repel moths and larvae. Use experimentally; see page 219.
- Pheromone dispensers can be used to confuse males and stop mating but may not be effective in small orchards.
- Encourage birds.
- Pheromone traps are available that catch males (not the same as mating-disruption lures). These can be used to monitor population levels and, in small areas, to help control populations.
- Spray dormant lime-sulfur spray (diluted 1:15) before the pink stage and after petal fall.

Pear Psylla

Description

- Nymphs are very tiny and yellow, green, or light brown. They feed on the top sides of leaves until only the veins remain.
- Adults are tiny (1⁄10″), light brown to dark orange-red, and have clear wings. Before buds open, adults lay tiny yellowish orange eggs in cracks and crevices, in the base of terminal buds and in old leaf scars. Also check tender growing tips of the highest shoots. Nymphs hatch in 2–4 weeks. Most hatch by petal fall.
- Nymphs and adults suck plant juices, and can transmit fire blight and pear decline.
- Produces 3–5 generations per year.

Plant Affected: Pear

Where It Occurs: Eastern (east of the Mississippi) and northwestern states

Signs

- Yellow leaves
- Leaf drop
- Low vigor
- Honeydew excretion attracts yellow jackets and ants and supports black sooty mold. Blackened leaves and fruit.
- Scarred and malformed fruit
- Very damaging

Organic Remedies

- Apply kaolin clay spray every 7 to 14 days, depending on rainfall and severity of infestation.

- Spray insecticidal soap, at high pressure, as soon as females emerge and when leaf buds are just beginning to turn green. Continue through the season as needed.
- Dust tree and leaves with limestone.
- Destroy all debris, which harbors the eggs. Adults and eggs spend winter on or near the tree.
- Spray light horticultural oil in fall and again in spring at the green tip stage; continue to spray every 7 days until larvae emerge.
- Plant tolerant varieties. (Bartlett and D'Anjou are the most susceptible.)

Pearslug

also known as Cherryslug

Description

- Larvae (½″) are dark green–orange, covered with slime, tadpole-shaped, and look like small slugs with large heads.
- Larvae feed for 2–3 weeks on upper leaf surfaces. Larvae in apples feed just under fruit skin until about one-third grown, then bore through the fruit. After feeding they drop to the ground to pupate.
- The adult is a small black-and-yellow sawfly, a little larger than a housefly, with 2 sets of transparent wings hooked together. At bloom time, the adult emerges from a cocoon in the soil. The sawfly inserts its eggs into leaves or into the skin of fruit.
- Produces 2 generations per year.

Plants Affected: Apple, cherry, pear,* plum

**Plant most frequently attacked by the insect*

Where It Occurs: Widespread

Signs

- Pink-brown patches on upper surface of leaves
- Lacy skeletonized leaves
- Defoliation
- Streaks of chocolate-covered sawdust on apples

Organic Remedies

- Shallow cultivation, no more than 2″ deep, at the tree base right before full bloom. This exposes cocoons to predators.
- Dust trees with wood ashes, slightly moistened to prevent blowing, which will dry out larvae and kill them—use experimentally; see page 219. Wash trees with water after 5 days.
- Pick up fallen fruit every day.

Pecan Casebearer

Description

- This small (½″) caterpillar is olive gray to jade green with a yellow-brown head. When buds open, caterpillars feed on buds and shoots.
- Adult moths emerge when the nut forms. They lay single, light-colored eggs on the blossom end of the nut. Larvae then feed on developing nuts.
- Produces 2 generations in northern climates, 4 generations in southern climates.

Plant Affected: Pecan

Where It Occurs: Present wherever pecans are grown

Signs

- Small cocoons at the base of the bud indicate over-wintering larvae.
- Tunneled shoots
- Signs of eaten nuts in the early maturation phase
- Trees will experience little damage, but nut yields are reduced.

Organic Remedies

- Black-light traps (1 for every 3 trees) will reduce populations.
- Collect all prematurely dropped nuts; at harvest-time, collect all shucks. If legal, burn. Otherwise, destroy in hot water or water laced with insecticidal soap. (Don't use kerosene—it is toxic to the soil and difficult to dispose.)
- **Biological control:** Trichogramma wasps—release 3 times per season (once in mid-April; again 2 weeks later; and a third time 2 weeks following).

Pecan Weevil

Description

- Similar to the chestnut weevil. The adult (¾″) is light brown, and as it ages it may become dark brown. Its needle-thin snout can be as long as its body. Adults feed on husks and young nuts.
- Grubs are white with reddish brown heads. They feed on kernels, emerge, and pupate in "cells" as much as 12″ below the soil surface. Adults may not emerge for 2–4 years.
- Has 1 emergence per year.

Plants Affected: Hickory, pecan

Where It Occurs: Present wherever pecan and hickory are grown.

Signs: Premature nut drop and hollowed kernels

Organic Remedies

- Use same controls as for Chestnut Weevil and Plum Curculio (see page 228 and at right, respectively).
- Burlap bands wrapped around trees (See "Sticky bands" on page 197.)
- **Botanical control:** Neem

Phylloxera Aphid

see Aphid

Pickleworm

Description

- This medium-size (¾″) caterpillar is green or copperish. The first generation emerges midsummer.
- Damage is worst late in the season when the broods are largest.
- The adult nocturnal moth is yellowish. It lays eggs that develop into small caterpillars that are pale yellow with black dots. These change color as they mature.
- Produces 3–4 generations per year.

Plants Affected: Cucumber, melon, squash

Where It Occurs: Prevalent primarily in the Southeast and the Gulf states, particularly Florida and Louisiana

Signs

- Holes in buds, blossoms, and fruits of most cucurbits
- Masses of rotting green excrement

Organic Remedies

- Plant susceptible crops as early as possible to avoid pest.
- Destroy all plant debris after harvest.
- Cultivate the soil deeply in early fall, after harvest.
- Plant resistant varieties.

Pill Bug

also known as Roly-poly

See Sow Bug, page 265. (Unlike sow bugs, pill bugs roll up into tight balls about the size of a pea.)

Plum Curculio

Description

- This small (¼″), dark brown beetle has a long down-curving snout and 4 humps on its back. It emerges at blossom time when temperatures climb above 70°F/22°C. When disturbed, it folds its legs and drops to the ground. It lays eggs in a crescent-shaped fruit wound.
- Grubs are gray-white with brown heads and curled bodies. They feed at the fruit center for 2 weeks and emerge only after the fruit falls to ground. They pupate in the ground. Adults emerge in about 1 month.
- Produces 1–2 generations per year.

Plants Affected: Apple, apricot, blueberry, cherry, peach, pear, plum*

**Plant most frequently attacked by the insect*

Where It Occurs: East of the Rockies

Signs

- Eaten leaves and petals
- Crescent-shaped cavities in fruits
- Sap exudates from apple fruit dries to a white crust.
- Misshapen fruit
- Premature fruit drop
- Brown rot disease

Organic Remedies

- Hang several white sticky traps (8″ × 10″) per tree at chest height for monitoring and control. Remove after 3–4 weeks.
- Starting at blossom time, every day in the early morning spread a sheet or tarp under the tree and knock branches with a padded board or pole. Shake collected beetles into a bucket of water laced with insecticidal soap. (Don't use kerosene—it is toxic to the soil and difficult to dispose.)
- Remove all diseased and fallen fruit immediately. Destroy larvae by burning fruit or burying it in the middle of a hot compost pile.
- Keep trees pruned; curculios dislike direct sun.
- Encourage chickadees, bluebirds, and purple martins. Domestic fowl will also eat these insects.

Plume Moth

Description: Larvae bore into the fruit, blemish the scales, and tunnel into the heart. Nocturnal adult brown moths (1″ wingspan) have feathery wings and fly near the plant. They lay eggs on leaf undersides.

Plant Affected: Artichoke

Where It Occurs: Lives on the Pacific and Texas coasts.

Signs

- Irregular holes in stems, foliage, and bud scales
- Small worms are on bud scales and new foliage.
- Damage is year-round but worst in spring.

Organic Remedies

- Pick and destroy all wormy buds.
- Remove and destroy all plant debris in fall.
- Remove all nearby thistles.
- **Biological control:** Spinosad and Bt are effective.

Potato Bug

see Colorado Potato Beetle

Potato Flea Beetle

see Flea Beetle

Potato Leafhopper

also known as Bean Jassid; *see also* Leafhopper.

Description

- This leafhopper causes "hopperburn": A triangular brown spot appears at leaf tips, leaf tips curl, yellow, and become brittle.
- Reduces yields in potatoes.
- Produces 2 generations in mid-Atlantic states.

Plants Affected: Apple,* bean (South), peanut, potato (East and South)*

**Plants most frequently attacked by the insect*

Where It Occurs: Lives primarily in eastern and southern United States. It migrates south for winter and returns north in spring to feed first on apples, then on potatoes.

Organic Remedies

- See Leafhopper on page 245.
- Potato leafhoppers are said to be trapped by black fluorescent lamps—use experimentally; see page 219.

Potato Tuberworm

also known as Tuber Moth

Description

- The gray-brown adult moth is small with narrow wings. It lays eggs on the leaf undersides or in tubers.

- Larvae (¾″) are pink-white with brown heads. They tunnel into stems and leaves.
- They pupate on the ground in cocoons covered with soil, and can emerge in storage to pupate.
- Produces 5–6 generations per year.

Plants Affected: Eggplant, potato,* tomato

**Plant most frequently attacked by the insect*

Where It Occurs: Present in the South from coast to coast, and northward to Washington, Colorado, Virginia, and Maryland. Worst in hot, dry years.

Signs

- Wilted shoots and stems
- Dieback

Organic Remedies

- Plant as early as possible.
- Keep soil well cultivated and deeply tilled.
- Cut and destroy infested vines before harvesting.
- Destroy all infested potatoes.
- Screen storage areas and keep storage area cool and dark. (Darkness discourages moth activity.)

Rabbit

Description: A small white or gray mammal with long ears and short tail that travels primarily by hopping.

Plants Affected: Bean, carrot, lettuce, pea, strawberry, tulip shoots, bark of fruit trees

Where It Occurs: Widespread

Signs: Rabbits eat vegetables, herbs, and flowers and chew on young fruit trees.

Organic Remedies

- Sprinkle any of these around plants: Blood meal, moistened wood ashes, ground hot peppers, chili or garlic powder, crushed mint leaves, talcum powder. Use experimentally; see page 219. Replenish frequently, especially after rain. You can also sprinkle black pepper right on the plants, which gives rabbits sneezing fits and keeps them away.
- Cover seedlings with plastic milk jugs that have the bottoms cut out. Anchor them well in the soil, and keep the cap off for ventilation. This can also be used as a season extender in the spring.
- Place old smelly leather shoes on the garden periphery—use experimentally; see page 219.
- Place fake snakes near garden—use experimentally; see page 219.
- Wrap base of fruit trees with hardware cloth.
- Set rabbit traps.
- Encourage owls and sparrow hawks with nest boxes.
- Hinder is reputed to be an effective repellant. Spray on foliage, borders, and animal paths. When painted on bark, it prevents tree girdling by rabbits.
- Fine-woven fences are effective deterrents.
- Garlic, marigold, and onion are said to deter rabbits—use experimentally; see page 219.

Raspberry Caneborer

Description

- Medium-size (½″) adult is a long-horned black-and-yellow beetle. It lays 1 egg between a double row of punctures on the stems near the cane tip.
- A small worm hatches and burrows 1″–2″ deep near the base of the cane to hibernate.
- This is a major cane pest.
- Produces 1 generation per year.

Plants Affected: Blackberry, raspberry

Where It Occurs: Present in Kansas and eastward

Signs

- Sudden wilting of tips
- 2 rows of punctures about 1″ apart

Organic Remedies

- Cut off cane tips 6″ below the puncture marks, and burn or destroy.

Raspberry Root Borer

also known as Raspberry Crown Borer

Description

- Larvae are small, white, and hibernate at the soil level near canes. They tunnel into cane crowns and bases.
- The adult moth has clear wings and a black body with 4 yellow bands.
- Produces 1 generation.

Plants Affected: Blackberry, raspberry

Where It Occurs: Prevalent in eastern United States

Signs: Wilting and dying canes in early summer, usually when berries are ripening

Organic Remedies: Cut out infected canes below the soil line.

Raspberry Sawfly

see Blackberry Sawfly

Rednecked Cane Borer

see Caneborer

Root Fly and Root Maggot

see Corn Maggot *and* Cabbage Maggot

Rose Chafer

also known as Rose Bug

Description

- This slender, adult beetle (⅓″–½″) is tan, with a reddish brown head and long, spiny, slightly hairy legs.
- It emerges in late May to early June and feeds for 3–4 weeks, attacking flowers first, then fruit blossoms and newly set fruit.
- Eggs laid in the soil hatch in 1–2 weeks.
- Larvae (¾″) feed on grass roots, then pupate 10″–16″ deep in the soil.
- Produces 1 generation annually.

Plants Affected: Grape,* peony, rose,* other fruits and flowers

**Plants most frequently attacked by the insect*

Where It Occurs: Prevalent east of the Rockies; primarily a pest in sandy soils and north of New York City

Signs

- Chewed foliage
- Destroyed grass roots

Organic Remedies

- Apply kaolin clay spray every 7 to 14 days, depending on rainfall and severity of infestation.
- Handpick adults.
- Cheesecloth fences, stretched higher than the plants, will deter the beetle as it doesn't fly over barriers.
- Do not allow chickens to clean garden because these beetles are poisonous to chickens.
- Great Lakes IPM sells a rose chafer pheromone-based lure that is used typically to alert growers to the presence of a beetle but can be adapted to a large container that can trap hundreds or thousands of rose chafers at a time.

Roundworm

see Nematode

Sap Beetle

many species; also known as Corn Sap Beetle, Strawberry Sap Beetle

Description

- This small (³⁄₁₆″), black, oblong beetle invades ears through the silk channel or via holes in the husk caused by other pests. This is often associated with corn borer or corn earworm damage. A smaller, brown, oval beetle attacks small fruit.
- White, maggotlike larvae eat inside kernels and infested fruit. They scatter when exposed to light.

Plants Affected: Corn, raspberry, strawberry

Where It Occurs: Widespread

Signs

- Brown hollowed-out kernels at the corn ear tip. Sometimes individual damaged kernels are scattered throughout.
- Round cavities eaten straight into ripe strawberries
- Feeding injury between the raspberry and stem. Injury predisposes small fruit to secondary rot organisms.

Organic Remedies

- Clean and complete harvesting of small fruit and removal of damaged, diseased, and overripe berries helps to reduce populations.
- Deep plowing in fall or early spring reduces overwintering populations of the corn sap beetle.
- Destroy alternate food sources, such as old vegetable crops beyond harvest.
- Mineral oil, applied just inside the tip of each ear, suffocates the worms. Apply only after the silk has wilted and started to brown at the tip, or pollination will be incomplete. Use ½ of a medicine dropper per small ear, and ¾ of a dropper per large ear. You might add red pepper to the oil to see if it increases the effectiveness. Apply 2 or more applications of oil, spaced at 2-week intervals.
- Practice fall cultivation. In spring, cultivate the top 2″ of soil.
- Plant resistant varieties with tight husks. Or clip husks tightly with clothespins. You can also try covering ears with pantyhose.
- **Biological controls:** Minute pirate bugs. Lacewings. Trichogramma wasps and tachinid flies lay eggs in the moth eggs and prevent hatching. Inject beneficial nematodes into infested ears; they seek out and kill worms in 24 hours. Bt can be applied to borers before they move into the stalks. Then wettable Bt, applied every 10–14 days, is effective.
- **Botanical controls:** Pyrethrin. Use pheromone traps to identify moth flight paths before spraying. Spray moths before they lay eggs.
- **Allies:** Corn, marigold, soybean (See chart on pages 280–94.)

Scale

many species

Description

- Scales are extremely small and suck plant nutrients from bark, leaves, and fruit.
- You may see the insect's "armor," which is either a part of its body or, in some species, is made up of old exoskeletons and a waxy coating that shields them from attacks. This armor may look like flaky, crusty parts of the bark.
- The immature insect (1⁄16″) crawls to a feeding spot, where it stays for the remainder of its life.
- Ants carry scales from plant to plant.
- Produces 1–3 or more generations per year.

Plants Affected: Fruit trees, nut trees, shrubs

Where It Occurs: Different species occur throughout the United States.

Signs

- Small spots of reddened tissue on leaves or branches
- Fine dusty "ash"
- Hard bumps on fruit
- Dead twigs or branches
- Limbs lose vigor, leaves yellow, and the plant dies, usually from the top down. Honeydew excretions support black fungus and attract ants.

Organic Remedies

- Spray insecticidal soap.
- Apply horticultural oil spray late in spring, right at bud break. One spray should be sufficient.
- Mix ¼ pound glue in a gallon of water; let stand overnight. Spray on twigs and leaves. Use experimentally; see page 219. When dried it will flake off,

taking trapped mites with it. Spray 3 times, every 7–10 days.

- Scrape scale off plants or touch them with an alcohol-soaked cotton swab. Repeat every 3–4 days until the scale falls off.
- **Biological controls:** Several species of chalcid wasps can be used to control scale: *Aphytis melinus* for California red scale; *Aphytis lingnanensis* for various soft scale insects, including black scale; *Metaphycus helvolus* for soft scale or black scale; *Comperiella bifasciata* for California red scale or yellow scale. Use the vedalia ladybug for cottony cushion scale, and the *Chilocorus nigritus* ladybug for all scales.

Seedcorn Maggot

see Corn Maggot

Skipjack

see Wireworm

Slug (many species) and Snail

Description

- Slugs are large (½″–10″ long), slimy, wormlike creatures that resemble snails without shells. They are mollusks but have no outer protective shells. Their eyes are at the tips of 2 tentacles. They come in all colors—brown, gray, purple, black, white, and yellow—and can be spotted. They feed mainly from 2 hours after sundown to 2 hours before sunrise. Females lay clusters of 25 oval white eggs in damp soil, which hatch in about 1 month.
- Snails, also in the mollusk family, have hard shells and scrape small holes in foliage as they feed and lay masses of eggs. Eggs are large (⅛″) and look like clusters of white pearls. Snails can go dormant in periods of drought or low food supply.

Plants Affected: Artichoke, asparagus, basil, bean, brassicas, celeriac, celery, chard, cucumber, eggplant, greens, lettuce, onion, pea, pepper (seedling), sage, squash, strawberry; most fruit trees

Where It Occurs: Widespread, but they rank as one of the top pests (if not the top one) in the western United States. They thrive in temperatures below 75°F/24°C.

Signs

- Large, ragged holes in leaves, fruits, and stems, starting at plant bottom
- Trails of slime on leaves and soil

Organic Remedies

- Reduce habitat by removing garden debris, bricks, boards, garden clippings, and weeds. Use mulches that are slug irritants, such as shredded bark, crushed rock, or cinders.
- Make the habitat less conducive to this pest by watering in the morning instead of at night. Swiss researchers found slug consumption of lettuce leaves with morning watering was less than one-fifth of the consumption with evening watering.
- Cultivation or spading in spring or times of drought will help destroy dormant slugs and eggs.
- A spray of 2 parts vinegar and 1 part water can be effective against snails and slugs, but may result in phytotoxicity; a ratio of 1:1 was found to be an effective control with less plant damage.
- Place stale beer in shallow pans, the lip of which must be at ground level—use experimentally; see page 219. Replace every day and after rain, and dispose of dead slugs. Because slugs are attracted to the yeast, an even more effective solution is made by dissolving 1 teaspoon dry yeast in about ¼ cup water. Where slugs are too numerous for this solution (e.g., in the West), try the following other traps.
- Use the weed plantain as a trap crop, but first be sure it will not become a pest in your area—use experimentally; see page 219.
- Spray with wormwood tea—use experimentally; see page 219.

- Researchers in India suggest that both garlic powder and raw garlic contain the toxic substance allicin, which can kill snails.
- **Board trap:** Set a wide board about 1″ off the ground in an infested area. This provides daytime shelter for slugs and easy collection for you.
- **Gutter trap:** Set aluminum gutter around the garden beds and coat it with Ivory soap. The slugs will get trapped in this. Empty and kill them regularly.
- **Seedlings:** Keep seedlings covered until they're 6″ high, particularly pea seedlings. Try plastic jugs with the bottoms cut out, anchored firmly in the soil, with the caps off for ventilation. Make sure no slugs are inside.
- **Asparagus:** Plant crowns in wire baskets anchored several inches down in the ground.
- **Barriers for raised beds:**
  - Strips of aluminum screening about 3″ high, pushed about 1″ into the soil. Bend the top of the screen outward, away from bed, and remove 2 strands from the edge so it's ragged.
  - A 2″ strip of copper flashing tacked around the outside of beds, extending 1″ from top of bed. This carries a minor electrical charge that repels slugs. Copper bands around tree trunks work similarly.
  - Crushed eggshells around plants.
  - Strips of hardware cloth tacked onto top edges of the bed, extending 2″ above edge. Make sure there are sharp points along the top edge.
- Sprinkle diatomaceous earth around the plant base and work slightly into the soil. If that is not available, sprinkle moistened wood ashes around the plant base. Avoid getting ashes on plants.
- An Oregon master gardener devised a moat that reportedly protects her young seedling brassicas. Seedling pots are placed on plywood supported by bricks in a shallow plastic tub filled with soapy water. She reports no more losses. Use experimentally; see page 219.
- Don't apply mulch until the soil has warmed to 75°F/24°C, which is warmer than slugs like.
- Destroy all eggs. Find them under rocks, pots, and boards.
- Encourage predators such as birds, ducks, lightning bug larvae, ground beetles, turtles, salamanders, grass, and garter snakes. Ducks have a voracious appetite for these pests.
- Uscharin, a glycoside compound found in the latexlike sap of *Calotropis procera* (mudar, native to the Middle East and grown as green houseplant in temperate areas), is extremely toxic to the white garden snail (*Theba pisana*). Home experimenters can lay parts of this plant around mollusk-susceptible plants.
- An Oregon recipe for slug bait combines 3 cups water, 1 tablespoon granulated yeast, and 2 tablespoons sugar. Slugs are attracted to the yeast. Put in a pan with the edge at least ½″ above the soil surface, to keep beneficial ground beetles out. Use experimentally; see page 219.
- Flowers said to be "distasteful to slugs" include the genera *Achillea, Ageratum, Alyssum, Arabis, Armeria, Aster, Astilbe, Calendula, Campanula, Cosmos, Dianthus, Dicentra, Eschscholzia, Galium, Hemerocallis, Iberis, Kniphofia, Lobelia, Mentha, Paeonia, Penstemon, Phlox, Portulaca, Potentilla, Ranunculus, Rudbeckia, Saxifraga, Sedum, Thymus, Tropaeolum, Verbena, Vinca, Viola, Zinnia*—use experimentally; see page 219.
- **Biological control:** Predatory snail *Rumina decollata* will feed on brown garden snails. It can't be shipped to most places, like northern California or the Northwest, because it kills native snails.
- **Allies:** Fennel, garlic, rosemary (See chart on pages 280–94.)

Southern Corn Rootworm

see Cucumber Beetles

Sow Bug

also known as Dooryard Sow Bug

Description

- These bugs are crustaceans. They are small (¼″–½″), oval, humpbacked bugs with 14 legs. Sow bugs scurry when disturbed and generally hide under leaves and debris. The pill bug will roll itself into a ball for protection.
- Produces 1 generation per year.

Plants Affected: Seedlings

Where It Occurs: Widespread. Common in gardens but not usually a severe problem.

Signs: Chewed seedlings, stems, and roots

Organic Remedies

- Apply wood ashes or an oak-leaf mulch.
- Water plants with a very weak lime solution. Mix 2 pounds per 5 gallons, and let sit for 24 hours before using.
- Bait with half of a potato placed cut side down on the soil surface. In the morning, collect and kill the bugs. Use experimentally; see page 219.

Spider Mite

see Mite

Spinach Flea Beetle

see Flea Beetle

Spittlebug

many species; also known as Froghopper

Description

- Adults (⅓″) are dull brown, gray, or black, sometimes with yellow markings. They hop and look like short, fat leafhoppers.
- They lay eggs in plant stems, and in grasses between the stem and leaf sheath. "Spittle" (foam) covers the eggs, which overwinter.
- In spring when nymphs hatch, they produce even more froth for protection.
- Adults and nymphs suck plant juices from leaves and stems.
- Produces 1 or more generations per year.

Plants Affected: Corn; many others

Where It Occurs: Widespread, but worst in the Northeast, Oregon, and high-humidity regions

Signs

- Foamy masses ("frog spit"), usually at stem joints
- Faded, wilted, curled, or discolored leaves
- Stunted, weakened, and sometimes distorted plants

Organic Remedies

- Many species are not a serious problem, so you may want to leave them alone.
- If seriously damaging, cut out plant parts with "spittle" or simply remove the foamy mass. Destroy egg masses or nymphs contained inside.

Spotted Asparagus Beetle

Description

- This slender reddish brown–orange beetle has 6 black spots on each side of its back.
- It lays single greenish eggs on leaves; orange larvae develop in 1–2 weeks.
- Larvae bore into the berry and eat seeds and pulp, then pupate in the soil.
- Produces 1 generation per year.

Plants Affected: Asparagus,* aster, cucurbits,* zinnia

**Plants most frequently attacked by the insect*

Where It Occurs: East of the Mississippi

Signs

- Defoliation and misshapen fruit
- It usually appears in July.

Organic Remedies

- Apply kaolin clay spray every 7 to 14 days, depending on rainfall and severity of infestation.
- Handpick in the morning, when the beetle can't fly due to cool temperatures.
- See Organic Remedies for Asparagus Beetle, page 221.

Spongy Moth

formerly known as Gypsy Moth

Description

- This hairy gray or brown caterpillar (1⁄16″–2″) has 5 pairs of blue and 6 pairs of red spots. Larvae crawl to top of trees and dangle on silky threads to be blown to another tree. When more mature (2½″), they hide during the day and feed at night.
- The adult female white moth doesn't fly, but lays tan eggs in 1″-long masses on trunks, branches, and under rocks. The adult male moth is large (1½″ wingspan) and brown. Adults live less than 2 weeks.
- Larvae pupate and overwinter in dark cocoons or tie themselves to a branch with silken threads.
- Produces 1 generation per year.

Plants Affected: Apple, apricot, basswood, birch, linden, oak, peach, pear, willow

Where It Occurs: Prevalent primarily in the East, but moving south and west. Worst attacks follow a dry fall and warm spring.

Signs

- Rapid defoliation; defoliation in successive years may kill deciduous trees.
- Masses of worms feeding
- Large holes in leaves
- No tents

Organic Remedies

- ***August–April:*** To destroy egg masses, paint with creosote or drop into water laced with insecticidal soap. (Don't use kerosene—it is toxic to the soil and difficult to dispose of safely.)
- ***Late April–early June:*** Attach a 12″-wide burlap strip to a tree, about chest height, by draping it over a string. Caterpillars will hide under the cloth during the day. Every afternoon, using gloves, sweep the worms into soapy water. Apply sticky bands; remove them in mid-July.
- ***Fall:*** Check lawn furniture, woodpiles, walls, and outbuildings for egg masses. Also check all vehicles for egg masses to avoid transporting eggs to new areas. Destroy all egg masses.
- Use spongy moth pheromone traps to monitor and control populations.
- **Biological controls:** Bt is effective when applied every 10–14 days starting in April and continuing through mid-June until the caterpillars are 1″ long. Trichogramma and chalcid wasps provide limited control. Lacewings, tachinid flies, predaceous ground beetles, and white-footed mice can all help. Also try *Glyptapanteles flavicoxis* and *Cotesia melanoscelus*. Use beneficial nematodes at the tree base to prevent migration.
- **Botanical controls:** Pyrethrin, neem

Squash Bug

Description

- These medium (⅝″), brown-black bugs feed by sucking plant sap and injecting toxins. When crushed at any age, they emit a foul odor. They like moist, protected areas and hide in deep, loose mulch like hay or straw, as well as in debris or under boards.
- They lay clusters of yellow, red, or brown eggs on the undersides of leaves along the central vein. Eggs hatch in 7–14 days.
- Young bugs have red heads and bright green bodies that turn to gray as they mature.

- Bugs overwinter under vines, in boards and buildings, and under dead leaves.
- Produces 1 generation per year.

Plants Affected: Cucumber, muskmelon, pumpkin,* squash,* watermelon

**Plants most frequently attacked by the insect*

Where It Occurs: Widespread

Signs

- Rapidly wilting leaves dry up and then turn black.
- No fruit development

Organic Remedies

- Apply kaolin clay spray every 7 to 14 days, depending on rainfall and severity of infestation.
- Use row covers. When female blossoms (fruit blooms) open, lift the edges of covers for 2 hours in the early morning, twice a week, until blossoms drop. This permits pollination.
- Handpick bugs.
- Sprinkle a barrier of wood ashes, moistened to prevent blowing, around the plant base—use experimentally; see page 219. Don't get ashes on the plant. Renew periodically.
- In fall, leave a few immature squash on the ground to attract the remaining bugs. Destroy squash covered with bugs.
- Trellised plants are less susceptible to this bug.
- Pull vulnerable plants as soon as they finish bearing, place in a large plastic bag, tie securely, and place in direct sun for 1–2 weeks. This destroys all eggs.
- Spray insecticidal soap, laced with isopropyl alcohol to help it penetrate the bug's shell. Soap, however, is not very effective against hard-bodied insects.
- Time plantings to avoid bugs.
- Rotate crops.
- Use heavy mulch materials. Avoid aluminum and white or black plastic mulch, which can increase squash bug populations.
- Place boards in the garden under which the bugs will hide and be easy to catch—use experimentally; see page 219.
- Plant resistant varieties.
- Encourage birds.
- **Biological controls:** Praying mantises eat eggs and nymphs. Tachinid flies are natural predators.
- **Allies:** Borage, catnip, marigold, mint, nasturtium, radish, tansy (See chart on pages 280–94.)

Squash Vine Borer

Description

- This long (1″), dirty white worm, with brown head and legs, bores into stems, where it feeds for 4–6 weeks. It overwinters 1″–2″ below the soil surface.
- The adult wasplike moth (1½″ wingspan) has transparent copper-green forewings, clear rear wings, and rings on its abdomen colored red, copper, and black. It lays rows or clusters of individual tiny, longish, brown or red eggs near the base of the plant's main stem.
- Produces 1 generation per year in the North, and 2 generations per year in the southern and Gulf states.

Plants Affected: Cucumber, gourd, muskmelon, pumpkin, squash

Where It Occurs: East of the Rockies

Signs

- Sudden wilting of plant parts
- Moist yellow sawdust-like material (frass) outside small holes near the plant base

Organic Remedies

- Use row covers. When female blossoms (fruit blooms) open, lift cover edges for just 2 hours in early morning, twice a week, until blossoms drop. This permits pollination.
- Reflective mulch such as aluminum foil will repel them—use experimentally; see page 219.
- Stem collars can prevent egg laying.
- If not grown on a trellis, pinch off the young plant's growing tip to cause multistemming. For trailing

squash stems, bury every fifth leaf node to encourage rooting. When one part becomes infested, cut it off and remove. Leave other sections to grow. Mound soil over vines up to blossoms.
- Slit stem vertically to remove and destroy borers. Mound soil around the slit stem to encourage new rooting. Remove and destroy damaged stems.
- Handpick the eggs.
- Sprinkle wood ashes, crushed black pepper, or real camphor around plants to deter borer—use experimentally; see page 219.
- Time planting to avoid borer. In the North, plant a second crop in midsummer to avoid borer feeding.
- Plant resistant varieties.
- Remove plants as soon as they finish bearing, place in a plastic bag, tie securely, and place in direct sun for 1–2 weeks to destroy borers and eggs.
- **Biological controls:** Inject beneficial nematodes into infected vines at 4″ intervals over bottom 3′ of vine, using 5000 nematodes per injection; use them in mulch around vines as well. Spinosad or Bt are also effective controls; inject it into the vine after the first blossoms and again 10 days following. Clean the syringe between injections. Trichogramma wasps attack borer eggs. Lacewings are also predators.
- **Allies:** Borage, nasturtium, radish (plant radishes around the plant base) (See chart on pages 280–94.)

Squirrel

Description: One of the most physically variable mammals. Fur on head may range from red to black; long furry tail; tufts of hair on ears. All except those with black fur have white underbellies.

Plants Affected: Fruit, nuts, seeds

Where It Occurs: Widespread

Signs: The presence of squirrels is obvious: you'll see the squirrel digging in the garden or scurrying in and around the bottom of your fruit and nut trees. They steal seeds, fruit, and nuts.

Organic Remedies
- Before planting corn try mixing 1 teaspoon pepper with 1 pound corn seed—use experimentally; see page 219.
- Gather fruits and nuts every day. You may need to harvest fruit slightly underripe, for squirrels can clean out every single ripe fruit in one night.

Stink Bug

many species

Description
- The medium-size (⅓″–¾″) adult is an ugly gray, brown, green, or black. Its back is shaped like a shield.
- It emits a very unpleasant odor when touched or frightened.
- Adults lay eggs on plants in midspring, and hibernate in debris.
- Adults and nymphs suck sap.
- Some stink bugs prey on the Colorado potato beetle.
- Produces 1–4 generations per year.

Plants Affected: Bean,* cabbage, cucumber,* mustard, okra, pepper,* snapdragon, tomato*

**Plants most frequently attacked by the insect*

Where It Occurs: Widespread; many different species

Signs
- Tiny holes in leaves and stems, particularly in new growth
- Holes are surrounded by milky spots.
- Stunted, distorted, and weak plants

Organic Remedies
- Main control is to keep the garden well weeded.

- Insecticidal soap sprays must be laced with isopropyl alcohol to help penetrate the bug's outer shell; soap alone is not very effective against hard-bodied insects.
- Handpick and destroy.
- **Botanical controls:** Pyrethrin

Strawberry Clipper

see Strawberry Weevil

Strawberry Corn Borer

Description

- Small yellow grubs bore into strawberry roots and crowns, and turn pink the longer they feed.
- The small (⅕″) adult snout-nosed beetle is brown, with reddish patches on its wings. It feeds on stems and leaves.
- Adults overwinter just below the soil surface, and lay eggs in spring in shallow holes at the base of leaf stalks in the plant's crown.
- Produces 1 generation per year.

Plant Affected: Strawberry

Where It Occurs: East of the Rockies, particularly in Kentucky, Tennessee, and Arkansas

Signs

- Stunted or weakened plants
- Chewed leaves and stems

Organic Remedies

- If a patch is infested with crown borer, plant new strawberries at least 300 yards away from the area. Beetles can't fly and won't migrate.
- Pull and destroy plants that show damage. Replacement plants can be established immediately.
- Make sure plants are healthy and fed with compost; healthy plants can usually tolerate these beetles.
- **Ally:** Borage (See chart on pages 280–94.)

Strawberry Leaf Roller

Description

- Yellow-green-brown larvae (½″) feed inside rolled leaves.
- Small (½″) adult moths, gray to reddish brown, emerge in May to lay eggs on leaf undersides.
- Produces 2 or more generations per year.

Plant Affected: Strawberry

Where It Occurs: Northern United States, Louisiana and Arkansas

Signs

- Rolled-up leaves
- Skeletonized leaves that turn brown
- Withered and deformed fruit

Organic Remedies

- For minor infestations, remove and burn leaves.
- For larger infestations, mow or cut plants off 1″ above the crowns. Burn or destroy plants.
- Handpick eggs in winter.
- Spray light horticultural oil in early spring before buds appear.
- Garlic Barrier, a product containing only garlic oil and water, is supposed to repel leaf rollers.
- **Predators:** Trichogramma wasps will eat the caterpillars.
- **Biological control:** Spinosad and DiPel Bt are also effective controls; be sure to spray inside the rolled leaf.

Strawberry Root Weevil

many species

Description

- Beetles are small to large (1⁄10″–1″), shiny brown, gray to black. Females lay eggs on the soil surface in spring.
- Small, white to pinkish, thick-bodied, legless curved grubs feed on roots and then hibernate in soil.
- Produces 1 generation annually.

Plant Affected: Strawberry

Where It Occurs: Prevalent in the northern United States

Signs

- Adults eat notches into leaves.
- Larvae eat roots and crown, which weakens, stunts, and eventually kills the plants.

Organic Remedies

- Remove and destroy plants showing damage.
- Planting annual crops can, in some areas, help avoid weevil damage.
- **Botanical controls:** Generally ineffective because of the difficulty in timing sprays to coincide with adult emergence.

Strawberry Weevil

also known as Strawberry Clipper

Description

- These small (1⁄10″), reddish brown beetles, with black snouts, feed at night and hide in daylight. Females lay eggs in buds, then sever them.
- Small white grubs feed inside severed buds and emerge after the fruit is picked in July.
- Produces 1 generation per year.

Plants Affected: Brambles, strawberry

Where It Occurs: Northern United States

Signs: Holes in blossom buds and severed stems

Organic Remedies

- Remove and destroy all stems hanging by threads. These carry the eggs.
- Remove mulch, maintain open-canopy beds, and renovate immediately after harvest to discourage new adults.
- Plant late-bearing strawberries.
- **Biological controls:** Beneficial nematodes are effective, especially the new Hh strain.
- **Botanical controls:** Pyrethrin (apply 2 treatments 7–10 days apart, starting at early bud development); neem
- **Ally:** Borage (See chart on pages 280–94.)

Striped Blister Beetle

Description

- Slender adult beetles (½″) are black with a yellow stripe. They swarm in huge numbers and can destroy everything in sight. They lay eggs in the soil that hatch midsummer. Other blister beetles may be less damaging.
- Larvae are heavy-jawed, burrow in the soil, and eat grasshopper eggs. They become hard-shelled as pseudopupae and remain dormant for under 1 year up to 2 years.
- Produces 1 generation per year.

Plants Affected: All vegetables

Where It Occurs: East of the Rockies

Signs

- Eaten blossoms, chewed foliage, eaten fruit
- Human skin that contacts a crushed beetle will blister.

Organic Remedies

- Handpick with gloves to protect skin.
- Use row covers or netting.

Striped Flea Beetle

see Flea Beetle

Tarnished Plant Bug

Description

- Small (¼″), highly mobile adults suck juice from young shoots and buds. They inject a poisonous substance into plant tissue and can spread fire blight.
- Generally brownish and oval, this insect can have mottled yellow, brown, and black triangles on each side of its back. It lays light yellow, long, curved eggs inside stems, tips, and leaves.
- Adults hibernate through winter under stones, tree bark, garden trash, or in clover and alfalfa.
- Nymphs are green-yellow with black dots on the abdomen and thorax.

- Over half of the cultivated plant species grown in the United States are listed as host plants for tarnished plant bugs; 385 hosts have been recorded.
- Produces several generations per year.

Plants Affected: Bean, celery, most vegetables; peach, pear, raspberry, strawberry

Where It Occurs: Widespread

Signs

- Deformed, dwarfed flowers, beans, strawberry, and peaches
- Wilted and discolored celery stems
- Deformed roots
- Black terminal shoots
- Pitting and black spots on buds, tips, and fruit
- Fire blight

Organic Remedies

- Remove all sites of hibernation.
- Use row covers.
- Use white sticky traps.
- Spray insecticidal soap weekly in the early morning, though this is not very effective against hard-bodied insects.
- **Biological controls:** Try beneficial nematodes in fall to kill overwintering forms.
- **Botanical controls:** Pyrethrin (in 3 applications 2–3 days apart). Spray in the early morning when bugs are sluggish.

Tent Caterpillar

also known as Eastern Tent Caterpillar, Apple Tree Caterpillar

Description

- Large (2″) caterpillars are black, hairy, with white and blue markings and a white stripe down the back. They feed in daylight on leaves outside the tent.
- Adults (1¼″) are red-brown moths.
- Females lay egg masses in a band around twigs, and cover them with a foamy substance that dries to a dark shiny brown, hard finish. Eggs hatch the following spring.
- Produces 1 generation per year.
- Worst infestations come in 10-year cycles.

Plants Affected: Apple,* cherry, peach, pear

**Plant most frequently attacked by the insect*

Where It Occurs: Prevalent east of the Rockies; a similar species exists in California.

Signs

- Woven tentlike nests, full of caterpillars, in tree forks
- Defoliation

Organic Remedies

- Destroy nests by hand. Wearing gloves, in early morning pull down nests and kill caterpillars by crushing or dropping into a bucket of water laced with insecticidal soap. (Don't use kerosene—it is toxic to the soil and difficult to dispose.)
- Use sticky burlap bands. Remove pests daily.
- In winter, cut off twigs with egg masses and burn. Check fences and buildings for eggs as well.
- Remove nearby wild cherry trees.
- Attract Baltimore orioles, bluebirds, digger wasps, and chickadees.
- **Biological control:** Spinosad and/or Bt, sprayed every 10–14 days
- **Botanical controls:** Pyrethrin, neem
- **Ally:** Dill (See chart on pages 280–94.)

Thrips

many species

Description

- Tiny (1⁄25″) straw-colored or black slender insects with two pairs of slender wings edged with hairs.
- Nymphs and adults both suck plant juices and scrape and sting the plant. They transmit spotted wilt to tomatoes.

- Adults insert eggs inside leaves, stems, and fruit. Eggs hatch in 1 week.
- Produce 5–8 generations per year.

Plants Affected: Bean, corn, onion, peanut, pear, squash, tomato

Where It Occurs: Widespread

Signs

- Damaged blossoms, especially those colored white and yellow
- Buds turn brown.
- Whitened, scarred, desiccated leaves and fruit
- Pale, silvery leaves eventually die.
- Dark fecal pellets

Organic Remedies

- Apply a kaolin clay spray every 7 to 14 days, depending on rainfall and severity of infestation.
- Immediately remove infested buds and flowers.
- A reflective mulch like aluminum foil is reported to repel them—use experimentally; see page 219.
- Control weeds.
- Spray insecticidal soap.
- Spray a hard jet of water in the early morning, 3 days in a row.
- Dust with diatomaceous earth.
- Garlic or onion sprays—use experimentally; see page 219. Garlic Barrier, a product containing only garlic oil and water, is supposed to repel thrips.
- Spray light horticultural oil twice, 3–4 days apart, in the morning.
- Ensure sufficient water supply.
- Rotate crops.
- **Biological controls:** Spinosad. Predatory mites (*Amblyseius andersoni* and *Euseius tularensis*). Green lacewing larvae, ladybugs, and predatory thrips prey on thrips. Beneficial nematodes may work in soil control in the greenhouse. Also in the greenhouse, PFR (*Paecilomyces fumosoroseus*) is a beneficial microorganism available in granule form that attacks whiteflies, mites, aphids, thrips, mealybugs, and certain other greenhouse pests, and is claimed to be safe for humans and beneficials.
- **Botanical controls:** Pyrethrin, neem. A mix might work best. Sulfur and tobacco dusts also work.
- **Allies:** Carrots, corn (See chart on pages 280–94.)

Tobacco Hornworm

also known as Southern Hornworm

Description: Virtually the same as the Tomato Hornworm (see below), except this worm has a red horn.

Plants Affected: Eggplant, pepper, tomato

Where It Occurs: Worst in the Gulf States and on ornamentals in California

Signs: See Tomato Hornworm.

Organic Remedies: See Tomato Hornworm.

Tomato Fruitworm

see Corn Earworm

Tomato Hornworm

Description

- This very large (3″–4″) green worm has white bars down both sides and a black or green horn at its tail end.
- The large (4″–5″ wingspan) adult moth emerges in May and June and is sometimes called the hawk moth or hummingbird moth. It has long, narrow gray wings, yellow spots on its abdomen, flies at dusk, and feeds like a hummingbird. It lays single, green-yellow eggs on leaf undersides. Pupae (2″) emerge and overwinter 3″–4″ under the soil in a hard-shelled cocoon.
- Produces 1 generation per year in the North, and 2 per year in the South.

Plants Affected: Dill, eggplant,* pepper,* potato,* tomato*

**Plants most frequently attacked by the insect*

Where It Occurs: Widespread

Signs

- Holes in leaves and fruit
- Dark droppings on leaves
- Defoliation

Organic Remedies

- Handpick larvae and eggs. Look for green droppings under the plant.
- Do not pick worms with cocoons on their backs. Eggs of the braconid wasp, a predator, are in the cocoons. If you see these, make the NPV control spray described under the Organic Remedies for Cabbage Looper (see page 223). Also, do not pick eggs with dark streaks, which means they're parasitized by the trichogramma wasp.
- Apply hot pepper or soap and lime sprays directly on worms—use experimentally; see page 219.
- Encourage birds.
- Black-light traps and bug zappers are effective against the adult as well. But these kill beneficial insects. Use experimentally; see page 219.
- Practice fall cultivation.
- **Biological controls:** Lacewings, braconid and trichogramma wasps, and ladybugs attack the eggs. Release at first sign of adults laying eggs. Spinosad and/or Btk (Berliner *kurstaki* strain), sprayed every 10–14 days, is very effective.
- **Botanical controls:** Pyrethrin, neem
- **Allies:** Borage and dill (both used as trap crops), opal basil, marigold (See chart on pages 280–94.)

Vine Borer

see Squash Vine Borer

Vole (Field Mouse)

see Mouse

Walnut Caterpillar

Description

- This black caterpillar (2″), with long white hairs, lifts its head and tail when disturbed. At night they gather at branch bases. Pupae overwinter 1″–3″ below the soil surface.
- Adult moths emerge in spring. They are dark tan with 4 brown transverse lines on their forewings. They lay clusters of eggs on leaf undersides.
- Produces 1 generation per year in northern climates, 2 generations in southern climates.

Plants Affected: Hickory, pecan, walnut

Where It Occurs: Prevalent in the eastern United States south to Florida, and west to Texas and Wisconsin

Signs

- Defoliation, usually in large branches first
- Black walnuts are prime targets.

Organic Remedies

- In late evening, brush congregating caterpillars into water laced with insecticidal soap. (Don't use kerosene—it is toxic to the soil and difficult to dispose.)
- Spray with dormant horticultural oil. Make sure all parts of the tree are covered.

Walnut Husk Fly and Maggot

Description

- Small larvae feed on the outer husk, then drop to the ground. Pupae hibernate under the trees in the ground in hard brown cases.
- Adult flies, the size of houseflies, emerge in midsummer. They are brown with yellow stripes across their backs and have transparent wings. Females lay eggs inside husks.
- Produces 1 generation per year.

Plants Affected: Peach (in West), walnut

Where It Occurs: Various species occur throughout the United States.

Signs

- Dark liquid stain over the walnut shell, and sometimes the kernels. This is a by-product of larvae feeding.
- Kernels may have an off taste.

Organic Remedies

- Destroy worms in infested nuts by dropping husks into a pail of water. Remove dead maggots when removing the husk.
- Practice fall cultivation.
- Plant late-maturing cultivars in eastern United States.
- For large orchard sprays, consult your Extension agent or Richard Jaynes, *Nut Tree Culture in North America*.

Webworm (Garden)

see Garden Webworm

Weevil

many species

Description

- Family of hard-shelled, snout-nosed, tear-shaped small beetles. Usually brown or black, they feed at night and hide during the day.
- Small, white larvae feed inside fruit, stems, or roots. Adults usually lay eggs on the plant, sometimes inside.
- Bean and pea weevil larvae feed in young seed and emerge when beans are in storage. They can do extensive damage in storage.
- Usually produces 1 generation per year.

Plants Affected: Apple, bean, blueberry, brassicas, carrot, celeriac, cherry, pea, peach, pear, pepper, plum, raspberry, strawberry, sweet potato

Where It Occurs: Widespread

Signs: Zigzag paths in roots, fruit, stems.

Organic Remedies

- Heat beans and peas before storing: beans at 135°F/58°C for 3–4 hours, peas at 120°F–130°F/49°C–55°C for 5–6 hours. Store in a cool, dry place.
- Clean cultivation is essential.
- Deep cultivation exposes larvae.
- ***Pea weevil:*** Plant crops early.
- ***Sweet potato weevil:*** Rotate crops, and use certified disease-free slips.
- ***Brassicas:*** Rotate crops.
- Try dusting with lime when the leaves are wet or dew-covered.
- Encourage songbirds.
- See Organic Remedies under Carrot Weevil, Plum Curculio, Strawberry Clipper, and Strawberry Root Weevil for additional controls.
- **Biological controls:** Beneficial nematodes are helpful when applied in early spring near planting time.
- **Botanical controls:** Pyrethrin, neem
- **Allies**: Radish, summer savory, tansy (See chart on pages 280–94.)

Whitefly

Description

- Tiny (1/16″) insects with white wings suck plant juices from the undersides of leaves, stems, and buds. They lay groups of yellow, conical eggs on leaf undersides. Nymphs hatch in 4–12 days and are legless white crawlers.
- Produces several generations per year.

Plants Affected: Greenhouses, most fruits, most vegetables, rosemary

Where It Occurs: Widespread

Signs

- Leaves yellow and die
- Black fungus

- Honeydew excretions coat leaves and support black fungus.

Organic Remedies

- Spray insecticidal soap, every 2–3 days for 2 weeks.
- Use yellow sticky traps. In greenhouses, place them at plant canopy height and shake the plants.
- Mix 1 cup alcohol, ½ teaspoon Volck oil or insecticidal soap, and 1 quart water. Spray twice, at 1-week intervals, to the point of runoff. This suffocates whiteflies but doesn't harm plants.
- Use forceful water jet sprays, in early morning at least 3 days in a row.
- Hot pepper and garlic sprays—use experimentally; see pages 192–93. Garlic Barrier, a product containing only garlic oil and water, is supposed to repel whiteflies.
- Apply cooking oil spray mix, as recommended by USDA (see page 191).
- Check phosphorus and magnesium levels; whitefly may be a sign of a deficiency. Magnesium may be applied by mixing ½ cup Epsom salts in 1 gallon water and thoroughly soaking the soil with the solution.
- Increase air circulation.
- Marigold root secretion is alleged to be absorbed by nearby vegetables and repel whiteflies—use experimentally; see page 219.
- **Biological controls:** Ladybugs and green lacewings. Trichogramma and chalcid parasitic wasps. Whitefly parasites, *Encarsia formosa*, can be used in greenhouses. In the greenhouse, PFR (*Paecilomyces fumosoroseus*) is a beneficial microorganism available in granule form that attacks whiteflies, mites, aphids, thrips, mealybugs, and certain other greenhouse pests and is claimed to be safe for humans and beneficials.
- **Botanical controls:** Neem, pyrethrin
- **Allies:** Mint, nasturtium, thyme, wormwood (See chart on pages 280–94.)

White-Fringed Beetle

Description

- Larvae (½″) are yellow-white, curved, legless, and emerge in May, with the greatest numbers in June and July. They feed for 2–5 months and may travel ¼–¾ mile. They overwinter in the top 9″ of the soil and pupate in spring.
- Adult beetles (½″) are brownish gray with broad, short snouts, have short pale hairs all over and nonfunctional wings banded with white. They feed in large numbers.
- Produces 1–4 generations per year.

Plants Affected: Virtually all vegetation

Where It Occurs: Appears in the Southeast (Alabama, Arkansas, Florida, Georgia, Kentucky, Louisiana, Missouri, North Carolina, South Carolina, Tennessee, Virginia), but is moving north and has been seen in New Jersey.

Signs

- Severed roots
- Chewed lower stems, root tissue, tubers
- Plants yellow, wilt, and die.
- Extremely damaging

Organic Remedies

- Large-scale government quarantine and eradication measures have eliminated this in some areas, but home gardeners have limited methods of dealing with the beetle. If you experience this pest, notify your Extension agent. The Cooperative Extension Service should be alerted to the movement of this pest and may be able to help you with control measures.
- Deep spading in spring can help destroy overwintering grubs.
- Dig very steep-sided ditches, 1′ deep, to trap crawling beetles. Capture and destroy.

White Grub

larvae of June *and* Japanese Beetles

Description

- Medium to large (¾″–1½″), plump, white, curved worms have brown heads and several legs near the head. They feed on plant roots. The adult is usually either the May or June beetle.
- It takes them 10 months to several years to complete 1 life cycle.
- Has 1 emergence per year.

Plants Affected: Apple (young), blackberry, corn,* grain roots,* lawns,* onion, potato,* strawberry*

**Plants most frequently attacked by the insect*

Where It Occurs: Widespread

Signs

- Sudden wilting, especially in early summer
- See Signs under June Beetle, page 244.

Organic Remedies

- Fall and spring cultivation
- Don't plant susceptible crops on areas just converted from untilled sod, as grubs will come up through the grass.
- Allow chickens to pick over garden following fall and spring cultivations.
- Encourage birds.
- **Biological controls:** Beneficial nematodes in spring or early summer, as mulch or dressing. Milky spore disease, which takes a few years to spread enough to be effective.
- **Botanical control:** Neem

Wireworm

many species

Description

- Large (1½″), slender, fairly hard-shelled worms, with 3 pairs of legs near the head; feed underground; do not curl when disturbed. They core into roots, bulbs, and germinating seeds. Corn, grasses, and potatoes may be badly damaged.
- The adult beetle is also known as the click beetle or skipjack. It flips into the air with a clicking sound when placed on its back. It can't fly well or long. The egg-adult cycle takes 3 years—2 of which are in the larval feeding phase.
- Overlapping generations are present at all times.

Plants Affected: Bean,* cabbage, carrot,* celeriac, corn,* lettuce,* melon, onion,* pea, potato,* strawberry,* sweet potato, turnip

**Plants most frequently attacked by the insect*

Where It Occurs: Widespread, but particularly a problem in poorly drained soil or recently sodded soil.

Signs

- Plants wilt and die.
- Damaged roots
- Thin and patchy crops

Organic Remedies

- Frequent, at least once weekly, fall and spring cultivation to expose worms to predators
- Don't grow a garden over grass sod. Plow or till the soil once every week for 4–6 weeks in fall before beginning a garden.
- Alfalfa is said to repel wireworms; white mustard and buckwheat are alleged to repel wireworms; and clover and timothy (and other grass hays) are said by some to repel wireworms, others say they attract them. Use experimentally; see page 219. You might try it as a trap crop, away from your garden.
- ***Potato trap:*** Cut potatoes in half, spear them with sticks, and bury 1″–4″ in soil, with the sticks as handles aboveground. Set 3′–10′ apart. Pull the potatoes in 2–5 days. Destroy the potatoes and all worms. Some gardeners reported capturing 15–20 worms in 1 potato. Use experimentally; see page 219.

- Put milkweed juice on the soil around affected plants; this supposedly repels worms. Use experimentally; see page 219.
- **Biological controls:** Apply beneficial nematodes 2 months before planting.
- **Allies:** Alfalfa, clover (See preceding tip on alfalfa and clover; also see chart on pages 280–94.)

Woolly Aphid

see Aphid

CHAPTER SIX

allies & companions

Allies are said to actively repel insects or to enhance the growth or flavor of the plant they help, the target plant. Companions, by contrast, are said to share space and growing habits well but do not necessarily play an active role in each other's pest protection or growth. Allies can be and are considered companions, but companions are not necessarily allies.

There is considerable controversy concerning allies and companions. Efforts to test claims scientifically with proper controls have been few, and results are often difficult to interpret. For example, in field trials a particular species of marigold was shown to repel nematodes, but only in mass plantings. Small plantings of marigolds next to the target crop resulted in decreased yields. Therefore, in the chart that follows every effort has been made to include information from as many scientific trials as possible, among them those in which a putative ally was shown to carry with it some negative effects. Though an ally may effectively deter one insect pest, it may simultaneously attract other insect pests.

Plant Allies and What They Do

The chart lists a plant ally; the plant(s) enhanced; the pest(s) it controls; the method of control, if known (e.g., visual masking); the test site where the data on its effects were gathered, if known; and its other benefits (e.g., repels insects, aids growth). Potential drawbacks are italicized and enclosed in parentheses.

Some sources claim to have evidence supporting the efficacy of a certain ally but fail to mention the nature of the evidence. *Evidence* constitutes a one-time occurrence for some, whereas others maintain a more rigorous, scientific standard, requiring multiple occurrences. When there is no clear scientific evidence for the effectiveness of an ally or when the source of the claim is unidentified, the method of control is designated *anecdotal*. Such claims may derive from folklore, word of mouth, or personal observation and may or may not be valid.

Approach companion planting with skepticism, curiosity, and a healthy experimental attitude. Conduct your own trials. The success of allies and companions depends greatly on your microclimate, soil conditions, and cropping history, to name just a few variables.

PLANT ALLY	PLANT ENHANCED	PEST CONTROLLED	METHOD OF CONTROL	NOTES
Alder	Fruit trees	Red Spider Mite	Attracts beneficial predators.	
Alfalfa	Barley	Aphid	Attracts beneficial predators.	
	Corn	Wireworm	*Anecdotal*	
	Strawberry	Lygus Bug (use Alfalfa as trap crop)		
Alliums	Pepper	Green Peach Aphid	Deters insects from settling on pepper plant.	
Allysum (Sweet)	Grapes	Aphid	Attracts beneficial predators.	
	Lettuce	Aphid	Attracts beneficial predators.	
Anise	Cabbage	Cabbageworm		*(May reduce cabbage yield.)*
	Most vegetables	Aphid	*Anecdotal*	
	General		Chemical repellent contained in plant (essential oil mixed with sassafras [*Sassafras albidum*])	General insecticide
Asparagus	Some vegetables	Nematodes: Asparagus roots contain a toxin	*Anecdotal*	
Barley (as cover crop)	Many vegetables		*Anecdotal*	Reduces nematode populations.
	Soybean	Soybean pests	Attracts beneficial predators.	
Basil	Asparagus	Asparagus Beetle	*Anecdotal*	Improves growth.
	Most vegetables	Flies	*Anecdotal*	Improves growth and flavor.

PLANT ALLY	PLANT ENHANCED	PEST CONTROLLED	METHOD OF CONTROL	NOTES
Basil, *continued*	Tomato	Fruit Flies, Thrips	Chemical repellent contained in plant (essential oil); masks tomato plant from thrips	
	Tomato		*Anecdotal*	Improves growth and flavor.
	Tomato	Tomato Hornworm (with Opal Basil)	Chemical repellent contained in plant (essential oil)	
	Tomato	Yellow-Striped Armyworm	Reduces egg-laying behavior.	
	Onions	Thrips (they prefer red onions to white)	Chemical repellent contained in plant (essential oil)	
Beans	Corn	Leaf Beetle, Leafhopper, Fall Armyworm	Attracts beneficial predators; physical interference so pest can't reach target.	Fixes nitrogen in the soil.
	Cucumber		*Anecdotal*	Adds nutrients.
	Eggplant	Colorado Potato Beetle	*Anecdotal*	
	Potato	Colorado Potato Beetle, Leafhopper	*Anecdotal*	(*May reduce potato yield.*)
French Beans	Brussels Sprouts	Aphid	Physical interference so pest can't reach target.	
Green Beans	Potato		*Anecdotal*	Repels insects and increases potato tuber size.
Snap Beans	Potato		*Anecdotal*	
Bee Balm (*Monarda didyma*)	Tomato		*Anecdotal*	Improves growth and flavor.
Beet	Onion		Provides alternate host to target plant.	Improves growth.
Blackberry	Grape	Leafhopper (Pierce's disease)	*Anecdotal*	
Black Salsify	Various vegetables	Carrot Rust Fly	*Anecdotal*	
Borage (as trap crop)	Squash	Squash Vine Borer	*Anecdotal*	Improves growth and flavor.
	Strawberry	Strawberry Crown Borer	*Anecdotal*	Improves growth and flavor.
	Tomato	Tomato Hornworm		Improves growth and flavor.

PLANT ALLY	PLANT ENHANCED	PEST CONTROLLED	METHOD OF CONTROL	NOTES
Bramble Berries (e.g., Raspberry)	Fruit trees	Red Spider Mite	Attracts beneficial predators.	
Brassicas	Pea	Root Rot (*Rhizoctonia*)	*Anecdotal*	
Broccoli	Beet (Sugar)	Green Peach Aphid	Attracts beneficial parasitic wasps.	
	Cucumber	Striped Cucumber Beetle	Physical interference so pest can't reach target	
Buckwheat (as cover crop)	Fruit trees	Codling Moth	Attracts beneficial parasites.	
Calendula (Pot Marigolds)	Collards	Aphid	Deters aphids from feeding on collards.	Attracts beneficial insects.
Candytuft	Brassicas	Flea Beetle	Masking by chemical repellent confuses pest.	
Caraway	Fruit trees		*Anecdotal*	Attracts beneficial insects.
	Gardens		*Anecdotal*	Loosens soils.
	Onion	Thrip	Visual masking	Improves growth.
	Peas		*Anecdotal*	Improves growth.
	Pepper		*Anecdotal*	Improves growth.
Catnip	General		Chemical repellent contained in plant (nepetalactone in essential oil of catnip found comparable to DEET).	General insecticide
	Beans	Flea Beetle (plant in borders)	*Anecdotal*	(*May also increase whiteflies on snap beans.*)
	Broccoli	Cabbageworm, Flea Beetle		(*Some evidence suggests that catnip increases cabbageworms and decreases cabbage yields.*)
	Cucumber	Cucumber Beetle	*Anecdotal*	
	Pepper	Green Peach Aphid		(*Catnip may compete with pepper.*)
	Potato	Colorado Potato Beetle		
	Squash	Squash Bug		(*Squash may not grow as large.*)

PLANT ALLY	PLANT ENHANCED	PEST CONTROLLED	METHOD OF CONTROL	NOTES
Catnip, *continued*	All vegetables	Aphid, Flea Beetle, Japanese Beetle	*Anecdotal*	
Celery	Beans		*Anecdotal*	Improves growth.
	Brassicas	Cabbageworm	Chemical repellent contained in plant	
Chamomile	Beans		*Anecdotal*	Improves growth.
	Brassicas		*Anecdotal*	Improves growth and flavor.
	Cole crops	Cabbageworm	Chemical repellent contained in plant (essential oil)	
Chervil	Radish		*Anecdotal*	Improves growth and flavor.
Chive	Carrot		*Anecdotal*	Improves growth and flavor.
	Celery	Aphid	*Anecdotal*	
	Lettuce	Aphid	*Anecdotal*	
	Pea	Aphid	*Anecdotal*	
	All vegetables	Japanese Beetle	*Anecdotal*	
Cilantro	Cabbage	Aphid	Attracts beneficial insects/ predators.	
	Eggplant	Colorado Potato Beetle	Attracts beneficial insects/ predators.	
Clover				
Crimson	Many vegetables	Thrips	Attracts beneficial insects, such as predaceous spiders.	
Dutch White	Turnip	Cabbage Maggot	Masking by chemical repellent confuses pest.	
Green Chop	Cabbage	Flea Beetle		
Medium Red	Squash		Suppresses weeds by acting as living mulch.	Fixes nitrogen in soil.
New Zealand White	Oats	Fruit Fly	Physical interference so pest can't reach target	
Red	Barley	Aphid	Attracts beneficial predators.	
Red and White	Cabbage, Cauliflower	Aphid, Imported Cabbage Butterfly	Physical interference so pest can't reach target; attracts beneficial predators.	
Unspecified	Corn	Corn Borer	Physical interference so pest can't reach target	

PLANT ALLY	PLANT ENHANCED	PEST CONTROLLED	METHOD OF CONTROL	NOTES
Clover, *continued*				
Unspecified	Fruit trees	Aphid, Codling Moth	Attracts beneficial parasites.	
Unspecified	Fruit trees	Reduces Leafhopper population	*Anecdotal*	*(Can also attract leaf-hoppers, which will then damage susceptible crops.)*
Unspecified	Many vegetables	Repels Wireworm	*Anecdotal*	Suppresses weeds by acting as a living mulch.
White	Cabbage	Cabbage Maggot	Reduces egg-laying behavior and attracts beneficial predators.	
White	Blueberry, Strawberry		Suppresses weeds by acting as a living mulch.	Fixes nitrogen in soil.
White	Brussels Sprouts	Aphid, Cabbage Butterfly, Maggot	Visual masking	
Collard Greens (as trap crop)	Broccoli	Diamondback Moths		
	Cabbage	Diamondback Moths		
	Cauliflower	Diamondback Moths		
	Kale	Diamondback Moths		
Coriander	All fruit trees		*Anecdotal*	Attracts beneficial insects.
	Eggplant	Colorado Potato Beetle	*Anecdotal*	
	Potato	Colorado Potato Beetle	*Anecdotal*	Attracts beneficial insects.
	Tomato	Colorado Potato Beetle	*Anecdotal*	
	Many vegetables	Aphid	Chemical repellent contained in plant (essential oil)	
	Many vegetables	Spider Mite	*Anecdotal*	
	Various vegetables	Carrot Rust Fly	*Anecdotal*	
Corn	Beans		*Anecdotal*	Improves growth.
	Cucumber	Striped Cucumber Beetle	Physical interference so pest can't reach target	
	Cucurbits		*Anecdotal*	Improves growth.
	Peanut	Corn Borer	Visual masking	

PLANT ALLY	PLANT ENHANCED	PEST CONTROLLED	METHOD OF CONTROL	NOTES
Corn, *continued*	Pumpkin		*Anecdotal*	Improves growth.
	Soybean	Corn Earworm	Attracts beneficial parasitic wasps.	
	Squash	Cucumber Beetle	Physical interference so pest can't reach target	
	Squash	Western Flower Thrip	Attracts beneficial predators.	
	Many vegetables	Nematode (plant Corn as cover crop)	*Anecdotal*	
Corn Spurry (*Spergula arvensis*)	Cauliflower	Aphid, Flea Beetle, Cabbage Looper	Attracts beneficial predators.	
Cosmos	Cole crops	Aphid	Attracts beneficial insects/ predators.	
Cover Grass	Brussels Sprouts	Aphid	Physical interference so pest can't reach target	
Cucumber	Radish		*Anecdotal*	Repels insects.
Dead Nettle (*Lamium* species)	Potato	Colorado Potato Beetle	*Anecdotal*	
	Potato		*Anecdotal*	Improves growth and flavor.
Dill	Brassicas	Cabbage Looper, Imported Cabbageworm	*Anecdotal*	Improves growth and vigor.
	Cabbage	Spider Mite, Caterpillars	*Anecdotal*	
	Cole crops	White Cabbage Butterfly	Chemical repellent contained in plant (essential oil)	
	Eggplant	Colorado Potato Beetle	Attracts beneficial insects/ predators.	
	Fruit trees	Codling Moth, Tent Caterpillar	*Anecdotal*	
	Lettuce	Aphid	Attracts beneficial insects/ predators.	
	Tomato	Tomato Hornworm (use dill as trap crop)	*Anecdotal*	
	General		Chemical repellent contained in plant (essential oil)	General insecticide
Eggplant	Potato	Colorado Potato Beetle (use Eggplant as trap crop)	*Anecdotal*	

PLANT ALLY	PLANT ENHANCED	PEST CONTROLLED	METHOD OF CONTROL	NOTES
Fennel	Most vegetables	Aphid	Attracts beneficial insects/ predators.	
	General		Chemical repellent contained in plant (essential oil)	General insecticide
Flax	Carrot		*Anecdotal*	Improves growth and flavor.
	Potato		*Anecdotal*	Improves growth and flavor.
	Onion	Colorado Potato Beetle	*Anecdotal*	
	Onion		*Anecdotal*	Improves growth and flavor.
Garlic	Beet		*Anecdotal*	Improves growth and flavor.
	Brassicas	Cabbage Looper, Maggot, Worm	*Anecdotal*	Improves growth and flavor.
	Celery	Aphid	*Anecdotal*	
	Fruit trees	Codling Moth	*Anecdotal*	
	Lettuce	Aphid	*Anecdotal*	
	Peach tree	Peach Borer	*Anecdotal*	
	Raspberry		*Anecdotal*	Improves growth and health.
	Rose		*Anecdotal*	Improves growth and health.
	Many vegetables	Japanese Beetle, Mexican Bean Beetle, Nematode, Slug, Snail	*Anecdotal*	
	General	Aphids, flies, mosquitoes	Chemical repellent contained in plant (essential oil)	
Goldenrod[a]	Peach tree	Oriental Fruit Moth		
	Various vegetables	Cucumber Beetle	*Anecdotal*	
Goosegrass (*Eleusine indica*)	Beans	Leafhopper	Masking by chemical repellent confuses pest.	
Hairy Indigo	Various vegetables	Nematode	*Anecdotal*	
Horseradish	Potato	Potato Bug (planted in patch corner)	*Anecdotal*	

PLANT ALLY	PLANT ENHANCED	PEST CONTROLLED	METHOD OF CONTROL	NOTES
Hyssop	Cabbage	Cabbage Looper, Moth, and Worm	Chemical repellent contained in plant (essential oil)	
	Grape		*Anecdotal*	Increases yields.
Johnson Grass (*Sorghum halepense*)	Grape	Pacific Mite	Attracts beneficial predators.	(*While Johnson grass may help with Pacific mites, one Arkansas grower noted that it killed his vines, so you may want to make sure the grass is not allowed close to the vines.*)
	Grape	Willamette Mite	Attracts beneficial predators.	
Lamb's Quarters[b]	Collards	Green Peach Aphid	Attracts beneficial predators.	
	Cauliflower	Imported Cabbage Butterfly	Attracts beneficial predators.	
	Peach tree	Oriental Fruit Moth		
Lettuce	Carrot	Carrot Rust Fly	*Anecdotal*	
	Radish		*Anecdotal*	Improves growth.
Marigold (*Tagetes* sp.)[c]	Asparagus	Asparagus Beetle	*Anecdotal*	
	Beans	Mexican Bean Beetle	*Anecdotal*	(*May reduce bean yield.*)
	Cabbage	Flea beetle	*Anecdotal*	(*May reduce cabbage yield and quality.*)
	Eggplant	Nematode	Roots excrete toxic substances.	
	Lima Bean	Mexican Bean Beetle	*Anecdotal*	
	Lima Bean	Nematode	Roots excrete toxic substances.	
	Onion	Onion Fly	Reduces egg-laying behavior.	
	Rose	Aphid	*Anecdotal*	
	Squash	Beetles, Nematode	*Anecdotal*	
	Tomato	Aphid, Tomato Hornworm	*Anecdotal*	(*May reduce tomato yield.*)
	Many vegetables	Cabbage Maggot	*Anecdotal*	

PLANT ALLY	PLANT ENHANCED	PEST CONTROLLED	METHOD OF CONTROL	NOTES
Marjoram	Vegetables		*Anecdotal*	Improves flavor.
Mint	Brassicas	Cabbage Looper, Moth, and Worm	Attracts parasitic wasps.	Improves growth and flavor.
Mint, *continued*	Broccoli	Ant	*Anecdotal*	
	Pea		*Anecdotal*	Improves growth and flavor.
	Squash	Squash Bug	*Anecdotal*	
	Tomato		*Anecdotal*	Improves growth and flavor.
	Many vegetables	Whitefly	*Anecdotal*	
	Many vegetables	Caterpillar	Attracts parasitic wasps.	
Mirabilis (Four-o'Clocks)		Japanese Beetle	Acts as trap crop.	
Mustard (White or Black)	Many vegetables	Nematode	*Anecdotal*	
Mustard (Yellow)	Summer squash		Suppresses weeds by acting as a living mulch.	Relieves soil compaction, increases water infiltration (can become invasive).
Mustard Greens (Chinese) (as trap crop)	Cole crops	Flea Beetle		(*Some claim cauliflower next to mustard increases flea beetles.*)
	Cole crops	Harlequin Bug		
Nasturtium	Asparagus	Carrot Rust Fly	*Anecdotal*	
	Beans	Mexican Bean Beetle	*Anecdotal*	(*May increase whiteflies.*)
	Brassicas	Aphid, Beetles, Cabbage Looper and Worm	*Anecdotal*	
	Celery	Aphid	*Anecdotal*	
	Cucumber	Aphid, Cucumber Beetle	*Anecdotal*	
	Fruit trees		*Anecdotal*	Provides general protection (under tree).
	Pepper	Green Peach Aphid		
	Potato	Colorado Potato Beetle		

PLANT ALLY	PLANT ENHANCED	PEST CONTROLLED	METHOD OF CONTROL	NOTES
Nasturtium, *continued*	Radish		*Anecdotal*	Provides general protection.
	Squash	Beetles, Squash Bug		
	Many vegetables	Whitefly	*Anecdotal*	
	Zucchini	Squash Bug		
Onion family	Beet	Insects	*Anecdotal*	
	Brassicas	Cabbage Looper, Maggot, and Worm	*Anecdotal*	
	Carrot	Carrot Rust Fly	Masking by chemical repellent confuses pest.	
	Potato	Colorado Potato Beetle	*Anecdotal*	
	Swiss Chard		*Anecdotal*	Improves growth.
	Many vegetables	Aphid	*Anecdotal*	
Green Onions	Chinese Cabbage	Flea Beetle		
Oregano	Beans		*Anecdotal*	Improves flavor and growth.
	Cucumber		*Anecdotal*	Deters pests.
	Squash		*Anecdotal*	General pest protection
Parsley	Asparagus	Asparagus Beetle	*Anecdotal*	Helps growth.
	Tomato		*Anecdotal*	Improves growth.
Pea	Carrot, Corn		*Anecdotal*	Improves growth and flavor by adding nutrients to the soil.
	Turnip		*Anecdotal*	Improves growth.
	Lettuce			Provides nitrogen to the soil.
Pennyroyal	Various vegetables	Carrot Rust Fly	Attracts beneficial parasitic wasps.	
	General	Fleas, mosquitoes, gnats, and ants	Chemical repellent contained in plant (essential oil)	
Peppers (Hot Cherry) (as trap crop)	Bell peppers	Pepper Maggot		

PLANT ALLY	PLANT ENHANCED	PEST CONTROLLED	METHOD OF CONTROL	NOTES
Pigweed (*Amaranthus* spp.)	Collards	Green Peach Aphid (*A. retroflexus*)	Attracts beneficial predators.	
	Corn	Fall Armyworm (*A. hybridus*)	Attracts beneficial predators; attracts beneficial parasitic wasps.	
	Corn, Onion, Potato		*Anecdotal*	Brings nutrients to soil surface where available to plants.
***Phacelia* spp. (herbs)**	Apple	Aphid, San Jose Scale	Attracts beneficial predators.	
	Cole crops	Aphid	Attracts beneficial predators.	
Potato	Beans	Mexican Bean Beetle	*Anecdotal*	
	Corn		*Anecdotal*	Repels insects.
	Eggplant	Useful as trap plant	*Anecdotal*	
Radish	Brassicas	Cabbage Maggot	*Anecdotal*	
	Cucumber	Striped Cucumber Beetle	*Anecdotal*	
	Lettuce		*Anecdotal*	Improves growth.
	Squash	Squash Bug, Vine Borer (use Radish as trap crop)	*Anecdotal*	
	Sweet Potato	Sweet Potato Weevil	*Anecdotal*	
Ragweed[d]	Collards	Flea Beetle	Masking by chemical repellent confuses pest.	
Giant	Corn	Corn Borer	Provides alternate host plant.	
Normal	Peach tree	Oriental Fruit Moth	Provides alternate host for parasitic wasps.	
Red Sprangletop (*Leptochloa mucronata*)	Beans	Leafhopper	Masking by chemical repellent confuses pest.	
Rosemary	Beans	Mexican Bean Beetle	*Anecdotal*	
	Brassicas	Cabbage Moth	*Anecdotal*	Repels insects.
	Carrot	Carrot Rust Fly	*Anecdotal*	Repels insects.
	Many vegetables	Slug, Snail	*Anecdotal*	
Rue	Cucumber	Cucumber Beetle	*Anecdotal*	
	Raspberry	Japanese Beetle	*Anecdotal*	
	Rose	Japanese Beetle	*Anecdotal*	

PLANT ALLY	PLANT ENHANCED	PEST CONTROLLED	METHOD OF CONTROL	NOTES
Rue, *continued*	Many vegetables	Flea Beetle	*Anecdotal*	
	General	Fleas	Chemical repellent contained in plant (essential oil)	
Rye (as cover crop)	Asparagus		Suppresses weeds by acting as a living mulch.	(*Requires more watering.*)
	Cabbage	Flea Beetle		(*May reduce cabbage yields.*)
	Fruit trees	Aphid	Attracts beneficial predators.	
	Fruit trees	Leafhopper	*Anecdotal*	
	Many vegetables	Nematode (turn cover crop under)	Roots excrete toxic substances.	
	Soybean	Seedcorn Maggot	Physical interference so pest can't reach target	
Rye (mulch)	Fruit trees	European Red Mite	Attracts beneficial predators.	
Sage	Brassicas	Cabbage Looper, Maggot, Moth, and Worm	*Anecdotal*	
	Cabbage	White Cabbage Butterfly	Chemical repellent contained in plant (essential oil)	(*May attract cabbageworm.*)
	Carrot	Carrot Rust Fly	*Anecdotal*	Improves growth.
	Marjoram		*Anecdotal*	Improves growth.
	Strawberry		*Anecdotal*	Improves growth.
	Tomato		*Anecdotal*	Improves growth.
Savory (Summer)	Beans	Mexican Bean Beetle	*Anecdotal*	Improves growth and flavor.
	Onion		*Anecdotal*	Improves growth and flavor.
	Sweet potato	Sweet Potato Weevil	*Anecdotal*	
Shepherd's Purse	Brassicas	Flea Beetle	Masking by chemical repellent confuses pest.	
	Corn	Black Cutworm	Attracts beneficial parasitic wasps.	
Smartweed[e]	Peach tree	Oriental Fruit Moth		
Sorghum (cover crop mulch)	Cowpea	Leaf Beetle	Masking by chemical repellent	
	Fruit trees	European Red Mite	Attracts beneficial predators.	

PLANT ALLY	PLANT ENHANCED	PEST CONTROLLED	METHOD OF CONTROL	NOTES
Southernwood	Cabbage	Cabbage Moth	*Anecdotal*	
Soybeans	Corn	Corn Earworm	Attracts beneficial predators	
	Corn	Cinch Bug	*Anecdotal*	
Squash (Blue Hubbard) (as trap crop)	Melon	Squash Bug		
	Pumpkin	Squash Bug		
	Squash	Squash Bug and Squash Vine Borer		Attracts squash bees.
	Zucchini	Squash Bug		
Strawberry	Peach tree	Oriental Fruit Moth	Attracts beneficial predators	
	Spinach		*Anecdotal*	Improves growth.
Sudan Grass	Grape	Willamette Mite	Attracts beneficial predators	
Sweet Potato	Corn	Leaf Beetle	Attracts beneficial parasitic wasps	
Tansy	Brassicas	Cabbageworm, Cutworm		(*Some evidence suggests that tansy increases cabbageworms.*)
	Cucumber	Ants, Cucumber Beetle, Squash Bug	*Anecdotal*	
	Fruit trees	Ants, Aphid, Japanese Beetle	*Anecdotal*	
	Fruit trees (especially Peach)	Borer	Chemical repellent contained in plant (when planted under tree)	
	Peppers	Aphids		(*Competes vigorously with pepper plant*)
	Potato	Colorado Potato Beetle	Chemical repellent contained in plant (essential oil)	
	Raspberry	Ants, Japanese Beetle	*Anecdotal*	
	Squash	Squash Bug		(*May make squash plants smaller.*)
		Sweet Potato Weevil		
	Sweet Potato	Flea Beetle, Japanese Beetle	*Anecdotal*	
	All vegetables		*Anecdotal*	

PLANT ALLY	PLANT ENHANCED	PEST CONTROLLED	METHOD OF CONTROL	NOTES
Thyme	General	Mosquitoes	Chemical repellent contained in plant (citronella in lemon thyme)	
	Brassicas	Cabbage Looper and Worm, Insects	Reduces egg-laying behaviors	*(May reduce cabbage yields)*
	Strawberry	Worms	*Anecdotal*	
	Many vegetables	Whitefly		*(May cause higher whitefly population in beans)*
Tomato[f]	Asparagus	Asparagus Beetle	*Anecdotal*	
	Brassicas	Imported Cabbage Butterfly	*Anecdotal*	
	Cabbage	Diamondback Moth, Flea Beetle		
	Collards	Flea Beetle	Masking by chemical repellent	
Turnip	Pea		*Anecdotal*	Improves growth.
Vetch	Fruit trees	Aphid	*Anecdotal*	
Weedy Ground Cover	Apple	Tent Caterpillar	Attracts beneficial parasitic wasps.	
	Apple	Codling Moth	Attracts beneficial parasitic wasps.	
	Brussels Sprouts	Cabbage Butterfly, Cabbageworm	Attracts beneficial predators.	
	Collards	Flea Beetle	Visual masking	
	Collards	Cabbage Aphid	Attracts beneficial parasitic wasps.	
	Mung Bean	Beanfly	Physical interference so pest can't reach target	
	Walnut	Walnut Aphid	Provides alternate host for parasitic wasps.	
Wheat (as cover crop)	Soybean	Soybean pests	Attracts beneficial predators.	
	Many vegetables	Nematode	*Anecdotal*	
Wheat (mulch)	Fruit trees	European Spider Mite	Attracts beneficial predators.	
Wildflowers	Fruit trees		*Anecdotal*	Attracts beneficial insects
Wormseed Mustard	Brassicas	Flea Beetle	Masking by chemical repellent	

PLANT ALLY	PLANT ENHANCED	PEST CONTROLLED	METHOD OF CONTROL	NOTES
Wormwood (pulverized)	Brassicas	Cabbage Maggot	*Anecdotal*	
	Cabbage	Flea Beetle		(*May reduce cabbage yield and quality.*)
Wormwood, *continued*	Fruit trees	Codling Moth	*Anecdotal*	
	Many vegetables	Mice, Whitefly	*Anecdotal*	
	Carrot	Carrot Rust Fly	*Anecdotal*	

*Note: Most information included in this table is from studies referenced in *Designing and Maintaining Your Edible Landscape Naturally* by Robert Kourik (Santa Rosa, Calif.: Metamorphic, 2004) and *Plant Partners: Science-Based Companion Planting Strategies for the Vegetable Garden* by Jessica Walliser (North Adams, Mass.: Storey Publishing, 2020). Where a footnote is listed, information was gathered from an additional source below.

A specific method of control is listed in this table when explicitly shared in these books. If nothing is listed in the method of control, a specific method was not shared in these books. Consult the book for further information on the original research articles.

[a]Clausen, C. P. *Ann Entomol Soc Am 29* (1936): 201–23. Quoted in Kourik, *Designing and Maintaining Your Edible Landscape*.

[b]Ibid.

[c]Research at the Connecticut Agricultural Experiment Station has shown that small French marigolds (*Tagetes erecta*) suppress meadow, or root lesion, nematodes for up to 3 years and one or more other nematodes for 1 or more years. Marigolds are effective when rotated or grown in the entire infested area for a full season. Interplanting is not as effective, and can reduce crop yields, but some beneficial nematicide effects may be seen the following year. To reduce competition, interplant marigolds 2 weeks or more after other plants. Two theories exist on how marigolds work: (1) They produce a chemical from their roots that kills nematodes; (2) they do not serve as a host to nematodes and, in the absence of a host, the nematode population dies.

[d]Clausen, C. P. *Am Entomol Soc Am 29* (1936): 201–23. Quoted in Kourik, *Designing and Maintaining Your Edible Landscape*.

[e]Ibid.

[f]Raros, R. S. "Prospects and Problems of Integrated Pest Control in Multiple Cropping." *IRRI Saturday Seminar Proc* (Los Banos, Philippines, 1973), 1–20. Quoted in Kourik, *Designing and Maintaining Your Edible Landscape*.

Afterword

How can you or I, as small backyard gardeners, know whether our gardens are truly organic?

Since the late 1980s, when this book first started to take shape, the term *organic* has evolved significantly. When home gardeners talk about growing organically, they are likely sharing their philosophical attitude of stewardship of the earth, meaning they are striving to support, nurture, and work in harmony with natural ecosystems. Typically, these gardeners share a range of values that nurture both environmental and human health in the broadest terms, such as:

- Use local and regional renewable resources and recycled materials to the greatest extent possible.
- Support diversity within the garden by growing a variety of cultivars and crops, as well as protecting and supporting diverse local plant and wildlife habitat.
- Nurture long-term soil health through planning, design, and maintenance of the garden, which may include practices such as growing green manure, biodynamic preparations, rotating crops, composting, and attracting beneficial insects and animals that help control harmful insects and diseases.
- Minimize (or avoid altogether) the use of any substances that may harm soil health, native plants or wildlife, or human health.
- Provide a safe environment for anyone working in the garden.

However, *organic* has come to mean something very different when discussed in a commercial context at the farm stand, farmers' market, or grocery store. In 1993 a federal mandate required that anyone labeling their produce as organic and selling more than $5000 per year must obtain an annual certification. Certification programs quickly sprang up throughout the United States, beginning the entry of organics into mainstream commercial food culture. Nearly 10 years later, in 2002, the federal government implemented the National Organic Program that created uniform national standards for production and handling of foods labeled organic.

By law, the federal standard of approved and prohibited substances for organic production must be reviewed and updated at least every 5 years. This mandated review reflects an understanding that the definition of *organic* will necessarily evolve as field and laboratory research provide new information about the effects that certain substances have on soil and food crops. A core part of this program is the National List of Allowed and Prohibited Substances; it also has continued to be updated and should not be considered the final word on what is organic. Nor should the "approved methods" be considered the final word on what we should and should not do if we want to grow organic.

To this day there continues to be heated controversy over what is and is not allowable in commercial organic production. For some, the National Organic Program created a helpful pathway—even an incentive—for conventional farmers to transition to more sustainable cultivation practices, making organic foods more widely accessible to people everywhere. Others have argued that the national standards were a betrayal of the core values of organic agriculture, with politics leading to the permitting of practices that do not reflect true organic values. A few key points of contention are:

- Should the common practice of spreading human waste in the form of biosolids, or sludge, to fertilize agricultural fields be allowable on organic fields?
- Should the use of genetically modified seed be allowable in organic soils? Are genetically modified organisms (GMOs) inherently at odds with organic or are they, as some argue, merely an accelerated form of hybridization?
- Should antibiotics be allowed under certain conditions, or never?
- Can irradiation be used to provide longer shelf life for foods labeled organic?
- Can chickens be labeled organic if they are raised in large poultry houses where they may have access to an outdoors area but are not free roaming?
- Can hydroponically grown produce (i.e., foods not grown in soil) be labeled organic? Does the term *organic*, historically and philosophically rooted in soil health and food nutrition provided by healthy soils, automatically rule out hydroponic growing methods?
- Should small farmers be subject to the same requirements designed for industrial-scale production?

These are but a sampling of the heated debates that continue to surround the term *organic* in commercial venues. In addition to these issues, many small commercial farmers consider the organic certification process and requirements too costly and administratively onerous. This combination of philosophical, economical, and administrative barriers for small farmers have led to a proliferation of different labels that avoid the requirement for certification but still convey to the consumer the grower's values and practices. Examples include and are not limited to: beyond organic, sustainable, grass-fed, free range, free roaming, no-spray, pesticide-free, and regenerative.

Thankfully, for most of us these issues are not relevant. We can make our gardens organic, we can call our gardens organic, and we can share our organic produce with family and friends. Gardening is one of the top pastimes in the United States, and people at all socioeconomic levels garden. Some garden because they must grow food for their table; some garden to grow healthy foods; some garden to grow unusual foods; some garden to grow cultural foods from their homeland; some garden for physical and emotional health; and others garden for the sheer pleasure of seeing things grow. The good news is that, regardless of how large the garden, home gardeners anywhere can choose to make their gardens organic. An organic garden is just as easy as a conventional garden, but it is healthier for you and your family, the soil, the environment, and critters. And many times more rewarding.

Bibliography

GENERAL GARDENING & VEGETABLE GROWING

Appelhof, Mary, and Joanne Olszewski. *Worms Eat My Garbage, 35th Anniversary Edition: How to Set Up and Maintain a Worm Composting System*. North Adams, Mass.: Storey Publishing, 2017.

A small, easy-to-read paperback. Appelhof tells you all you need to know about how to grow earthworms without much effort. Not as complete as Minnich's book, but most people don't need the detail that Minnich offers.

Arms, Karen. *Environmental Gardening*. Savannah, Ga.: Halfmoon, 1992.

A fun and informative resource for all gardeners. A biologist by training, Arms covers general principles and numerous specifics, such as water gardening, attracting wildlife, saving water and energy, annuals, shrubs, trees, lawns, and edible plants. She accomplishes her goal of providing a guide to which gardening practices are environmentally sound and which are dangerous or unethical.

Ball, Jeff. *Jeff Ball's 60-Minute Garden: Just One Hour a Week for the Most Productive Vegetable Garden Possible*. New York: Collier, 1992.

One of my favorite books, not only because of its goal of low-time gardening, but also because it is so well written and fun to read. Practical, informative, and easy to follow. Includes diagrams of useful garden tools as well as shopping lists and instructions. Diagrams and construction plans are provided for a boxed bed with PVC foundations, tunnels, trellis and orchard fence, compost bin and sifter, seedling box, garden sink, and birdhouse.

Bartholomew, Mel. *All New Square Foot Gardening*. Minneapolis, Minn.: Cool Springs, 2006.

Another fun book, good for both novice and experienced gardeners, based on the PBS television series. The square foot method is an interesting, practical method of intensive gardening, in some ways more formulaic (and therefore easier) than French intensive. The back of the book contains cultural notes on vegetables and square foot spacing rules for each vegetable.

Bubel, Nancy. *The New Seed-Starters Handbook*. Emmaus, Penn.: Rodale, 2018.

For those who want an in-depth discussion of how to get plants off to a good start, Bubel covers everything from germinating to transplanting. She also explains how to save your own seeds. The last third of the book includes cultural briefs on how to start from seed vegetables, fruits, herbs, flowers, wildflowers, trees, and shrubs. Useful charts on soil deficiency, symptoms and treatment, and more.

Coleman, Eliot. *Four-Season Harvest: Organic Vegetables from Your Home Garden All Year Long*. White River Junction, Vt.: Chelsea Green, 2012.

See annotation below.

———. *The New Organic Grower: A Master's Manual of Tools and Techniques for the Home and Market Gardener*. White River Junction, Vt.: Chelsea Green, 2018.

I love this book, not just because one reviewer called it the perfect companion to *Gardening at a Glance* (the self-published precursor to this book), but because it really is the perfect companion. While the book you're reading now is strong on information for individual crops and pest control, Coleman's book is strong on understanding, approach, and techniques. Coleman is a joy to read and learn from. The sections on green manure rotations and crop rotations are especially useful. There are many useful charts, but I especially like the rotation charts for green manure and vegetable crops.

Creasy, Rosalind. *Edible Landscaping*. Berkeley, Calif.: Counterpoint, 2010.

An excellent book on how to make your garden an attractive landscape and your landscape into an attractive garden. Useful to all gardeners. Major principles of edible landscaping are covered in this timely book. Creasy also discusses gardening techniques, culture, hygiene, diseases, and insects. The last half of the book is a useful "encyclopedia" of fruit, vegetable, herb, and nut culture, and includes varieties and sources.

———. *Rosalind Creasy's Recipes from the Garden.* North Clarendon, Vt.: Tuttle, 2008.
A gem filled with valuable growing information and visual beauty. Creasy creates and explores specialty gardens of different countries, traditions, colors, and flavors. She shares a wealth of information on varieties known for such things as color, flavor, and heirloom history. Mouthwatering recipes accompany every section, including such wonders as violet vichyssoise and lavender ice cream. The book concludes with an encyclopedia on how to grow each type of vegetable.

Fukuoka, Masanobu. *The One-Straw Revolution: An Introduction to Natural Farming.* New York: New York Review, 2009.
Now considered a classic on the subject, this book discusses the importance and methods of no-till cultivation. Some of the methods may not be generally applicable in the United States, however, because they're designed for a mild Japanese climate.

Hamilton, Geoff. *Organic Gardening: The Classic Guide to Growing Fruit, Flowers, and Vegetables the Natural Way.* New York: D.K., 2011.
Excellent color photographs and diagrams make this book special. The photographs cover everything from different soil types to how to harvest different vegetables. Includes photos of the various methods of training fruit trees and provides good cultural notes. Concludes with a good list of gardening activities that is broken down by season and type of garden (ornamental, fruit, vegetable, greenhouse).

Hill, Lewis. *Secrets of Plant Propagation: Starting Your Own Flowers, Vegetables, Fruits, Berries, Shrubs, Trees, and Houseplants.* North Adams, Mass.: Storey, 1985.
A complete guide to starting new plants.

Jeavons, John. *How to Grow More Vegetables.* Berkeley, Calif.: Ten Speed Press, 2012.
An excellent discussion on the importance and methods of French intensive raised-bed gardening. Jeavons is well known for advocating high-yield, intensive techniques. Here's a good, detailed description on how to double-dig. Useful charts include a 4-year garden plan; companion plants; growing data on vegetables, fruits, grains, and fertilizers and their components.

Kourik, Robert. *Designing and Maintaining Your Edible Landscape Naturally.* White River Junction, Vt.: Chelsea Green, 2005.
For the novice and experienced gardener, this is essential reading on edible landscaping, the gardening wave of the future. Unusual, informative, and fun. Kourik's book discusses everything from aesthetics to specific gardening techniques—how to plan gardens, the pros and cons of tillage, how to prune, and much more. Useful charts include companion planting research summaries; intercropping for pest reduction; green manure plants; dynamic accumulators; seven-step rotation for fertility; multipurpose edibles; soil indicators (plants); ripening dates for fruit and nut varieties; fruit tree rootstocks; disease-resistant trees; and more.

———. *Drip Irrigation for Every Landscape and All Climates.* Santa Rosa, Calif.: Metamorphic Press, 2009.
A step-by-step guide to easy and simple drip irrigation. This book demystifies drip irrigation and includes illustrations, charts, and sources.

Lappé, Frances Moore, and Anna Lappé. *Hope's Edge: The Next Diet for a Small Planet.* New York: Tarcher/Putnam, 2003.
A journey to different parts of the world to meet interesting people who are developing new ways of growing food, the book also addresses hunger and social change. Lappé demonstrates that the links between what we grow and eat, our health, and our economy extend to the very root and soul of our societies. Demonstrates the rich possibilities for solutions all around us and the power of individuals to initiate change. A must-read for those interested in sustainability, it will challenge and inspire gardeners everywhere.

Maynard, Donald N., and George J. Hochmuth, eds. *Knott's Handbook for Vegetable Growers,* 6th ed. Hoboken, N.J.: Wiley, 2023.
A professional's resource book and authority on all aspects of vegetable growing. Just when you thought you had a handle on the issues involved in vegetable growing, this book can both humble and stimulate. Covers everything from hydroponic

solutions to irrigation rates. A small ring binder, it's easy to carry around and fun to browse through for both trivia and essentials. Charts that might be appropriate for the nonprofessional include the following: composition of fresh raw vegetables; diagnosis and correction of transplant disorders; soil temperature conditions for germination; days required for seedling emergence; composition of organic material; key to nutrient-deficiency symptoms; practical soil moisture interpretation; disease control for vegetables; insect control for vegetables.

Rodale's Ultimate Encyclopedia of Organic Gardening. New York: Rodale, 2018.
A good general reference book that covers to a greater or lesser extent every plant one might be curious about. It also discusses general topics such as fertilizer, fruit cultivation, landscaping, and much more. Useful charts include planting dates (based on average last frost date); shrubs: recommended shrubs for the home grounds; straw: mineral value of straws; trace elements: chart on signs of deficiency and accumulator plants; wild plants; and edibles, among others.

Rogers, Marc. *Saving Seeds: The Gardener's Guide to Growing and Storing Vegetable and Flower Seeds.* North Adams, Mass.: Storey, 1990.
This helpful guidebook to saving seeds presents general principles and specifics for each vegetable.

Roulac, John W. *Backyard Composting.* Ojai, Calif.: Harmonious, 1995.
A great little gem of a handbook that makes composting super simple and easy. This is all you need to get your backyard compost pile started. It also provides information for those trying to be more environmentally sensitive.

Sunset Books and Sunset Magazine, eds. *The New Sunset Western Garden Book.* New York: Time Home Entertainment, 2012.
Often considered the western gardener's bible, this book covers all growing areas west of the Rockies. Among other goodies, it includes a plant selection guide for different growing conditions and a huge encyclopedia of more than 6000 plants. A great book.

Thomson, Bob. *The New Victory Garden.* Boston: Little, Brown, 1987.
Based on the popular PBS television series, this book emphasizes how to achieve maximum yield per unit of effort. Perhaps most unique is its monthly guide on what to do for each vegetable. It also includes a short but useful section on fruit cultivation, as well as interesting chapters on cider-making and bird feeders and sample pages of a gardening journal.

Whealy, Kent, ed. *Garden Seed Inventory.* Decorah, Iowa: Seed Savers Exchange, 2004.
As director of the Seed Savers Exchange, Whealy compiles a complete listing of all nonhybrid varieties (more than 5000) offered by more than 200 seed companies. Each entry describes the variety, provides synonyms, provides a range of maturity dates, and lists all known sources. Known by some as the "seed savers bible."

FRUITS AND NUTS

Hill, Lewis. *The Fruit Gardener's Bible.* North Adams, Mass.: Storey, 2012.
A good book on all aspects of fruit culture. Both entertaining and informative, Lewis goes the extra mile to explain the whys and hows behind so many orchard practices.

———. *Pruning Made Easy: A Gardener's Visual Guide to When and How to Prune Everything from Flowers to Trees.* North Adams, Mass.: Storey, 1997.
A great guide on how to prune everything from evergreens and ornamentals to fruit and nut trees. Useful illustrations of before and after proper pruning.

Otto, Stella. *The Backyard Orchardist: A Complete Guide to Growing Fruit Trees in the Home Garden.* Maple City, Mich.: OttoGraphics, 2015.
A super resource and excellent guide for the fruit hobbyist. While not strictly organic in approach, Otto provides the information you need to take an organic approach if you so choose. She covers everything from site preparation to pest control, harvest, and storage. Useful charts include best fruit choices for U.S. regions; common fruit tree insect pests in various U.S. regions; period of active

insect pressure; a question-and-answer chart for troubleshooting seasonal problems; and a monthly almanac of things to do and watch for in the orchard.

———. *The Backyard Berry Book: A Hands-on Guide to Growing Berries, Brambles, & Vine Fruit in the Home Garden.* Maple City, Mich.: OttoGraphics, 1995.
See annotation above.

See also Creasy, *Rodale's Ultimate Encyclopedia of Organic Gardening,* Hamilton, Kourik (charts on rootstocks, diseases, resistant fruits, ripening dates, and excellent section on pruning); and Thomson under General Gardening, beginning on page 297.

HERBS

Editors of Reader's Digest. *Magic and Medicine of Plants.* Pleasantville, N.Y.: Reader's Digest, 1986.
A wonderful resource for learning about the medicinal purposes of almost 300 plants, including herbs. With instructive illustrations and excellent color photographs, this book features chapters on the history of plants in magic and medicine, an exceptionally clear chapter on the anatomy of plants, and plant entries that differentiate between folk medicine and medicinal purposes that have been scientifically proved. Herb gardeners will also enjoy the chapters that offer designs for herb gardens and recipes for culinary and medicinal purposes.

Garland, Sarah. *The Herb Garden.* New York: Frances Lincoln, 2006.
Comprehensive coverage of how to grow fragrant herbs for culinary and other purposes.

Hartung, Tammi. *Homegrown Herbs.* North Adams, Mass.: Storey, 2011.
Tammi and her husband grow medicinal plants on an organically certified farm in southern Colorado.

Hutson, Lucinda. *The Herb Garden Cookbook.* Austin: University of Texas Press, 2003.
A good book on how to grow and how to cook with herbs, including many recipes. Useful information for Southwestern gardeners.

Jacobs, Betty E. M. *Growing and Using Herbs Successfully.* North Adams, Mass.: Storey, 1981.
Complete information about herbs.

Kowalchik, Claire, and William H. Hylton, eds. *Rodale's Illustrated Encyclopedia of Herbs.* Emmaus, Penn.: Rodale, 2000.
Hands down the best and most complete book I've seen on herbs, covering everything from herb culture to how to use herbs for healing. Includes useful charts on companion planting, dangerous herbs, herbs for dyeing, herb pests, herb diseases, and more.

See also Bubel, Creasy, and *Rodale's Ultimate Encyclopedia of Organic Gardening* under General Gardening, beginning on page 297.

INSECTS AND DISEASES

Bradley, Fern Marshall. *Rodale's Find-It-Fast Answers for Your Vegetable Garden.* Emmaus, Penn.: Rodale, 2007.
A good book specifically on organic disease and insect control for major plants. Easy to use, you can problem-solve by plants or by the specific insect or disease.

Olkowski, William, Sheila Daar, and Helga Olkowski. *Common-Sense Pest Control: Least-Toxic Solutions for Your Home, Garden, Pets and Community.* Newtown, Conn.: Taunton, 1991.
The definitive word on integrated pest management, this hefty reference makes scientific advancements accessible to the nonprofessional. The authors (one horticulturist and two entomologists) have been leaders in reporting on advancements through the nonprofit Bio-Integral Resource Center (BIRC) in Berkeley, California. Discover ways to control garden, household, and community pests, and learn just about anything you ever wanted to know about pest control, from pesticide toxicity levels and effects on different organs, to different garden mulches for weed control. There are too many useful charts to list here, but organic gardeners will be particularly interested in the chart of plants that attract beneficial insects.

Yepsen, Roger, Jr., ed. *The Encyclopedia of Natural Insect & Disease Control.* Emmaus, Penn.: Rodale, 1984.
An excellent reference covering major insects and diseases. Excellent color photos. Page numbers for the charts are given because of the potential difficulty of locating them. Useful charts on insect- and disease-resistant vegetable varieties; insect emergence times, divided into 16 zones.

See also Rodale's Ultimate Encyclopedia of Organic Gardening and Kourik under General Gardening, beginning on page 297.

HARVEST AND STORAGE

Bubel, Mike, and Nancy Bubel. *Root Cellaring: Natural Cold Storage of Fruits & Vegetables.* North Adams, Mass.: Storey, 1991.
The only reference on root cellars I'm aware of that has been thoroughly researched by investigating what has and hasn't worked over the years. Many other books are pure theory; this one isn't. Many useful diagrams.

Recommended Reading

Books

2015 Directory of Least-Toxic Pest Control Products. Berkeley, Calif.: The Bio-Integral Resource Center, 2015.
Lists more than 2000 pest control items in four sections: insects and mites, plant disease, vertebrates, and weeds. Supplier addresses and cross-references are available.

Bowe, Patrick. *The Complete Kitchen Garden: The Art of Designing and Planting an Edible Garden.* New York: Macmillan, 1996.

Campbell, Stu. *Let It Rot!: The Gardener's Guide to Composting,* 3rd ed. North Adams, Mass.: Storey, 1998.
Explains the technical aspects of composting in simple, easy-to-understand terms, provides detailed information on selecting the right materials, and covers the mechanics clearly and comprehensively.

———. *Mulch It!* North Adams, Mass.: Storey, 2001.
Explains the labor-saving way to maintain a healthy garden. Nothing beats mulch for controlling weeds, retaining moisture, and fertilizing and insulating soil, with minimum effort. Explains how to make your own mulch, when to mulch, and which ones to use in various types of gardens.

Editors of Garden Way Publishing. *The Big Book of Gardening Skills.* North Adams, Mass.: Storey, 1993.
Comprehensive, illustrated guide to growing flowers, fruits, herbs, and vegetables, on a small or large scale. Numerous charts on planting, garden design, organic pest and disease control, succession planting, and more.

Edwards, Linda. *Organic Tree Fruit Management.* Vernon, B.C.: Organic BC, 2023.

Gilkeson, Linda, Pam Pierce, and Miranda Smith. *Rodale's Pest & Disease Problem Solver: A Chemical-Free Guide to Keeping Your Garden Healthy.* Emmaus, Penn.: Rodale, 2000.

Hart, Rhonda Massingham. *Bugs, Slugs, and Other Thugs.* North Adams, Mass.: Storey, 1991.
Explains how to stop pests without risk to the environment. Chapters are organized by predator, and each is illustrated with descriptions of habitat, life cycle, habit, favorite garden targets, and damage caused.

———. *Vertical Vegetables & Fruit: Creative Gardening Techniques for Growing Up in Small Spaces.* North Adams, Mass.: Storey, 2001.
Explains the benefits of using trellises and ways to improve and increase yields, cut time input, and use less space. Also shows how to design and construct different types of garden supports and how to plant and grow more than two dozen varieties of vegetables, fruits, and flowering vines on trellises.

Larkcom, Joy. *The Salad Garden.* London: Frances Lincoln, 2017.
A fun book for those interested in salad greens and cooking.

Lee, Andy. *Day Range Poultry: Every Chicken Owner's Guide to Grazing Gardens and Improving Pastures.* Shelburne, Vt.: Good Earth, 2002.
This permaculture book explains in detail how chickens and bottomless cages can improve soil fertility.

Leighton, Phebe, and Calvin Simonds. *The New American Landscape Gardener: A Guide to Beautiful Backyards and Sensational Surroundings.* Emmaus, Penn.: Rodale, 1987.
Numerous charts of both edible and nonedible plants for different landscapes makes this a helpful aide. General design principles and design flaws are discussed in-depth. Extremely readable. Useful charts include plants for meadows, plants for a sunspot, plants for a rock garden, plants for a winter landscape, plants for a water garden, plants for a wildlife garden, and plants for a woodswalk.

McClure, Susan. *The Harvest Gardener.* North Adams, Mass.: Storey, 1993.
A compendium of tips and advice about choosing cultivars, scheduling plantings, organizing garden space, coping with the vagaries of weather and pests, harvesting and storing the crop. Also includes an encyclopedia of culture, harvest, and storage of fruits, herbs, and vegetables.

Medic, Kris. *The New American Backyard: Easy Organic Techniques and Solutions for a Landscape You'll Love.* Emmaus, Penn.: Rodale, 2001.
Demonstrates how organic techniques can save homeowners money and time.

Miloradovich, Milo. *Growing and Using Herbs and Spices.* Mineola, N.Y.: Dover, 2011.

Phillips, Michael. *The Apple Grower: A Guide for the Organic Orchardist.* White River Junction, Vt.: Chelsea Green, 2005.

Pleasant, Barbara. *The Gardener's Bug Book: Earth-Safe Insect Control.* North Adams, Mass.: Storey, 1994.
An easy-to-use guide to identifying both the beneficial and harmful insects in your garden. Includes instructions for homemade pest control remedies that are safe for you and your garden.

Poisson, Leandre, and Gretchen Vogel Poisson. *Solar Gardening: Growing Vegetables Year-Round the American Intensive Way.* White River Junction, Vt.: Chelsea Green, 1994.
A practical text filled with concrete particulars, not abstract generalities. Includes photos, plans of existing gardens, tools, and apparatus.

Prakash, Anand, and Jagadiswari Rao. *Botanical Pesticides in Agriculture.* Boca Raton, Fla.: Lewis (CRC Press), 1997.

Riotte, Louise. *Carrots Love Tomatoes: Secrets of Companion Planting for Successful Gardening.* North Adams, Mass.: Storey, 1998.
Vegetables and fruits have natural preferences; the author explains how to plan a garden to take advantage of these productive relationships.

———. *Roses Love Garlic: Companion Planting and Other Secrets of Flowers.* North Adams, Mass.: Storey, 1998.
The author explores companion planting with flowers and shows how to combine flower and vegetable gardens for striking display of color, form, and productivity.

Shaudys, Phyllis V. *Herbal Treasures: Inspiring Month-by-Month Projects for Gardening, Cooking, and Crafts.* North Adams, Mass.: Storey, 1990.

A month-by-month collection of herb crafts, recipes, and gardening ideas. Also included are projects with herbs, reference materials, and suppliers.

Wirth, Thomas. *Victory Garden Landscape Guide.* Boston: Little, Brown, 1984.
A fun and useful month-by-month guide to landscaping. Wirth offers interesting and useful ideas and charts on everything concerning landscaping, from terraces and patios to fruit trees. He divides each month into four categories: landscaping opportunities, plants for a purpose, materials and constructions, and plants by design.

Magazines, Newsletters, and Websites

American Vegetable Grower
Meister Media Worldwide
https://growingproduce.com/magazine/american-fruit-grower

Common Sense Pest Control Quarterly and IPM Practitioner (monthly)
Bio-Integral Resource Center
https://birc.org
Two journals offering the least-toxic solutions to pest problems of the home and garden. Available to members of the Bio-Integral Resource Center.

Fine Gardening
Taunton Press, Inc.
https://finegardening.com
A collector's magazine to be savored, like all other Taunton Press publications. Articles on edibles (vegetables, fruits, and herbs), landscaping, ornamentals, insects, diseases, and gardening methods. Well-researched information; superb photography.

Mother Earth News
Ogden Publications, Inc.
https://motherearthnews.com
A bimonthly publication about country living skills, including a regular section on organic gardening.

Sunset
S Media International Corporation
https://sunset.com
A monthly magazine that features a regular section on gardening and landscaping in the Western United States. Highly recommended for Western gardeners.

Resources

State and local organic growers associations are excellent resources. Joining your local association offers an ideal opportunity to learn more about trends in organic growing and to network and make new friends.

I urge you to contact your state and local organic growers' association for a list of locally recommended insect and disease controls. Issues of disease and insect control vary widely from region to region: pests in the Northeast may never be seen on the West Coast, in the Southwest, or in Florida, and vice versa. State and local associations will have the most accurate information for your location.

Also, be aware that many state associations have compiled lists of substances that are permitted, regulated, or prohibited in organic growing within the state. Some states may even have standards that are stricter than the federal guidelines stipulated in the National Standards.

Last, state and local associations may be able to direct you to cooperatives that may be able to assist with producing and marketing issues as they arise.

California Certified Organic Farmers
https://ccof.org

Canadian Organic Growers
https://cog.ca

National Center for Appropriate Technology's Sustainable Agriculture Project
https://attra.ncat.org

National Gardening Association
https://garden.org

Northeast Organic Farming Association
https://nofa.org

Organic Crop Improvement Association
https://ocia.org

Organic Farming Research Foundation
https://ofrf.org

Organic Trade Association
https://ota.com

Metric Conversions

Temperature

To convert	to	
Fahrenheit	Celsius	subtract 32 from Fahrenheit temperature, multiply by 5, then divide by 9

Length

To convert	to	multiply
inches	millimeters	inches by 25.4
inches	centimeters	inches by 2.54
inches	meters	inches by 0.0254
feet	meters	feet by 0.3048
feet	kilometers	feet by 0.0003048
yards	centimeters	yards by 91.44
yards	meters	yards by 0.9144
yards	kilometers	yards by 0.0009144
miles	meters	miles by 1,609.344
miles	kilometers	miles by 1.609344

Acknowledgments

This book represents a rich landscape of infinite gratitude to my husband, Cecil Cobb, for his steadfast support of all aspects of my life, and especially for his loving and gentle reminders to tend the garden of my life. He would have been most proud to see this book born anew.

For the wonderful folks at Storey Publishing, I am most grateful to Carleen Madigan and Deborah Balmuth for their vision of bringing this book into the Backyard Homestead family and for their editing support in different phases, and to Storey's in-house editor Sarah Slattery for her careful tending of the book's progress to keep it moving forward. In an amazing and delightful twist of events, for the principal substantive editing we turned to Anne Nelson Stoner, who had worked closely with me at the Institute for Engagement & Negotiation at the University of Virginia during her graduate studies in Urban and Environmental Planning. I am deeply indebted to the marvelous Anne Nelson for her commitment to excellence, consummate professionalism, and for taking on this work even when the unexpected loss of my husband rendered me unavailable for several months. The enduring compassion of Anne Nelson and the entire Storey family throughout this time allowed me to ease back into this work, slowly but surely, like a seedling taking root. Above all, the rebirth of this book is a reminder to me of the cycle of life and comes with an abundance of thanks and appreciation for all gardeners who, year after year, plant seeds with hope and faith that they will grow.

For contributions to the previous versions of the book, many thanks to Marlene Denckla, for her research work on updating the information on vegetables and herbs, and her continual technical support and enthusiasm through the first years of researching and writing the book; to Alia Anderson, for her research work on updating the information on fruit; Todd Davidson, for his research work on updating the information on disease and insect pest controls; Jennifer Taylor, for updating the entire contents of the self-published volume, enabling it to metamorphose into the first edition; Doug Britt, president of Ag Life, for reviewing the insect and disease charts; John Brittain, president of Nolin River, for numerous helpful suggestions on nut varieties; Rosalind Creasy, author and edible landscaper, for a detailed review and helpful contributions to the entire manuscript, as well as for suggestions about regional issues; Galen Dively, Ph.D., entomologist, University of Maryland, for a detailed review of the macropest charts, and many valuable contributions; Frank Gouin, Ph.D., horticulturist, Chairman of the University of Maryland's Department of Horticulture, for reviewing the herb entries, and for kindly arranging review of the vegetable section; Patrick J. Hartmann, president of Hartmann's Plantation, Inc., for suggesting appropriate blueberry cultivars and for help with *Phytophthora cinnamomi*; Richard A. Jaynes, Ph.D., geneticist, president of the Northern Nut Growers Association, for reviewing the nut entries and for thoughtful suggestions on nut varieties; Clay Stark Logan, president of Stark Bro's Nurseries and Orchards Co., and Joe Preczewski, Ph.D., director of Stark Bro's Field Research and Product Development, for reviewing the fruit entries and suggesting appropriate fruit varieties; Alan MacNab, Ph.D., plant pathologist, Pennsylvania State University, for valuable contributions to vegetable disease remedies and especially for raising critical issues of presentation; Charles McClurg, Ph.D., horticulturist, University of Maryland, for reviewing the vegetable entries; John E. Miller, president of Miller Nurseries, for reviewing the fruit entries and suggesting appropriate fruit varieties; Tom Mills, president of Indiana Walnut Products, for suggesting nut varieties; Carl Totemeier, Ph.D., horticulturist, retired vice-president of the New York Botanical Garden, for a very detailed review and contributions to the entire manuscript; and to Jeff Ball, author, communicator, president of New Response, Inc.; Judy Gillan, of the Organic Foods Production Association of North America (OFPANA); Lewis Hill, author, former owner of Hillcrest Nursery; Richard Packauskas, Ph.D., entomologist, University of Connecticut; and Robert D. Raabe, Ph.D., plant pathologist, University of California, Berkeley.

Index

Page numbers in **bold** indicate charts.

A

B

C

D

E

F

fall and spring armyworm, 236–37
fall cultivation, 176, 192
fall webworm, 237
fences, electrical, 177
fennel (*Foeniculum vulgare*), 150–51
  seed-starting dates, **150**
  storage requirements, **151**
fertilizer, 11
  earthworms and, 3
  high-nitrogen, 175
filbert (*Corylus* spp.), 108–11
  storage requirements, **111**
filbert mud mite, 237–38
filbert weevil, 238
filbertworm, 238
fire blight, 211
flathead borer, 238–39
flea beetle, 239–240
flowers, examining, 179
fly/flies. *See also* sawfly
  carrot rust, 226
  cherry fruit, 227
  hover, 190
  parasitic, 190
  walnut husk, 273–74
  whitefly, 274–75
freezing temperatures, plant protection and, 176
frost date(s), 13, 14
frost-tender vegetables, 14
fruit. *See specific type*
fruit trees. *See also specific tree*
  about, 87
  chilling requirement, 12
  examining, environment and, 179–180
  growing and bearing, 12
  planting, 88
  pollination, 12
  pruning, 12–13
  rootstocks, 15
  shaping, 12–13
  siting of, 10–11
  training, 12
fruit tree leaf roller. *See* leaf roller
fungal diseases, 186–87
fusarium wilt, 211–12

G

gall wasp, 240
garden. *See also* self-sustaining garden
  location of, 8
  monitoring of, 179
  pest breeding grounds and, 175–76
  plant location/selection, 174
  raised beds, 9
garden structures, 177
garden symphylan or centipede, 240
garden webworm, 240–41
garlic (*Allium sativum*), 152–53
  seed-starting dates, **152**
  storage requirements, **153**
garlic spray, 192
germination of seeds, 11, 13, 17
"ghost" gardens, 171
gophers, 241
grafting, 15
grape (*Vitis* spp.), 112–14
  storage requirements, **114**
grape berry moth, 241
grass, mowing orchard, 176
grasshopper, 241–42
gray mold. *See* botrytis
greenhouse leftier. *See* celery leaftier
groundhogs, 241
grub, white, 276

H

handpicking insect pests, 192
harlequin bug, 242
harvesting
  prompt timing of, 176
  vegetables, 15
hazelnut (*Corylus* spp.), 108–11
  storage requirements, **111**
height of plant, 11
herbs. *See also specific herb*
  about, 139
  borders of, 176–77
  frost dates and, 13, 14
  maturity of plants, 13
  propagation of, 12
  seed starting, 13
  transplanting, 13
hickory shuckworm, 242–43
hornworm
  tobacco, 272
  tomato, 272–73
horticultural oil, 193
hot pepper spray, 193–94
hot-water seed treatment, 194
hover fly, 190

I

imported cabbageworm, moth, and butterfly, 243
inchworm. *See* cankerworm, fall and spring
incompatibles, plants as, 15
insecticidal soap spray, 194
insect(s), 8. *See also* beneficial insects; bug; *specific type*
  birds, bats and, 7
  dessicating, 192
  pest prevention, 10
insect pests
  diseases and, 14
  handpicking, 192
  symptoms, remedies and, 188–89
integrated pest management (IPM), 178, 195
intercropping, 174
iron (Fe), 183–84

J

Japanese beetle, 243–44
June beetle, 244–45

K

kale (*Brassica oleracea* var. *acephela*), 57–58
  seed-starting dates, **57**
  storage requirements, **58**
kaolin clay, 195
kiwi (*Actinidia* spp.), 115–17
  storage requirements, **117**

L

lace bug, 245
lacewings, 190
lavender (*Lavandula angustifolia*), 154–55
  storage requirements, **155**
leaf beetle. *See* bean leaf beetle
leaf blight, 212
leaf-footed bug, 245
leafhopper, 245–46
  beet, 222
  potato, 259
leaf miner, 246–47
leaf roller, 247
  strawberry, 269
leaf spot
  cherry, 207–8
  plum, 207–8
leaftier, celery, 226–27
leaves of plant, examining, 179
lettuce (*Lactuca sativa*), 59–60

M

N

synthetic, 200
pheromone traps, 198
pH range, 11
phylloxera aphid. *See* aphid
phytochemicals, 10
pickleworm, 258
pill bug, 258
planning a garden, 8–10
location of garden, **172**
organic remedies and, 172–74
plant(s). *See also specific type*
beneficial insects and, 190
certified disease-free, 174
diseased, removal of, 176, 191
environment and, 179–180
harvesting and, 176
maintenance of, 175–76
measurements and, 11–12
shading in hot weather, 176
plant allies. *See* allies
planting depth, 11
plant location/selection, 174
plant names, 10
plum (*Prunus domestica* and *P. salicina*), 126–29
rootstock pests/diseases, **128–29**
rootstocks, 128, **128**
storage requirements, **127**
plum curculio, 258–59
plume moth, 259
plum leaf spot, 207–8
pollination, fruit and nut trees, 12
potassium (K), 182
potato (*Solanum tuberosum*), 73–75. *See also* sweet potato
seed-starting dates, **73**
storage requirements, **75**
potato bug. *See* Colorado potato beetle
potato flea beetle. *See* flea beetle
potato leafhopper, 259
potato tuberworm, 259–260
potting soil, 173–74
powdery mildew, 213–14
prevention, plant problems and, 10, 174–79
problem identification, gardening, 179–180
propagation (herbs), 12
pruning fruit and nut trees, 12–13
psyllid yellows, 214–15
pyrethrin, 199
pyslla, pear, 256–57

R

rabbit, 260
raised beds, 9, 173
raspberry (*Rubus idaeus*, *R. occidentalis*, and *R. strigosus*), 130–31
storage requirements, **131**
raspberry caneborer, 260
raspberry root borer, 261
raspberry sawfly. *See* blackberry sawfly
rednecked can borer. *See* caneborer
remedies. *See* organic remedies
root depth, 11
root fly and root maggot. *See* cabbage maggot; corn maggot
rootstocks, 15
apple, 92–93, **94–95**
plum, 128, 128-129
rose chafer, 261
rosemary (*Rosmarinus officinalis*), 162–63
storage requirements, **163**
roundworm, 261
row covers, 177, 196
rust
asparagus, 203–4
cedar apple, 207
orange, 212–13

S

sage (*Salvia officinalis*), 164–65
  storage requirements, **165**
sap beetle, 261–62
sawfly
  blackberry, 223
  cherry fruit, 227
  European apple, 235–36
scab, 215–16
scale, 262–63
seed(s)
  certified disease-free, 174
  germination of, 11, 13, 17
  hot-water seed treatment, 194
  starting, vegetables and herbs, 13
seedcorn maggot. *See* corn maggot
self-fruitful fruit/nut trees, 12
self-sustaining garden
  described, 2
  partners in, 3–8
  steward role in, 1, 2
short-day (SD) factor, 13
side-dressing, 11
siting, fruit/nut trees, 10–11
skipjack. *See* wireworm
slug, 263–64
  pearslug, 257
smut, 216
snail, 263–64
soap and lime spray, 196
soap spray (homemade), 196
soil. *See also* cultivation
  acid, 181
  additions to, 11
  alkaline, 181
  amendments, 11
  compaction of, 173
  condition of, 173
  earthworms and, 3–4
  examining, environment and, 180
  needs, 11
  nutrients in, 8, 10
  organic remedies and, 191
  potting, pasteurizing, 173–74
  solarizing, 173
  testing and amending, 8, 10
  water transport and, 10
solarization of soil, 173
sour cherry. *See* cherry, sour
southern blight (*Sclerotium rolfsii*), 216–17
southern corn rootworm. *See* cucumber beetles (striped/spotted)
southern wilt. *See* southern blight
sow bug, 265
spacing of plants, 11–12, 12
spider mite. *See* mite
spiders, 7
spinach (*Solanum tuberosum*), 76–77
  seed-starting dates, **76**
  storage requirements, **77**
spinach flea beetle. *See* flea beetle
spinosad, 199–200
spittlebug, 265
spongy moth, 266
spotted asparagus beetle, 265–66
spotted wilt, 217
spray(s)
  cooking oil spray mix, 191–92
  garlic, 192
  insecticidal soap, 194
  soap (homemade), 196
  soap and lime spray, 196
squash (*Cucurbita pepo* and others), 78–80
  seed-starting dates, **78**
  storage requirements, **80**
squash bug, 266–67

T

V

viral diseases, 188
vole (field mouse). *See* mouse

W

walnut (*Juglans regia*, *J. nigra*, *J. cinerea*, and *J. ailantifolia*), 135–37
  storage requirements, 137
walnut bunch, 218
walnut caterpillar, 273
walnut husk fly and maggot, 273–74
walnut wilt, 184
wasp, **178**
  gall, 240
  parasitic, 190
water/watering
  earthworms and, 3
  needs, 11
  prevention of problems and, 175
  soil type and, 10
  too little/too much, 181
water-based white paint, 177
webworm
  fall, 237
  garden, 240–41
weeds
  clean cultivation and, 191
  controlling, 175
weevil, 274
  carrot, 226
  chestnut, 228
  filbert, 238
  pecan, 258
  strawberry, 270
  strawberry root, 269–270
western yellow blight. *See* curly top
whitefly, 274–75
white-fringed beetle, 275
white grub, 276
wildlife. *See* animals; birds
wilt
  bacterial, 204–5
  fusarium, 211–12
  oak, 212
  spotted, 217
  walnut, 184
winter injury. *See* sunscald
wire cages, 177
wireworm, 276–77
woolley aphid. *See* aphid
worm. *See also* cabbageworm; earthworms; hornworm; webworm
  armyworm, fall and spring, 236–37
  cabbageworm, 225
  cankerworm, fall and spring, 225–26
  cherry fruitworm, 228
  corn earworm, 230–31
  corn rootworm (northern and western), 232
  cutworm, 233–34
  filbertworm, 238
  hickory shuckworm, 242–43
  parsleyworm, 254–55
  pickleworm, 258
  potato tuberworm, 259–260
  roundworm, 261
  wireworm, 276–77

Y

yellows, 218–19